THE OFFICIAL INDONESIAN QUR'ĀN TRANSLATION

The Official Indonesian Qur'ān Translation

The History and Politics of *Al-Qur'an dan Terjemahnya*

Fadhli Lukman

OpenBook Publishers

https://www.openbookpublishers.com

Digital material and resources associated with this volume are available at https://doi.org/10.11647/OBP.0289#resources

ISBN Paperback: 9781800643987
ISBN Hardback: 9781800643994
ISBN Digital (PDF): 9781800644007
ISBN Digital ebook (EPUB): 9781800644014
ISBN Digital ebook (AZW3): 9781800644021
ISBN XML: 9781800644038
ISBN HTML: 9781800649224
DOI: 10.11647/OBP.0289

Cover image by Johanna Pink

Design by Anna Gatti

For
Milla, Aksa,
Ama, Apa, Uda, Nita

Table of Contents

About the Author ix

Acknowledgments xi

Figures xv

Notes on Transliteration and Translation xvii

Glossary and Abbreviations xix

Introduction 1

Approach 7

The History of Indonesian State Qur'an Projects 11

Qur'an Translation as a Sub-Genre of *Tafsīr* 17

Structural Overview 22

1. **Islam and Muslims in the State of Indonesia: A Brief Overview** 25

Sunnism and the Islamization of Indonesia 27

Governing Religion: The Relationship between the State and Religious Groups 36

The Role of Religious Mass Movements 42

The Ahmadiyya and Its Publication Projects 52

2. **An Introduction to *Al-Qur'an dan Terjemahnya*** 59

The Contributing Institutions and the Publishers of *Al-Qur'an dan Terjemahnya* 62

The Various Editions of *Al-Qur'an dan Terjemahnya* 64

The Various Forms of *Al-Qur'an dan Terjemahnya* 86

Conclusion 101

3. **The Political Significance of *Al-Qur'an dan Terjemahnya*** 103

Sukarno and the Ideologization of *Al-Qur'an dan Terjemahnya* 104

Suharto and the De-ideologization of *Al-Qur'an dan Terjemahnya* 116

The Post-Suharto Period: 122

Al-Qur'an dan Terjemahnya and the State's Preoccupation with Language 133

Conclusion 140

4. The Hermeneutical Production 143

The General Structure of *Al-Qur'an dan Terjemahnya* 144

The Development of the Collaborative Translation Process 147

Methodology 156

The Legacy of the *Gandul* Method 171

The Sources Consulted by the Translation Teams 176

Conclusion 185

5. Between Official Translation and the Official Reform 187

Q 4:1, The Creation Verse 190

Q 4:3, Marriage and Polygamy 197

Q 4:34, The Political Rights of Women 209

Q 1:7 and Q 3:19: Religious Tolerance and Pluralism 217

Conclusion 224

6. The Official Translation and Ideological Vocabulary of the State 227

Esa and *Khalifah:* Pancasila or Islamic Caliphate 228

Q 5:51, *Awliyāʾ*: '*Pemimpin-pemimpin*' ('Leaders') or '*Teman Setia*' ('Loyal Friend') 238

Q 6:123, *Akābir Mujrimīha*: '*Penjahat Terbesar*' or '*Pembesar yang Jahat*' 253

Q 4:59 and 83, *Ūlu al-Amr*: '*Pemegang Kekuasaan*' 261

Conclusion 267

7. One Translation, Two Faces: The Ambivalent Authority of the Official Qur'an Translation 269

Ahok and Q 5:51: A Politicized Verse 271

The Accusation of Religious Blasphemy 275

Al-Qur'an dan Terjemahnya and the Interpretive Dimension of the Blasphemy Allegations 285

Imagining the State Authority in the Translation 285

Conclusion 301

Concluding Remarks: What Is an Official Qur'an Translation? 303

Bibliography 311

Index 333

About the Author

Fadhli Lukman is a faculty member at the Department of Qurʾānic Studies (Ilmu Al-Qur'an dan Tafsir) of Universitas Islam Negeri Sunan Kalijaga Yogyakarta, Indonesia. He is also an associate researcher at *Laboratorium Studi Qur'an-Hadis* (LSQH). He completed his basic Islamic disciplines in Madrasah Sumatera Thawalib Parabek, continued his Bachelor's and Master's studies in Qurʾān and Tafsīr studies at Universitas Islam Negeri Sunan Kalijaga Yogyakarta, and then completed his Ph.D at the Department of Islamic Studies, Orientalisches Seminar, Albert-Ludwigs-Universität Freiburg in 2019. His work mainly deals with Qurʾānic hermeneutics and the history of tafsīr in Indonesia.

Acknowledgments

This book is a revised version of my Ph.D. thesis, submitted to the Orientalisches Seminar at Albert-Ludwigs-Universität Freiburg in 2019. I wish to thank the many people without whom the completion of my doctoral dissertation, and later this book, would not have been possible.

First and foremost, I would like to express my gratitude to my supervisor, Professor Johanna Pink, for her full and kind support throughout my Ph.D. As well as guiding my research with her insightful advice and through our many discussions, Prof. Pink has also trained me to be an academic in a more general sense. I may have completed my Ph.D. the day I nervously sat the final examination in her office back in 2019, but her assistance has extended well beyond that particular moment: she not only guided me through my intellectual journey, but was also a welcoming and generous host to me and my wife while we were in Freiburg.

My journey to Freiburg would not have been possible without the support of Prof. Pink and the DFG (Deutscher Forschungsgemeinschaft). Prof. Pink invited me to Freiburg to work with her as part of the project 'Ein Nationalstaat als religiöser Akteur: Das Indonesische Religionsministerium (Kementerian Agama) und die Deutungshoheit über den Koran' with financial support from the DFG from 2016 to 2019, and it was a great privilege to be able to undertake my Ph.D. research through this program. I also extend my gratitude to Dr Moch. Nur Ichwan, who first introduced me to Prof. Pink in 2015, only a couple of weeks after my graduation with a Master's degree from the Graduate Program at UIN Sunan Kalijaga Yogyakarta. This book is essentially an extension of a small part of his scholarship, and I have benefited a great deal from his research.

I am also indebted to Jun.-Prof. Ruth Bartholomä, who acted as one of the examiners of my thesis, and to Majid Daneshgar, who provided me with valuable discussions and reading materials while I was revising my Ph.D. thesis into its current form, for which I am very grateful. I would also like to thank Prof. Peter Riddell who kindly located a copy of *Tarjumān al-mustafīd* for me. We had planned to meet in Nuremberg in February 2019 but this proved impossible, however I still hope that one day I can meet Professor Riddell in person.

I also express my gratitude to the Ministry of Religious Affairs, most importantly the Lajnah Pentashihan Mushaf Al-Qur'an (LPMQ), the Puslitbang LKKMNO, and the members of the translation committee, especially Prof. Quraish Shihab, Prof. Muhammad Chirzin, Drs Abdul Gaffar Ruskhan, M.Hum., Dr K.H. Malik Madani, Dr Lilik Ummi Kaltsum, and Pak Junanda P. Syarfuan, who have been helpful and supportive during my research in Jakarta. I am especially grateful in this regard to Dr Muchlis M. Hanafi for allowing me to attend the sessions of the committee, and to Dr Ali Akbar, Dr Reflita, and Zarkasi Afif, MA, who guided me while I was undertaking research at the LPMQ. My encounters with the members of the committee were an enriching experience for me: I learned a great deal from simply being around them, listening to their discussions, and engaging in conversation.

I completed this manuscript while working at UIN Sunan Kalijaga Yogyakarta, alongside my normal duties, and I would like to take this opportunity to thank the Rector Prof. Dr phil. Al Makin, the Dean of Fakultas Ushuluddin dan Pemikiran Islam Dr Inayah Rohmaniyah, S.Ag., M.Hum, M.A., and the Head of the Department of Qur'anic Studies Program, Dr Ali Imron, M.S.I. for their continuous encouragement and support. My regular meetings with them, and with other academic staff in the university, provided me with the motivation to move through the next chapter of my academic life. I am especially thankful to my mentors with whom I have discussed my research: Dr phil. Sahiron Syamsuddin, Ahmad Rafiq, Ph.D., Dr Jajang A. Rohmana, Ervan Nurtawab, Ph.D., Dr Islah Gusmian, Dr Faried F. Saenong, Dr Yusuf Rahman, and Dr phil. Syafiq Hasyim.

In the latter stages of preparing this book, several colleagues read the manuscript and provided me with valuable comments and suggestions. I express my grateful thanks to them: Lien Iffah Naf'atu Fina, Dr phil. Muammar Zayn Qadafy, Dr Ahmad Muttaqin, Dr phil. Imam Ardianto, Dr phil. Zacky Khoirul Umam, Zakia El Muarifa & Ahmadi, Dluha

Luthfillah, Afifurrahman Sya'rani, and Asep Nahrul Musaddad. I should also mention the names of others, with whom I discuss all manner of topics, including my book: Dr Abdul Jalil, Dr Hamam Faizin, Said Muhammad, Syamsul Wathani, Burhan Ali, Dr phil. Sita Hidayah, Dr phil. Munirul Ikhwan, Dr Riki Saputra, and Alex Medani. Muhammad Hanafi and Syahrul Wilda helped me greatly with my research in Jakarta. I also thank Helen Blatherwick and Melissa Purkiss for patiently correcting my English during the preparation of this book.

Last but not the least, I acknowledge the support from my family in the completion of my studies. Apa, Ama, Uda, and Nita have always been with me, providing their support, encouragement, prayers, and love. Special thanks are due to my beloved wife, Imroati Karmillah, and my little daughter, Aksara Mutia. The time I spent working towards my Ph.D. was made especially precious to me by the presence of my wife and our discussions about our hopes for our future little Aksara. I sincerely dedicate this book to my family!

Figures

Chapter Two

1 The tabular layout of QT (first edition), author's personal collection. 97

2 The combination of gloss and interlinear layout from QT (third edition), the collection of Muhammad Dluha Luthfillah, CC-BY 4.0. 99

Chapter Four

3 The printed version of a manuscript of translation undertaken using the *gandul* method. The commentary flows around the inner box that contains the Qur'anic text and its interlinear translation, the collection of Muhammad Dluha Luthfillah, CC-BY 4.0. 173

Notes on Transliteration and Translation

This text follows the IJMES transliteration system for Arabic words. Indonesian words derived from Arabic, most notably *ulama* and *mushaf*, are written in plain italics without transliteration. The English Qur'an translation in use is that of M.A.S. Abdel Haleem, with some adjustments when necessary, unless otherwise indicated.

The title of the Qur'an translation that is the focus of this study has been written differently in different contexts, owing to a combination of developments in the Indonesian spelling and transliteration systems, and also to inconsistencies in usage in the sources. It has been penned variously as *Al Quräan dan Terdjemahnja, Al Quräan dan Terjemahnya, Al Qur'an dan Terjemahnya*, and *Al-Quran dan Terjemahnya*. The most popular title in current use is *Al-Qur'an dan Terjemahnya*. However, the most recent edition (2019), *Al-Qur'an dan Terjemahannya*, has updated the title once more, although this form is yet to gain wider recognition. This study uses the most popular title, *Al-Qur'an dan Terjemahnya*, throughout, or simply its acronym, QT.

In some parts of the book, where I take a close look at the development of the translation, I present the first edition and only those subsequent editions that introduce changes to the translation. Thus if, for example, I address the first and third editions, this means that the changes to which I am referring occurred in the third edition, and did not feature in the second or fourth editions.

Glossary and Abbreviations

ABI	Aksi Bela Islam (Defending Islam Action)
BNPT	(Badan Nasional Penanggulangan Terorisme, National Body of Eradication of Terrorism)
BP7	Badan Pembina Pendidikan Pelaksanaan Pedoman Penghayatan dan Pengamalan Pancasila (The Supervisory Body for Implementation of Guidance for Comprehension and Practice of Pancasila)
BPIP	Badan Pembinaan Ideologi Pancasila (The Agency for Pancasila Ideology Education)
BPPB	Badan Pengembangan dan Pembinaan Bahasa (The Language Cultivation and Development Agency)
BPUPKI	Badan Penyelidik Usaha Persiapan Kemerdekaan Indonesia (The Investigation Committee for Preparation for Indonesian Independence)
DDI	Darul Dakwah Wal Irsyad (House of Predication and Guidance)
FPI	Front Pembela Islam (The Islamic Defenders Front)
FUI	Front Umat Islam (Front of the Muslim Community)
GAI	Gerakan Ahmadiyah Indonesia (Indonesian Ahmadiyyah [Lahore] Movement)
GBPPSB	Garis-garis Besar Pola Pembangunan Semesta Berencana (The Outline of the Comprehensive National Development Plan)
GNPF MUI	Gerakan Nasional Pengawal Fatwa MUI (The National Movement of the Escort of the Fatwa of MUI)
HTI	Hizbut Tahrir Indonesia (the Indonesian Brach of Hizb ut-Tahrir)
IAIN	Institut Agama Islam Negeri (State Institute for Islamic Studies)
JAI	Jajasan Api Islam (Fire of Islam Foundation)
JAI	Jemaat Ahmadiyah Indonesia (Indonesian Ahmadiyya [Qadian] Congregation)
JAT	Jama'ah Ansharut Tauhid

KBBI	Kamus Besar Bahasa Indonesia (The Main Dictionary of Indonesian Language)
KHI	Kompilasi Hukum Islam (The Compilation of Islamic Law)
LPMQ	Lajnah Pentashihan Mushaf Al-Qur'an (The Qur'anic Text Review Board)
LPPKSA	Lembaga Penyelenggara Penterjemah Kitab Suci Al-Qur'an (The Organizing Committee for the Translation of the Holy Qur'an)
Masyumi	Majelis Syura Muslimin Indonesia (Consultative Council of Indonesian Muslims)
MIAI	Madjlis Islam A'laa Indonesia (The Supreme Islamic Council of Indonesia)
MMI	Majelis Mujahidin Indonesia (Council of Indonesian Warriors)
MPRS	Majelis Permusyawaratan Rakyat Sementara (The Provisional People's Consultative Assembly)
MUI	Majelis Ulama Indonesia (Indonesian Ulama Council)
NU	Nahdlatul Ulama
Parmusi	Partai Muslimin Indonesia (Muslim Party of Indonesia)
PDI-P	Partai Demokrasi Indonesia Perjuangan (Indonesian Democratic Party of Struggle)
Persis	Persatuan Islam (Islamic Union)
Perti	Persatuan Tarbiyah Islamiyah (Union for Islamic Education)
PKB	Partai Kebangkitan Bangsa (National Awakening Party)
PKS	Partai Keadilan Sejahtera (Prosperous Justice Party)
PPIM	Pusat Pengkajian Islam dan Masyarakat (The Centre for Islamic and Social Studies)
PPKI	Panitia Persiapan Kemerdekaan Indonesia (Committee for the Preparation of Indonesian Independence)
PPP	Partai Persatuan Pembangunan (United Development Party)
PRRI	Pemerintahan Revolusioner Republik Indonesia (Revolutionary Government of the Republic of Indonesia)
PUEBI	Pedoman Umum Ejaan Bahasa Indonesia (The General Guidelines of The Indonesian Language's Spelling)
RIS	Republik Indonesia Serikat (The United Indonesian Republic)
SI	Sarekat Islam (Islamic Union)
UIN	Universitas Islam Negeri (State Islamic University)
YPPA	Yayasan Penyelenggara Penterjemah/Pentafsir Al-Qur'an (The Foundation of the Organizing Committee for Translating/Interpreting the Qur'an)

Introduction

> Di dalam suasana semakin meningkatnya taraf revolusi dan Nation & Character-Building kita yang kian terkonsolidasikan, maka terbitnya terjemahan Kitab Suci Al-Qur'an merupakan sumbangan amat besar bagi seluruh lapisan rakyat kita...
>
> ... ayo gali dan sebar-sebarkan terus Api Islam! Justru Al-Qur'an adalah satu-satunya sumber paling hebat dan dahsyat daripada Api Islam.
>
> [During a time of increasing revolutionary feeling, and the more consolidated our Nation & Character Building became, the publication of the translation of the holy scripture Al-Qur'an is a profound endowment to the whole of our people...
>
> ... [C]ome, elaborate and share the spirit of the Fire of Islam! Indeed, the Qur'an is the sole and ultimate source of the Fire of Islam.]
>
> Sukarno (1901–70), the first President of the Republic of Indonesia

What happens if a government with particular political interests commissions a Qur'an translation? What does it mean when this Qur'an translation is introduced with the privileged status of official state Qur'an translation? How is the meaning of a particular Qur'anic word or idiom decided if the translation is a collaborative process, in which a group of translators work on the translation and the target text is supposedly arrived at through consensus? How is the translation affected, in terms of both the actual translation process itself and other technical aspects, when the target text is designed to meet various political interests of the state, especially if it can also be read in a way that does not accord with those interests?

These questions highlight three interrelated problems, the most fundamental of which is the issue of Qur'an translation itself. According to doctrine, Muslims believe that Arabic is one of the essential features of the Qur'an (which is often described as the *qurʾān ʿarabī*, the 'Arabic Qur'an'); Arabic was the language in which the scripture was revealed

 https://doi.org/10.11647/OBP.0289.09

to the prophet Muhammad in the seventh century, a fact that has shaped Muslims religious practices ever since. This belief in the 'Arabic Qur'an' implies that any translation of the Qur'an into another language is not the Qur'an—a notion that led Marmaduke Pickthall (1875–1936), one of the earliest modern Muslim Qur'an translators, for example, to testify that his rendering could not capture 'that inimitable symphony [of the Qur'an], the very sounds of which move men to tears and ecstasy.'[1] There is also a hermeneutical issue that complicates the task of the translator: the linguistic style of the Qur'an is such that it often mentions events without explaining their historical background. This is further complicated by the fact that a given word might be used in different contexts with different meanings. According to another translator of the Qur'an, Muhammad Abdel Haleem, these hermeneutical issues of context are frequent causes of mistranslation.[2] Equally problematically, the meaning of the Qur'an is often multi-layered, as can be seen from even a cursory glance at the multitude of Qur'an commentaries produced over the course of history. When translating a particular verse, a translator will generally find Arabic dictionaries insufficient and turn their attention to *tafsīr* instead. However, taking recourse to *tafsīr* is far from a clear-cut solution, precisely because commentators are likely to have different interpretations of a given word or phrase, not to mention the fact they often provide a range of interpretive possibilities rather than straight answers.

The second problem relates to the practice of translation by committee. The twentieth century has seen the emergence of various modern institutions, either social, educational, or political, which act as producers of Qur'an commentaries, creating a new form of *tafsīr*, i.e., institutional *tafsīr*.[3] Some commentaries of this type are written by a committee of translators specifically selected and established by sponsoring institutions. In the face of this development, some

1 Cf. Abdur Raheem Kidway, 'Muhammad Marmaduke Pickthall's English Translation of the Quran (1930): An Assessment', in *Marmaduke Pickthall: Islam and the Modern World*, ed. by Geoffrey P. Nash (Leiden; Boston: Brill, 2017), xxi, pp. 231–48 (p. 231).

2 M. A. S. Abdel Haleem, *The Qur'an* (Oxford: Oxford University Press, 2004), pp. xxi–xxv.

3 Johanna Pink, 'Tradition, Authority and Innovation in Contemporary Sunnī Tafsīr: Towards a Typology of Qur'an Commentaries from the Arab World, Indonesia and Turkey', *Journal of Qur'anic Studies*, 12.1/2 (2010), 56–82 (p. 61).

unprecedented issues have arisen. On the one hand, the production of a Qur'an translation by collective amplifies the issues of Qur'an translation outlined above, because the interpretation and commentary on the text that emerges from a collaborative process will ultimately be the embodiment of negotiation within the committee. The question of how such negotiations are conducted, and how these impact on the interpretive process, is currently understudied. Additionally, this kind of collaborative process implies the existence of further, extra-hermeneutical procedures. The soliciting institution might, for example, provide the committee with pre-approved guidelines, a list (or school) of references to use,[4] pre-decided theological/sectarian principles, etc. At this point, the production of institutional commentaries should be investigated more thoroughly, not simply from an interpretive perspective, as the distinct processes involved in collaborative production might have different degrees of relevance in shaping the general form of institutional *tafsīr.*

The third problem is state involvement in the production of Qur'an commentaries and translations. Nation-states, especially Muslim ones, have been vital in shaping contemporary *tafsīr*. At the interpretive level, the translation must deal with issues that are subject to state regulation, such as political leadership, domestic violence, polygamy, and interreligious relationships. The parallel between the Qur'an translation produced by the state and state regulations on such issues is thus worthy of attention. Beyond the interpretive context, the production of a particular Qur'an translation represents just one facet of the broader structures of national policies. Policies concerning religion come to mind first; states populated mostly by Muslims, such as Turkey, Egypt, Saudi Arabia, or Indonesia, would have a strong incentive to approve a religious discourse that ensures the sustainability of the state (or the ruling government). State-funded schools where religion is taught require standard textbooks and references, and this might include an 'official' Qur'an translation. Such state intervention also feeds in to higher education and influences the

4 Al-Azhar manages its translations of the Qur'an using this procedure: their first English translation appeared in 1993, and was based on the interpretations provided in pre-selected commentaries. See Stefan Wild, 'Muslim Translators and Translations of the Qur'an into English', *Journal of Qur'anic Studies*, 17.3 (2015), 158–82 (p. 165), https://doi.org/10.3366/jqs.2015.0215.

educational development of those individuals who will later go on to produce their own commentaries. The politics of national languages is another relevant factor in this respect. In fact, the production of modern Qur'an translations in a number of nation-states, such as Turkey and Indonesia, has been strongly—although not exclusively—prompted by the growing significance of their national languages.[5]

These three problems are perfectly encapsulated in the publication history of *Al-Qur'an dan Terjemahnya* (henceforth QT), the most important Qur'an translation currently in circulation in Indonesia. The introduction to this translation puts emphasis on the fact that it is the official Qur'an translation of the state. The presence of the state in the work is apparent, as the quotation of Sukarno cited at the opening of this Introduction makes clear. Not only is the translation intended to fulfill the normal expected function of a Qur'an translation—that is, to be an instrument through which Indonesians can gain understanding of the Qur'an's religious and spiritual message—but it also has a connection to the specifically governmental ideas of 'revolution and Nation & Character building.' To this end, throughout its history, this translation has been overseen by a working committee, run by a special institution whose duty it is to supervise state affairs with regards to the Qur'anic text and its interpretation, that oversees its continued socio-cultural relevance. The committee's duties include drafting and revising the text, as well as undertaking all necessary measures to maintain the translation's relevance. Finally, as a Qur'an translation catering to Indonesian readers, the committee has to deal with translation issues arising from historical and cultural discrepancies between the milieu inhabited by the Arabic Qur'an and that of contemporary Indonesia, as well as linguistic disparities between Arabic and Indonesian.

Consider, for example, Q 5:51:

يَـٰٓأَيُّهَا ٱلَّذِينَ ءَامَنُوا۟ لَا تَتَّخِذُوا۟ ٱلْيَهُودَ وَٱلنَّصَـٰرَىٰٓ أَوْلِيَآءَ ۘ بَعْضُهُمْ أَوْلِيَآءُ بَعْضٍ ۚ وَمَن يَتَوَلَّهُم مِّنكُمْ فَإِنَّهُۥ مِنْهُمْ ۗ
إِنَّ ٱللَّهَ لَا يَهْدِى ٱلْقَوْمَ ٱلظَّـٰلِمِينَ

5 Johanna Pink, *Muslim Qur'ānic Interpretation Today: Media, Genealogies, and Interpretive Communities*, Themes in Qur'ānic Studies (Sheffield: Equinox, 2019), pp. 210–14.

> You who believe, do not take the Jews and Christians as *awliyāʾ*: they are *awliyāʾ* only to each other. Anyone who takes them as *awliyāʾ* becomes one of them—God does not guide such wrongdoers...

What does the word *awliyāʾ* mean here? How do works of *tafsīr* elaborate on the kind of relationship between Muslims and non-Muslims that is forbidden by the verse? Finally, how should the word be rendered in the state's official translation? The answers to these questions may have (and indeed, in the Indonesian context, have had) a profound social or political impact.

In the case of this example, the word *awliyāʾ* is mentioned in forty-two places across the Qur'an,[6] and each occurrence may have different linguistic and non-linguistic contextual situations, each of which can result in a different meaning. Even a brief survey of Qur'an commentaries and other literature that focuses on Qur'anic terms and vocabulary reveals a great diversity of semantic options, ranging from meanings with an emphasis on the concepts of leadership, management, authority, power, or legal power over someone (in terms of family relationships, inheritance, marriage, and ownership of slaves), to those conveying the idea of help and support, or love and intimacy, in the context of relationships between friends, allies, cousins and neighbors, or arbitration of disputes. As a result, to achieve a proper translation for this particular word, one must first decide which meaning is the most suitable out of a number of possibilities. To achieve this, consideration of the linguistic and historical context of the verse, or phrase, in question is necessary. In the case of Q 5:51, the following verse intimates that the word *awliyāʾ* is used here in context of the historical tendency of some people to seek protection or support from the Jews and Christians when faced with an undesirable situation. Once the translators then go on to consult works of *tafsīr* and find that reports on the verse's historical context support this meaning, the approach they should take to translating it becomes clear, and this specific case does not seem so difficult.

In this particular instance, the translation process conducted by an individual might at this point be complete. However, when it comes to a translation conducted by a committee, there is a good chance

6 For a detailed discussion of this issue, see Chapter Six.

that one of the members might wish to consider literature from other disciplines, let us say political Islam (*fiqh siyāsa*). The strategy illustrated in the previous paragraph is typical of the *tafsīr* process, yet some of the members may be better acquainted with jurisprudence than *tafsīr* proper, meaning that alternative perspectives on the verse are inevitable. Q 5:51 talks about 'the Jews and the Christians,' and we have classical *fiqh* literature, which discusses the issue of non-Muslim leadership over Muslim populations. The fact that the semantic range covered by *awliyā'* encompasses the dimensions of leadership, management, and the exercise of power justifies a consideration of this aspect of meaning. Here, negotiation is needed. Which interpretation to choose: support/protection or leadership/management/power?

A Qur'an translation that is produced by the state, such as QT, will entail further considerations beyond issues of exegetical precedents. Indonesia is not an Islamic state, and the constitution guarantees the rights of citizens to follow and perform their various faiths. In fact, one of the state's key aims is to build a society in which citizens with different beliefs live in harmony. Given this, it would simply be irresponsible to produce a translation that might spark a disharmonious relationship. In this context, the translation of this particular verse, Q 5:51, has far-reaching social and political implications, a facet of the translation process that also, of course, applies to other similar cases. In addition to long-term political goals and ideology, such as that influencing the translation of Q 5:51, there is also the possibility that developing political situations may influence the decisions made by the working committee, as well as readers' reception of the published translation.

This book seeks to analyze the issue of state participation in the production of Qur'an translations by considering the resulting translation, the technical procedures surrounding the production of the work, and the reception of the translation. The relevance of this topic lies in the underlying assumption that because QT is produced by a state, the nature of its production is driven by political interests and the resulting translation reflects such interests. Historically speaking, within the Islamic tradition, exegetical authority goes back to individuals, and the growth of exegetical materials recorded in literature is the result of a centuries-long intellectual venture undertaken and developed by individual religious scholars over generations. Thus, the participation of an institution in the production of a Qur'an commentary is an unusual authorial situation when it comes to *tafsīr;* the responsibility for a Qur'an commentary in this context is assumed by an institution instead of a person. With this background in mind, this book discusses the case of QT, the official Qur'an translation of the State of Indonesia, initially published in 1965. It seeks to cast light on the notion of officiality ascribed to QT and to highlight the influence of the state's position as the 'actor' in the interpretive processes at work in the text. It also examines the widespread assumption that the production of QT was undertaken with the intention of creating a standardised Islamic discourse in Indonesia.

Approach

Given that this is a study of a Qur'an translation, readers might expect it to place great emphasis on word choices. Furthermore, given that it focuses on the issue of the politics of translation as found in an official state Qur'an translation, readers might also expect it to uncover the political interests of the state or ruling government behind these word choices. Indeed, this is an approach that is often taken in discussions of Qur'an translations, and holds true for a number of previous studies of QT itself.[7] There are indeed some discussions on word choices in this book (in Chapters Five and Six), and rightly so. Nevertheless, my aim is not to contribute to the body of scholarship that seeks to find inadequacies and 'mistakes' in translations, or what Brett Wilson refers to as studies that discuss Qur'an translations in terms of 'a tragic series of failures rather than as a dynamic and crucial chapter in the

7 The first work that comes to mind is *Koreksi Tarjamah Harfiyah Al-Qur'an Kemenag RI: Tinjauan Aqidah, Syari'ah, Muamalah, Iqtishadiya* by Muhammad Thalib, a polemical work questioning the method and word choices of QT (more on this in Chapter Three). The study of Nashruddin Baidan also falls into this category. Then we also have *Falsifikasi Terjemah Al-Qur'an* by Ismail Lubis, concerning the quality of the translation of QT published in 1990, and *Studi Kritis terhadap Al-Qur'an dan Terjemahnya Departemen Agama Republik Indonesia* by Moh. Mansyur, which seeks to understand whether the QT 1990 edition follows a certain method of translation. See: Muhammad Thalib, *Koreksi Tarjamah Harfiyah Al-Qur'an Kemenag RI: Tinjauan Aqidah, Syariah, Mu'amalah, Iqtishadiyah* (Yogyakarta: Ma'had An-Nabawy, 2011); Nashruddin Baidan, *Terjemahan Al-Qur'an: Studi Kritis terhadap Terjemahan Al-Qur'an yang Beredar di Indonesia* (Yogyakarta: Pustaka Pelajar, 2017); Isma'il Lubis, *Falsifikasi Terjemahan Al-Qur'an Departemen Agama Edisi 1990* (Yogyakarta: Tiara Wacana, 2001); Moh. Mansyur, 'Studi Kritis terhadap Al-Qur'an dan Terjemahnya Departemen Agama Republik Indonesia' (unpublished doctoral dissertation, IAIN Syarif Hidayatullah, 1998).

history of the Qur'an.'[8] Rather, the primary interest of this book is to understand the officiality of a particular Qur'an translation. Thus, it approaches word choices as a means of understanding whether QT's status as the official Qur'an translation of the state may or may not have had an impact on its content. That is not all, however. The issue of state involvement is so central to this study that the analysis goes beyond exploring the complexity and interest of the translation choices made by the translators. Instead, my inquiry considers every element of QT, including the working procedures of the committee, the forewords from government officials incorporated in the various editions of the translation, the spelling systems used, the typesetting and publication formats, and the reception of the various editions by their readerships. In short, the notion of Qur'an translation in this study goes beyond the actual rendering of the Qur'anic text into another language, and the notion of politicization is more complex than simply whether or not the state's choice of words indicates an explicitly political agenda.

In addition to investigating the involvement of the state in the production of QT, this study will analyze the presence of the *tafsīr* tradition (this terminology will be addressed later in this chapter). As such, this study does not approach Qur'an translation from the perspective of translation studies: an investigation of the accuracy, readability, and 'acceptability' of the translation, or of the concept of equivalence in general, is not its aim. There are many studies on Qur'an translation that situate the source and target texts at the heart of their analysis, while giving too little attention to *tafsīr*. This study, in contrast, acknowledges the important role of *tafsīr* in the production of Qur'an translations, because, as I would argue, Qur'an translation is a part of the *tafsīr* tradition. As a result, this study considers Qur'an translation as an intrinsic element of *tafsīr*. For this reason, at some points in this book, I call QT a commentary, depending on the context. As such, I am interested in the exegetical decisions made by the translation committees involved in each edition, and how these reflect the *tafsīr* tradition. In other words, my main interest does not lie in the question of what a precise Indonesian equivalence for a certain Qur'anic word might be, but rather how an Indonesian rendering of a certain Qur'anic word is derived from the vast and longstanding *tafsīr* tradition. I should also

8 M. Brett Wilson, *Translating the Qur'an in an Age of Nationalism: Print Culture and Modern Islam in Turkey* (London: Oxford University Press, 2014), p. 5.

underline from the beginning that this study is not concerned with the issue of the (un)translatability of the Qur'an, especially given that when QT was published the controversy surrounding this issue had died down (having said that, I do include a relatively short discussion that touches on (un)translatability, as this issue reared its head once again during a period covered by this study).

Since the publication of QT in 1965, this translation has evolved, both in terms of its content and publication format. Three comprehensive revisions have taken place, and this study deals with each of these editions. The analysis of the materials covers three different areas: the actual production process, the textual material, and the reception of the translation by its readers.

The first area relates to the actual production of QT. It deals with the hermeneutical aspects of the preparation of the translation, as well as technical decisions on its presentation. In this context, this study investigates the formation of the committee and the working procedures surrounding the translation. Given that the production of any state-produced publication involves bureaucratic procedures, this study also takes into account all of the bureaucratic documents and state employees who were responsible for the production of the work. The QT project may have begun in the early 1960s, but the most recent revision was ongoing between 2016 and 2019, when research for this book was being conducted. This means that I had the opportunity to attend several meetings of the committee, as well as other events related to the revision of the work, and was able to witness directly how the production of QT was developing.

When it comes to the technical aspects of the actual printing process, I focus on the layout design, the spelling and transliteration systems used, and the mediums in which QT is published. These technical aspects are by no means unimportant to meaningful discussion of the formation of an institutional translation such as QT, as differences in layout design can be indicative of the different ideas and approaches on the part of the person or organization producing a translation.[9] For example, the use of a particular translation and spelling system reflects a standard that was imposed upon the translators by the state, and the variety of mediums

9 Johanna Pink, 'Form Follows Function: Notes on the Arrangement of Texts in Printed Qur'an Translations', *Journal of Qur'anic Studies*, 19.1 (2017), 143–54, https://doi.org/10.3366/jqs.2017.0274.

of publication shows how the production of the work keeps pace with information technology to retain its significance.

The second area, the textual material of QT, relates to the interpretive outcome of the translation. For the interpretive outcome, this study reads QT in conjunction with various Qur'an commentaries, both those that are widely read by Indonesian intellectuals, and more importantly those that are listed in the bibliography of the various editions of QT, so as to understand the relationship of QT to the wider *tafsīr* tradition. Additionally, the readings of the Qur'an presented in QT will be juxtaposed with relevant government policies, so as to clarify the position of QT vis-à-vis the broader structures of state policies. A topical approach is inevitable in this case. The verses I have selected to use as case studies for this fall into the following categories: (i) verses that have become the subject of contention in the development of Islamic thought in Indonesia and (ii) verses that are closely related to the ideological idioms of the state such as *esa* (one) and *penguasa* (person with power). The first group of verses is analyzed in order to understand whether QT reflects the religious reforms implemented by the Ministry of Religious Affairs in other projects, while the second group is addressed to understand the extent of the presence of ideological vocabularies of the state in QT and how these function and become incorporated into the target text. Last but not least, in addition to the interpretive outcome of the translation, the paratext is of great importance. Freed from the restrictions of the Qur'anic text, elements of the paratext, especially the foreword, provide the producer of the work, in this case the state or ruling government, with an entirely blank space to exploit for their own interests. This makes the paratextual elements of QT critical to my analysis. Indeed, as we shall see, in these complementary texts, the governments of the day deploy their ideological vocabularies, providing vital clues about the role of QT in the state's political structures.

In order to consider the reception of the text, the third area of analysis, this book draws upon a case study, namely the 2017 Jakarta gubernatorial election, in which QT played a central role. This political contest grew into a polemic-fueled battle sparked by identity politics and encapsulates the issues surrounding questions of religious defamation and non-Muslim leadership in Indonesia. QT was central to this political crisis because the various editions that were available to readers rendered the particular phrase about *awliyāʾ* in Q 5:51 cited above differently, and these differences shaped the contradicting positions on the subject of political leadership that dominated the election. At one point, the arguments expanded to revolve around the issue of trust and distrust of the government. This study examines the extent to which QT played a role in this dispute, and what this can contribute to our understanding of the implications of its status as an official state translation. A case like this also provides insights into how the public perceived QT at the time and the extent to which its reading of the Qur'an is privileged due to this official status.

The History of Indonesian State Qur'an Projects

The foundation of Indonesia as an independent nation-state led to the establishment of a particular ministry to oversee state religious projects. Established on 3 January 1946, the Ministry of Religious Affairs (MORA) has remained significant for every ruling government in Indonesian post-colonial history; a number of ministries have ceased to exist for various reasons, but MORA has remained. Throughout the various early phases of nation-building and national identity implemented between 1945 and 1967 by Sukarno, the first president of Indonesia, the period of economic developmentalism and political stability between 1967 and 1998 under his successor Suharto (1921–2008), and the post-Suharto Reformation-era governments' preoccupation with state security amidst growing Islamism, terrorist attacks, and civil conflicts, the MORA has dutifully served the state in the pursuit of the political ends of each ruling government.[10]

Although MORA projects are predominantly concerned with the administration of religion,[11] the ministry also oversees projects that touch upon a more fundamental aspect of the epistemological formation of the Islamic intellectual tradition, namely the production of editions of the

10 Moch. Nur Ichwan, 'Official Reform of Islam: State Islam and the Ministry of Religious Affairs in Contemporary Indonesia, 1966–2004' (unpublished doctoral dissertation, Tilburg University, 2006), pp. 352–61, https://pure.uvt.nl/portal/en/publications/official-reform-of-islam(f07a60f1-bf55-4979-8ea1-bab6e45a42ac).html.

11 Martin van Bruinessen, 'Secularism, Islamism, and Muslim Intellectualism in Turkey and Indonesia: Some Comparative Observations', in *Ketika Makkah Menjadi Las Vegas: Agama, Politik dan Ideologi*, ed. by Mirza Tirta Kusuma (Jakarta: Gramedia, 2014), pp. 130–57 (p. 140).

Qur'anic text, i.e., the *mushaf*, and Qur'an commentaries. A particular division within the ministry, Lajnah Pentashihan Mushaf Al-Qur'an (LPMQ, The Qur'anic Text Review Board), has commissioned several projects closely related to state supervision of the Qur'an in Indonesia, including the production and publication of the *Mushaf Standar Indonesia* (the Indonesian standardized Qur'anic text), *Al-Qur'an Juz ʿAmma*, *Al-Qur'an dan Terjemahnya* (the Qur'an and its translation; QT), *Al-Qur'an dan Tafsirnya* (the Qur'an and its commentary), *Tafsir Ringkas* (a concise commentary), *Tafsir Tematik* (a thematic commentary), *Tafsir Ilmi* (a scientific commentary), and *Tajwid Warna* (a color-coded *tajwīd*). Thanks to the Qur'an printing industry, the standardized Qur'anic text and QT have a much wider audience than the others. While these MORA Qur'an projects enjoy varying degrees of public recognition and reception, they also make Indonesia one of the very few countries actively producing official, state-approved Islamic texts.

QT is the first official state Qur'an translation project, and it marks an unprecedented event in contemporary history; the claim of authority over the interpretation and reading of the Qur'an by a political institution. QT is distinct from other regular translations due to the palpable presence of the state in its very production. While regular translations and commentaries are strongly connected with either the intellectual or religious credentials of the translators or authors, such criteria are discernibly absent in QT. The privilege of being the official Qur'an translation of the state entails certain consequences. At the formative level, QT is the product of collective work coordinated by several individuals, and can be said to fall into a new category of *tafsīr*, which we will term institutional *tafsīr*.[12] The notion of collectivity in QT, however, is different from that in edited volumes or co-authored books, where the relative contribution of each individual is laid bare. In QT, individual contributions are entirely unidentifiable, although the names of the contributors are listed. This collaborative format has yet to receive serious attention from scholars. A further consequence of QT's status as the official Qur'an translation of the state is the fact that its own history is read in light of the history of the state. QT has existed throughout the rise

12 Pink, 'Tradition, Authority and Innovation in Contemporary Sunnī Tafsīr: Towards a Typology of Qur'an Commentaries from the Arab World, Indonesia and Turkey', p. 61.

and fall of all the major regimes of modern Indonesia: the Old Order, the New Order, and the Reformation era. It is also closely connected to the development of the national language and the religious modernization of the state. In addition to its three comprehensive revisions, and an uncountable number of reactive and ad hoc revisions that have taken place since its initial printing,[13] an agreement between the MORA and the Saudi authorities in 1989 brought about a further edition that has since been consistently published by the King Fahd Complex for the Printing of the Holy Qur'an (henceforth: King Fahd Complex) and which is annually distributed to Indonesian pilgrims as a gift. The range of its distribution amongst Indonesian Muslims is exceptional, and QT is the translation that is recited on official Islamic festivals commissioned by the state, which expands its reach even further. With these dynamics in mind, two questions arise: what does the official status of such a work mean, and what role has the translation played in the political stages of the state's development?

Pre-existing studies either take these issues for granted or simply disregard them. Of course, it is impossible to ignore the fact that QT is produced by the state. Nevertheless, only a few studies have placed this feature at the center of their analysis. The studies that are concerned with identifying the translation methods or techniques employed by QT, or with investigating the inadequacy of certain word choices of this translation, such as those by Nashruddin Baidan, Moh. Mansyur, Tardi, and Fahmi Gunawan treat QT as a regular translation and attribute no significance to its official status.[14] If the state's involvement is mentioned, it is usually in the context of the theological aspect of the translation, the idea that because QT is a widely-read, state-sanctioned work its first priority should be theological accuracy.[15] Some other studies do provide a comprehensive historical account of the production of QT, which places the involvement of the state front and center. Ismail Lubis' *Falsifikasi*

13 The different kinds of revision of QT will be discussed in Chapter Two.

14 Tardi, 'Koherensi Terjemahan Al-Qur'an: Analisis Struktural Terjemahan al-Qur'an Depag Edisi Tahun 2002' (unpublished master's thesis, Universitas Islam Negeri Syarif Hidayatullah, 2008); Fahmi Gunawan, 'The Effect of Translation Technique to Its Quality at The Holy Book of Indonesian Moslem Society', *Lisan: Jurnal Bahasa dan Linguistik*, 8.2 (2019), 101–09, https://doi.org/10.33506/jbl.v8i2.377.

15 Nasrullah Nurdin, 'Terorisme dan Teks Keagamaan: Studi Komparatif atas Terjemah Al-Qur'an Kemenag RI dan Terjemah Tafsiriyah MMI' (unpublished master's thesis, Universitas Islam Negeri Syarif Hidayatullah, 2016).

Terjemahan Al-Qur'an Departemen Agama Edisi 1990 (The Falsification of the Qur'an Translation of the Ministry of Religious Affairs 1990 Edition, 2001), for example, is a very important work that records the production of the first and second editions of QT. However, Lubis' historical account merely provides the introductory context for his study of QT, and the subsequent analysis is concerned primarily with the linguistic features of the translation, leaving its production history completely unaddressed.[16] Hamam Faizin's recent monograph, *Sejarah Penerjemahan Al-Qur'an di Indonesia* (The History of Qur'an Translation in Indonesia, 2022), presents a more comprehensive history of QT, and covers all existing editions. Unlike Lubis, Faizin consistently situates each edition of QT in its respective historical context. However, he is more interested in situating QT in dialogue with the changing intellectual milieu in recent Indonesian history than exploring the state's role in its production. Even though he connects his argument with the development of Indonesian politics from the Old Order, the New Order, and the Reformation era, this development plays a role more as a time frame for his study, which does not thoroughly address QT's official privilege.[17]

Other studies seem to take the official status of QT for granted, and essentially suggest that by publishing official Qur'an commentaries Indonesia is showing that it wants to provide a standard reference work for its Muslim population. R. Michael Feener suggests that QT 'may be seen as officially-sponsored attempts to provide Indonesian Muslims with 'standard' works of reference and thus ensure greater uniformity in national discourses on the sacred text.'[18] Likewise, Howard M. Federspiel suggests that the state's Qur'an projects were carried out to gain Muslims' trust by proving that the state endorses Islamic values, demonstrating the intellectual credential of Indonesian scholars, and

16 Isma'il Lubis, *Falsifikasi Terjemahan Al-Qur'an Departemen Agama Edisi 1990* (Yogyakarta: Tiara Wacana, 2001).

17 Hamam Faizin, *Sejarah Penerjemahan Al-Quran di Indonesia* (Ciputat: Gaung Persada, 2022).

18 R. Michael Feener, 'Southeast Asian Qurʾānic Literature', in *Encyclopaedia of the Qurʾān*, ed. by Jane Dammen McAuliffe (Leiden; Boston; Köln: Brill, 2006), pp. 98–101 (p. 100), http://referenceworks.brillonline.com/entries/encyclopaedia-of-the-quran/southeast-asian-quranic-literature-EQCOM_00190; See also: R. Michael Feener, 'Notes Towards the History of Qur'anic Exegesis in Southeast Asia', *Studia Islamika*, 5.3 (1998), https://doi.org/10.15408/sdi.v5i3.739.

standardizing commentaries and translations of the Qur'an.[19] Johanna Pink,[20] Peter G. Riddell,[21] and Munirul Ikhwan[22] all take a similar stance to Feener and Federspiel. This is unsurprising: since QT is a product of the state, scholars are quick to simply assume that it represents the state's political motives. The problem with this thesis is that it is an oversimplification, which on some occasions goes so far as to imply manipulation and abuse (more on this in Chapter Seven). Instead of emerging from a close investigation of the nature of QT's officiality, this claim comes from a perception that its position as the official Qur'an commentary is in itself a telling clue of its political significance, that its production is the result of an agenda concerned with advocating a state-approved Islamic discourse. These scholars do not seem to be interested in seeking to provide any explanation for how exactly the translation works to shape that discourse.

Several other studies question the issue of the state's participation in the production of the Qur'an translation. Moch. Nur Ichwan, in his article "Negara, Kitab Suci dan Politik Terjemah Resmi Al-Qur'an di Indonesia" (The State, Scripture, and Politics of Official Qur'an Translation in Indonesia, 2009), seeks to answer this question through a historical overview of QT and discussions on gender, politics, and sectarian biases. He is, in principle, on board with the previous studies, suggesting that by commissioning QT government officials have in fact presented themselves as supporters of the Muslim community in the country, whilst also pursuing an agenda of establishing a standardized religious discourse of the state. Nevertheless, unlike previous studies, Ichwan's analysis comes to a more specific conclusion: that the history of QT mirrors the internal political development of MORA, which is

---

19 Howard M. Federspiel, *Popular Indonesian Literature of the Qur'an*, 72nd edn (Ithaca, NY: Cornell Modern Indonesia Project, 1994), pp. 27; 65.

20 Johanna Pink, '"Literal Meaning" or "Correct ʿaqīda"? The Reflection of Theological Controversy in Indonesian Qur'an Translations', *Journal of Qur'anic Studies*, 17.3 (2015), 100–20.

21 Peter G. Riddell, 'Menerjemahkan Al-Qur'an ke dalam Bahasa-bahasa di Indonesia', in *Sadur Sejarah Terjemahan di Indonesia dan Malaysia*, ed. by Henri Chambert-Loir (Jakarta: Kepustakaan Populer Gramedia, 2009), pp. 397–416 (p. 403); Peter G. Riddell, 'Translating the Qurʾān into Indonesian Languages', *Al-Bayān: Journal of Qurʾān and Ḥadīth Studies*, 12.I (2014), 1–27 (p. 13).

22 Munirul Ikhwan, 'Challenging the State: Exegetical Translation in Opposition to the Official Religious Discourse of the Indonesian State', *Journal of Qur'anic Studies*, 17.3 (2015), 157–21 (pp. 146; 155), https://doi.org/10.3366/jqs.2015.0214.

reflected in the politics, gender, and sectarian biases of the various editions of the translation. However, the source material consulted in Ichwan's study is rather limited: his analysis pertains only to the introduction and a modest selection of the Qur'anic verses.[23] In a 2019 article co-authored with Ichwan and Syihabuddin Qalyubi, Akmad Supriadi addresses gender issues further, but essentially proposes the same view as Ichwan.[24] Another work worth mentioning is Islah Gusmian's *Tafsir Al-Qur'an dan Kekuasaan di Indonesia* (Qur'an Commentaries and Power in Indonesia, 2019). Investigating the relationship between Qur'an commentaries and the New Order government in Indonesia, Gusmian highlights that the absence of critical voices speaking out against the New Order government in QT indicates that the committee fell into *otosensor* (self-censorship) in an effort to avoid direct confrontation between the translation and the authoritarian governance.[25] Finally, Jajang A. Rohmana and Muhamad Zuldin have written on the various Qur'anic projects undertaken in West Java, including the production of a Qur'an translation by the regional government, and the translation of QT into Sudanese, and have argued that these Qur'an projects represent a process of religious politicization by the government, with the aim of containing Islam as a potential political force. The authors specifically argue that the fact that QT in principle follows Sunnism illustrates that the translation is the government's attempt to define an ideal Islam, at least from its own point of view.[26]

---

23 Moch. Nur Ichwan, 'Negara, Kitab Suci dan Politik: Terjemahan Resmi Al-Qur'an di Indonesia', in *Sadur Sejarah Terjemahan di Indonesia dan Malaysia*, ed. by Henri Chambert-Loir (Jakarta: Kepustakaan Populer Gramedia, 2009), pp. 417–33 (p. 418).

24 Akhmad Supriadi, Moch. Nur Ichwan, and Syihabuddin Qalyubi, 'Menuju Kesetaraan Ontologis dan Eskatologis?: Problematika Gender dalam Perubahan Terjemahan Ayat-ayat Penciptaan Perempuan dan Pasangan Surgawi dalam Al-Qur'an dan Terjemahnya', *SUHUF Jurnal Pengkajian Al-Qur'an dan Budaya*, 12.1 (2019), 1–20, https://doi.org/10.22548/shf.v12i1.395.

25 Islah Gusmian, *Tafsir Al-Qur'an dan Kekuasaan di Indonesia: Peneguhan, Kontestasi, dan Pertarungan Wacana* (Yogyakarta: Yayasan Salwa Indonesia, 2019), p. 301.

26 Jajang A. Rohmana and Muhamad Zuldin, 'Negara Kitab Suci: Pewacanaan Al-Qur'an di Jawa Barat', *KALAM*, 12.1 (2018), 127–58, https://doi.org/10.24042/klm.v12i1.1945; Jajang A Rohmana, 'Negosiasi, Ideologi, dan Batas Kesarjanaan: Pengalaman Penerjemah dalam Proyek Terjemahan Al-Qur'an Bahasa Sunda', *SUHUF Jurnal Pengkajian Al-Qur'an dan Budaya*, 12.1 (2019), 21–55 https://doi.org/10.22548/shf.v12i1.407.

Qur'an Translation as a Sub-Genre of *Tafsīr*

Let us start this section with a basic question: what is Qur'an translation? The prevalent answer, both in general terms and in terms of Indonesian scholarship in particular, would view Qur'an translation as the transfer of the Qur'an from Arabic into another language. This conception is derived from modern translation theories based on European practices of Biblical translation.[27] Implicit in this view—although often ignored—is the idea of replication, or the notion that the translated text should assume all features of the source text. However, the idea of replication is rejected by the vast majority of Muslims on the basis of the doctrine of the inimitability of the Qur'an. The common solution for this is to make a distinction between *tarjama ḥarfiyya* (literal translation) and *tafsīriyya* (interpretive translation). While *tarjama ḥarfiyya* is regarded as forbidden—of course with some dissent—*tarjama tafsīriyya* is viewed as justifiable, as it serves only to explain the meaning of the Qur'an, instead of aiming to actually replace it.[28]

While this concept of Qur'an translation has its merits, it also has drawbacks. This view fails to capture the complexity and diversity of Qur'an translation practices across history. Travis Zadeh has eloquently presented this argument with reference to pre-modern Qur'an translations into Persian,[29] whereas Pink makes the same case about modern Javanese pedagogical Qur'an translations.[30] Zadeh argues that the modern ideas surrounding Qur'an translation that stress the notion of substitution ignore the fact that Muslims have long translated the Qur'an, but have never considered their translations as a replacement for the divine Arabic text of the original. Pink, on the other hand, suggests that, contrary to the prevalent theory that translations should be as faithful as possible to the source text, the history of Qur'an translations in Javanese shows the translators' eagerness to provide their own voice.

---

27 Johanna Pink, 'The "Kyai's" Voice and the Arabic Qur'an; Translation, Orality, and Print in Modern Java', *Wacana*, 21.3 (2020), 329–59 (p. 333), https://doi.org/10.17510/wacana.v21i3.948.

28 Johanna Pink, 'Translation', in *The Routledge Companion to the Qur'ān*, ed. by Daniel A Madigan and Maria Dakake (London: Routledge, 2021), pp. 364–76 (p. 364).

29 See Travis Zadeh, *The Vernacular Qur'an: Translation and the Rise of Persian Exegesis* (New York: Oxford University Press, 2012).

30 See Pink, 'The "Kyai's" Voice and the Arabic Qur'an; Translation, Orality, and Print in Modern Java'.

The 'substitution' idea of translation, more often than not, also overlooks the importance of the *tafsīr* tradition in the history of Qur'an translation. As will be shown later, in Chapter Four, while the visibility of translators is an important issue in translation studies in general, the visibility of the *tafsīr* tradition is just as important when it comes to translations of the Qur'an.

Although the relationship between Qur'an translation and *tafsīr* will not be studied in depth until Chapter Four, it is necessary at this point to make some general observations about it. This study situates Qur'an translation as *tafsīr,* but from a slightly different perspective than the norm. It follows the theoretical assumption that Qur'an translation can be classified as one sub-genre of the *tafsīr* tradition. This classification is based on Walid Saleh's proposal that *tafsīr* is a genealogical tradition:

> By 'genealogical' I mean a certain dialectical relationship that each new commentary, and hence, each exegete, had with the previous tradition as a whole. At every moment the tradition was in its totality available to the exegete. [...] Designating this genre as genealogical has certain implications for the proper study of, and approach to, tafsīr. One cannot study any given Qur'an commentary in isolation. It has to be seen in conjunction with the tradition that produced it and the influences it left behind.[31]

Here, Saleh underlines the idea that *tafsīr* is never a single independent book; there is always a continuous relationship between any commentator and his predecessors which paves the way for *tafsīr* to become a coherent and internally consistent body of literature. The exegete, in many ways, is not independent since he has to deal with established and limited hermeneutical principles. Even when he disagrees with certain views or opinions, he cannot discard them outright. Saleh has also proposed the idea that there are two sub-genres of *tafsīr*: the encyclopaedic and the *madrasa*-style commentary. Encyclopaedic commentaries are those that provide the foundation for the tradition, and are compilations of materials drawn from various sources. This characteristic explains the polyvalent nature of classical commentaries (which are of this sub-genre). *Madrasa*-style commentaries, on the other hand, provide a 'shorthand summary of the encyclopaedic commentaries. [...] [They]

31 Walid A. Saleh, *The Formation of The Classical Tafsīr Tradition: The Qur'ān Commentary of al-Thaʿlabī (d. 427/1035)* (Leiden; Boston: Brill, 2004), p. 14.

summarized, omitted, elaborated, and highlighted interpretations or views already adduced in the encyclopaedic commentaries.'[32] Within this schema, I would introduce Qur'an translation as a third sub-genre.

While *madrasa*-style commentaries are shortened versions of encyclopaedic commentaries, translations of the Qur'an are the super-compendiums of the *tafsīr* tradition. A Qur'an translation is essentially a commentary presented in a more concise format, and is intended to provide a straightforward reading of the meaning of the Qur'an in the target language. The translator, in most cases, has to decide on only one meaning from a number of possibilities. A translation, therefore, is diametrically opposed in format to the classical commentaries, which tend to provide different views on the meaning of certain words or verses, mostly without a clear preference for one over another. In a translation, the only way the translator can elaborate on a specific term, or provide alternative readings or opinions, is through the use of brackets or footnotes. A translation of the Qur'an is, therefore, intended to be monovalent.

Despite this contrast, a Qur'an translation shares the same working principles as *madrasa*-style commentaries. First of all, both *madrasa*-style commentaries and translations of the Qur'an are founded upon a *selection* of views from a wider pool provided by the tradition. Secondly, the main task of commentator and translator alike lies in understanding and interpreting the complexities contained in key terms. A *madrasa*-style commentary both examines and contests the views introduced in encyclopaedic commentaries, and the debates and challenges are visible. While it necessarily covers all verses of the Qur'an, the subjects of dispute are always key terms and verses. The same is essentially true for translations of the Qur'an, although there is a major difference in that this process of dispute takes place in the background and is not visible to the readers. While in translations conducted by an individual debates unfold in the translator's mind, in translations produced by a committee, as in the case of QT, those debates are carried out in person, and resolution can be harder to achieve.

Saleh's description of genealogy has parallels with the production processes of a Qur'an translation. It is clear that most existing Qur'an

---

32 Saleh, *The Formation of The Classical Tafsīr Tradition: The Qurʾān Commentary of al-Thaʿlabī (d. 427/1035)*, p. 21.

translations have a dialectical relationship with the *tafsīr* tradition, not least because they often make reference to Qur'an commentaries available to the translators who wrote them. When one attempts to translate the Qur'an, one has to deal—to various degrees—with the vast *tafsīr* tradition in order to determine the precise meaning intended by certain Qur'anic words and phrases before translating them into the target language. Furthermore, in many contexts, especially educational situations, a Qur'an translation is never read as a standalone work, divorced from the wider tradition. Traditionally trained *ulama* will read a translation in conversation with *tafsīr* and often compare a range of existing Qur'an translations. Furthermore, there is usually a conversation between 'new' Qur'an translations and their predecessors, which often rank among the sources used by translators when authoring their own versions. Indeed, QT lists seven pre-existing Qur'an translations among its sources. It is even plausible that a Qur'an translation might be entirely grounded in preceding translations rather than the original Arabic: H.B. Jassin's translation is one such example.[33]

The impact of Qur'an translations on the *tafsīr* tradition is somewhat paradoxical. On the one hand, by making the message of the Qur'an more central in Muslims' life,[34] Qur'an translation is a genre that helps perpetuate the importance of *tafsīr.* Translation of the Qur'an into a language widely spoken by a certain community of readers

---

33 H.B. Jassin was a decorated Indonesian literary critic who was not traditionally trained in the Islamic disciplines. After the passing of his wife in 1962, he was drawn to the Qur'an, therein gaining a new spiritual experience that later led him to a close reading and translation of it. Jassin appreciated the beauty of the structure and meaning of the Qur'an and questioned why all the texts and translations he encountered were written in blocks of prose instead of in poetic form. This led him to translate the Qur'an into a poetic text entitled *Al-Qur'an al-Karim Bacaan Mulia* (The Glorious Qur'an: A Noble Recitation) and later inspired him to 'rewrite' the Qur'anic text in a poetic format that he called *Al-Qur'an Berwajah Puisi* (The Qur'an with Poetic Face). Both works generated nationwide controversy even though he initially received support from quite a number of *ulama*. See Yusuf Rahman, 'The Controversy Around H.B. Jassin: A Study of His Al-Quranu'l-Karim Bacaan Mulia and Al-Qur'an al-Karim Berwajah Puisi', in *Approaches to the Qur'an in Contemporary Indonesia*, ed. by Abdullah Saeed (Oxford: Oxford University Press, 2005), pp. 85–105; Webb Keane, 'Divine Text, National Language, and Their Publics: Arguing an Indonesian Qur'an', *Comparative Studies in Society and History*, 60.4 (2018), 758–85, https://doi.org/10.1017/S0010417518000282; Fadhli Lukman, 'Epistemologi Intuitif dalam Resepsi Estetis H.B. Jassin terhadap Al-Qur'an', *Journal of Qur'an and Hadith Studies*, 4.1 (2015), 37–55, https://doi.org/10.15408/quhas.v4i1.2282.

34 Pink, *Muslim Qurʾānic Interpretation Today: Media, Genealogies, and Interpretive Communities*, p. 17.

ensures entanglement with local religious and literary culture, thereby encouraging the production of new works of *tafsīr* as well as consolidating the significance of established writings. Not only does Qur'an translation help to maintain the importance of the *tafsīr* tradition, but it also broadens its reach beyond the conventional readership of *tafsīr,* i.e., traditionally-educated Islamic intellectuals. It is in this context that an individual without competency in Arabic could eventually produce a translation of the Qur'an, as in the aforementioned case of H.B. Jassin. Furthermore, translation of the Qur'an expands the reach of the tradition outside the formal genre of *tafsīr,* through its inclusion in school textbooks, as well as other books from a wide range of disciplines and genres, marketing or political posters, and memes; actually, the list of genres or formats in which Qur'an translation citation occurs is endless.

On the other hand, Qur'an translation in a way distances its readers from the *tafsīr* tradition. *Tafsīr* has long been the preserve of the Muslim intellectual community, and both encyclopaedic and *madrasa*-style commentaries are written for exegetes or future exegetes. In other words, they are written for specialized communities who have spent a lifetime engaging with Islamic scholarship, or are preparing to do so. Qur'an translations, on the other hand, expose *tafsīr* to a broader community, thereby creating a distinctive hermeneutical community with, I argue, its own distinctive approach to the text (I will deal with this in more detail in Chapter Seven). Readers of Qur'an translations are not necessarily people who have engaged, or ever would engage, with the tradition as a whole, and they hence have significantly less familiarity with the hermeneutical principles of *tafsīr.* These monovalent Qur'an translations might be the only part of the tradition with which they engage. As will be evident in Chapter Seven, this situation creates a sense of hermeneutical absolutism, a consequence of which is the dismissal of tradition by readers. This is how translations of the Qur'an simultaneously bridge the gap between the tradition and a broader readership, whilst also distancing them from it.

Viewing Qur'an translation as a sub-genre of *tafsīr* has consequences. Despite the fact that 'equivalence' has become a buzzword in translation studies, this approach very much relegates equivalence to the background. The committee that produced QT, and most probably many (if not all) other Qur'an translators, are indeed concerned with equivalence in most instances. However, when it comes to interpreting and translating the most problematic Qur'anic terms, such as words and phrases that pose doctrinal, sectarian, semantic, or hermeneutic problems, most of the time these translators opt to go with selected interpretive views provided by the *tafsīr* tradition instead of pursuing equivalence and using a corresponding local term in the target language, or, alternatively, leaving the word untranslated. That is why, as we will see in Chapter Four, the (in)visibility of *tafsīr* is of greater concern here than the (in)visibility of translators.

None of the above goes to say that no terminology from translation studies will be relevant to the study undertaken here, but translation studies theories do not represent the core hermeneutic in my inquiry, or the main focus of my analysis. Emphasizing the genealogical nature of the *tafsīr* tradition, this study situates the production of QT both in the general *tafsīr* tradition, and in Indonesia specifically, attempting to understand the *tafsīr*'s contribution to the formation of QT and the state's participation therein.

Structural Overview

This book is divided into seven chapters.

Chapter One provides the context for our understanding of QT by painting a brief picture of the history of Islam and Muslims in the State of Indonesia. The chapter elaborates on three essential features of Islam in the country: the Islamization of the region and the establishment of Sunnism as the predominant denomination, the institutionalization of religious mass organizations during the twentieth century, and the religious politics of the state following its declaration of independence. The first line of inquiry seeks to make sense of Muslims' adherence to Sunnism in the country, and additionally gives a brief description of the situation of non-Sunnī Muslims in Indonesia. The history of the Ahmadiyya in the country is interesting, and is particularly significant to the growth of Qur'an translation as a practice in Indonesia. For this reason, a great deal of attention is devoted to the Ahmadiyya in this chapter. As for the second line of inquiry, this chapter introduces two of the most important Muslim organizations in the country, the Muhammadiyah and Nahdlatul Ulama. The third line of inquiry deals directly with state political developments, particularly regarding Islam. The discussion elaborates on the issue of the relationship between the state and Islam, focusing on Pancasila—the Indonesian state ideology—and the Ministry of Religious Affairs.

In Chapter Two, QT is introduced. This chapter initially provides a very brief overview of the history of Qur'an translation in Indonesia, and then moves on to deal with the production and the development of QT from two perspectives. The first perspective sheds light on the evolution of the content of QT, through an analysis of the revisions made across its six-decade history. Arguing that the most important aspects in the development of this translation go beyond merely the evolution of the target text in its various incarnations, this chapter also deals with the more technical aspects of the production of QT, namely issues relating to format, decisions on layout, the transliteration and spelling system used, and the online and hard-copy versions of the work. This chapter argues that, as the official Qur'an translation of the state, QT is set to maintain its readership among Indonesian Muslims.

The third chapter discusses the political interests behind the production of QT. Focusing on its paratextual elements, through which the consecutive ruling governments have conveyed their particular agendas, this chapter shows that QT has been embroiled with the different political interests of different ruling governments since its initial publication. It argues that the production of QT is closely related to the struggles to maintain or restructure power relations that took place during the political development of the state in the Sukarno, Suharto, and post-Suharto periods. Additionally, this chapter elaborates on the motivations behind the production of an official Qur'an translation in the context of the development of the national language. There has been a move away from the use of Arabic or regional languages with Arabic-modified script (*Pegon*)—mainly found in traditional institutions such as *pesantren*—to the use of the Indonesian language in Latin script, which is nowadays prevalent in Islamic higher education. Given this development, this chapter argues that QT has led to the increased use of the Indonesian national language amongst Muslim citizens, and has also contributed to a shift in the language of Islamic scholarship.

The fourth chapter elaborates on the hermeneutical aspects of the production of QT. Starting with a description of the general structure of QT, this chapter goes on to elaborate on the collective, collegiate nature of the translation, and situates it in conversation with the *tafsīr* tradition through consideration of its interpretive method and sources. This chapter demonstrates how the state gives full interpretive authority to the *ulama,* and how the selection of committee members ensures that the translation relies heavily on Sunnī sources. However, the production procedures are such that the translation is generally attributed to the state instead of the individual translators, for whom this translation presumably has greater value than other projects. This chapter also raises a hypothesis concerning the Indonesian school of the *tafsīr* tradition.

The next two chapters, Chapters Five and Six, deal with the interpretive outcomes of QT across its editions. Both chapters investigate the extent to which the translation provided in QT represents the interests of the state. In doing so, Chapter Five compares QT and various reform projects in the arenas of Islamic law and education that have been brought about by MORA, through an exploration of a number of relevant issues that have been the focus of Islamic theological disputes in Indonesia, including marriage and polygamy, the political rights of women, the creation verse, and religious tolerance and pluralism. Chapter Six elaborates on the translation of selected verses, alluding to vocabulary or issues closely related to the ideological idioms of the state. This includes words such as *'esa'* (a keyword of Pancasila) as well as other words related to leadership and power. Both chapters argue against the narrative that QT creates the standard religious discourse in the country in that, even though the interpretive views provided by QT in a number of verses do exhibit a relatively subtle politicization, this is not the general trend of the work. Instead, I argue that QT is essentially a separate project, which was implemented in isolation from other MORA projects that aimed to advocate particular discourses.

Chapter Seven discusses the reception of QT through the analysis of a particular political scenario that was riven with disputes and controversy, namely the 2017 Jakarta gubernatorial election. This chapter shows that the various renderings of particular Qur'anic verses, notably Q 5:51, proposed by different editions of QT led to partisanship that influenced the outcome of the election. This case study also illustrates how the state's Qur'an translation is read as authoritative. This chapter shows that QT holds more than simply hermeneutical merit, because the translation is invested with authority by its official, state-sanctioned status.

1. Islam and Muslims in the State of Indonesia: A Brief Overview

Before beginning our discussion of QT as the official Qur'an translation of the state, this chapter will provide a brief sketch of the historical context and background, highlighting the most important features of Islam in Indonesia. Indonesia has always been predominantly Sunnī, as is evident in the history of the Islamization of the region and its intellectual networks, as well as the literature read, taught, and written by Indonesian Islamic scholars. This dominant loyalty to Sunnism has historically hindered the growth of other branches of Islam, and Shīᶜism has so far not succeeded in establishing a significant presence in the country, let alone overcoming the growing resistance of the majority to Shīᶜī beliefs, especially after the collapse of the New Order regime. However, another branch of Islam, the Ahmadiyya movement, will receive particular attention in this study. Even though this movement has also been marginalized in Indonesia, its contribution to the Islamic intellectual discourse of the early-twentieth century cannot be denied. The Ahmadiyya is also relevant to this particular study because it has either produced or contributed to the publication of translations of the Qur'an in several languages spoken across the Indonesian archipelago, and has also had a significant impact on QT—the very first edition of which copied the translation methodology used by the Ahmadiyya in their publications (as will be discussed in the following chapter).

The division of modernist and traditionalist tendencies in the region has also deeply affected the history of Islam and Muslims in Indonesia, and is another important feature of Indonesian Islam. As will become clear in this chapter, both tendencies were the result of the adoption

 https://doi.org/10.11647/OBP.0289.01

of Islamic discourse from abroad (most importantly the Ḥijāz until at least the nineteenth century, and Egypt and India since the turn of the twentieth century). This dichotomy, whilst not always so clear-cut over time, has had a remarkable impact on the history of Islam in Indonesia, and is strongly linked to the creation of religious mass organizations that are adept at working within the socio-political confines of the state. There are several such organizations, but the most important are Muhammadiyah and Nahdlatul Ulama, currently the two largest Islamic mass organizations in Indonesia. Constantly vying with one another to steer the religious discourse of the state, both organizations have contributed to every ruling government in the history of Indonesia.

The significant role played by Muslims in the creation of the Indonesian nation means that the state cannot ignore the aspirations of its Muslim population and their potential political power. It is because of this dynamic that a number of the most important material and non-material state infrastructures have emerged in their particular forms, as they embody a process of compromise between different ideologies, the most important of which are secular nationalism and Islamism.[1] Pancasila (The Five Principles) is the first such 'compromise' elaborated in this chapter. In accordance with the principles of Pancasila, Indonesia's state philosophy, Indonesia subscribes neither to strong secularism—in the sense of a full separation of religion and state affairs—nor to Islamic theocracy. To use Jeremy Menchik's terminology, Pancasila dictates that Indonesia is a 'Godly nation.'[2] The second instance of compromise relevant to this study is the establishment of a special ministry dedicated to dealing with the religious affairs of the state. As the first pillar of Pancasila recognizes God as one of the foundations of the state, and the constitution guarantees the freedom of faith of the citizens, Muslim leaders have demanded state involvement in religious affairs, and this

1 See Moch. Nur Ichwan, 'Official Reform of Islam: State Islam and the Ministry of Religious Affairs in Contemporary Indonesia, 1966–2004' (unpublished doctoral dissertation, Tilburg University, 2006), pp. 23–64, https://pure.uvt.nl/portal/en/publications/official-reform-of-islam(f07a60f1-bf55-4979-8ea1-bab6e45a42ac).html.

2 For more on Godly nationalism, see Jeremy Menchik, 'Productive Intolerance Godly Nationalism in Indonesia', *Comparative Studies in Society and History*, 56.3 (2014), 591–621, https://doi.org/10.1017S0010417514000267; Jeremy Menchik, *Islam and Democracy in Indonesia: Tolerance without Liberalism* (Cambridge: Cambridge University Press, 2016).

led to the establishment of the Ministry of Religious Affairs (MORA). MORA's remit is to deal with the administration of religion but, in reality, the ministry has also played an important role in each ruling government of Indonesia.

Sunnism and the Islamization of Indonesia

The majority of Muslims living in the Malay-Indonesian archipelago are followers of the Sunnī school of Islam. Accordingly, the Nahdlatul Ulama describe the core of their religious ideas as conforming to the ideas of *ahl al-sunna wa al-jamāᶜa* (those who adhere to the [Prophet's] Sunna and community),[3] a phrase that essentially denotes Sunnī beliefs. They base their religious practices on the Shāfiᶜī (767–820) school of law, the Ashᶜarī school of theology, and the Ghazalian school of mysticism. The Muhammadiyah also essentially follows Sunnī doctrine, though without emphasizing strict adherence to a particular *madhhab*.[4] Likewise, at state level, references to 'Islam' as one of the six religions recognized by the State are generally interpreted by Indonesian Muslims to mean 'Sunnī Islam'. Thus, when one looks, for example, at the formation of the *fatwa*s of the Majelis Ulama Indonesia (MUI, Indonesian Ulama Council), it is quite apparent that they consistently refer to Sunnī religious precepts.[5] In contrast, there are only very limited historical records about the existence of Shīᶜism in the country.[6] The Ahmadiyya, on the other hand, played a considerable role in Indonesian history and religious culture

3 Zamakhsyari Dhofier, 'The Pesantren Tradition: A Study of the Role of the Kyai in the Maintenance of the Traditional Ideology of Islam in Java' (unpublished doctoral dissertation, The Australian National University, 1980), pp. 297–98.

4 Muhamad Ali, 'The Muhammadiyah's 47th Congress and "Islam Berkemajuan"', *Studia Islamika*, 22.2 (2015), 382–83, http://journal.uinjkt.ac.id/index.php/studia-islamika/article/view/1978/1557.

5 See Nadirsyah Hosen, 'Behind the Scenes: Fatwas of Majelis Ulama Indonesia (1975–1998)', *Journal of Islamic Studies*, 15.2 (2004), 147–79.

6 According to Zulkifli, historians are divided about the arrival of Shīᶜism in Indonesia. The widely held belief is that Shīᶜism arrived in Indonesia more recently, and was closely linked to the Iranian Revolution. Azyumardi Azra, for example, rejects the notion that Shīᶜism wielded significant power prior to the Iranian Revolution. An alternative theory contends that Shīᶜism was the first branch of Islam to arrive in Indonesia. Despite their support for the early influence of Shīᶜism, the proponents of this theory, according to Zulkilfi, agree that most of their impact has faded over time. See Zulkifli, *The Struggle of The Shiᶜis in Indonesia*, Islam in Southeast Asia Series (Canberra: ANU E Press, 2013), pp. 2–3.

during the early twentieth century. However, both Shīᶜī and Ahmadiyya beliefs were considered heretical, particularly after the reformation era.

The history of Islam in Southeast Asia clearly reveals the reasons behind the dominance of Sunnism in Indonesia. Accounts of the early Islamic history of the peninsula[7] report the visit in around 1345 of Ibn Battuta (1304–77), who found that the rulers of the Samudra Pasai—one of the ancient kingdoms on the northern island of Sumatra—adhered to the Shāfiᶜī school. Later on, in the seventeenth century, it is quite certain that the *aṣḥāb al-jāwiyīn* (the *Jawi* community), who were indigenous to Southeast Asia, played a significant role in the Islamization of what is now Indonesia.[8] 'It is clear then that,' Michael F. Laffan suggests, 'an active scholarly tradition lay at the core of the relationship between the Muslim students of Southeast Asia and Middle East.'[9] In this section, I will elaborate on two features of this tradition: the intellectual network of native Indonesian scholars that has been in place since the seventeenth century with links to the center of Islamic intellectualism in the Ḥijāz, and the literature about the various Islamic sciences that has been disseminated in the region.

Let us first consider the intellectual climate of the Ḥijāz in the seventeenth century. Naser Dumairieh's recent study suggests that global changes that took place during the sixteenth century worked in favor of the establishment of the Ḥijāz as the hub for Islamic intellectual dissemination.

> The rise of a powerful and wealthy Islamic dynasty, the Mughals, and their massive donations to the Ḥijāz helped establishment of

---

7 An overview of theories of the Islamization of Indonesia is provided in Azra's *The Origins of Islamic Reformism in Southeast Asia*. This study uses two editions of the book: the English edition published by Allen & Unwin and University of Hawai'i Press in 2004 and the Indonesian (and extended) edition published in 2013. The latter edition contains an additional chapter about the Islamization of Indonesia, which does not exist in the English edition. Accordingly, the overview of the theories of Islamization in Indonesia in this study refers to the Indonesian edition. See Azyumardi Azra, *The Origins of Islamic Reformism in Southeast Asia: Networks of Malay-Indonesian and Middle Eastern ᶜUlamāʾ in the Seventeeth and Eighteenth Centuries*, Southeast Asia Publication Series (Allen & Unwin and University of Hawai'i Press, 2004); Azyumardi Azra, *Jaringan Ulama Timur Tengah dan Kepulauan Nusantara Abad XVII & XVIII: Akar Pembaruan Islam Indonesia* (Jakarta: Kencana, 2013), pp. 2–18.

8 Martin van Bruinessen, *Kitab Kuning, Pesantren dan Tarekat*, trans. by Farid Wajidi and Rika Iffati (Yogyakarta: Gading Publishing, 2012), p. 10.

9 Michael Francis Laffan, *Islamic Nationhood and Colonial Indonesia: The Umma Below the Winds* (London; New York: Routledge Curzon, 2003), p. 20.

> numerous educational institutions and maintain endowments there. The Ottoman expansion into the Ḥijāz, as well as to all of the Levant, Egypt, and most of North Africa, facilitated travel across these areas. Alongside facilitating travel, the Ottomans made numerous efforts to secure pilgrimage routes and provided generous economic supports for the region. Generous donations from the Mughals and the Ottomans helped increase investments in the region's educational institutions and maintain endowments that provided their teachers and students with all the necessities of life. Finally, the conversion of Iran to Shīᶜism forced numerous Sunni scholars there to disperse to other parts of the Islamic world, carrying their knowledge with them to other intellectual centers in the Indian Subcontinent, Anatolia, Damascus, Cairo, and the Ḥijāz.[10]

These external actions by the Mughals, the Ottomans, and Iran meant that the Ḥijāz became the focal point for Islamic intellectual development in the seventeenth century: many mosques, *madrasas*, *ribāṭ*s, kitchens, libraries, and other infrastructures were built, and scholars and students were supported with stipends. Moreover, one should not forget the internal privileges of this region: it was the birthplace of Islam, the location of the home of the Prophet, and the destination of pilgrims for the annual *ḥajj*—all of these facts play an essential role in its history. The Ottomans sought to protect the *ḥajj* routes, so increasing numbers of pilgrims visited the Ḥijāz, either for a short stay as part of a pilgrimage, or as part of a longer intellectual journey. Additionally, European navies were able to sail more safely in the Indian Ocean, which increased the number of pilgrims, scholars, and students coming to the Ḥijāz from Europe, as well as from Southeast Asia.[11]

For Southeast Asian Muslims, Mecca and the *ḥajj* stand at the heart of the process of Islamization of the area. The indigenous cosmology of several areas in Southeast Asia after Islamization clearly conceptualizes Mecca as the center of the world. As well as its link to the *ḥajj*, a performative ritual with a very high religious value, Mecca was regarded as the locus of political legitimacy, and the fount of religious knowledge.[12] The prosperity of the Malay-Indonesian Muslim states, the efforts made by the Ottomans to protect the *ḥajj* routes, and the development

10 Naser Dumairieh, *Intellectual Life in the Ḥijāz before Wahhabism: Ibrāhīm al-Kūrānī's (d. 1101/1690) Theology of Sufism*, Islamicate Intellectual History: Studies and Text in the Late Medieval and Early Modern Periods, 9 (Leiden; Boston: Brill, 2022), p. 18.

11 Dumairieh, pp. 18–49.

12 van Bruinessen, *Kitab Kuning, Pesantren dan Tarekat*, p. 4.

of economic, diplomatic, and socio-religious relations between Malay-Indonesian and Middle Eastern states in the fourteenth and fifteenth centuries all encouraged Malay-Indonesian Muslims to undertake the *ḥajj*. This in turn led to the establishment of non-Arab intellectual communities in the Ḥijāz, including the *asḥāb al-jāwiyīn*.[13] Later, the invention of the steamship and the construction of the Suez Canal in the mid-nineteenth century made the journey to the Ḥijāz shorter and easier, and consequently bolstered the number of *ḥajj* travelers.[14] Many of these travelers stayed in the Ḥijāz for a while to study, becoming students of leading scholars and joining the cosmopolitan scholarly communities they found there. Most of these travelers eventually went back home to the archipelago, and once there transmitted the intellectual tradition of the Ḥijāz to the Malay-Indonesian world.

This background explains the predominance of Sunnism and the Shāfiʿī *madhhab* in the Indonesian archipelago. Sunnism was popular in the Ḥijāz, and the Sharīf of Mecca was a Shāfiʿī.[15] Other leading and influential scholars in the Ḥijāz in the seventeenth century, such as Shibghatullāh (d. 1606) and Aḥmad al-Shinnawī (1567–1619) could

13 Azyumardi Azra, *The Origins of Islamic Reformism in Southeast Asia: Networks of Malay-Indonesian and Middle Eastern ʿUlamāʾ in the Seventeeth and Eighteenth Centuries*, Southeast Asia Publication Series (Allen & Unwin and University of Hawai'i Press, 2004), p. 3; Laffan, *Islamic Nationhood and Colonial Indonesia: The Umma Below the Winds*, p. 18; *Sejarah Kebudayaan Islam Indonesia: Tradisi, Intelektual, dan Sosial*, ed. by Taufik Abdullah and Endjat Djaenuderadjat, 2nd edn (Jakarta: Direktorat Sejarah, Direktorat Jenderal Kebudayaan, Kementerian Pendidikan dan Kebudayaan, 2017), p. 5.

14 van Bruinessen, *Kitab Kuning, Pesantren dan Tarekat*, pp. 13–14; Eric Tagliacozzo, *The Longest Journey: Southeast Asian and the Pilgrimage to Mecca* (Oxford: Oxford University Press, 2013), p. 64; M. Dien Majid, *Berhaji di Masa Kolonial* (Jakarta: CV. Sejahtera, 2008), p. 55.

15 Martin van Bruinessen noted in 1994 that between the sixteenth and eighteenth centuries in the Ḥijāz, the Hanafī *madhhab* was dominant. It is probable that, because the official *madhhab* adopted by the Ottomans and the Mughals was Ḥanafī, Bruinessen assumed that this would also hold true of the Ḥijāz. However, a later study by Laffan suggests that the Shāfiʿī *madhhab* predominated in the region. See Martin van Bruinessen, 'Pesantren and Kitab Kuning: Continuity and Change in a Tradition of Religious Learning', in *Texts from the Islands: Oral and Written Traditions of Indonesia and the Malay World*, ed. by Wolfgang Marschall (Berne: The University of Berne Institute of Ethnology, 1994), pp. 121–46 (p. 19), the citation is from the online copy on the author's site: https://www.academia.edu/2524271/Pesantren_and_kitab_kuning_Continuity_and_change_in_a_tradition_of_religious_learning; For the alternative viewpoint, see Laffan, *Islamic Nationhood and Colonial Indonesia: The Umma Below the Winds*, p. 20.

trace their intellectual genealogies back to notable names in the Sunnī-Shāfi^{c}ī milieu, such as Ibn Ḥajar al-^{c}Asqalānī (1372–1449), Shams al-Dīn al-Ramlī (d. 1004/1595–96, also known as 'the little Shāfi^{c}ī' [*al-Shāfi^{c}ī al-ṣaghīr*]), Jalāl al-Dīn al-Ṣuyūṭī (d. 911/1505), and Ibn ^{c}Arabī (1165–1249). It was Aḥmad al-Qushashī (1538–1661)—the most influential student of Shibghatullāh (d. 1606) and Aḥmad al-Shinnawī (1567–1619)—and his student, Ibrāhīm al-Kūrānī (1614–90) who were responsible for the development of the intellectual network in the Ḥijāz in the seventeenth century. Both al-Qushashī and al-Kūrānī were the followers of the Shāfi^{c}ī *madhhab*. Al-Kūrānī is well-known for being a *mujaddid* (reformer) during the seventeenth century, and the leading *mujtahid* among the Shāfi^{c}ī *fuqahā*ʾ and *muḥaddiths*. He had a large number of students, including leading figures of the *aṣḥāb al-jāwiyīn*, whom al-Kūrānī mentioned in many of his works, including *Itḥāf al-dhākī*. ^{c}Abd al-Raʾūf al-Singkīlī (1615–93) and Yūsuf al-Maqassarī (1627–99), who were eventually influential in transmitting the Sunnī-Shāfi^{c}ī intellectual tradition in the Malay-Indonesian region, were both students of his.[16] It was here that the virtually uninterrupted development of Sunnism in Indonesia began.

The establishment of the Sunnī-Shāfi^{c}ī *madhhab* in Indonesia can also be traced through the production, reproduction, and hence the pedagogy, of religious texts within scholarly circles in the archipelago, which intensified in the seventeenth and eighteenth centuries.[17] It is not a coincidence that these texts were often written by pupils of al-Kūrānī, such as ^{c}Abd al-Raʾūf al-Sinkilī, Yūsuf al-Maqassarī and ^{c}Abd al-Ṣamad al-Falimbānī (1704–c. 1789).[18] The records we have that list the works

16 Azra, *The Origins of Islamic Reformism in Southeast Asia: Networks of Malay-Indonesian and Middle Eastern ^{c}Ulamāʾ in the Seventeeth and Eighteenth Centuries*, pp. 12–20; Dumairieh, pp. 122; 128.

17 Azyumardi Azra, 'Naskah Terjemahan Antarbaris: Kontribusi Kreatif Dunia Islam Melayu-Indonesia', in *Sadur Sejarah Terjemahan di Indonesia dan Malaysia*, ed. by Henri Chambert-Loir (Jakarta: Kepustakaan Populer Gramedia, 2009), pp. 435–43 (p. 438); In this article, Azra mistook interlinear translation as the indigenous textual innovation of the Malay-Indonesian Muslims. Certainly, Azra does not consider the early Persian interlinear Qur'an translations for this claim. See also: Travis Zadeh, *The Vernacular Qur'an: Translation and the Rise of Persian Exegesis* (New York: Oxford University Press, 2012), p. 16.

18 Azra, 'Naskah Terjemahan Antarbaris: Kontribusi Kreatif Dunia Islam Melayu-Indonesia', p. 438; Laffan, *Islamic Nationhood and Colonial Indonesia: The Umma Below the Winds*, p. 21.

of literature disseminated in Islamic traditional education institutions in the country[19] indicate the institutionalization of the Shāfiᶜī *madhhab*. Perhaps the most obvious evidence for this can be seen in the kind of *fiqh* works that were in circulation during that time, given that *fiqh* is arguably the Islamic science that has the most practical, concrete impact in daily life. *Fatḥ al-wahhāb* by Zakariyya al-Anṣāri (1420–1520) (translated by ᶜAbd al-Raᵓūf al-Singkīlī and entitled *Mirᵓat al-ṭullāb*, but rarely available now), *Sullam al-tawfīq* and *al-Ghāya wa al-taqrīb* by Abū Sujāᵓ al-Iṣfahāni (1041–1166), and *Fatḥ al-qarīb* by Ibn Qāsim al-Ghazzi (1455–1512) were amongst the most popular works studied by beginners. *Fatḥ al-muᶜīn*, written by Zayn al-Dīn al-Malibari (d. 1579), a student of Ibn Ḥajar, in the sixteenth century has long been popular in Indonesia, and we also find records of its use. A commentary on this work, *Iᶜānat al-ṭālibīn*, written by Abū Bakr Shaṭṭā (1849–93) (who also compiled the *fatwas* of his colleague Aḥmad ibn Zayni Daḥlān (1816–86), a Shāfiᶜī *muftī* in Ḥijāz), was also widely read. Aḥmad Khaṭīb al-Minangkabawī (1860–1916), one of the important tutors among the *aṣḥāb al-jāwiyīn* in Mecca, was a disciple of Abū Bakr Shaṭṭā and specialized in teaching this book to his *jāwī* students.[20] When it comes to *ḥadīth* works, those frequently on the curricula included *Bulūgh al-marām*, *Riyāḍ al-ṣāliḥīn*, and *Durrat al-nāṣiḥīn*, while *ᶜaqīda* and *taṣawwuf* works included *Faṭḥ al-majīd* by Muḥammad Nawāwī al-Bantānī (1813–97), *Iḥyāᵓ ᶜulūm al-dīn*, *Taᶜlīm al-mutaᶜallim*, and *al-Ḥikam*.[21]

The dominance of Sunnism is also discernible in the field of *tafsīr*. Martin van Bruinessen notes that *Tafsīr al-Jalālayn*, the famous exegesis

19 This school's name varies, i.e., *pesantren* in Jawa, South Kalimantan, pondok in Kalimantan, South Sulawesi, Malay, portions of Sumatera, *surau* in West Sumatera, and dayah in Aceh. According to Azra, what makes it traditional is that until the early years of the twentieth century, teachers gave instruction almost exclusively in classical Islamic traditions of knowledge. Azyumardi Azra, Dina Afrianty, and Robert W. Hefner, 'Pesantren and Madrasah: Muslim Schools and National Ideals in Indonesia', in *Schooling Islam: The Culture and Politics of Modern Muslim Education*, ed. by Robert W. Hefner and Muhammad Qasim Zaman (Princeton and Oxford: Princeton University Press, 2007), pp. 172–98 (p. 175).

20 Laffan, *Islamic Nationhood and Colonial Indonesia: The Umma Below the Winds*, p. 107.

21 Martin van Bruinessen, 'Kitab Kuning: Books in Arabic Script Used in the Pesantren Milieu: Comments on a New Collection in the KITLV Library', *Bijdragen Tot de Taal-, Land- En Volkenkunde*, 146.2/3 (1990), 226–69 (pp. 236–53); van Bruinessen, 'Pesantren and Kitab Kuning: Continuity and Change in a Tradition of Religious Learning', pp. 12–15.

co-authored by Jalāl al-Dīn al-Ṣuyūṭī and Jalāl al-Dīn al-Maḥallī (d. 864/1460), was popular in *tafsīr* pedagogy in the Malay-Indonesian world from the sixteenth to eighteenth century, whilst al-Bayḍāwī's (d. 791/1388) *Anwār al-tanzīl* was mentioned by name, even though it was not widely taught to students.[22] The earliest report of the use of *al-Jalālayn* in the Southeast Asian *tafsīr* tradition dates back to its use as the core source of the first complete rendition of the Qur'an into Malay, *Tarjumān al-mustafīd* by ᶜAbd al-Raʾūf al-Sinkīlī (1615–93).[23] The earliest surviving manuscript of *Tafsīr al-Jalālayn* held in the collection of the National Library of Indonesia in Jakarta was written around the same period, namely in 1673. Accordingly, we can conclude that this *tafsīr* has had an influential role in the archipelago since the seventeenth century, presumably, according to Ervan Nurtawab, because of its brevity. The widespread translation of the commentary into vernacular languages such as Malay, Javanese, Sundanese, and Madurese provides further evidence of its influence. It has maintained its prominence in centers of Islamic education in Indonesia ever since, even though the modern pedagogical culture of *tafsīr* has seemingly developed at the expense of this commentary.[24]

References made to al-Bayḍāwī's *Anwār al-tanzīl*, although quite rare in pedagogical settings, are also indicative of the transmission of *tafsīr* norms from the Ḥijāz to Indonesia. As Martin van Bruinessen has already argued, the use of *al-Jalālayn* and *Anwār al-tanzīl* in the pre-modern *tafsīr* curriculum in Indonesia mirrored its use in the *madrasa*s and *zawiya*s in the Ḥijāz.[25] Walid Saleh, following Ibn ᶜAshūr, asserts that *Anwār al-tanzīl* by al-Bayḍāwī was the most important commentary

22 van Bruinessen, 'Kitab Kuning: Books in Arabic Script Used in the Pesantren Milieu: Comments on a New Collection in the KITLV Library', p. 253; van Bruinessen, 'Pesantren and Kitab Kuning: Continuity and Change in a Tradition of Religious Learning', p. 14.

23 Peter G. Riddell, *Malay Court Religion, Culture and Language: Interpreting the Qur'ān in 17th Century Aceh*, Texts and Studies on the Qur'ān, 12 (Leiden; Boston: Brill, 2017), p. 61.

24 Ervan Nurtawab, 'Jalalayn Pedagogical Practice: Styles of Qur'an and Tafsir Learning in Contemporary Indonesia' (unpublished doctoral dissertation, Monash University, 2018), pp. 8–11; Ervan Nurtawab, 'Tafsīr Al-Jalālayn at the Crossroads: Interpreting the Qur'ān in Modern Indonesia', *Australian Journal of Islamic Studies*, 6.4 (2021), 4–24, https://doi.org/10.55831/ajis.v6i4.429.

25 van Bruinessen, 'Pesantren and Kitab Kuning: Continuity and Change in a Tradition of Religious Learning', p. 19.

in pre-modern Sunnī *tafsīr* history.[26] In this light, it is noteworthy that al-Kūrānī studied this commentary not just once but twice: once in Baghdad and later in Medina,[27] and it is safe to assume that the arrival of al-Bayḍāwī's commentary in Indonesia had a connection to al-Kūrānī's role in transmitting religious knowledge from the Ḥijāz to Indonesia.

As well as being keen readers of literature originating from outside Southeast Asia, native *jāwīs* also wrote their own works on the Qur'an and the Islamic sciences. I have already mentioned the seventeenth-century Malay commentary on the Qur'an written by ᶜAbd al-Raʾūf al-Singkīlī. In addition to this, there was also an anonymous Malay who wrote a commentary on *Sūrat al-Kahf* (Q. 18), which is now kept in Cambridge University Library (catalogued as MS li.6.45). Both commentaries were based on Sunnī sources, including the *tafsīrs* of al-Baghāwī, al-Jalālayn, al-Khāzin (d. 725/1324), and al-Bayḍāwī.[28] The prolific Nawāwī al-Bantānī wrote *Tafsīr al-Munīr li maᶜālim al-tanzīl*, also known as *Maraḥ labīd*, which owes much to *Tafsīr al-Kabīr* by Fakhr al-Dīn al-Rāzī (d. 1210).[29] The trend is maintained in later examples of Indonesian-authored *tafsīr*, such as those by Ahmad Hassan (1887–1958), Hasbi Ash-Shiddieqy (1904–75), Hamka (1908–81), and Muhammad Quraish Shihab, among others.[30]

Whilst they were established territory for the followers of Sunnī-Shāfiᶜī Islam, the other three legal *madhhabs* of Sunnism are found

26 Walid A. Saleh, 'The Qur'an Commentary of al-Bayḍāwī: A History of *Anwār al-tanzīl*', *Journal of Qur'anic Studies*, 23.1 (2021), 71–102, https://doi.org/10.3366/jqs.2021.0451.

27 Dumairieh, p. 99.

28 The primary source of the commentary of al-Kahf is the commentary of al-Baghāwi, whilst that of *Tarjumān al-mustafīd* is *al-Jalālayn*. They share the use of al-Bayḍāwī and al-Khāzin as secondary sources. For more on the commentary of al-Kahf and *Tarjumān al-mustafīd*, see Riddell, *Malay Court Religion, Culture and Language: Interpreting the Qur'ān in 17th Century Aceh*, pp. 60–64; See also Peter G. Riddell, 'Menerjemahkan Al-Qur'an ke dalam Bahasa-bahasa di Indonesia', in *Sadur Sejarah Terjemahan di Indonesia dan Malaysia*, ed. by Henri Chambert-Loir (Jakarta: Kepustakaan Populer Gramedia, 2009), pp. 397–416 (p. 402); Peter G. Riddell, 'Translating the Qurʾān into Indonesian Languages', *Al-Bayān – Journal of Qurʾān and Ḥadīth Studies*, 12.1 (2014), 1–27 (p. 10), https://doi.org/10.1163/22321969-12340001.

29 R. Michael Feener, 'Southeast Asian Qurʾānic Literature', ed. by Jane Dammen McAuliffe, *Encyclopaedia of the Qurʾān* (Leiden; Boston; Köln: Brill, 2006), 98–101, http://referenceworks.brillonline.com/entries/encyclopaedia-of-the-quran/southeast-asian-quranic-literature-EQCOM_00190.

30 More on the sources of exegetical works in Indonesia in Chapter Four.

only rarely in Indonesia, and then most notably after the rise of modernist Islamic thought which advocates a fluid attitude with respect to the different streams of *madhhab*. In contrast to established practice in the traditional *pesantren*, in the growing body of modernist *pesantren/madrasas*, works on the curriculum include Ibn Rushd's *Bidāyat al-mujtahid*, which emphasizes a comparative perspective, and *Fiqh al-sunna* by Sayyid Sābiq.[31] This inclusive attitude, however, applies only to legal *madhhabs* within the Sunnī stream and other streams, such as the Ahmadiyya and Shīᶜism, have a minority status. It is true that the Islamic Revolution in Iran eventually inspired a limited number of Indonesian Muslims to adopt Shīᶜism, yet they remain a minority.[32] The Ahmadiyya, despite being appealing to some of the 'new intellectuals' in the first quarter of the twentieth century, has experienced the same fate.[33] Recently, the situation has become even less favorable for both of these denominations due to the failure of the *Reformasi* to properly manage religious diversity in the state. With the passing of the blasphemy law[34] alongside public support of MUI's *fatwas*,[35] as well as the general turn towards conservatism[36] among Indonesian Muslims after the collapse of Suharto (1921–2008), the activities and dissemination of non-Sunnī schools nowadays tend to be classified as heresy (*aliran sesat*) and

31 van Bruinessen, 'Kitab Kuning: Books in Arabic Script Used in the Pesantren Milieu: Comments on a New Collection in the KITLV Library', p. 244.

32 More on the history of Shi'ism in Indonesia, see Zulkifli, *The Struggle of The Shiᶜis in Indonesia*; Umar Faruk Assegaf, 'The Rise of Shi'ism in Contemporary Indonesia: Orientation and Affiliation' (unpublished master's thesis, The Australian National University, 2012).

33 Menchik, *Islam and Democracy in Indonesia: Tolerance without Liberalism*, pp. 73–90.

34 Noorhaidi Hasan, 'Religious Diversity and Blasphemy Law: Understanding Growing Religious Conflict and Intolerance in Post-Suharto Indonesia', *Al-Jāmi'ah: Journal of Islamic Studies*, 55.1 (2017), 105–26, https://doi.org/10.14421/ajis.2017.551.105-126.

35 On *fiqh* matters, besides the MUI, the Muhammadiyah and NU have issued several *fatwas* through their respective *fatwa* councils. On *ᶜaqīda*, there seems to be a silent agreement between those organizations that *fatwas* are the responsibility of MUI alone. This, in turn, creates an impression that the MUI has a monopoly on *ᶜaqīda*, and that with support from the ruling government, most notably during Susilo Bambang Yudhoyono's administration, the *fatwas* of MUI on *ᶜaqīda* have greater legitimacy than those on other matters. Syafiq Hasyim, 'Fatwa Aliran Sesat dan Politik Hukum Majelis Ulama Indonesia (MUI)', *Al-Ahkam*, 25.2 (2015), 241–66 (pp. 250–51), https://doi.org/10.21580/ahkam.2015.25.2.810.

36 Martin van Bruinessen, 'Introduction: Contemporary Development in Indonesian Islam and the "Conservative Turn" of the Early Twenty First Century', in *Contemporary Development in Indonesian Islam: Explaining the 'Conservative Turn'*, ed. by Martin van Bruinessen (Singapore: ISEAS Publishing, 2013), pp. 1–20.

considered blasphemous. As a consequence, followers of both streams have experienced public hate and violent attacks.[37]

Governing Religion: The Relationship between the State and Religious Groups

Islam has been the religion of the state for quite a long time in the Malay-Indonesian world. This is not to say that Indonesia ascribes to theocracy or aspires to be an Islamic state, but rather that the history of Islam in Indonesia has been consistently intertwined with the history of consecutive political institutions in the archipelagic peninsula, from the era of the pre-colonial kingdoms,[38] to that of Dutch[39] and Japanese colonialism,[40] and the post-colonial Indonesian State. For the state of Indonesia, the most important product of this close contact between religion and the state is Pancasila, as expressed in its first principle,

37 Hasyim, 'Fatwa Aliran Sesat dan Politik Hukum Majelis Ulama Indonesia (MUI)', p. 253; M. Adlin Sila, 'Kerukunan Umat Beragama di Indonesia: Mengelola Keragaman Dari Dalam', in *Kebebasan, Toleransi, dan Terorisme: Riset dan Kebijakan Agama di Indonesia*, ed. by Ihsan Ali-Fauzi, Zainal Abidin Bagir, and Irsyad Rafsadi (Jakarta: PUSAD Paramadina, 2017), pp. 117–58 (p. 130).

38 Rulers from kingdoms in the archipelago sought political legitimation through Islamization. The ruler of Samudera Pasai, an ancient kingdom in Aceh, competed or colluded with Bengal's rulers during the fourteenth century to have their names mentioned in the Friday prayer in Calicut, where the *jāwī* community met Indians, Persians, and the Arab communities. ʿAbd al-Raʾūf al-Singkīlī (1615–93) and Yūsuf al-Maqassarī (1627–99) had political influence in Aceh and Banten, respectively, upon their arrival from Mecca. Van Bruinessen uncovers the same story with regard to Javanese kings in Mecca during the seventeenth century. Some figures returning from *ḥajj* made an impact in those kingdoms. The 'Nine Saints' (*Wali Songo*), who are considered responsible for the Islamization of Jawa, were not only members of the religious elite but also the political elite. See Jajat Burhanudin, 'The Triumph of Ruler: Islam and Statecraft in Pre-Colonial Malay-Archipelago', *Al-Jāmiʿah: Journal of Islamic Studies*, 55.1 (2017), 211–40, https://doi.org/10.14421/ajis.2017.551.211-240; Michael Francis Laffan, *The Makings of Indonesian Islam: Orientalism and the Narration of a Sufi Past* (Princeton: Princeton University Press, 2011), p. 5; Azra, *The Origins of Islamic Reformism in Southeast Asia: Networks of Malay-Indonesian and Middle Eastern ʿUlamāʾ in the Seventeeth and Eighteenth Centuries*, pp. 52–108; van Bruinessen, *Kitab Kuning, Pesantren dan Tarekat*, p. 4.

39 Karel A. Steenbrink, *Kaum Kolonial Belanda dan Islam di Indonesia (1596–1942)*, trans. by Suryan A. Jamrah (Yogyakarta: Gading Publishing, 2017), pp. 144–53; B. J. Boland, *The Struggle of Islam in Modern Indonesia* (Dordrecht: Springer Netherlands, 1971), pp. 13–14, https://doi.org/10.1007/978-94-017-4710-3.

40 Boland, pp. 9–13; Ichwan, 'Official Reform of Islam: State Islam and the Ministry of Religious Affairs in Contemporary Indonesia, 1966–2004', pp. 29–35.

'Belief in one Almighty God,' and the establishment of MORA. Both define the nature of the relationship between the state and religion as neither secular nor religious, which means that all developments with regard to state and religious life in the country arguably revolve around the interpretation of, and policies derived from, Pancasila and/or the strategic position taken by MORA, which is tasked with realizing *Ketuhanan Yang Maha Esa* in public life.[41]

'Pancasila' as a political theory is a compromise that emerged from an intense debate about the relationship between the state and religion. In 1945, during the build-up to Indonesian independence, discussion on the issue of the foundation of the state divided the leaders of the future Indonesia into two groups: the secular nationalists and the Islamic nationalists. It is important to note that these categories were not mutually exclusive. Among the secular nationalists, there were devout Muslims who did perceive religion as an important moral basis for the future state of Indonesia, but posited that religions ought to be the concern of their respective followers. These groups were stuck at an impasse on the issue of the basis of the state. To use B.J. Boland's formulation, it was a question of whether '[...] the official basis of the Indonesian state [would] be formed by Islamic principles, expressed in an Islamic terminology, or would Indonesia be based on Pancasila and become a model of multi-religious state, where followers of different religions (together with an increasing number of 'humanists') live and work together with respect for one another?'[42] The Islamic nationalist group advocated for the first option, while the secular nationalists preferred the latter.

These debates, which had been taking place since the early twentieth century, essentially shaped the arguments that took place during the meetings of the official committee established to prepare for freedom in 1945, namely Dokuritsu Junbi Chōsakai, known in Indonesian as Badan Penyelidik Usaha Persiapan Kemerdekaan Indonesia (BPUPKI, The Investigation Committee for Preparation for Indonesian Independence).[43]

41 Boland, p. 108; Ismatu Ropi, *Religion and Regulation in Indonesia* (Singapore: Springer Singapore, 2017), p. 3, https://doi.org/10.1007/978-981-10-2827-4.

42 Boland, p. 23.

43 Bakhtiar Effendy, *Islam dan Negara: Transformasi Gagasan dan Praktik Politik Islam di Indonesia*, trans. by Ihsan Ali-Fauzi and Rudy Harisyah Alam, Digital (Democracy Project, 2011), p. 97.

The first session of the committee specifically dealt with the issue of the basis of the state, and was not conclusive. Nevertheless, it set an important milestone for what lay ahead. During this meeting, two important speeches, given by Mohammad Yamin (1903–62) and Sukarno (1901–70), shaped what the future formulation of the state philosophy would look like. Yamin proposed five principles as a basis for the future state of Indonesia: *Peri Kebangsaan* (nationalism), *Peri Kemanusiaan* (humanitarianism/internationalism), *Peri Ketuhanan* (belief in God), *Peri Kebangsaan* (democracy), and *Kesejahteraan Rakjat, Keadilan Sosial* (public welfare, social justice). On the last day of the session, 1 June 1945, Sukarno proposed a draft that would later be widely recognized as the first form of Pancasila, as he named these principles.[44] Sukarno's proposal consisted of Indonesian nationalism (*kebangsaan Indonesia*), internationalism or humanitarianism (*internasionalisme atau perikemanusiaan*), deliberation or democracy (*konsensus atau demokrasi*), social welfare (*kesejahteraan sosial*), and belief in God (*ketuhanan*). With this proposal, Sukarno suggested that Indonesia should be neither a secular state, nor a religious one, but a Pancasila state instead. The fifth pillar, 'belief in God' (*ketuhanan*) represented the aspirations of Islamic leaders, whilst the remaining pillars accommodated the secular nationalist group, without contradicting the Islamic view.

To resolve the gridlock, the debate was henceforth confined to a smaller team, *Tim Sembilan* (The Committee of Nine). On 22 June 1945, this smaller committee came to an agreement on a draft document that was intended to become the Preamble to the Constitution. Later known as Piagam Djakarta (The Jakarta Charter), this draft stipulated a new formulation of the five principles, as follows: Belief in God with the obligation to enforce Islamic sharia for Muslim believers (*Ketuhanan dengan kewajiban menjalankan syariat Islam bagi pemeluk-pemeluknya*); just and civilized humanity (*kemanusiaan yang adil dan beradab*); the unity of Indonesia (*persatuan Indonesia*); democracy guided by inner wisdom founded in consensus derived from deliberation amongst political representatives (*kerakyatan yang dipimpin oleh hikmat kebijaksanaan dalam permusyawaratan perwakilan*); and social justice for all of the people of Indonesia (*keadilan sosial bagi seluruh rakyat Indonesia*). The first principle

44 Boland seems to prefer associating the birth of Pancasila with Yamin's speech instead of Sukarno's. Boland, p. 17.

of the Jakarta Charter explicitly mentions Islam, granting Muslims a better position in the state. However, this agreement was not endorsed by members from Protestant and Christian backgrounds, namely A.A. Maramis (1897–1977) and Latuharhary (1900–59).[45] Eventually, after the declaration of Indonesian independence on 17 August 1945, the first principle was modified for the sake of the unity of the state to acknowledge those non-Muslim citizens who mostly resided in the eastern region. It was reduced by seven words to 'belief in One Almighty God' (*Ketuhanan Yang Maha Esa*), and this later version was recorded in the constitution and officially recognized as Pancasila.

As mentioned above, the amendment of the first pillar, or principle, of Pancasila to *Ketuhanan Yang Maha Esa* was the result of a compromise following protests among some Christian circles living in the eastern part of Indonesia, as they thought that the additional phrase relating to the enforcing of sharia law for Muslims in the Jakarta Charter would prevent them from being equal citizens of the Republic of Indonesia. Mohammad Hatta (1902–80), the first Vice President of Indonesia, referred to this amendment as one of 'the greatest changes that unite the nation.'[46] This new formulation of Pancasila gave voice to a conceptualization of Indonesia as neither a secular nor a religious state, and the revision of the first verse of Pancasila to *Ketuhanan Yang Maha Esa* accommodated the nationalist leaders' rejection of a theocracy or a state based on Islam, while still meeting Muslim demands that the state should not be radically separated from religion.[47]

The other major compromise relating to religion that was achieved during the formation of the state was the establishment of a particular ministry dealing with religious affairs (MORA), currently known by the name Kementerian Agama. The idea of establishing such a department initially emerged during the Dutch colonial era, in April 1941, when

45 Boland, pp. 27–28.

46 Cf. Ichwan, 'Official Reform of Islam: State Islam and the Ministry of Religious Affairs in Contemporary Indonesia, 1966–2004', p. 53.

47 Ibid.; Moch. Nur Ichwan, 'The Making of a Pancasila State: Political Debates on Secularism, Islam and the State in Indonesia', in *SOIAS Research Paper Series*, 6 (Japan: Institute of Asian Cultures, 2012), p. 8; Andrée Feillard, 'Traditionalist Islam and the State Indonesia: The Road to Legitimacy and Renewal', in *Islam in an Era of Nation-States : Politics and Religious Renewal in Muslim Southeast Asia*, ed. by Robert W. Hefner and Patricia Horvatich (Honolulu: University of Hawaii Press, 1997), pp. 129–55 (p. 132).

Indonesians were given the chance to become members of the Netherlands Indies Parliament. At the time, Islamic leaders proposed the establishment of a Kementerian Urusan Islam Khusus (Special Ministry for Islamic Affairs). Their proposal was not approved. However, this aspiration was eventually accommodated by the Japanese with the establishment of Shūmubu (Kantor Urusan Agama; The Office for Religious Affairs), which dealt specifically with Muslim affairs, despite working in the interests of the Japanese colonial military government.[48]

The establishment of a particular ministry providing state oversight of all religious affairs was eventually achieved in the first year of Indonesian independence, when President Sukarno officially announced the establishment of MORA on 3 January 1946. Many observers regarded the establishment of this ministry as compensation for Muslims' aspirations following the erasure of the 'seven words' of the Jakarta Charter. In his study of *Religion and Regulation in Indonesia*, Ismatu Ropi views this compensation narrative as partly true, in that it was strongly related to the shift from a presidential to parliamentary governmental system in late 1945, which saw the share of power between the executive—the President—and various political parties with diverse interests shift in such a way as to allow for compromises and concessions. As far as Muslims' political interests were concerned, this situation opened up the opportunity for negotiations over the establishment of MORA.[49] In addition, Moch. Nur Ichwan suggests that the establishment of MORA could also be viewed as a political decision made with the intention of winning the confidence of Muslims, by accommodating their demands for such a ministry. At the time the decision to set up MORA was made, it was being reported that the Dutch had initiated measures to reoccupy their former Indonesian territories. This meant that the state needed the full support of the Indonesian people, and, by announcing the establishment of MORA, the newly formed cabinet was engaging in an attempt to win the support of the Muslim population.[50]

Ever since the codification of Pancasila and the establishment of MORA, they have formed the fundamental bedrock of the government's

48 Boland, p. 9.

49 Ropi, pp. 102–03.

50 Ichwan, 'Official Reform of Islam: State Islam and the Ministry of Religious Affairs in Contemporary Indonesia, 1966–2004', pp. 58–63.

regulation of religion. Pancasila is the yardstick by which all Indonesian religious movements are measured. During Sukarno's administration, those who took arms to fight for the establishment of an Islamic state, such as Darul Islam, were denounced as rebels. The Masyumi (*Majelis Syura Muslimin Indonesia*/Consultative Council of Indonesian Muslims) was also accused of taking the side of one of the rebel movements and was therefore dissolved. Suharto's government went a step further in enforcing the doctrine of Pancasila. Sukarno's support for communism was heavily criticized by Muslim activists in the final years of his presidency; and although Suharto secured support from Muslims due to his purging of the communist influence during his rise to power, he was suspicious of political Islam. Loyalty to Pancasila was set as the main criteria for any movement's survival, and to publicly criticize the nationalist ideology meant running the risk of imprisonment or life in exile. This indoctrination became even more pervasive when, in 1985, Suharto made all parties and organizations recognize Pancasila as their sole foundation (*asas tunggal*).[51] When the fall of Suharto marked the end of his authoritarian regime and the rise of democracy, one of the main outcomes was the rise of Islamist ideologies, which benefited from the new freedom of speech. Radical groups were more vocal in proselytizing strict adherence to their interpretations of doctrine, posing a challenge to both democracy and Pancasila. However, mainstream groups, such as the Nahdlatul Ulama and the Muhammadiyah, officially recognized Indonesia as a legitimate state and Pancasila as its foundation,[52] and proved a major force in shaping Indonesian Muslims' acceptance of, and support for, Pancasila. All the post-New Order governments have used Pancasila as a force to counter those particular strands of Islamism that seek to turn Indonesia into an Islamic state or to establish a global and

---

51 Ahmad Najib Burhani, 'Defining Indonesian Islam: An Examination of the Construction of the National Islamic Identity of Traditionalist and Modernist Musilms', in *Islam in Indonesia: Contrasting Images and Interpretations*, ed. by Jajat Burhanudin and Kees van Dijk, ICAS Publication Series (Amsterdam: Amsterdam University Press, 2013), xvi, pp. 25–48 (p. 31).

52 Robert W. Hefner, 'Indonesia in the Global Scheme of Islamic Things: Sustaining the Virtuous Circle of Education, Associations and Democracy', in *Islam in Indonesia: Contrasting Images and Interpretations*, ed. by Jajat Burhanudin and Kees van Dijk, ICAS Publication Series (Amsterdam: Amsterdam University Press, 2013), xvi, pp. 49–62 (pp. 7–11).

transnational caliphate, and MORA plays a critical role in all of these efforts.

At this point, it suffices to say that the politicization of Islam in Indonesia is inevitable and there is a constant, ongoing process of negotiation that shapes the contours of state authority and religious policies and regulations. Ropi explores a number of religious regulations that point to the underlying cross purposes that exist between the executive and the majority of the Islamic community. While the need to maintain social and political order requires the government to regulate religious affairs, they are in a position where they need to take into account the interests of the majority, and these majorities believe firmly in the political power that is provided them by their numerical superiority.[53] Given this, Menchik's arguments for the co-evolution of the state and religion only seem reasonable.[54] As he has pointed out, social forces drive the collaborative relationship between state and religion in Indonesia, and, in turn, affect the development of both. This development, Menchik argues, has given rise to what he terms 'Godly nationalism', 'an imagined community bound by a common orthodox theism and mobilized through state support for religious orthodoxy over liminal and heterodox faiths.'[55] This explains why the notion of Islam in Indonesia, not only culturally, but also politically, is overwhelmingly Sunnī, to the extent that other streams, such as the Ahmadiyya and Shīᶜism, are nowadays considered heretical and are relegated to the status of outcasts in the democratic state of Indonesia.

The Role of Religious Mass Movements

The history of the Islamization of the Indonesian world illustrates the importance of the international connections between local Indonesian *ulama* and the wider Islamic world. As previously stated, in the seventeenth century this connection was made possible through *ḥajj* to the Ḥijāz, which was the international intellectual hub at the time. Later, in the nineteenth century, that intellectual hub expanded to include

53 Ropi, p. 223.

54 Menchik, *Islam and Democracy in Indonesia: Tolerance without Liberalism*, p. 93.

55 Menchik, 'Productive Intolerance Godly Nationalism in Indonesia'; Menchik, *Islam and Democracy in Indonesia: Tolerance without Liberalism*, p. 65.

Egypt and India. The intellectual connections that were forged in the seventeenth century introduced to Indonesia a traditional Sunnī Islam that essentially followed the Shāfiᶜī *madhhab* in *fiqh* and jurisprudence, Abū al-Ḥasan al-Ashᶜarī (874–936) and Abū Manṣūr al-Māturīdī (853–944) for *kalām* or theology, and Abū Ḥāmid al-Ghazālī (1058–1111) and Junayd al-Baghdādī (830–910) for *taṣawwuf* or mysticism.[56] The primary trait of this conceptualization of Sunnism is close reliance on the legal interpretations and practices of the medieval *ulama*. Classical texts, commonly known as *kitab kuning* in the Indonesian context and widely perceived as a finite body of knowledge,[57] played a role as the reference point for religious thought, with close-knit teacher-student supervision that ensured the continuation of religious knowledge and practices.

The expansion of the Islamic intellectual hub to include Egypt and India in the nineteenth century was perhaps partly the result of the political turmoil that occurred in the Ḥijāz in the late eighteenth century, during which the Ottoman Empire lost control of the two holy cities of Mecca and Medina.[58] As a result, Cairo began to wield greater influence during the early twentieth century, as reflected in the growing number of Indonesian students who attended al-Azhar University.[59] Furthermore, in the 1920s, the Ahmadiyya sent missionaries to Indonesia, and they had notable success in introducing India as an alternative destination for scholars seeking further education in the Islamic sciences.[60] With these developments, the movements of Muḥammad ibn ᶜAbd al-Wahhāb (1115–1206/1701–93) in the Ḥijāz, Jamāl al-Dīn al-Afghānī (1838–97) and Muḥammad ᶜAbduh (1849–1905) in Egypt, and the Ahmadiyya movement, exerted their influences in Indonesia to varying degrees. Although differing in many respects, these movements introduced to the *Jawi* community the ideas of *al-rujūᶜ ilā al-Qurʾan wa al-sunna* (return

56 Faried F. Saenong, 'Nahdlatul Ulama (NU): A Grassroots Movements Advocating Moderate Islam', in *Handbook of Islamic Sects and Movements*, ed. by Muhammad Afzal Upal and Carole M. Cusack, Brill Handbook on Contemporary Religion, 21 (Leiden - Boston: Brill, 2021), pp. 129–50 (p. 132).

57 van Bruinessen, 'Pesantren and Kitab Kuning: Continuity and Change in a Tradition of Religious Learning', p. 1.

58 Carool Kersten, *Islam in Indonesia: The Contest for Society, Ideas and Values* (London: C. Hurst & Co., 2015), p. 55.

59 Laffan, *Islamic Nationhood and Colonial Indonesia: The Umma Below the Winds*, p. 114.

60 Martin van Bruinessen, 'Global and Local in Indonesian Islam', *Southeast Asia Studies*, 37.2 (1999), 158–75 (p. 169).

to the Qur'an and the Sunna) which underlined direct reference to the foundational religious texts of Islam, a mistrust of *ṭarīqa* and Sufism, and advocacy of *ijtihād* (independent reasoning) at the expense of loyal adherence to the traditional *madhhab*s, which were negatively dubbed *taqlīd* (the blind acceptance of earlier teachings). Above all, this new and growing segment of Islamic intelligentsia believed that Islamic civilization was suffering from a serious decline into backwardness. This undesirable situation, they thought, was brought about by an uncritical loyalty to tradition inherited from the Middle Ages, and the fact that religious practices had become defiled by scripturally unjustifiable external practices and values.[61]

These new ideas brought about friction, dividing Indonesian Muslim society into what were then termed as *kaum muda* (young people) against *kaum tua* (old people), or reformists (some also calls modernist) against traditionalists. The reformists sought religious and social reform, while the traditionalists sought to preserve the ideas transmitted from the formative centuries of Islam.[62] The return of those who had gone on *ḥajj* in the late nineteenth century, for example, often led to violent encounters with traditional *ulama*. Many of those returning from *ḥajj* in the twentieth century took inspiration from more recent reformist figures, such as ᶜAbduh and Rashīd Riḍā (1865–1935), who was known for founding the widely-read journal *al-Manār* as well as for forming enduring relationships with some of his Indonesian pupils.

By the first half of the twentieth century, the division between modernist and traditionalist tendencies had manifested in two blocks of mass organizations. In the traditionalist camp, these included Nahdlatul Ulama, Persatuan Tarbijah Islamijah (Perti, the Union for Islamic Education), Nahdlatul Wathan, and the DDI (Darul Dakwah Wal Irsyad, House of Predication and Guidance), whilst the modernist camp included Syarikat Islam (The Islamic Union), Persis (Persatuan Islam, The Islamic Union), Thawalib, and Masyumi. The modernist groups were established earlier than their traditionalist counterparts, and their members were motivated by a growing awareness of the

61 Ahmad Najib Burhani, 'Pluralism, Liberalism, and Islamism: Religious Outlook of Muhammadiyah', *Studia Islamika*, 25.3 (2018), 433–70 (pp. 436–37), https://doi.org/10.15408/sdi.v25i3.7765.

62 Dhofier, p. viii.

need for self-organization, which was partly a result of their Western education, and partly a response to colonialism. The traditionalist movements did not emerge until later, primarily because they were triggered by the establishment of the modernist groups they sought to counter. The story behind the establishment of Nahdlatul Ulama, as will be discussed briefly below, is a good illustration of the typical pattern of the competition between the two camps.[63]

The NU and the Muhammadiyah are nowadays the two largest and most important religious mass organizations in Indonesia. Partly owing to their involvement in political developments on the national level, as will become clear later, they are the two most successful such organizations, and are able to wield significant influence at a national level.[64] The ample research that has been undertaken on both organizations and their role in the country has given rise to a discourse according to which the modernist and traditionalist factions are understood to have been overwhelmingly co-opted by these two groups. More often than not, this has led to the problematic impression that all modernists are Muhammadiyah and all traditionalists are NU.

The Muhammadiyah was established in Yogyakarta by K.H. Ahmad Dahlan (1868–1923) in 1912, and only received official approval from the Dutch government two years later. This organization engages in three main ways: as an advocate for religious reform, an agent of social change, and a political force.[65] The religious significance of the Muhammadiyah as articulated in its founding statute concerns the spread of Islamic teaching among the Indonesian people and the promotion of religious life among its members. It is commonly stated that the modernist agenda pursued by the Muhammadiyah was

63 Laffan, *Islamic Nationhood and Colonial Indonesia: The Umma Below the Winds*, p. 232; Saenong, p. 131.

64 Both organizations, van Bruinessen argues, have societal penetration at the national level, whereas the significance of other organizations is limited to the regional level. See Martin van Bruinessen, 'Overview of Muslim Organizations, Associations and Movements in Indonesia', in *Contemporary Development in Indonesian Islam: Explaining the 'Conservative Turn'*, ed. by Martin van Bruinessen (Singapore: ISEAS Publishing, 2013), pp. 21–59 (pp. 21–30).

65 Alfian, 'Islamic Modernism in Indonesian Politics: The Muhammadijah Movement during the Dutch Colonial Period (1912–1942)' (unpublished doctoral dissertation, The University of Wisconsin, 1969), p. 212; Burhani adds one more character, i.e., a form of resistance to Christianity. See: Burhani, 'Pluralism, Liberalism, and Islamism', p. 436.

influenced by the ideas of Muhammad ᶜAbduh. However, in addition to this, observers also acknowledge that the Muhammadiyah's theological position is also rooted in Ashᶜarī thought (through Rashīd Riḍā) and the ideas of Ibn Taymiyya (1263–1328).[66] As a modernist movement, the Muhammadiyah disapproves of *taqlīd*, and otherwise promotes *ijtihād*, is concerned with *tachayyul* (heretical phantasms), *bidᶜa* (unlawful innovations), and *churafat* (superstitions), and follows the hermeneutics of *al-rujūᶜ ilā al-Qurᵓan wa al-sunna*. The Muhammadiyah's theological vision also places a great deal of emphasis on social welfare, stressing that the basic tenets of the religion are not limited to belief and ritual, but are integral to the refinement of the individual's quality of life. They promote a holistic view of religion that emphasizes the idea that religion is not limited to the salvation of the afterlife, and that worldly affairs are equally important. Despite its reputation as a religious movement, the Muhammadiyah is active in educational, social, and welfare affairs:[67] by 2015, as many as 2,604 elementary schools, 1,722 middle schools, 745 high schools, 546 vocational schools, 160 *pesantrens*, and 177 colleges and universities were affiliated with the Muhammadiyah, and by 2016, it was responsible for hundreds of orphanages, as well as hospitals, polyclinics and other medical services.[68]

Politically, the Muhammadiyah has in general cooperated with the authorities throughout its history. In its formative period, the Muhammadiyah's political power was overshadowed by that exerted by Sarekat Islam, thanks to the insistence of its founder, Ahmad Dahlan, that it was a non-political movement. However, the Muhammadiyah formed an alliance with Sarekat Islam, and some of its leading figures also had prominent roles in that party.[69] The Muhammadiyah was also

66 This religious position is quite ambivalent compared to NU and has also led to the association of Muhammadiyah with Wahhabism. Nevertheless, Muhammadiyah denies its association with Wahhabism, PKS, Hizb al-Tahrir and Wahdah Islamaiyah. Carool Kersten, *A History of Islam in Indonesia: Unity in Diversity*, The New Edinburgh Islamic Surveys (Edinburgh: Edinburgh University Press, 2017), p. 113; Burhani, 'Pluralism, Liberalism, and Islamism', pp. 435–36.

67 Achmad Jainuri, 'The Formation of the Muḥammadīyah's Ideology, 1912–1942' (unpublished doctoral dissertation, McGill University, 1997), pp. 5; 48.

68 Ahmad Najib Burhani, 'Muhammadiyah', ed. by Kate Fleet, Gudrun Krämer, and Everett Rowson, *Encyclopaedia of Islam*, p. 146, https://referenceworks.brillonline.com/entries/encyclopaedia-of-islam-3/*-COM_36688.

69 Alfian, pp. 241–52.

involved in the struggle for Indonesian independence. During the New Order government, the Muhammadiyah participated in the formation of Parmusi (Partai Muslimin Indonesia, the Indonesian Muslim Party) but, since 1969, the organization has adopted a neutral position towards political parties, although it does not prevent its members from engaging in politics.[70]

The rise of the Muhammadiyah, and modernist movements in general, in the early twentieth century posed a threat to the traditionalists in two main arenas: religion and economics. The different points of view on religious subjects held by the two factions led to fierce competition for social influence. Most of the differences of opinion related to particularities in *ᶜibāda* (ritual) matters, such as the recitation of *uṣallī*[71] at the beginning of prayer, the *qibla* direction, and the method used to determine the beginning and the end of *Ramaḍān* and *ᶜĪd al-Fiṭr,* to name only a few. At some point, the modernists became harsher in their criticism of the traditionalists. They mocked the competency of the *kyais*[72] to make decisions on religious matters, and their culture more broadly. In return, the *kyais* questioned the modernists' motivations. The modernists denounced the traditionalists as polytheists (*mushriks*), and the latter deplored the former as infidels (*kāfirs*). On the economic front, the growth of modernist organizations in various towns in which new recruits included rich businessmen and landlords threatened the economic foundations of the traditionalist *pesantren* and *kyais.* Conflict between the two divisions grew especially heated in 1926 when, during the preparations for sending a delegation to the International Congress of Islam in Mecca that was held following the rise of Ibn Saud to power, the personalities and ideas of Indonesian traditionalists were traduced and marginalized.

Frustrated and disappointed by the delegation debacle, a number of prominent traditionalist *ulama* gathered in Surabaya in January 1926 to discuss forming a *Komite Hijaz* (the Hijāz Committee) which would represent Indonesian traditionalist religious interests at the

70 Burhani, 'Pluralism, Liberalism, and Islamism', p. 437.

71 *Uṣallī* is an Arabic term which means 'I pray', which in this context refers to the debate between modernists and traditionalists over the proper way to perform obligatory prayers.

72 *Kyai* is an honorific for religious teachers at *pesantrens* used widely in the Javan context.

International Congress. In addition to the formation of this committee, the group also made the decision to establish a new organization that represented their view of Islam, namely Nahdlatul Ulama (NU). Like the Muhammadiyah, the NU was originally founded as a religious and social organization but went on to play a significant role in politics. As a response to the modernist religious tendency, the NU explicitly mentioned the obligation to follow one of the four *madhhabs* in their founding charter, defined their religious ideas with the term *ahl al-sunna wa al-jamāʿa*, and implied that modernists were *ahl al-bidʿa* (people who adopted unlawful religious innovations). In this formative period, the NU was not concerned with political issues, a hesitation that is linked to the fact that the political interests of Muslims during this period were represented by Sarekat Islam, which was dominated by modernist figures. Additionally, many traditionalist *ulama* were accustomed to Dutch colonial policy, which gave full freedom on purely religious affairs and repressed Islamic political movements.

In the 1930s, the NU gradually started to move into politics. This period also saw a rapprochement between the NU and the Muhammadiyah.[73] Whilst their respective religious views differed, both groups were united in their protests against Dutch colonial policies that were considered discriminatory against Islam.[74] Such policies included the *Guru Ordonnantie* (Teacher Ordinance), which placed strict limits on Islamic education; the marriage law, which forbade polygamy; the government's objection to Muslims' demands to be exempt from conscription; and the fact that the government gave larger subsidies to Christian schools than Islamic schools. The rapprochement of the NU and the Muhammadiyah on these issues led to the establishment in September 1937 of Madjlis Islam A'laa Indonesia (MIAI, the Supreme Islamic Council of Indonesia), whose objective was to enhance communication and cooperation among the Muslim community. The NU and the Muhammadiyah formed the backbone of the MIAI and accounted for more than half of its members. However, the MIAI was short-lived, as it was dissolved by the Japanese during the Japanese

73 Robin Bush, *Nahdlatul Ulama and the Struggle for Power within Islam and Politics in Indonesia* (Singapore: ISEAS Publishing, 2009), pp. 40–43.

74 Laffan, *The Makings of Indonesian Islam: Orientalism and the Narration of a Sufi Past*, p. 235.

occupation of 1942–45 and replaced with a new organization, Masyumi, which K.H. Hasyim Asy'ari (1871–1947), an NU leader, was appointed to lead. Masyumi was established to deal with religious issues, and was ostensibly non-political, however it was an instrument through which the Japanese government hoped to win Muslim support for their military interests. This meant that the *kyais* were effectively tasked with ensuring the Japanese interests were furthered among grassroots Muslims.[75] The foundation of Masyumi had far-reaching consequences: not only did it pave the way for the NU to become more proactively involved in politics, but their experience during this period also provided NU leaders with the confidence to take on strategic political positions.[76]

In September 1945, following the Indonesian declaration of independence, Masyumi became a political party representing the Muslim community, and by the 1950s it had become the largest political party in the newly formed state of Indonesia. During this time, the NU and the Muhammadiyah held vital positions in the party. Nevertheless, there was a complex tension at work within Masyumi, the most significant cause of which was the divide between its traditionalist and modernist elements. In 1949, during the party's fourth annual congress, the modernists, led by Mohammad Natsir (1908–93), made a bid to take control of the party that destroyed the balance of power: leaders from the NU were marginalized and their power became increasingly limited. Finally, after a series of conflicts that grew heated, the NU withdrew from Masyumi on 31 July 1952 and established a party of their own, the NU party.[77] Thus, two parties were now representing the Muslim community: Masyumi and the NU. Unsurprisingly, Masyumi was aligned with modernist Islam, while the NU channeled traditionalist Islamic interests. Equally unsurprisingly, in 1955, as the election drew nearer, the two parties participated in heated campaign debates. With their established network of *ulama* (mostly based in Java), as well as their entrenched cultural influence in rural areas, the NU party had

75 Ichwan, 'Official Reform of Islam: State Islam and the Ministry of Religious Affairs in Contemporary Indonesia, 1966–2004', pp. 29–35.

76 Greg Fealy, *Ijtihad Politik Ulama: Sejarah NU 1952–1967*, trans. by Farid Wajdi and Mulni Adelina Bachtar (Yogyakarta: LKiS, 2011), pp. 28–37; 93–113.

77 Bush, pp. 43–53.

great success in the 1955 election: Masyumi won 20.9% of the votes, whereas NU, surprisingly, received 18.4%.[78]

Unlike the NU, the Muhammadiyah never transformed itself into a political party. Instead, the political aspirations of the Muhammadiyah were channeled through the membership of Muhammadiyah figures in political parties such as Sarekat Islam and Masyumi. The direct involvement of the NU in politics, however, was a matter of constant internal debate over the *raison d'être* of the organization. Eventually, in 1984, the NU announced its withdrawal from formal politics in a move known as *Kembali ke Khittah 1926* (Return to the Guidelines of 1926) that dissolved the NU as a political party.[79] This withdrawal, however, did not mean a complete repudiation of politics and, like the Muhammadiyah, the NU continues nowadays to play an important role in defining the political paths taken by the state, especially with regards to Islam.

Given that the traditionalist-modernist dichotomy, more often than not dominated by the NU and the Muhammadiyah, has heavily influenced not only religious but also socio-political life for Muslims in Indonesia, the state's policies towards and involvement in religion have always been a battlefield for both groups. Fully aware of this situation, Abdurrahman Wahid (1940–2009), the fourth president of the Republic of Indonesia, described MORA as a 'marketplace where belief and devotion are negotiated'.[80] This reflects the fact that MORA has always been regarded highly by both traditionists and modernists in the development of their respective movements, and was seen as providing valuable career opportunities for graduates from *madrasas* or *pesantrens* who otherwise had limited opportunities to obtain governmental positions. Unsurprisingly, each ruling government preferred either the traditionalists or modernists over the other, and shifts in power led to the rise and fall of each group, especially in terms of their representation within MORA. Ichwan has termed this situation 'NU-ization' or 'Muhammadiyah-ization'.[81] Sukarno, during the Guided Democracy era, for example, was very close to traditionalist leaders due to their

78 Boland, p. 53.

79 Bush, p. 72.

80 Ichwan, 'Official Reform of Islam: State Islam and the Ministry of Religious Affairs in Contemporary Indonesia, 1966–2004', pp. 236–37.

81 Ichwan, p. 362.

flexible view of Nasakom (*Nasionalisme, Agama, Komunisme;* nationalism, religion, communism),[82] while at the same time, the same internal disagreements in Masyumi that had led to the withdrawal of the NU had put the latter in desperate need of greater political affiliation,[83] something that Sukarno could assure. The position of Minister of Religion, and the staff of the ministry, were dominated by NU members during this time. This balance of power later shifted when, after having been helped by traditionalists to expunge the threat of communism in the country, Suharto turned to the modernists, believing that they could help develop a state-approved religious discourse and would support development policies.[84] His appointment of Abdul Mukti Ali, a Muhammadiyah figure, as the Minister of Religious Affairs in 1971 sparked a wave of Muhammadiyah-ization in the ministry. As for the current Joko Widodo administration, his intimacy with the traditionalists is very discernible, to the extent that one of the NU leaders, K.H. Ma'ruf Amin, has become his Vice President for the second term of his presidency.

In sum, political interactions between the NU and the Muhammadiyah in the country have been very dynamic. This political relationship is well summed up by Ichwan:

> As the consequence of this contestation between various interests, State-defined 'Islamic [religious] affairs' are overlapping discourses, which represent the overlapping interests and goals of some actors. In this context, Islamic affairs were mainly defined by hegemonic Muslim groups... During the New Order, the hegemonic Muslim groups were represented by some 'modernist' and 'corporatist' Islamic organizations, at the expense of 'traditionalist' and oppositional Islamic organizations which were marginalized and disarticulated. The Post-New Order situation turned out otherwise; NU increasingly took over the leadership of MORA, at the expense of the former hegemonic 'modernist' groups...[85]

82 Nasakom is Sukarno's ideological experiment that attempted to fuse three conflicting factions during the early decades of Indonesian independence, namely the nationalists, Islamists, and communists.

83 Mochtar Naim, 'The Nahdlatul-Ulama Party (1952–1955): An Inquiry into the Origin of Its Electoral Success' (unpublished master's thesis, McGill University, 1960), p. 204.

84 Martin van Bruinessen, 'What Happened to the Smiling Face of Indonesian Islam? Muslim Intellectualism and the Conservative Turin in Post-Suharto Indonesia', in *RSIS Working Paper* (Nanyang Technological University, 2011), p. 14.

85 Ichwan, 'Official Reform of Islam: State Islam and the Ministry of Religious Affairs in Contemporary Indonesia, 1966–2004', pp. 362–63.

The Ahmadiyya and Its Publication Projects

The Ahmadiyya is one of the most important producers of modern Qur'an translations at the global level.[86] They are typically among the first to publish a Qur'an translation in a particular vernacular[87] and their translations have contributed to shaping the development of modern Qur'an translations.[88] Their sway may have waned in recent years, but in early twentieth-century Indonesia their influence was important. They were warmly welcomed on their initial arrival from India in the 1920s, particularly by reformist groups such as the Muhammadiyah and Sarekat Islam, successfully impressed Indonesian leaders, and managed to win the confidence of Indonesian Muslims as a result of their publication program and positive media coverage. Overall, the movement was considered a bright success.[89]

The initial friendly cooperation between the Ahmadiyya and indigenous Indonesian reformist groups was due to the paradigmatic similarity between the ideals brought in by the Ahmadiyya and those of the existing reformist Muslims in Indonesia, both of which proposed a modernized version of Islam in the face of a changing world and European colonialism. The Ahmadiyya teach harmony between religion and science, and stress that the Qur'an is the self-sufficient solution to

86 Hartmut Bobzin suggests that the first person to translate the Qur'an from the Muslim world was Sayyid Ahmad Khan with his Persian-language version, published in 1866. The Ahmadiyya came later along with Kemal Attatürk's government's effort to latinize the Qur'an. For Stefan Wild, the Ahmadiyya was one of the pioneers of the translation of the Qur'an into English, and despite the criticism, it contributed to boosting Muslims' confidence in translating the Qur'an. See Hartmut Bobzin, 'Translation of the Qur'an', ed. by Jane Dammen McAuliffe, *Encyclopaedia of the Qur'ān* (Leiden; Boston; Köln: Brill, 2006), 340–54 (pp. 341–42); Stefan Wild, 'Muslim Translators and Translations of the Qur'an into English', *Journal of Qur'anic Studies*, 17.3 (2015), 158–82 (p. 168), https://doi.org/10.3366/jqs.2015.0215.

87 Pink, 'Translation', p. 368.

88 M. Brett Wilson, 'Translations of the Qur'an: Islamicate Languages', in *The Oxford Handbook of Qur'anic Studies*, ed. by Mustafa Shah and M. A. S. Abdel Haleem (Oxford: Oxford University Press, 2020), pp. 552–64 (p. 554).

89 Ahmad Najib Burhani, 'When Muslims Are Not Muslims: The Ahmadiyya Community and the Discourse on Heresy in Indonesia' (unpublished doctoral dissertation, University of California, 2013), p. 5; Menchik, 'Productive Intolerance Godly Nationalism in Indonesia'; Menchik, *Islam and Democracy in Indonesia: Tolerance without Liberalism*, pp. 65–92; Alfitri, 'Religious Liberty in Indonesia and the Rights of Deviant Sects', *Asian Journal of Comparative Law*, 3.1 (2008), 1–27, https://doi.org/10.2202/1932-0205.1062.

all problems in the world. Having already been confronted with Dutch colonialism and the introduction of Christianity and European scientific thought, Indonesians saw the Ahmadiyya missionaries as allies and a source of inspiration in their efforts to combat the expansion of Christian missionaries and the clash of values between Islam and Dutch modernity, both of which had caused the Muslim intelligentsia to lose confidence in their religion.

Despite initially being met with enthusiasm, the Ahmadiyya have more recently encountered a number of challenges in the Indonesian context, particularly after the fall of the New Order. The Ahmadiyya, particularly the JAI (Jemaat Ahmadiyah Indonesia, the Indonesian Ahmadiyya Congregation), the official organization of the Qadiani Ahmadiyya in Indonesia, has been on the receiving end of public anger, and even violence, due to their adherence to a number of religious tenets that are considered heretical by mainstream Muslims. The main focal point of Sunnī objections towards the Qadiani Ahmadiyya lie in the messianic claims made by his followers that the movement's founder, Mirza Ghulam Ahmad, was a prophet, which is considered a serious deviation from normative Islamic doctrine. To the mainstream Sunnī, one cannot proclaim oneself Muslim if one disputes the idea that Muhammad was the final prophet. At the international level, in 1974 the World Muslim League recommended that all Muslim organizations and countries take measures against all of the Qadiani's activities and label them non-Muslims.[90] Accordingly, in 1980, the MUI issued a *fatwa* declaring them a deviant sect and recommended that the government take action against them, and in 1984 MORA requested that the Ministry of Justice reconsider the legal status of the JAI in Indonesia. After the fall of Suharto, tensions increased further and the Ahmadiyya community experienced several physical attacks, including those carried out in Lombok in 2002 and 2006, and in Parung, a village in West Java Province, in 2005. The attack in Parung used the 1980 *fatwa* issued by the MUI as justification, and, in the opinion of some analysts, was intended to deliver a message to the MUI's national congress, due to take place two weeks after, urging it to take more definitive action against the Ahmadiyya. Ichwan suggests that the rise of Islamist political attitudes and the conservative and puritanical turn after the fall of Suharto, as

90 Alfitri, 'Religious Liberty in Indonesia and the Rights of Deviant Sects', p. 20.

well as the subsequent conservative and puritanical turn within the MUI itself, had shifted the MUI's exclusively anti-Qadiani Ahmadiyya attitude to an indiscriminately anti-Ahmadiyya attitude.[91] Whether this is true or not, at the 2005 congress the MUI shifted from being harsh towards the Qadiani branch but lenient to the Lahore branch, to condemning both equally. Despite criticism of the new *fatwa* issued by the MUI in 2005, and continuous advocacy to protect the Ahmadiyya community on the part of some NGOs, it was generally accepted in Indonesia, as is reflected in a survey conducted by Pusat Pengkajian Islam dan Masyarakat (PPIM, the Centre for Islamic and Social Studies) in 2006, which revealed that 47% of the respondents supported the *fatwa* and 28.7% agreed with the eviction of Ahmadiyya communities from their homes.[92] The government justified the *fatwa* in 2008 through a joint ministerial decree that practically forbade all Ahmadiyya activities.[93]

The publication and translation of works pertaining to Islam are essential activities for the Ahmadiyya, as one of the key features of their teaching is the modification of the doctrine of physical *jihād* into the *jihād* of word and pen, and this forms a vital element of their proselytization activities (*daʿwa*).[94] Consequently, they have published numerous books to disseminate their modernist view of Islam, and habitually translate those into languages spoken by communities that they are targeting. In the Indonesian context, their books were read by modernist-leaning Muslims, mostly those with a Dutch education who were fluent in English or Dutch but had no competency in Arabic, and many of whom were members of modernist organizations such as Persis, the Muhammadiyah, and Jong Islamieten Bond (Young

91 Moch. Nur Ichwan, 'Towards a Puritanical Moderate Islam: The Majelis Ulama Indonesia and the Politics of Religious Orthodoxy', in *Contemporary Development in Indonesian Islam: Explaining the 'Conservative Turn'*, ed. by Martin van Bruinessen (Singapore: ISEAS Publishing, 2013), pp. 60–104 (p. 86).

92 Ichwan, 'Towards a Puritanical Moderate Islam: The Majelis Ulama Indonesia and the Politics of Religious Orthodoxy', p. 87.

93 Martin van Bruinessen, 'Ghazwul Fikr or Arabization? Indonesian Muslim Responses to Globalization', in *Southeast Asian Muslims in the Era of Globalization*, ed. by Ken Miichi and Omar Farouk (New York: Palgrave Macmillan, 2014), pp. 61–85 (p. 17), the citation is from the online copy on author's site: https://www.academia.edu/2839951/Ghazwul_fikri_or_Arabisation_Indonesian_Muslim_responses_to_globalisation.

94 As has been suggested by Johanna Pink in *Muslim Qurʾānic Interpretation Today: Media, Genealogies, and Interpretive Communities*, p. 27.

Islamic League).[95] This readership generally did not have access to the traditional Arabo-Islamic intellectual legacy or to the modernist ideas disseminated in Arabic publications such as *al-Manār*. The Ahmadiyya publications were particularly appealing to this particular segment of modernists precisely because it was very different to the intellectual legacy recorded in the Arabic *kitab kuning* that was consumed by their traditionalist counterparts, and they were unable to access the modern Arabic sources (mostly from Egypt) that were available to their fellow modernists who had received a *madrasa* education. The reach of their publications was striking, even influencing such figures as Sukarno and H.O.S. Tjokroaminoto (1883–1934), two of the greatest leaders of the Indonesian independence movement. In sum, the contribution made by the Ahmadiyya to modernizing the religious vision of younger, Western-educated Indonesians during the twentieth century cannot be overstated.[96]

When it comes to Ahmadiyya publication activities, the translation of the Qur'an is one of their most successful enterprises, and has a global reach. It is safe to say that the Ahmadiyya Qur'an translation project has contributed to the acceptance by mainstream Sunnī Muslims of the permissibility of translating the Qur'an.[97] In the Indonesian context, almost immediately after the Lahore Ahmadiyya was established on 10 December 1928,[98] their main activity was not recruiting new

95 Steenbrink, pp. 231–41.

96 Burhani, 'When Muslims Are Not Muslims: The Ahmadiyya Community and the Discourse on Heresy in Indonesia', pp. 99–103.

97 Stefan Wild speculates that 'the almost sensational success' of the Ahmadiyya in the field of Qur'an translation, which were disseminated throughout the world, including in Egypt, may have been facilitated by the silence of al-Azhar on the issue, a silence which indicated a shift of attitude towards the idea of translating the Qur'an. If this is true, it is ironic that in 1952 al-Azhar burned the Ahmadiyya's translation in a very public rejection of it. Rashīd Riḍā's famous answer over the question of the issue of the translatability of the Qur'an raised by his Indonesian pupil, Basuni Imran, also had a strong anti-Ahmadiyya tone. Apparently, more recently, the Egyptian religious authorities have given up their opposition to this translation, indicating that Wild's ideas may well be valid. See Wild, p. 169; Moch. Nur Ichwan, 'Differing Responses to an Ahmadi Translation and Exegesis: "The Holy Qur'ân" in Egypt and Indonesia', *Archipel*, 2001, pp. 143–61 (p. 152), https://doi.org/10.3406/arch.2001.3668; Wilson, 'Translations of the Qur'an: Islamicate Languages', p. 552; Pink, 'Translation', p. 369.

98 It was not legally acknowledged by the Dutch government until almost a year later, on 28 September 1929.

members, but translating the Qur'an into Dutch, Javanese, and Malay. Iskandar Zulkarnain conveys that the Qadiani branch of Ahmadiyya had intended to produce Qur'an translations in a hundred different languages by 1989, in order to commemorate a hundred years of the Ahmadiyya movement. However, by 2000, they had seemingly only managed to translate it into sixty-four languages.[99]

What does the Ahmadiyya preoccupation with Qur'an translation mean to Indonesia? The first Ahmadiyya English translation of the Qur'an, *The Holy Qur'an*, was authored by Muhammad Ali (1874–1951), the leader of the Lahore branch of the Ahmadiyya, and published in 1917. It has since acted as the main source for many later translations into other languages. This translation had a significant readership among Indonesian intellectuals and inspired them to render it into local languages. In 1925, Tjokroaminoto started to translate *The Holy Qur'an* into Malay, while Soedewo (1906–71) translated it into Javanese a decade later. Tjokroaminoto's translation was a failure. His work was rejected, amidst some uproar, by the delegates at the al-Islam Congress held on 26–29 January 1928, and this led to the termination of the project. Unlike Tjokroaminoto's effort, Soedewo's translation met with great success, and was reprinted several times in Indonesia and a number of Dutch-speaking countries, such as South Africa, Suriname, and the Netherlands. In fact, it was so popular that it was said to have been possessed by every member of the Muslim intelligentsia during the late colonial era. It was also the translation that was frequently quoted by Sukarno in his writings and speeches. The Ahmadiyya themselves also translated the Qur'an into various Indonesian local languages: the Lahore Ahmadiyya translated the Qur'an into Javanese in a version titled *Qur'an Sutji Djarwa Djawi Dalah Tafsiripun* by R. Ng. H. Minhadjurrahman Djajasugita and M. Mufti Sharif (first published in 1958), whereas the Qadiani Ahmadiyya translated selected verses of the Qur'an into Sundanese (*Ayat-ayat Panilih Tina Al-Qur'an* by Djajadi, J.D. Narasoma, Anwari, and Ahmad Anwar), Balinese (*Kutipan-kutipan saking al-Qur'an sui ring Bahasa Bali*), and Bataknese (*Ayat-ayat na*

99 Iskandar Zulkarnain, *Gerakan Ahmadiyah di Indonesia* (Yogyakarta: LKiS, 2005), pp. 305–06.

Tarpilit siat al-Qur'an tu Hata Batak). These translations had a significant readership in Indonesia until at least a few decades after independence.[100]

When it comes to QT, the legacy of the Ahmadiyya translation project is significant. The first edition of QT draws some material from *The Introduction to the Study of the Holy Qur'an* by Mirza Bashir-ud-din Mahmud Ahmad (1889–1965) (the second *khalīfa* of Mirza Ghulam Ahmad). Additionally, it also seems that the initial format of QT was heavily influenced by that of the Ahmadiyya's Qur'an translation (I will return to this in Chapter Two).

Ahmad Najib Burhani has suggested that the Ahmadiyya pioneered the production of modern translations of the Qur'an into Indonesian vernacular languages that were intended for a wider readership outside the pedagogical setting or missionary interests. He argues that prior to this, translation of the Qur'an in Indonesia had been condemned by the traditional *ulama* on the grounds of the doctrine of *iᶜjāz al-Qurᵓān* (Qur'anic inimitability) and the perceived untranslatability of the original Arabic text. His evidence for this is the fact that both the translations of Tjokroaminoto into Malay in 1925 and Soedewo into Dutch in 1934 were based on Ahmadiyya translations rather than other sources.[101] While the influence of Ahmadiyya activities on the history of Qur'an translation in Indonesia should not be belittled, Burhani's view is something of an overstatement. For starters, Tjokroaminoto was not the first person to translate the Qur'an into the Malay language—of course, unless we loosely classify his 'translation of the translation of the Qur'an' as Qur'an translation. Mahmud Yunus (1899–1982) had, in fact, started writing his own translation in 1922,[102] a couple of years before Tjokroaminoto, and he did not seem to have been inspired by

---

100 Ahmad Najib Burhani, 'Sectarian Translation of the Quran in Indonesia: The Case of the Ahmadiyya', *Al-Jāmiʿah: Journal of Islamic Studies*, 53.2 (2015), 251–82 (pp. 269–70), https://doi.org/10.14421/ajis.2015.532.251-282.

101 Burhani, 'When Muslims Are Not Muslims: The Ahmadiyya Community and the Discourse on Heresy in Indonesia', pp. 94–126; Burhani, 'Sectarian Translation of the Quran in Indonesia: The Case of the Ahmadiyya', p. 264; Ichwan, 'Differing Responses to an Ahmadi Translation and Exegesis: "The Holy Qur'ân" in Egypt and Indonesia', p. 158.

102 Yunus's work initially started in 1922. He worked individually for the first three juzᵓ, got assistance from his colleagues up to the eighteenth juzᵓ and later worked alone again until he reached the end of the Qur'an. He only finished his work in 1938. Nurtawab, 'Tafsīr Al-Jalālayn at the Crossroads: Interpreting the Qur'ān in Modern Indonesia', p. 6.

the Ahmadiyya movement. For Yunus, A.H. Johns' and Bruinessen's explanation—that the modernist-reformist movement in Egypt inspired Muslims to become more direct in their approach to Qur'an commentaries—is more feasible.[103] Whatever the case, the publication of QT and its dominant reach has disadvantaged other Qur'an translations in Indonesia, and the translations of the Ahmadiyya community were seemingly no exception to this rule.

103 Anthony H. Johns, 'Quranic Exegesis in the Malay World: In Search of a Profile', in *Approaches to the History of the Interpretation of the Qur'ān*, ed. by Andrew Rippin (Oxford: Clarendon Press, 1988), pp. 257–87 (p. 274); van Bruinessen, 'Kitab Kuning: Books in Arabic Script Used in the Pesantren Milieu: Comments on a New Collection in the KITLV Library', p. 229.

2. An Introduction to *Al-Qur'an dan Terjemahnya*

The Malay-Indonesian communities' first encounters with the textual culture of the Qur'an can be presumed to have occurred over five centuries ago. The two earliest surviving copies of the Qur'anic text in the region date back to the sixteenth and the seventeenth centuries. The first is a segment of Q 58 collected by a Dutch mariner in 1604, while the second is a complete copy of the Qur'an with a colophon in Javanese, probably written sometime between 1550–75, which the Sultan of Johor presented to the Dutch Admiral Matelieff De Jonge on 20 July 1606 as a gift. The earliest known translations of the Qur'an in the region also date to around the same period, and took the form of individual verses incorporated into works that did not necessarily belong to the genres of *tafsīr* or Qur'an translation. Hamzah Fansuri (d. *c.* 1590), Shams al-Dīn al-Sumatrāʾī (d. 1630), and Nūr al-Dīn al-Rānirī (d. 1658) were all prominent authors who included Qur'anic citations rendered into Malay in their writings. Another work worth mentioning, that comes closer to being *tafsīr*, is an anonymous commentary on an individual *sūra*, *Sūrat al-Kahf* (Q 18), now held in the Cambridge University Library under the code MS Or.Ii.6.45. The first complete translation of the Qur'an into the Malay language was *Tarjumān al-mustafīd*, which was written by ʿAbd al-Raʾūf al-Sinkīlī (1615–93) in around 1675.[1] These are all considered to be trailblazing works of Qur'anic scholarship in the Malay-Indonesian world.

1 Peter G. Riddell, 'Translating the Qurʾān into Indonesian Languages', *Al-Bayān–Journal of Qurʾān and Ḥadīth Studies*, 12.1 (2014), 1–27 (pp. 4–12), https://doi.org/10.1163/22321969-12340001; Peter G. Riddell, *Malay Court Religion, Culture and Language: Interpreting the Qur'ān in 17th Century Aceh*, Texts and Studies on the Qur'ān, 12 (Leiden; Boston: Brill, 2017), p. 6.

 https://doi.org/10.11647/OBP.0289.02

The following period witnessed a flourishing of Qur'anic literature. In an account covering Qur'anic commentaries and translations in three of the languages spoken in the Malay-Indonesian peninsula (Malay, Javanese, and Sundanese) from the earliest evidence to the early twentieth century, Ervan Nurtawab records numerous works from each region. Nurtawab suggests that at this point it was hard to identify works in terms of the properly defined genres of Qur'an translation or commentary. He instead classifies these works as 'Qur'anic texts,' despite their inclusion of interlinear translations or commentaries, either of individual verses and *sūras*, or of the complete Qur'an. Whilst some have suggested otherwise, his research proves that writing activity surrounding the Qur'an and its exegesis in Indonesia grew continuously in the years after al-Sinkīlī produced his *Tarjumān al-mustafīd*.[2]

In the early twentieth century, anti-colonial activism heightened the cultural and political significance of the Malay language. Originally used as the language of trade in the peninsula, it gained ideological significance during the struggle against Dutch colonial powers. To contextualize the importance of this for Islamic scholarship in the area, the transmission of Islamic scholarship in traditional institutions such as *surau* or *pesantren* had hitherto used Arabic and regional languages written with a modified Arabic script, known as *Jawi or Pegon* script. In the twentieth century, anti-colonial activists developed a greater sense of unity and sought a unitary language. They eventually turned to the Malay language, changing its name to *Bahasa Indonesia* (the Indonesian language) in 1928. This new development sparked the growth of Islamic scholarship in the newly recognized language and script, which began to overshadow the use of *Jawi* script, especially in *tafsīr* works.[3]

Islamic scholarship continued to use regional languages with *Jawi* script for some time, but the switch to writing Qur'anic commentaries in Indonesian using Latin script heralded the beginning of a bright future.

---

2 Ervan Nurtawab, 'Qur'anic Translation in Malay, Javanese, and Sundanese: A Commentary or Substitution', in *The Qur'ān in Malay-Indonesian World: Context and Interpretation*, ed. by Majid Daneshgar, Peter G. Riddell, and Andrew Rippin (London, New York: Routledge, 2016), pp. 39–57 (p. 41).

3 Moch. Nur Ichwan, 'The End of Jawi Islamic Scholarship? Kitab Jawi, Qur'anic Exegesis, and Politics in Indonesia', in *Rainbows of Malay Literature and Beyond: Festschrift in Honour of Professor Md. Salleh Yaapar* (Pulau Pinang: Penerbit Universiti Sains Malaysia, 2011), pp. 82–101.

The earliest trend in Indonesian-language Islamic scholarship seems to have been for translations of Qur'an translations and commentaries. H.O.S. Tjokroaminoto (1883–1934), as mentioned in the previous chapter, undertook a translation of Muhammad Ali's (1874–1951) *The Holy Qur'an* in 1925. The same year witnessed the translation of the first *juzʾ* (part) of *al-Manār* by Abdul Wahid-Nasserie, which was published in Batavia. Ahmad Hassan (1887–1958) went a step further and translated the Qur'an directly from the original Arabic in his *Al-Furqan: Tafsir Quraan* in 1928, and this was followed by the publication of Mahmud Yunus's *Tarjamah Al-Qur'an al-Karim* in 1938,[4] and *Tafsir Al Quraan* by Zainuddin Hamidy (1907–57) and Fakhruddin Hs. (b. 1906) in 1955.[5] As the Indonesian language grew more established and its use became the norm, more commentaries on and translations of the Qur'an with a wide range of features and approaches were written in the language. However, when QT arrived on the scene, it became the dominant player in the Indonesian Qur'an translation market, leaving all other translations in the dust. During a speech given by Muchlis M. Hanafi, the director of Lajnah Pentashihan Mushaf Al-Qur'an (LPMQ, The Qur'anic Text Review Board), in a public consultation on the revision of *Al-Qur'an dan Terjemahnya* on 14 February 2018, he stated that between seven and ten million copies of QT are produced and distributed per year; to put this estimate in perspective, the King Fahd Complex for Printing the Holy Qur'an produces about ten million copies of the Arabic *mushaf* annually for worldwide distribution.[6]

The rest of this chapter is devoted to the history of QT, and focuses particularly on two aspects: the evolution of the content itself and the technical aspects of the production of this translation. The former aspect deals with the translation in the context of how the authors or institutions involved view the interpretive value of the work, and the revision process from which the consecutive editions of QT stem. Comparison of different editions has often been a vehicle through which to describe the history of QT. However, this chapter suggests

4 Ervan Nurtawab, 'Tafsīr Al-Jalālayn at the Crossroads: Interpreting the Qur'ān in Modern Indonesia', *Australian Journal of Islamic Studies*, 6.4 (2021), 4–24 (p. 6), https://doi.org/10.55831/ajis.v6i4.429.

5 Riddell, 'Translating the Qurʾān into Indonesian Languages', pp. 12–14.

6 Bruce B. Lawrence, *The Koran in English: A Biography*, Lives of Great Religious Books (Princeton and Oxford: Princeton University Press, 2017), p. 123.

that this comparative perspective is not enough and that important aspects would be neglected should one only pay attention to revisions of content alone. This is because QT has undergone changes in more than just its wording. Thus, this section will also describe issues concerning presentation and the media used to convey the translation, including the spelling and transliteration system, the physical binding, its print and online forms, and the layout design. This section argues that such paratextual elements are by no means insignificant in shaping Qur'an translation as a genre.

The Contributing Institutions and the Publishers of *Al-Qur'an dan Terjemahnya*

Before going any further into the history of QT, it is necessary to start this section with a brief description of the institutions and publishers behind QT. Currently, the supervision of MORA Qur'anic projects has been assigned to LPMQ (the Qur'anic Text Review Board). As its name indicates, LPMQ is a body within MORA that is tasked with ensuring the validity of the Qur'anic text printed and distributed in Indonesia through a procedure called *taṣḥīḥ*, which is a thorough checking process carried out by LPMQ-affiliated *ulama* upon the text of the Qur'an in a prospective *mushaf* for publication. Only distribution of those editions of the *mushaf* with the *taṣḥīḥ* stamp is officially allowed: the ministry does not guarantee the validity of non-sanctioned editions.

The LPMQ was established in 1957.[7] However, even though the QT project started in the 1960s, LPMQ has not always been responsible for its translation and publication processes. QT was initially undertaken by a different, ad hoc committee established by the Ministry of Religious Affairs, through Ministerial Decision No. 91 of 1962 and No. 53 of 1963, namely Lembaga Penyelenggara Penterjemah Kitab Suci Al-Qur'an (LPPKSA, The Organizing Committee for the Translation of the Holy Qur'an). The duties of this committee were limited to actual

7 Lajnah Pentashihan Mushaf Al-Qur'an, 'Sejarah—Lajnah Pentashihan Mushaf Al-Qur'an', *Lajnah Pentashihan Mushaf Al-Qur'an Badan Litbang dan Diklat Kementerian Agama Republik Indonesia*, https://lajnah.kemenag.go.id/profil/sejarah; *Sejarah Penulisan Mushaf Al-Qur'an Standar Indonesia*, ed. by H. Muhammad Shohib and Zaenal Arifin Madzkur (Jakarta: Lajnah Pentashihan Mushaf Al-Qur'an, 2013).

translation of the Qur'an. When it came to printing duties, MORA established another team through Ministerial Decision No. 56 on 1 June 1963. The first volume of the first edition of QT was thus the product of both committees. Later, for the sake of reducing administrative procedures, LPPKSA was transformed into a foundation, namely Yayasan Penyelenggara Penterjemah/Pentafsir Al-Qur'an (YPPA, The Foundation of the Organizing Committee for Translating/Interpreting the Qur'an). This foundation was responsible for the translation and the printing of QT, and it undertook the translation and publication of the other two volumes of the first edition.

During the New Order era, the government next introduced Proyek Pengadaan Kitab Suci Al-Qur'an (the Project for the Procurement of the Holy Qur'an) through MORA. This project brought Qur'an translation affairs under the aegis of LPMQ. In 1974, the project instructed LPMQ to conduct a review of all MORA's Qur'an projects. However, because until 1982 LPMQ had been preoccupied with reviewing the text of the Qur'an, it only began to actually engage with QT in that year.[8] Since then, QT has always been subject to oversight by LPMQ.

Since 2011, MORA has also been interested in translating the Qur'an into regional languages. Indonesia is home to people from multiple ethnicities who speak many different regional languages, and translating the Qur'an into all of those languages is a huge task. While responsibility for translating the Qur'an into the national language (i.e., the QT project) remains with LPMQ, responsibility for translating the Qur'an into these regional languages has been assigned to Puslitbang Lektur, Khazanah Keagamaan, dan Managemen Organisasi (Puslitbang LKKMO, The Centre for Research and Development of Religious Literature and Tradition and Organizational Management). LPMQ is only involved in reviewing the Qur'anic text of these translations (more on this in the following sub-section).

When it comes to the actual printing of QT, there are three regular players. The first is MORA itself. In this context, MORA has typically welcomed the involvement of other parties. From the first edition through to the third edition, QT has been printed by a number of different companies and institutions, including Yamunu' (1965, 1967,

8 Isma'il Lubis, *Falsifikasi Terjemahan Al-Qur'an Departemen Agama Edisi 1990* (Yogyakarta: Tiara Wacana, 2001), pp. 140–41.

1970), PT. Intermasa (1974), PT. Bumi Restu (1978/1979), and Pustaka Agung Harapan (2006).[9] Since 1990, the King Fahd Complex has also been printing QT and distributing it for free to Indonesian pilgrims each year (the King Fahd Complex version of QT is also widely available in shops in Mecca and Medina). MORA and the King Fahd Complex, our first two players, have typically printed limited copies of QT. The third player is the wider Qur'anic printing industry; the huge demand for QT is largely met by private publishers.

In addition to these three categories, some institutions have also printed their own copies of QT. In 1993, the Muhammadiyah, in cooperation with al-Irshād al-Islāmiyya and a Kuwaiti organization, Jamᶜiyya Iḥyāᵓ al-Turāth al-Islāmī, printed QT and distributed the copies free to their communities. Other institutions, such as *pesantren*, banks, or private companies, might also print a customized copy of QT—typically through a particular publisher—and distribute it within their communities or amongst their employees, or provide it to mosques or orphanages during *Ramaḍān*. The King Fahd Complex and Jamᶜiyya Iḥyāᵓ al-Turāth al-Islāmī are also not the only foreign institutions that publish QT: Darussalam publishers in Riyadh chose to print the third edition of QT, which is interesting considering that the King Fahd Complex continues to print their adjusted version of the second edition.

The Various Editions of *Al-Qur'an dan Terjemahnya*

The idea of commissioning a government-produced Qur'an translation arose during the Guided Democracy era in 1960. The translation is said to have initially appeared on 17 August 1965 (although there are some difficulties with the date of publishing, as will be discussed later in this chapter), and it has been constantly published since then. There is no historic record of the number of print runs, but Ismail Lubis has suggested that QT was printed annually.[10] The printing of the work increased incrementally until, by 1990, production was on a huge

9 These names are gathered from the covers of the copies of QT that I have been able to find.

10 From my survey of many places, especially the library of LPMQ, I have only been able to find those copies before industrialization, printed in eight different years: 1965/67/69, 1971, 1974, 1977/78, 1982/83, 1984, 1987, 1989. Lubis, *Falsifikasi Terjemahan Al-Qur'an*, p. 141.

industrial scale, and today QT is the most printed Qur'an translation in Indonesia. This makes it impossible to account for all print runs, especially those by private publishers. The predominance of this translation has persisted throughout the separate administrations of every president of Indonesia, from Sukarno (1901–70) to Joko Widodo, and across the three different political phases of the Old Order, the New Order, and the Reformation Era. Now having been published for almost six decades, QT has unsurprisingly been subject to several revisions, resulting in several different editions.

Before discussing the editions of QT further, it is imperative to clarify the kinds of revision that have taken place. It is also necessary to clarify that the committee has not simply described their activity as 'revision'. Instead, they have used the words *penelitian* (research), *perbaikan* (correction), and *penyempurnaan* (perfection, consummation). During the production of the most recent, 2019, edition, the translators and LPMQ officials casually used the term *revisi* (revision). However, the official term that has frequently been used in official documents and press releases throughout QT's history has, in fact, been *penyempurnaan*.

The textual revisions implemented as part of the revision process can be split into two classifications: systematic and ad hoc revision. Systematic revision refers to instances where thorough investigation and a wide range of adjustments have been conducted by the committee, covering the editorial and/or interpretive dimensions of the translation. This kind of revision usually produces a distinct edition of QT. There are records of this kind of revision process, which has taken place in three different periods: 1989–90, 1998–2002, and 2016–19. This history of the revision of QT is the official account repetitively presented by LPMQ itself through speeches by its leader, in press releases, or in forewords to works published by LPMQ. Accordingly, this account has also been widely recognized in Indonesian scholarship on *tafsīr* or Qur'an translation.

Ad hoc revision, the second type of revision, does not employ a considered methodology, nor a complete and thorough investigation of the existing edition. It is conducted partly as a reaction against criticisms that have been directed at an existing edition of QT. Thanks to its broad readership, feedback evaluating and criticizing the translation is frequently received, and the committee will adjust the translation if they deem it necessary. There is a complete lack of information available on this type of revision. The reason for this is probably archival; there are a limited number of surviving documents on the early history of QT. Additionally, shifts in the organizational form of the translation working committee—such as the relocation of its office—has contributed to the scarcity of the relevant documents. Therefore, the precise number of ad hoc revisions is not realistically quantifiable.

One of the earliest criticisms directed against QT was an allegation of plagiarism which caused a media outcry in late 1973 and early 1974. An (interestingly) anonymous article published in *Tempo* on 12 January 1974, voiced concerns that the translators working on QT might have copied a significant chunk of material from a book written by Mirza Bashir-ud-din Mahmud Ahmad (d. 1965) (the second *khalīfa* of Mirza Ghulam Ahmad), entitled *The Introduction to the Study of the Holy Qur'an.*[11] A comparison between the *muqaddimah* (Introduction) of QT and Mirza Bashir-ud-din Mahmud Ahmad's *Introduction*, published in 2016,[12] exposed the fact that fifteen pages of material written in the introduction to QT (which discuss the place of the Qur'an within the history of the holy scriptures and argue for the need for the Qur'an) were lifted almost verbatim from Mirza Bashir-ud-din Mahmud Ahmad's work and translated into Indonesian with only minor adjustments. These adjustments included providing Arabic texts from the Qur'an where the source text provides only English translations of them, and elimination of some material considered unnecessary. After passing over the next forty pages, which criticize other scriptures, the *muqaddimah* in QT then includes a two-page summary of a forty-page elaboration in *The Introduction* on the issue of Muhammad's prefiguration as a prophet in earlier scriptures. This section is presented with the heading '*Perlunya Al-Qur'an Diturunkan*' (The Necessity of the Revelation of the Qur'an) as a part of a section on the history of the prophet Muhammad in the *muqaddimah.*

The *Tempo* article reported that concerns over this plagiarism did not only touch on the act of copying without providing appropriate references and acknowledgments, but also the fact that the book from which this content was copied was written by a prominent Ahmadiyya figure. It also revealed the ambivalent reaction of the then general

11 '"Jiplak-Menjiplak" Tafsir Qur'an', *Majalah Tempo*, 12 January 1974, p. 49.
12 Mirza Bashir-ud-din Mahmud Ahmad, *Introduction to The Study of The Holy Qur'ān* (Surrey: Islam International Publications Limited, 2016).

secretary of MORA, Bahrum Rangkuti, to these allegations: on the one hand, he was reported to have justified the act, suggesting that the content copied did not contradict normative Islamic ideas, while, on the other hand, he condemned the act of plagiarism.

The plagiarism controversy led to an impromptu revision of QT, and the committee eventually gave credit where it was due. I have not been able to obtain a copy of QT that was printed between 1974 and 1976, but in the edition printed during the Pelita (*Pembangunan Lima Tahun*, Five-Year Development Project) II, i.e., in 1977–78, the name of Bashir-ud-din Mahmud Ahmad was included in the bibliography. The way this new bibliography entry was actually included, however, provides even more evidence of the unsystematic nature of the revision that was undertaken. The bibliography of the edition printed in 1965 lists twenty-five titles, which seem to be sorted in an arbitrary way; their order is not alphabetical, nor is it based on the year the works in question were published. The list ends with a 'miscellaneous' entry that reads '*dan lain-lain buku/kitab tafsir dalam berbagai bahasa*' ('and other Qur'an commentaries which were written in various languages'), which presumably is intended to indicate less significant literatures that were referred to during the translation phase of QT and therefore were not named. Ideally, the reference to Mirza Bashir-ud-din Mahmud Ahmad's plagiarized work should have been included as the twenty-fifth, with the 'miscellaneous' entry coming next. Somehow, that is not the case: the Mirza Bashir-ud-din Mahmud Ahmad entry is instead inserted *after* the miscellaneous entry. To add insult to injury, the title of the book in question is also presented incorrectly, as *The Holy Qurän* instead of *The Introduction to the Study of the Holy Qur'an.*

A constant stream of other, more minor, unremarked and unsystematic revisions was also implanted by the committee. As early as 1971, R.H.A. Soenarjo (1908–98), the then head of the committee, indicated in his preface to the 1971 print run that corrections had been made to some mistakes in the previous publication. Moch. Nur Ichwan and Hamam Faizin have also found that the version of QT printed in 1974 introduced a number of changes to the initial first edition, both in the paratext and in the body of the translation.[13]

13 Moch. Nur Ichwan, 'Negara, Kitab Suci dan Politik: Terjemahan Resmi Al-Qur'an di Indonesia', in *Sadur Sejarah Terjemahan di Indonesia dan Malaysia*, ed. by Henri Chambert-Loir (Jakarta: Kepustakaan Populer Gramedia, 2009), pp. 417–33 (p.

Before moving on, it is important to clarify a point on terminology: this study uses the term 'edition' to refer to the initial translation and the three editions that resulted from the three comprehensive-systematic revisions that have been undertaken on the text. Changes made as a result of ongoing, undocumented, more minor ad hoc revisions are not counted as distinctive editions. Additionally, where 'revision' is mentioned in the following pages of this book, it refers to a comprehensive-systematic revision, whereas ad hoc revision is described as such in full. It is also necessary to note at this point that the LPMQ and many publishers often use the word 'edition,' or the Indonesian *edisi*, sporadically. Surveying the copies of QT printed in different years, one might find that some of them proclaim themselves to be *edisi baru* (a new edition) or *edisi terkini* (the latest edition), while others mention the word 'edition' followed by the year of the printing, such as *edisi 2010*. This study does not follow their use of the word.

As there have been three revisions,[14] there are, thus, four main editions of QT: the initial first edition (1965–70), the second edition (1990), the third edition (2002), and the fourth edition (2019).[15] In addition to these

420); Hamam Faizin, *Sejarah Penerjemahan Al-Quran di Indonesia* (Ciputat: Gaung Persada, 2022), pp. 154–62.

14 For this statement, I follow the official chronology provided by LPMQ, as mentioned by its chair, Muchlis M. Hanafi, in his "Introduction" to MORA's *Tafsir Ringkas*. Additionally, I also managed to index all the changes between the first, second, and third editions, the result of which affirms the aforementioned LPMQ chronology. I have not been able to include the fourth edition in the index because the revisions resulting in this edition were still in progress when I was conducting the research. See Lajnah Pentashihan Mushaf Al-Qur'an, *Tafsir Ringkas Al-Qur'an al-Karim*, 2 vols (Jakarta: Lajnah Pentashihan Mushaf Al-Qur'an, 2015), i, pp. xxxvii–xl.

15 Ichwan and Faizin identify the copy published in 1974 as a distinctive edition. However, in my opinion, the changes implemented are not sufficient to classify it as a comprehensive-systematic revision, and consequently a distinct edition. The editions proposed by Ichwan are as follows: the Yamunu' edition (1965), the Mukti Ali edition (1974), and the Saudi edition (1990). The way he names the editions follows his perspective on the underlying power relationships involved in the production of each edition. Yamunu' (Yayasan Mu'awanah Nahdlatul Ulama) was a foundation affiliated with Nahdlatul Ulama; Mukti Ali was the Minister of Religion from Muhammadiyah; and the Saudi edition refers to the fact that he considers that that particular edition was published thanks to collaboration between the Ministry of Religious Affairs and the King Fahd Complex for the Printing of the Holy Qurʾān. Although this article was published in 2009, his actual research took place in 1999, which explains the absence of the third edition (2002) in his chronology. Ichwan, 'Negara, Kitab Suci dan Politik: Terjemahan Resmi Al-Qur'an di Indonesia', pp. 419–22; Faizin, *Sejarah Penerjemahan Al-Quran di Indonesia*, p. 150.

four main editions, as mentioned above, The King Fahd Complex has become an active publisher of QT since 1990. For reasons elaborated later, I also refer to the copy published by the Saudi institution as a distinctive edition. MORA has also been working on the translation of QT into regional languages across Indonesia, and I identify these as one distinct edition.

The First Edition (1965, 1967, and 1970)

As a state-commissioned Qur'an translation, QT came about through constitutional procedures. The initial plan to produce such a translation came from the highest state institution, namely the Majelis Permusyawaratan Rakyat Sementara (MPRS, Provisional People's Consultative Assembly). The MPRS held their first general meeting from 10 November to 7 December 1960, after which they issued two resolutions, TAP MPRS No. I/MPRS/1960 and TAP MPRS No. II/MPRS/1960. The second resolution was concerned with the first phase of the national development plan, Garis-garis Besar Pola Pembangunan Nasional Semesta Berencana (The Outline of the Comprehensive National Development Plan), which took place between 1961 and 1969. One of the provisions of this plan was to translate holy scriptures into Indonesian.[16] On 13 December 1960, the MPRS handed both resolutions to President Sukarno. To follow up the mandate, the Ministry of Religious Affairs established the LPPKSA.

The LPPKSA was made up of scholars with positions in the Ministry of Religious Affairs, state-funded Islamic higher education, and Islamic mass organizations. It was chaired by Soenarjo,[17] a member of the first generation that had established the Ministry of Religious Affairs, in which he had risen to the position of general secretary under K.H. Masykur (1904–94) between 1947 and 1949. He also played an enormous role in the reform and development of Islamic higher education in Indonesia; he

---

16 Four scriptures were mentioned in this outline: the Qurʾān, the Bible, and Weda and Wiharma M.P.R.S dan Departemen Penerangan, *Ringkasan Ketetapan Madjelis Permusjawaratan Rakjat Sementara—Republik Indonesia* (Jakarta: M.P.R.S dan Departemen Penerangan, 1961), p. 224.

17 Machasin, 'Prof. Mr. R.H.A Soenarjo', in *Lima Tokoh IAIN Sunan Kalijaga Yogyakarta*, ed. by Muhammad Damami (Yogyakarta: Pusat Penelitian IAIN Sunan Kalijaga, 2000), pp. 71–102.

was one of a group who transformed existing Islamic higher education bodies into state-funded institutions, and he had assumed the first rectorship of the Institute Agama Islam Negeri (IAIN, State Institute for Islamic Studies) al-Jami'ah al-Islamiyah al-Hukumiyah, the embryo of all further Islamic higher-education institutions in Indonesia.

There were thirteen members of the LPPKSA committee. Some of them had a national reputation and a bright career either in academia, serving as dean or rector of a particular IAIN, or politics, while other members were relatively less well-known. Hasbi Ash-Shiddieqy (1904–75)[18] and Abdul Mukti Ali (1923–2004)[19] seem to be two names with the highest reputation. Hasbi Ash-Shiddieqy was known as a prolific scholar—his publications include two works of *tafsīr* and several textbooks on the various Islamic disciplines aimed at IAIN students—and, above and beyond this, for his much-appreciated idea of indigenizing Islamic law.[20] Abdul Mukti Ali had the privilege of assuming the highest position in MORA and served as Minister of Religious Affairs from 1971 to 1978. Four of the other members would go on to be appointed dean or rector of a particular Islamic higher-education institution: Muchtar Jahja (1907–96),[21] K.H. Anwar Musaddad (1909–2000), Bustami Abdul Ghani (1912–2001),[22] Toha Jahja Omar (1912–72) and Busjairi Madjdy (date of birth and death unknown). Another member, K.H. Ali Maksum (1915–89), has a unique profile compared to other members. He did not pursue a career in a state university/institute, nor in the ministry, but nevertheless was one of the most respected Indonesian *ulama* during his lifetime, and was a high-ranking Nahdlatul Ulama figure. There is relatively little, or even no, information available about some other names on the committee. Kamal Muchtar is on record as being a graduate of

---

18 Nourouzzaman Shiddiqi, 'Prof. Dr. Tengku Muhammad Hasbi Ash-Shiddieqy', in *Lima Tokoh IAIN Sunan Kalijaga Yogyakarta*, ed. by Muhammad Damami (Yogyakarta: Pusat Penelitian IAIN Sunan Kalijaga, 2000), pp. 149–214.

19 Muhammad Damami and others, 'Prof. Dr. H. A. Mukti Ali, M.A.', in *Lima Tokoh IAIN Sunan Kalijaga Yogyakarta*, ed. by Muhammad Damami (Yogyakarta: Pusat Penelitian IAIN Sunan Kalijaga, 2000), pp. 217–71.

20 R. Michael Feener, 'Indonesian Movements for the Creation of a "National Madhhab"', *Islamic Law & Society*, 9.1 (2002), 83–115.

21 Umar Asasuddin Sokah, 'Prof. Dr. H. Mukhtar Yahya', in *Lima Tokoh IAIN Sunan Kalijaga Yogyakarta*, ed. by Muhammad Damami (Yogyakarta: Pusat Penelitian IAIN Sunan Kalijaga, 1998), pp. 107–46.

22 Setyadi Sulaiman, *Sang Begawan Bahasa Arab: Potret Perjalanan Prof. Dr. Bustami Abdul Gani* (Ciputat: Adabia Press, 2013).

IAIN Sunan Kalijaga and a member of the committee of *Al-Qur'an dan Tafsirnya,* but there is not much information available about Masuddin Noor, Gazali Thaib, S. Siswopranoto, or Asrul Sani.[23]

In addition to the names listed above, there is also the possibility that other unidentified people were involved. For example, K.H. Maimoen Zubair (1928–2019), one of the most respected *ulama* from Nahdlatul Ulama, in February 2017 testified that he translated the *juzᵓ ᶜammā,* the last *juzᵓ* of the Qur'an, for the first edition of QT on behalf of his father, K.H. Zubair Dahlan. The names of such figures have never been included alongside those of the committee members. It does, however, seem very likely that the initial translation duties were more widely distributed than has previously been imagined. This is because it was actually common practice for the notable *ulama* to delegate participation in such activities to one of their valued students. The above example of K.H. Maimun Zubair indicates that this may well have also been the case for QT. It is highly probable that K.H. Maimun Zubair and his father were indeed not officially involved in the committee, but perhaps were assigned this translation duty by K.H. Ali Maksum, one of the committee members with whom they were close.

Despite the fact that the translation duties were handed out to a team, the initial translation was conducted on an individual basis. The team was divided into two groups: the Jakartas and the Yogyakartas. For the first volume, the Jakartas wrote the introduction (*muqaddimah*), while the Yogyakartas translated the first ten *juzᵓ* of the Qur'an. For the next two volumes, they distributed the amount of text to be translated equally. There are no records that give details about the actual distribution of translation duties.[24] After the completion of their individual translations, the groups exchanged their work for evaluation and, after that, a plenary meeting was held for the final phase. Again, at this point, there is no concrete record of these interchanges, or of how rigorous the final evaluation was. It seems likely that the work of each individual was examined by another member of the translation

---

23 Asrul Sani is the name of a renowned Indonesian poet, but this is not the same Asrul Sani who is a member of the committee for the translation of QT.

24 It is reported in R.H.A Soenarjo's biography that he wrote the subsection on "Kandungan Al-Qur'an" [lit. the content of the Qur'an] in the *muqaddimah,* for which he relied on Soedewo's translation of Muhammad Ali's *The Holy Qur'an* into Dutch. See Machasin, p. 96.

team. If this was the case, it explains the level of inconsistency in this first edition, a feature that was addressed in the next edition. After the completion of these steps, the work was then submitted to the Minister of Religious Affairs for authorization.

The task of translating the entire Qur'an is necessarily a time-consuming one, especially for those who may also have regular governance and academic duties. Because of this, instead of waiting for the whole translation to be finished, the first edition of QT was published in three different volumes. The first volume was published in 1965, followed by the other two volumes in 1967 and 1970, respectively.[25] This timeframe meant that the first edition of QT was essentially 'the product of transition of power' from the Old Order to the New Order government;[26] the project was started under the administration of Sukarno (when the first volume was completed and published), but only finished after Suharto (1921–2008) took charge.

There seems to be a tendency to match the date of the formal launch of the first edition of QT to the commemoration of one of the most historic days in Indonesia, namely the proclamation of independence on 17 August 1945. It seems that the commemoration of independence was thought to provide an appropriate moment for the state to introduce one of its most important religious projects, and was a mark of the official privilege accorded to QT. The foreword of the first volume, written by the then Minister of Religious Affairs, Saifuddin Zuhri (1919–86), begins with an appreciation of the fact that the commemoration of Indonesian independence was enhanced by the fact that it was also the publication date of QT. The foreword provided by President Suharto in the second volume adopts the same tone. In a more straightforward fashion, he states that 'the publication of the second volume of QT coincides with the twenty-second anniversary of the independence of Indonesia.' The ministry seems to want to stick to this narrative, as the *muqaddimah* of the latest edition of the translation explicitly mentions that the first edition was published on 17 August 1965.[27]

---

25 Lubis, *Falsifikasi Terjemahan Al-Qur'an*, p. 135.

26 Ichwan, 'Negara, Kitab Suci dan Politik: Terjemahan Resmi Al-Qur'an di Indonesia', p. 421.

27 Some observers take this narrative for granted. Lubis, for example, suggests that the first and second volumes of the first edition of QT were published on 17 August 1965 and 1967, respectively. Lubis, *Falsifikasi Terjemahan Al-Qur'an*, pp. 140–41.

The government certainly could have launched QT to commemorate Independence Day. While that might have been the ideal scenario, evidence indicates that although the work was formally launched on that date, it is unlikely that this actually meant that all the publishing processes had actually been completed and the translation was ready for distribution. It is more likely that the committee had almost finished their job, but not quite on time, and that, at the time its publication was formally announced by the government, a physical copy was not ready. It in fact appears that these formal introductions on the day of the anniversary of independence were merely symbolic, a feature that adds further to the official associations of the translation.

The reason for my skepticism over the launch date is that, I would argue, it is misleading to assume that, given the forewords of Saifuddin Zuhri and Sukarno, the dates of the launch of the project and its publication are identical. Unfortunately, we do not have any external information—such as media coverage—on either the formal introduction or the publication of the work other than the aforementioned forewords. With regards to the first volume, four forewords from government officials, including President Sukarno and Minister of Religious Affairs Saifuddin Zuhri, were dated to 17 August 1965; the fifth and final one was signed on 14 August 1965. Considering these dates, it is logistically impossible that this volume was actually printed and launched on 17 August 1965, because the process of actually printing the translation would take time once the full draft—including those forewords—were ready. The second volume suffered from the same problem, if not more so. President Suharto is clear in his foreword: the volume was published on 17 August 1967. Nevertheless, the forewords were signed on 17 August, 14 October, 31 October, 5 November, and 3 December 1967. Accordingly, the launch of this volume predated the actual printing and publication of the work by quite a significant amount of time.

The launch of the third volume of the first edition of QT did not have the momentum of the national Independence Day. Nevertheless, the ostensible date of its publication is also problematic. This volume reused Suharto's foreword from the 1967 edition verbatim; it did not even revise a paragraph that clearly mentions 'the publication of this second volume.' The other forewords included in this edition were signed on 9 October, 2 November 1969, and 1 January 1970 and, although the last date appended to one of the forewords is 1 January 1970, the cover of the volume states 1969 as the year of publication. In sum, we cannot accept those forewords as indicative of the actual printing and publication dates of the first two volumes of QT, and thus we cannot know that these volumes were actually published on Indonesian Independence Day. The selection of the commemoration day as the platform for QT's introduction is clearly strongly connected to its position as a governmental project, not to the day the work was actually published.

The Second and Saudi Editions (1990)

There has likewise been a misconception about the second edition of QT. Both previous scholarship and the LPMQ assert that the revision process that took place from 1989–90 resulted in the Saudi edition.[28] I do not agree with this prevailing narrative, and argue that the outcome of this revision should not be referred to as a solitary edition, but rather two distinct editions: the second or 1990 edition, and the Saudi edition. The former refers to the copies of the second edition printed in Indonesia, whereas the latter refers to those printed by the King Fahd Complex in Medina.

There are multiple grounds for this misconception. First, one of the factors leading to the 1990 revision of the translation was a proposal from the King Fahd Complex. The fact that this proposal was an influencing factor in the decision to undertake the revision has fed into the prevailing narrative that the Saudi authorities influenced the form and content of the revision process itself. Secondly, many accounts, either from LPMQ or from scholars who have studied the history of QT and its various revisions, refer to the second (1990) edition *and* the Saudi edition interchangeably, most probably owing to a lack of recognition of the difference between the copies printed in Medina by the King Fahd Complex and those printed by other parties. Thirdly, identification of the Saudi edition persists, because the King Fahd Complex have continued

---

28 Ichwan, 'Negara, Kitab Suci dan Politik: Terjemahan Resmi Al-Qur'an di Indonesia', p. 421; Lubis, *Falsifikasi Terjemahan Al-Qur'an*, pp. 140–48; Ahmad Najib Burhani, 'Sectarian Translation of the Quran in Indonesia: The Case of the Ahmadiyya', *Al-Jāmi'ah: Journal of Islamic Studies*, 53.2 (2015), 251–82 (p. 267), https://doi.org/10.14421/ajis.2015.532.251-282; Lajnah Pentashihan Mushaf Al-Qur'an, i; Faizin, *Sejarah Penerjemahan Al-Quran di Indonesia*, p. 163.

to print and distribute their version of QT to Indonesian pilgrims as a gift each year until recently,[29] whereas the Qur'anic printing industry in Indonesia has been publishing the third edition since 2004, meaning that the Indonesian version of the second edition has gradually ceased to exist since then.

Before articulating my arguments, let us consider the existing historical narrative on this issue and identify its problems.

After two and a half decades, the first revision of QT took place from 1989–90. This revision was driven by several motivations: there was an internal desire for it at the Ministry of Religious Affairs, as well as a proposal from King Fahd Complex, and demand from the Qur'an printing industry more broadly. MORA had also wanted to revise QT for some time. Nevertheless, LPMQ's attention was taken up by the project of the national *mushaf* (i.e., the Arabic Qur'an) during the 1970s and 1980s. After the readership of QT gradually grew, recommendations on corrections to the translation came in in increasing numbers. In 1982, through Ministerial Regulation No. 1/1982, MORA demanded that LPMQ execute revisions on all their Qur'anic publications, including the *mushaf* itself, as well as its interpretation and translation. Additionally, the seventeenth Musyawarah Kerja Nasional Ulama Al-Qur'an (National Congress of the Ulama of the Qur'an), an annual meeting of Qur'anic scholars in the country held on 23–25 March 1989, issued a recommendation on the necessity of revising the first edition of QT.[30]

In the meantime, the King Fahd Complex, funded in 1984 by the Ministry of Islamic Affairs of the Saudi Kingdom, had embarked on an ambitious project of translating the Qur'an into world languages, or as Stefan Wild has put it, into languages from Albanian to Zulu.[31] It was

29 During my pilgrimage in 2017, the Saudi authorities did not distribute their edition of QT to Indonesian pilgrims as they had consistently done in previous years. Instead, they only distributed the *mushaf* without translation. I obtained my copy of the King Fahd Complex version of QT from a bookshop in Mecca. During my interview with Muchlis M. Hanafi, the director of LPMQ, he revealed that the Saudi authorities had demanded that MORA hand in the latest edition of QT to them. MORA however intended to wait until the fourth edition was finished. Nevertheless, the new Saudi edition has not yet been published in 2022.

30 Ichwan, 'Negara, Kitab Suci dan Politik: Terjemahan Resmi Al-Qur'an di Indonesia', p. 421.

31 Stefan Wild, 'Muslim Translators and Translations of the Qur'an into English', *Journal of Qur'anic Studies*, 17.3 (2015), 158–82 (p. 167), https://doi.org/10.3366/jqs.2015.0215; See also: Lawrence, p. 122.

thus completely unsurprising when the Saudi authorities proposed that they would print QT themselves and distribute it to Indonesian pilgrims. Private publishers had also seen the potential of the Qur'an publication industry and requested that MORA allow them to publish the translation. Because this development would see a significant increase in the public profile and circulation of QT, MORA felt that it was necessary to revise it.

To realize this revision, MORA and the Saudi authorities established a joint committee. MORA's decree No. P/15/1989, issued on 4 July 1989, thus established Tim Penelitian dan Penyempurnaan Al-Qur'an dan Terjemahnya (The Committee for Research and Perfection of *Al-Qur'an dan Terjemahnya*) to assess the existing translation and to produce recommendations for its revision. LPMQ followed this up with their own set of recommendations for the revision of QT. The committees involved consisted of scholars affiliated with various institutions, including MORA, the leadership of Masjid Istiqlal (Istiqlal Mosque),[32] Majelis Ulama Indonesia (MUI, Indonesian Ulama Council), and academics from several Islamic higher-education institutions. The Saudi authorities, through the religious attaché of the Saudi embassy in Jakarta, set up a committee consisting of three Indonesian students who were studying at the University of Ummu al-Qurā, the Islamic University of Medina, and the Imam Mohammad ibn Saud Islamic University in Riyadh.[33] Finally, the conclusions of these joint committees were then presented to the King Fahd Complex for the printing phase. Their recommendations concerned the editorial presentation of the translation more than anything else. The Indonesian language had developed and changed over time, and some of the language used in the first edition now appeared dated. In other words, many words and phrases mentioned in the first edition made little sense to readers of the late 1980s. The King Fahd Complex initially printed three thousand copies of this edition

32 Masjid Istiqlal is a large mosque built on 22 February 1978 in Jakarta to commemorate Indonesian independence. The official Islamic festivals managed by the state predominantly take place in this mosque.

33 S. Sadhewo and W.H. Hartoyo, 'Quran yang Terpelihara', *Majalah Tempo*, 25 April 1992, p. 77; Ali Mustafa Ya'qub, *Makan Tak Pernah Kenyang* (Jakarta: Pustaka Firdaus, 2012), pp. 46–47.

and distributed a thousand each to the Muhammadiyah and Nahdlatul Ulama, giving the other thousand to the general public.[34]

This is the prevailing historical narrative on the production of the second edition of QT. It seems pretty straightforward, and there is no indication that two different versions emerged from this revision process. That is, until one learns that the edition of QT printed by the King Fahd Complex and the edition resulting from the 1989–90 revision that was printed in Indonesia contain a number of differences. What is missing from the above narrative is the fact that, in addition to being published by the King Fahd Complex, the first revision was also printed by other parties in Indonesia, such as the Muhammadiyah (who printed, for example, the 1993 copy) and other local printers in Indonesia. This opens up the possibility that the version of QT printed by each separate body might differ slightly from the others, especially given that each political entity involved has distinct interests from a theological, sectarian point of view. It is not a secret that the Saudi authorities are not interested in merely supporting the production of a particular Qur'an translation: they make that translation suit their own theological vision. For example, when it came to choosing an English translation, King Fahd Complex chose to use the translation by Abdullah Yusuf Ali (1872–1953). But, instead of printing Yusuf Ali's original text intact, the King Fahd Complex imposed significant adjustments to the text, before printing their own version in 1985. The King Fahd Complex continued to print this edition until they approved a translation that better suited their hermeneutical and theological position, that of Muhammad Taqiuddin al-Hilali (1893–1987) and Muhammad Muhsin Khan (1927–2021).[35] When it comes to QT, two members of the MORA committee, Badri Yunardi and Mazmur Sya'rani, have revealed that the King Fahd Complex indeed advised them to adjust the translation to fit their theological stance, and that this led to negotiations on several verses, especially those concerning the attributes of God.[36]

---

34 Lubis, *Falsifikasi Terjemahan Al-Qur'an*, p. 143; Faizin, *Sejarah Penerjemahan Al-Quran di Indonesia*, p. 167.

35 Lawrence, p. 124; Ziauddin Sardar, *Reading the Qur'an: The Contemporary Relevance of the Sacred Text of Islam* (Oxford: Oxford University Press, 2011), p. 47.

36 Faizin, *Sejarah Penerjemahan Al-Quran di Indonesia*, p. 165.

Far more significantly, the King Fahd Complex seems to have exerted considerable control over the interpretive aspects of the version of QT that they print. For example, they appointed an official with knowledge of the Indonesian language to review the translation, and this official read parts of the translation himself and requested that an Indonesian translators' committee authorized by the King Fahd Complex offer him their own versions of selected verses for approval and inclusion.[37] Later, the King Fahd Complex conducted their own independent revision of their version of QT, a revision which indeed had a distinctive trajectory. The initial Saudi edition retains the original introduction from QT the first edition with minimum adjustments, yet a later version of the Saudi edition completely rewrites it. Not only are the changes to the introduction extensive, there are also significant adjustments in the main text of the translation. For example, the translation of Q 1:7 in QT as printed by the King Fahd Complex adds mention of Jews and Christians in parentheses as a gloss for the Arabic word *al-maghḍūb* (those who incur anger) and *al-ḍāllīn* (those who have gone astray). Both of these glosses are absent from the original first edition of QT, nor do they exist in the 1992 and 1993 copies of QT printed in Indonesia. A later version of QT produced by the King Fahd Complex changes this passage again, so that it refrains from explicitly mentioning Jews and Christians by name but substitutes this with phrases that describe the characteristics of both of these religious groups (this will be discussed in more detail in Chapter Five).

It is true that both the second edition of QT and the Saudi editions were technically the product of the same revision process and that the number of interpretive differences between these versions is limited—although, if taken individually, those differences might still be significant. If we think in terms of the categories of systematic and ad hoc revision, the number of differences between these two versions could arguably put them into the latter group. Nevertheless, the way the Saudi edition came into existence and has since been developed shows that this process was not simply one of unsystematic revision, but

37 I thank Johanna Pink and her team in GloQur, especially Mykhaylo Yakubovych, who were also working on the translation activity of King Fahd Complex, for this particularly significant information, which I obtained through personal correspondence with them.

rather illustrates a firm discrepancy between the very different interests advocated by two different political powers. Because the King Fahd Complex represents a particular interest and authority outside the state of Indonesia (for more on the different Indonesian perceptions of the Saudi edition see Chapter Seven), it is not wrong to identify their QT as a distinctive edition, quite separate to the first revised edition produced in Indonesia itself. The Saudi edition is a slightly different text, produced by King Fahd Complex, to the second edition of the Indonesian QT that was produced within Indonesia.

The high visibility of the role played by the King Fahd Complex in the production of the second edition of QT and its Saudi counterpart led to criticism of this edition from the NU, which was concerned by the supposed Wahhabi tendencies that had been instilled in the translation. Under the leadership of Abdurrahman Wahid, the NU was initially not willing to accept the thousand copies of the Saudi edition that were delivered to them. In fact, they formed a committee to investigate the translation under the leadership of K.H. Ma'ruf Amin (then the Secretary of the NU, currently the Vice President of Indonesia).[38] I cannot obtain information about the results of their investigation, but it appears that the leadership of NU was not united in its views on this edition of QT. K.H. Syukron Ma'mun, the head of Lembaga Dakwah Nahdlatul Ulama (The Propagation Unit of Nahdlatul Ulama) found this edition to be acceptable, which indicates that he was not worried about any issues of theological discrepancy. K.H. Mustafa Ya'qub, a respected scholar and later a committee member for the third edition, also played down concerns, suggesting that the original QT was already in line with the Saudi theological ideas, and that only minor shifts had been introduced in the Saudi edition.[39]

The Third Edition (2002)

The second edition met with criticism with respect to its editorial quality, the accuracy of the translation (from the point of view of generally accepted mainstream Sunnī interpretations of the text), and even its

38 Sadhewo and Hartoyo, 'Quran yang Terpelihara', p. 77.

39 Faizin, *Sejarah Penerjemahan Al-Quran di Indonesia*, p. 167; Ya'qub, *Makan Tak Pernah Kenyang*, pp. 47–48.

format. Against this backdrop, another revision process (the second revision) was undertaken between 1998 and 2002, and the resultant third edition, often called 'the 2002 edition', was officially released in 2004. Ever since, private publishers have chosen to publish this edition. As was the case for the second edition, the production of the third edition also involved parties outside MORA and the LPMQ.

On 18 February 2000, an individual in East Java sent a letter to the President, copied to the Vice President, the Minister of Religious Affairs, and the Coordinator Minister of Public Welfare. In this letter, he delivered his recommendations for revisions to QT. In a totally separate move, a private institute, Yayasan Iman Jama' Jakarta,[40] distributed a questionnaire about reader responses to QT to 527 respondents, 98% of whom were students in Islamic universities in Jakarta. The questionnaire surveyed their familiarity with QT, and their expectations and perceptions of this particular translation of the Qur'an. The overall findings of this survey were that QT was read relatively frequently and widely, but that its quality was poor and it required improvement. From a technical perspective, a more stylish mode of publication, a smaller and less cumbersome size of volume, and a lower price point were all recommended.[41] Junanda P. Syarfuan, the director of Yayasan Iman Jama' Jakarta, presented the results of the survey to LPMQ and strongly recommended a revision. Junanda P. Syarfuan is an interesting figure who came to exert a not inconsiderable influence on the third edition of QT. A great Qur'an translation enthusiast, he regularly sent letters to the LPMQ outlining his proposed 'corrections' to QT. He was eventually appointed as a member of the revision committee, during the second revision process, and now represents those citizens who understand neither Arabic nor the *tafsīr* tradition and thus must rely on the translation of the Qur'an alone. In fact, he established a close personal relationship with Quraish Shihab, a prominent exegete in Indonesia and fellow committee member for the third edition of QT, and collaborated with him on his *Al-Qur'an dan Maknanya*. In addition to his passionate

---

40 QT is not the first time Yayasan Iman Jama' has played a role in the LPMQ's project. The foundation also took part in making the standardized *mushaf* of MORA.

41 H. Muhammad Shohib, 'Implementasi Pemahaman Memelihara Al-Qur'an di Indonesia: Studi tentang Upaya Pemerintah Republik Indonesia dalam Memelihara Al-Qur'an Melalui Kegiatan Lajnah Pentashih Mushaf Al-Qur'an' (unpublished master's thesis, Perguruan Tinggi Ilmu Al-Qur'an, 2003), p. 101.

scrutiny of QT, Syarfuan even agreed to provide financial support for the revision.[42]

The revision took four years to complete. The committee was initially composed of three members, two from LPMQ and Junanda P. Syarfuan, but over the years this increased to fourteen, as a result of structural changes within LPMQ. When the process began, LPMQ was headed by A. Hafizh Dasuki, and it continued under his successor Muh. Kailani, and was only finished under the subsequent leadership of Fadhal A.R. Bafadhal.[43] On the suggestion of Syarfuan, the intention was for the translation of each verse to be shorter and denser, so as to reduce the physical extent of the translation, resulting in a smaller volume. The introductory section (*muqaddimah*) and the opening and closing sections that framed every *sūra* in the previous edition were removed, and the number of footnotes was reduced by over a third from 1610 to 930.[44] These adjustments meant that the 2002 edition of QT had a considerably reduced overall length, and the total number of pages was reduced from 1,294 to 924. Copies of this edition published by private publishing houses are even shorter, at around six hundred pages. As for the translation itself, this edition is significantly different from the previous two editions, in terms of the style of diction and linguistic structures used, and, in some instances, the interpretive views included.

The Fourth Edition (2019)

After fourteen years, LPMQ set out to revise QT for a third time in 2016. The idea for the third revision emerged from a recommendation produced during the Musyawarah Kerja Nasional Ulama Al-Qur'an in August 2015. This conference raised a number of points about the existing QT, most notably with regards to consistency in the translation of several synonymous or even identical words and also, to some extent, the interpretive decisions behind the work. The possibility that the King Fahd Complex might also become involved in any potential revision

42 Personal interview with Junanda P. Syarfuan on 16 August 2016.

43 Faizin, *Sejarah Penerjemahan Al-Quran di Indonesia*, pp. 186–87.

44 Lajnah Pentashihan Mushaf Al-Qur'an, i, pp. xxxvii–xl; Lajnah Pentashihan Mushaf Al-Qur'an, 'Panduan Kajian Revisi Al-Qur'an dan Terjemahnya Kementrian Agama Tahun 2016'.

process also provided a minor impetus. In April 2015, talks took place between the Minister of Religious Affairs and the Saudi authorities about the possibility that the King Fahd Complex might print the latest edition of QT. This led LPMQ to propose the establishment of a joint committee, but in the end the Saudi authorities did not respond to this request.[45]

Muchlis M. Hanafi, the director of LPMQ, managed to put in place a better set of processes for this round of revisions. He established two sub-committees with distinctive yet intersecting duties. The first sub-committee was *tim substansi* (the Substance Team) which worked on the interpretive substance of QT. This team consisted of Islamic/ Qur'anic scholars affiliated with various institutions and organizations such as the Muhammadiyah, the NU, Persis, the MUI, and a number of Islamic higher-education institutions and *pesantren*. The team included Huzaemah T. Yanggo (1946–2021),[46] Muhammad Chirzin, Rosihan Anwar, Ahsin Sakho Muhammad, Abdul Ghafur Maimun, Malik Madani, Amir Faishol, Abbas Mansur Tamam, Lilik Ummi Kaltsum, and Junanda P. Syarfuan. It is also worth acknowledging that LPMQ invited a number of female scholars to participate as committee members during this revision process, namely Huzaeman T. Yanggo, Lilik Ummi Kaltsum, and Umi Husnul Khotiman. Quraish Shihab is not mentioned as a member of the committee of this edition, despite his occasional presence at the plenary meetings.

The second sub-committee was Hanafi's unprecedented initiative. He formally invited Badan Pengembangan dan Pembinaan Bahasa (BPPB, The Language Cultivation and Development Agency), a unit responsible for language policy within the Ministry of Education, to join the committee. The BPPB assigned four experts to LPMQ: Abdul Ghaffar Ruskhan, Dora Amalia, and Sriyanto, and Amran Purba. This was the *tim redaksi* (the Editorial Team), which worked on editorial aspects of the translation.

The main revision activity involved individual scrutiny of one particular segment of the Qur'an by each committee member, who would then propose his or her revision recommendations. Then, this

45 Interview with Muchlis M. Hanafi on 6 December 2016.

46 Prof. Huzaemah Tahido Yanggo passed away on 23 July 2021 from Covid-19. May she rest in peace with all those who died suffering from this disease.

recommendation would be put up for discussion in a series of meetings involving all committee members. (This process may be the reason for the omission of Quraish Shihab's name from the list of committee members, as, due to his seniority, he was not assigned a section of text for individual review.) In addition to this main activity, Hanafi introduced the idea of a *Konsultasi Public* (public consultation), a series of conferences held by LPMQ in cooperation with other institutions, in which LPMQ gathered as many recommendations for corrections as possible. These conferences targeted academics, *ulama,* the MUI, mass Muslim organizations, and *pesantren.* LPMQ also commissioned surveys of the reception of the translation across Indonesia, the results of which were reported in *SUHUF: Jurnal Pengkajian Al-Qur'an dan Budaya,* an academic journal produced by LPMQ.[47] Hanafi also set up an online platform through which the general public had the opportunity to deliver their recommendations. After this revision process had been completed, and all the recommendations from the various sources had been considered, the translation underwent two final inspections by two different congresses of the *ulama,* namely Musyawarah Kerja Nasional Ulama Al-Qur'an on 25–27 September 2018 and Forum Ijtima' Ulama Al-Qur'an Nasional (the National Meeting of the Ulama of the Qur'an) on 8–10 July 2019. At the end of this three-year process, MORA officially announced the publication of this edition on 18 October 2019, but it is yet to go into press at the time of writing. However, the PDF version of the translation has been made available online.

Al-Qur'an dan Terjemahnya in Indonesian Regional Languages

In 2011, MORA embarked on a project to translate the Qur'an into Indonesian regional languages. Indonesia is a land inhabited by people of diverse cultures and languages, and MORA feels a duty to preserve these cultural heritages through translation of the Qur'an. The intention is to manage national heritage (*pengelolaan kekayaan bangsa*), to

47 Jonni Syatri and others, 'Sikap dan Pandangan Masyarakat terhadap Terjemahan Al-Qur'an Kementerian Agama', *SUHUF Jurnal Pengkajian Al-Qur'an dan Budaya,* 10.2 (2017), 227–62; Zarkasi Afif and others, 'Preferensi Masyarakat dalam Penggunaan Al-Qur'an Digital', *SUHUF Jurnal Pengkajian Al-Qur'an dan Budaya,* 11.2 (2018), 185–214.

preserve regional cultures (*pelestarian budaya daerah*), and to strengthen religious service (*layanan keagamaan*) among the religious community. The ministry believes that one good way to aid the preservation of regional languages is through the translation of the Qur'an, because the privileged status of the scripture in the hearts of Muslims will ensure a continued readership of and relationship with the text in these various translations, a status which is not enjoyed by other texts such as newspapers or novels.

There are many regional languages in Indonesia, and the task of translating the Qur'an into all of these is huge: MORA is only realistically able to produce translations into three to five languages each year. Because of this, the ministry has set out a number of criteria to determine how to prioritize the various translation projects. Translations are only conducted into languages that are nearly extinct, but that also have more than one million speakers. The absence of any surviving Qur'an translation in the relevant regional language is a further criterion. By applying these criteria, the ministry has chosen to set aside languages that are well preserved, such as Javanese. In the case of Javanese, not only is the language spoken widely, but there are also a number of existing Qur'an translations in this language.[48] The project, however, has attracted the attention of both scholars and regional authorities whose languages do not fit the criteria, yet who are keen on having the Qur'an translated into their languages.

Although it falls under the aegis of MORA, the regional languages project is not overseen by LPMQ, but is instead run by Puslitbang LKKMO, a body within MORA concerned with research and development. To execute the project, Puslitbang LKKMO establishes joint committees with state-funded Islamic higher-education institutes in each region (UIN/IAIN/STAIN). Puslitbang LKKMO provides them with "Pedoman Penerjemahan Al-Qur'an ke dalam Bahasa Daerah" (Guidelines for Translating the Qur'an into Regional Languages), which set out three prerequisites: (1) the use of the 2010 copy[49] of QT, including

48 For more information about Qur'an translations in Javanese, see Islah Gusmian, 'Bahasa dan Aksara dalam Penulisan Tafsir Al-Qur'an di Indonesia Era Awal Abad 20 M', *Mutawatir*, 5.2 (2015), 223–47.

49 The guidelines use the term '2010 edition.' There is basically no 2010 edition of QT. The 2010 edition is also mentioned in some other documents produced by the LPMQ. It refers to the publication year instead of a distinctive edition.

the footnotes; (2) the use of the standardized *mushaf* published by the Ministry of Religious Affairs and issued in 2009; and (3) the use of the official Arab-Latin transliteration system issued in 1987. In 2018, MORA had published eighteen translations—nine translations in 2015,[50] and another three in each subsequent year.[51] At the time of writing, five further translations are in progress.

The committees for these various translations consist of experts in the Islamic disciplines, particularly in Qur'an and *tafsīr*, and the relevant language and culture. The members with expertise in Islamic disciplines conduct a personal initial translation, which is then submitted for the approval of all members of the team. The resulting first draft is handed to LPMQ to undergo *taṣḥīh*. The print run of QT in regional languages is limited. Copies are sent to the relevant Islamic state higher-education institutions, public libraries, and certain individuals who are authorized to distribute and disseminate translations, such as academics and other figures who lecture on Qur'an and *tafsīr*, researchers, and local *ulama*. At this point, none of these translations is available to buy, because MORA is only responsible for producing the primary copy of the translation.[52] Once MORA has handed these to the regional authorities, it is then their responsibility to publish the translation for mass consumption.

There are historical records of the translation of the Qur'an into regional languages such as Malay, Sundanese, Banjar, and Bugis. Scholarship on the Qur'an has long been disseminated in these languages, and in some cases translations and *tafsīr* existed in these regional languages long before the Indonesian language with Roman script even came into existence at the turn of the twentieth century.[53]

---

50 Choirul Fuad Yusuf, 'Pengantar Kepala Puslitbang Lektur dan Khazanah Keagamaan Badan Litbang dan Diklat Kementerian Agama', in *Al-Qur'an dan Terjemahnya Bahasa Minang* (Jakarta: Puslitbang Lektur dan Khazanah Keagamaan, 2015), pp. vii–viii.

51 antaranews.com, 'Kemenag Luncurkan Terjemahan Al Quran dalam Bahasa Daerah', *Antara News*, 2016, https://www.antaranews.com/berita/602379/kemenag-luncurkan-terjemahan-al-quran-dalam-bahasa-daerah; 'Menag Luncurkan Alquran Terjemah Tiga Bahasa Daerah', *Republika Online*, 2017, https://republika.co.id/share/p18slr335; 'Kemenag akan Luncurkan Alquran Terjemahan 3 Bahasa Daerah', *Republika Online*, 2018, https://republika.co.id/share/pjk6tr384.

52 Personal interview with Muhammad Zain, the head of Puslitbang LKKMO, on 10 August 2018.

53 Gusmian, 'Bahasa dan Aksara dalam Penulisan Tafsir Al-Qur'an di Indonesia Era Awal Abad 20 M', pp. 5–16.

Ironically, it was the promotion of Indonesian as the unifying, official language of the state, alongside the language policy pursued by the post-colonial governments, which gradually drove the practice of undertaking Qur'anic scholarship in regional languages into extinction.[54]

Moving beyond issues of language use, another important issue that factors in to the project is that of the script that these translations are written in. Before the move to the standardized use of Latin script for Indonesian, traditional Qur'anic scholarship had used *Jāwī, Pegon, Carakan,* and *Lontara* scripts. Ostensibly, MORA wants to rejuvenate the use of these older scripts, however, it is not an exaggeration to say that the ministry actually considers the choice of script to be a marginal element. This is clear from the fact that MORA gives full responsibility for the choice of script to organizing committee members, who may choose to write their translations in Latin script or a traditional script. So far only one translation (into Bugis) has been produced using a traditional script (in this case the *Lontara* script). The reason that the traditional scripts are being marginalized is, according to Muhammad Zain, the head of Puslitbang LKKMO, the fact that translations of QT into regional languages are intended for a broad readership, and traditional scripts are no longer comprehensible to the current generation. Because of this, the idea of producing a translation employing these scripts is usually deemed counterproductive.[55]

The Various Forms of *Al-Qur'an dan Terjemahnya*

Half a century is not a long time for a work as influential as QT. However, within this short space of time, QT has undergone many changes, primarily because of its status as the official state translation and the fact that a state institution, MORA, is responsible for supervising the production of the Qur'anic text and its interpretation. In other words, there is continuous oversight of the translation, and of how it is being received and responded to, and there are always designated individuals

54 Ichwan, 'The End of Jawi Islamic Scholarship? Kitab Jawi, Qur'anic Exegesis, and Politics in Indonesia', pp. 82–101; Kevin W. Fogg, 'The Standardisation of the Indonesian Language and Its Consequence for Islamic Communities', *Journal of Southeast Asian Studies*, 46.1 (2015), 86–110 (p. 93), https://doi.org/10.1017/S0022463414000629.

55 Personal interview, 10 August 2018.

whose job it is to take care of it. It is thus only to be expected that there will be a constant, ongoing process of revisions. As the official Indonesian state translation of the Qur'an, QT has developed and changed in tandem with the historical changes taking place in the politics, economy, and language of the state. Because of this, the dynamics of its revision process extend beyond changes or continuities in the substance of the translation itself, to issues such as language, the spelling system, script, and the form in which it is presented. As far as the history of QT is concerned, the changes to content only constitute one part of the revision process; the other aspect is technical.

The Publication Format: Multivolume and Single-Volume Versions

The format of QT follows the modern format followed by most Qur'an translations. The translation starts with a lengthy introduction (*muqaddimah*), providing information and basic technical knowledge on the Qur'an, the history of the Prophet Muhammad, the function and history of *tafsīr*, and the history of the translation of the Qur'an. To compose these materials, the committee drew on traditional *ᶜulūm al-Qurʾān* (Qur'anic sciences) literatures, the *sīra nabawiyya* (Biography of the Prophet), and Ahmadiyya-leaning literatures as their sources. The third edition of QT, however, as mentioned above, omits this entire section.

When it comes to the translation itself, QT follows the traditional canonical sequence, starting from *al-Fātiḥa* (Q. 1), the first *sūra,* all the way to *al-Nās* (Q. 144), the last *sūra.* The text of the translation is presented side by side with the original Arabic text. Each *sura* begins with an introduction which provides the basic necessary information about the name and merits of the *sūra,* and its key contents (*pokok-pokok isinya*). Furthermore, the Qur'anic text is arranged into groups consisting of several verses, each of which are given a distinct heading. Finally, at the end of every *sūra,* the conclusion of the *sūra* and how it connects to the next *sūra* are explained.

The first edition of QT was published in multiple volumes; the first volume consists of a 172-page introduction (*muqaddimah*) and the first ten *juzʾ*, whilst each of the second and third volumes consists of another ten *juz*ʾ. This multi-volume format was presumably a result of two combined factors: the length of time it took to produce the first edition, and the government's desire to support (and to be seen to support) this national project. It took ten years to complete the first edition of QT, a fact which is unsurprising, given the time and effort required to translate the entire Qur'an. Since QT was a national project, the government wished to demonstrate that it was coming to fruition as quickly as possible, and on a planned publication schedule. Waiting until the completion of the whole translation to publish would have contradicted this message, hence the government decided to publish QT in three separate volumes. After the translation was completed in its entirety, it is then logical that the government would combine the separate volumes as a single volume in later editions, especially given that single-volume translations were common at the time. The one-volume format made its first appearance in 1971, and has remained standard ever since.

The Arabic *Mushaf*

It is necessary at this point to very briefly outline the history of the publication of the Qur'anic text (the *mushaf*) in Indonesia. The oldest printed Qur'an known in Indonesia, which is also the oldest in Southeast Asia, is a lithographic text produced by Haji Muhammad Azhar bin Kemas Haji Abdullah and printed on 21 August 1848 (21 Ramadan 1264). The range of distribution for this *mushaf* cannot be identified due to a lack of surviving data. The Qur'an printing industry in Indonesia, which gradually developed during the twentieth century, prints two kinds of *mushaf*. The first (and most popular) kind reproduces the *mushaf* widely distributed in Southeast Asia since the nineteenth century, which originates from Singapore and Bombay, India—hence the reason it is known as *mushaf Bombay*. The second *mushaf*, better known as *mushaf bahriyya* (Ar. *al-muṣḥaf al-baḥriyya*), came from Turkey and Egypt. *Mushaf Bombay* uses *rasm uthmānī* (Uthmānic script) with bold lettering, whereas *mushaf bahriyya* uses *rasm imlāʾī* (Arabic script),[56] a

56 *Rasm* is a technique for writing the Qur'an script. *Rasm uthmānī* is the script that was believed to have been used in the text of the Qur'an issued by Uthmān ibn ʿAffān. This method of writing the Qur'an is preserved in *ʿulūm al-Qurʾān* literatures, such as *al-Itqān fī ʿulūm al-Qurʾān* by al-Ṣuyūṭī (d. 911/1505). *Rasm imlāʾī*, on the other

more stylistic and decorated calligraphy. The other significant difference is that *mushaf bahriyya* follows the *pojok or sudut* (both literally mean 'corner') mechanism, in which every page concludes with a verse ending, making it very helpful for students memorizing the Qur'an.

In 1984, the Ministry of Religious Affairs issued Mushaf Standar Indonesia (the standardized *mushaf* of Indonesia). The elements standardized in the *mushaf* include the writing script (*rasm*), vocalization marks (*ḥarakāt*), additional necessary recitational signs (such as *sakta, ishmām,* etc.), and stopping signs (*waqf*); all were decided by consensus of the National Congress of the Ulama of the Qur'an. There are three variants of the standardized *mushaf*: in addition to the *uthmānī* and *bahriyya mushafs*, there is also a braille *mushaf*.[57] Since the introduction of standardized *mushafs* the Qur'an printing industry has continued to produce either *mushaf Bombay, mushaf bahriyya,* or predominantly the standardized *mushaf*. Thanks to technological advancements, the Medina *mushaf* calligraphy produced by the King Fahd Complex has been adopted to fit into a standardized *mushaf*. This has been the predominant calligraphy in use until recently.[58]

In the context of this development, the first edition of QT uses the Bombay *mushaf* for its Arabic text. It is worth noting that when MORA initially made Qur'an printing a governmental project in 1960, the version printed was also a *mushaf Bombay*. Soon after the launch of the standardized *mushaf*, QT was printed using the *uthmānic* variant of this *mushaf*. I could not obtain a copy of the variants printed between 1985 and 1988, but the 1989 copy uses this variant. During the production of the Saudi edition of QT, there was little discussion on which *muṣhaf* was to be printed. The LPMQ wanted it to be the standardized Indonesian *mushaf*, but eventually the King Fahd Complex printed it with their own *mushaf* preference.[59] As for the second edition, it follows the standardized Indonesian *mushaf*. Nevertheless, I found a particular copy of the second edition of QT that was printed using *bahriyya* in 1992. Furthermore, after

---

hand, is the method of writing the Qur'an following the commonplace method in Arabic. See Shohib and Madzkur, p. 12.

57 Shohib and Madzkur, *Sejarah Penulisan Mushaf Al-Qur'an Standar Indonesia*, pp. 12–14.

58 Ali Akbar, 'Pencetakan Mushaf Al-Qur'an di Indonesia', *SUHUF*, 4.2 (2015), 271–87, https://doi.org/10.22548/shf.v4i2.57.

59 Faizin, *Sejarah Penerjemahan Al-Quran di Indonesia*, p. 166.

the publishers were able to adjust the calligraphy of the Medina *mushaf* into the standardized *mushaf*, QT has been widely printed with this new development.

The Spelling System

A relatively young language, Indonesian has developed both from a linguistic and a technical perspective over the last ninety-odd years. Since its initial introduction as the language of unity in 1928, and its eventual official recognition as the state language in 1945,[60] the Indonesian language has developed in various ways. Changes in the spelling systems used are discernible from a first look at any text, and the system of transliteration has also evolved. Developments in both are evident in QT.

Prior to the twentieth century, there was no such thing as conformity of orthography in the Malay and Indonesian languages. The way that Malay was written down in Latin script varied from one author to another. The first attempt to standardize spelling was made by Ch. A. Van Ophuijsen in 1901, in his *Kitab Logat Melajoe* (*The Book of the Malay Language*). This spelling system was officialized during the Dutch colonial period, but at the first Kongres Bahasa Indonesia (Congress on Indonesian Language), held in 1938 in Solo, the need for a spelling reform was voiced. It was not until 15 April 1954 that this call was finally answered with the introduction of a new standardized spelling system through a decree issued by the Ministry of Education and Culture. This system was known as Soewandi or Republik spelling. In 1954, at the second Congress on the Indonesian Language, an attempt to perfect a standardized spelling system was, once again, suggested. In 1957, the committee that was established to undertake this project proposed a new spelling system, known as Ejaan Pembaruan (lit. 'spelling update'). This spelling system, however, was never used as it was considered impractical due to its inclusion of several new letters.

60 Junaiyah H. Matanggui, *Bahasa Indonesia Serba Sekilas* (Jakarta: Indra Press, 1984), pp. 22–23; James Sneddon, *The Indonesian Language: Its History and Role in Modern Society* (Sydney: UNSW Press, 2003), pp. 9; 111; Fogg, 'The Standardisation of the Indonesian Language and Its Consequence for Islamic Communities', p. 88.

A congress held in Singapore in 1956, followed by a meeting between the Commission for the Implementation of Malay-Indonesian Cooperation in Jakarta on 4–7 December 1959, proposed yet another new system, one that unified the spelling of the two countries, namely Pengumuman Bersama Ejaan Bahasa Melayu-Indonesia (Joint Communiqué on Malay-Indonesian Spelling), better known as 'Melindo spelling'. Due to political disputes between Malaysia and Indonesia, this spelling system also failed to take off. After the two countries reconciled in 1966, a final initiative emerged. A commission headed by Anton M. Moeliono drafted a new system, in consultation with the Malaysian Spelling Committee. It was finally agreed to use this new system, although it was referred to by different names in each country; Ejaan Baru Bahasa Indonesia in Indonesia and Ejaan Baru Bahasa Malaysia in Malaysia. Facing both approval and criticism, the new system was introduced and then made official through Executive Order No. 57/1972 and an announcement by President Suharto before Parliament. This system came to be known by the name Ejaan yang Disempurnakan (Improved Spelling, EYD). In 2015, the Minister of Education and Culture, Anies Baswedan, changed its name to Pedoman Umum Ejaan Bahasa Indonesia (General Guidelines for Spelling in the Indonesian Language, PUEBI).[61]

The basic idea behind all these spelling reforms was to achieve simplification and a coherent spelling system that could be used at an international level. For this very reason, the Soewandi System abandoned the use of diaeresis, which had previously been used to differentiate between, for example, '*gulai*' (/*gu-lai*/, 'curry soup'—a noun), and *gulaï* (/*gu-la-ï*/, 'to put sugar into [something]'—a verb with the suffix -i), and in indicating open syllable boundaries, such as *saät* (*sa-at*) and *Koerän* (*Kur-an*) which were initially used in the Van Ophuijsen System. It also ended the use of apostrophes to indicate glottal stops, as in, for example *tida'* and *pende'*, and to indicate the sound of /ع/ from Arabic loanwords. The idea of simplification was often interpreted as

61 Tim Pengembang Pedoman Bahasa Indonesia, *Pedoman Umum Ejaan Bahasa Indonesia* (Jakarta: Badan Pengembang dan Pembinaan Bahasa Kementerian Pendidikan dan Kebudayaan, 2016).

'one-to-one correspondence between phoneme and grapheme.'[62] The older <oe> to represent /u/ in the Van Ophuijsen System was replaced with <u>, but it retained the use of <dj> and <tj>. They were then replaced with <j>, <c> and <u> respectively in Ejaan Baru and EYD.

When taking into account these developments to the Indonesian system of spelling, one can easily identify that the first edition of QT followed the Soewandi Spelling System, and that since EYD was officialized, QT has followed this system instead. In the first edition of QT, the phrase *'segala pudji dan utjapan sjukur'*[63] clearly shows the use of <dj>, <tj>, <sj>, and <u>, whilst the term *'machluk'* represents the use of <ch>. Both examples follow the Soewandi System. There are however minuscule exemptions and inconsistencies. In some cases, Arabic loanwords with the letter /ع/ use the apostrophe, which does not accord with the Soewandi System, for example *ni'mat* and *dita'ati.* Some other cases, however, do follow the Soewandi rules, such as *ibadat,* instead of *'ibadat.* (It should be stressed that the committee seems to be fully aware of the difference between presenting a lexical item as an Indonesian loan word and as a transliterated form of the original Arabic—*ibadat* for the former and *ᶜibaadat* for the latter.) Furthermore, in accordance with developments in policy in the area of spelling, QT also switches to the EYD System. While I could not obtain the translation published in 1972, when EYD was officially introduced, the 1977 edition uses it. Nevertheless, the problem of rogue apostrophes remained unchanged in this edition. The fourth edition uses the PUEBI System. As mentioned above, the LPMQ officially invited Badan Pengembangan dan Pembinaan Bahasa (BPPB, The Language Cultivation and Development Agency), who are responsible for language policy, to collaborate in the preparation of this edition. This may be why, when using this latest system, QT resolves the apostrophe problem.

62 Kridalaksana, Harimurti, 'Spelling Reform 1972: A Stage in the Process of Standardisation of Bahasa Indonesia', in *Papers from the Conference on the Standardisation of Asian Languages, Manila, Philiphines. Pacific Linguistic,* ed. by AQ Perez, AO Santiago, and Nguyen Dang Liem, C, 47 (Canberra: Australian National University, 1974), pp. 305–17, http://sealang.net/archives/pl/pdf/PL-C47.305.pdf; Lukman Ali, *Ikhtisar Sejarah Ejaan Bahasa Indonesia* (Jakarta: Pusat Pembinaan dan Pengembangan Bahasa, 1998).

63 Departemen Agama Republik Indonesia, *Al-Qurāan dan Terdjemahnja,* 3 vols (Jakarta: Jamunu', 1965), i, p. 3.

The Transliteration System

Until 1987, there was no such thing as a formal transliteration system for Arabic in use in Indonesia. However, there was a popular system. This essentially uses the double letter method. Emphatic consonants are marked with an additional *h*, as in <zh>, <dh>, <th>, and <sh> for <ظ>, <ض>, <ط>, and <ص>, respectively. The older version of this system would use <ch> for <خ> and <kh> for <ح>, but this changed so that <خ> is represented by <kh>, and <ح> with a single <h>, making it similar to <ه>. Dental fricatives such as <ذ> and <ث> are marked with <dz> and <ts>, respectively, and <ع> is designated by an apostrophe. The earlier system used vowels with diaeresis (ä, ï, and ü) for <ء>, while long vowels were typically marked with double letters (aa, ii, and uu). More recently, the popular system started to transcribe these using vowels with macrons (ā, ī, and ū) or circumflexes (â, î, and û). Nevertheless, many authors in the 1970s and 1980s just ignored this feature. The popular system typically did not use a hyphen to separate the prefix *al* from the main word.

The first edition of QT effectively used this popular system. Up until the early years of the second edition, QT includes the same note on transliteration, which describes a system similar to that outlined in the above paragraph. When it comes to actual usage, here is just one example, the listing for one of the Qur'an commentaries consulted in the bibliography: '*Allaama Al Alusy, Tafsir Ruuhul Ma'aani.*' This entry includes the use of double letters for long vowels and an apostrophe for <ع>. However, it also displays inconsistency; although the <ع> is indicated in the word *ma'aani*, one is also needed for *Allaama*, and the double vowel required for the long 'i' in *Tafsir* is also missing, for example. Another example can be found in the transcription of the word *al-qurʾān* in the actual title of the work as *Al Quräan*, without a hyphen between *al* and *Quräan* and using an 'a' with a diaeresis. This system is used for *al-qurʾān* across all earlier editions of the work, with only some minor inconsistencies. As a matter of fact, the title of the work continued to be written that way at least until 1987 (there is a slight change in the fourth edition to *Al-Qur'an dan Terjemahannya*, but it has nothing to do with transliteration). Given its use of the Soewandi Spelling System, the use of diaeresis in '*Al Quräan*' could be seen as inconsistent, yet that was not the case. The use of a diaeresis in '*Al Quräan*' does not relate to the spelling, but rather to transliteration. In this popular system, a diaeresis was used for <ء> with *fatḥa*.

This inconsistency is not unique at all. Indonesian scholars, at least until the end of the twentieth century, did not seem to bother much with uniformity and consistency in transliteration. This was also true for the texts produced by MORA itself. The transcripts of Sukarno's speeches published by the ministry, for example, were not uniform in their transliteration. In one instance we find *Al Qurän Membentuk Manusia Baru,*[64] but in another this appears as *Kalau akan Mentjari Tuhan Batjalah Al-Qur'an.*[65]

In 1987, through *Surat Keputusan Bersama* (The Mutual Decree, SKB), a decree issued by the Minister of Religious Affairs and the Minister of Education and Culture, No: 158/1987 and No. 0543b/U/1987, the government issued an official manual on the transliteration of Arabic words into Indonesian. This transliteration system ousts both the use of diaeresis and the double letter method. Long vowels are marked with macrons, <ā>, <ī>, and <ū>; and dental fricatives are marked with overdots, as in <ż> for <ذ> and <ṡ> for <ث>, while emphatic consonants are marked with underdots, as in <ḥ>, <ẓ>, and <ḍ> for <ظ> ,<ح>, and <ض> respectively. This system retains the use of <kh> and <sy> for <خ> and <ش>. The hyphen is to be used between the article *al* and the main word. This transliteration style has been set as the standard ever since. Academic publications have gradually adopted this system, and universities eventually instructed students to use it for their academic writing activities.

With the issuance of this transliteration system, one might expect that QT, as a state project, would have adjusted its own transliteration style sooner rather than later. Nevertheless, that was not the case. In the 1993 copy, the body of QT continued to use the old transliteration system, despite the fact that its title was changed. We see, for example, *Al Faatihah* instead of *al-Fātiḥah.* Again, there were inconsistencies—for example, the use of *Anwaruttanzil* instead of *Anwaaruttanziil.* In short,

---

64 Soekarno, 'Alqurän Membentuk Manusia Baru' (Djawatan Penerangan Agama Departemen Agama, 1961).

65 Soekarno, *Kalau akan Mentjari Tuhan Batjalah Al-Qur'an* (Jakarta: Departemen Agama R.I, 1963).

even though QT was first revised from 1989–90, the old transliteration style is still applied in the second edition. Upon seeing the title of this edition, *Al-Qur'an dan Terjemahnya*, one might assume that it follows the updated official transliteration system, but this is not the case. The title of the official MORA commentary printed in 1985 had already left out a diaeresis in its title, presenting the title as *Al-Qur'an dan Tafsirnya*, rather than *Al-Quräan dan Tafsirnya*. The version of QT printed in 1989 likewise used the title *Al-Qur'an dan Terjemahnya*. Instead of following the official transliteration system, the change in the title, in both cases, is because the word *Al-Qur'an* was written as an Indonesian word instead of an Arabic transliteration.

There is a high chance that the 1987 transliteration conventions were not applied until the third edition of QT was issued. In this edition, the note on transliteration explicitly refers to the SKB System, and the names of the *sūras*, the titles listed in the bibliography, and Arabic words included either in the body of the translation or the footnotes all follow this system. This third edition uses *al-fātiḥa, al-ḥajj,* and *yaumiddīn,* for example: overall it shows increased consistency, except for minor cases where it diverts from the system. These inconsistencies were ultimately corrected in the fourth edition.

Layout, Typesetting, and Innovations Introduced by Private Publishers

The actual format of the Qur'anic text has been almost completely overlooked by scholars, and that neglect extends to Qur'an translations as well. One of the very few people to pay proper attention to this facet of the Qur'an is Keith Small. In his book *Qurʾāns: Books of Divine Encounter* (2015), he elaborates on the underlying meaning of the format and stylistic appearance of Qur'an manuscripts. He suggests that the writing format and the various artistic elements of the manuscript serve more than merely aesthetic purposes. 'Ornamentation,' he suggests, 'developed using strictly Islamic themes that increasingly served the liturgical needs of recitation together with theological aspects of the text.' For example, third-century parchment from the Abbasid period shifted the main page format to landscape in order to allow 'greater artistic possibilities for the script and also made the Qur'an visually distinct from Christian and Jewish scriptures.'[66] When it comes to Qur'an translations, the first person to look at this aspect of these works is Johanna Pink. In an article entitled 'Form Follows Function: Notes on the Arrangements of Text in Printed Qur'an Translations' (2017) she argues that 'layout decisions in Qur'an translations stand in close relation to the target group envisaged by the translator or publisher and to the uses that the translation is supposed to be put to.'[67]

As a point of departure Pink looks at the common forms of layout used in Qur'an translations throughout history, and modern developments that have become popular in the print age. She finds that there were three main forms of classical translations: interlinear translations, paraphrastic translations, and glosses. Translations of the first sort are usually written as a comprehension aid. In the interlinear format, the meaning of each word is written between the lines without any effort to formulate a meaningful sentence in the target language. In the paraphrastic format, the translation is provided as a running text alongside the Qur'anic text with a visual distinction, such as the use of a different color. Glosses physically separate the target text from its source; the former is written in a central box on the page and the translation, or commentary, is situated outside it. Another format, the tabular layout, has become popular more recently. This format places the Arabic text and the translation side by side either on one page or on opposite pages. While each of the above forms is typically used for bilingual translations, a monolingual layout should also be added to the list. This layout is usually written by or intended for non-Muslim readers who have no interest in the original Arabic text, and therefore presents the target text as a typical running text, without the Arabic source text. For theological reasons, this form is not easily available in most Muslim-majority countries.[68]

---

66 Keith E. Small, *Qur'āns Books of Divine Encounter* (Oxford: Bodleian Library, 2015), pp. 15; 22.

67 Johanna Pink, 'Form Follows Function: Notes on the Arrangement of Texts in Printed Qur'an Translations', *Journal of Qur'anic Studies*, 19.1 (2017), 143–54 (p. 143), https://doi.org/10.3366/jqs.2017.0274.

68 Pink, 'Form Follows Function', pp. 144–45.

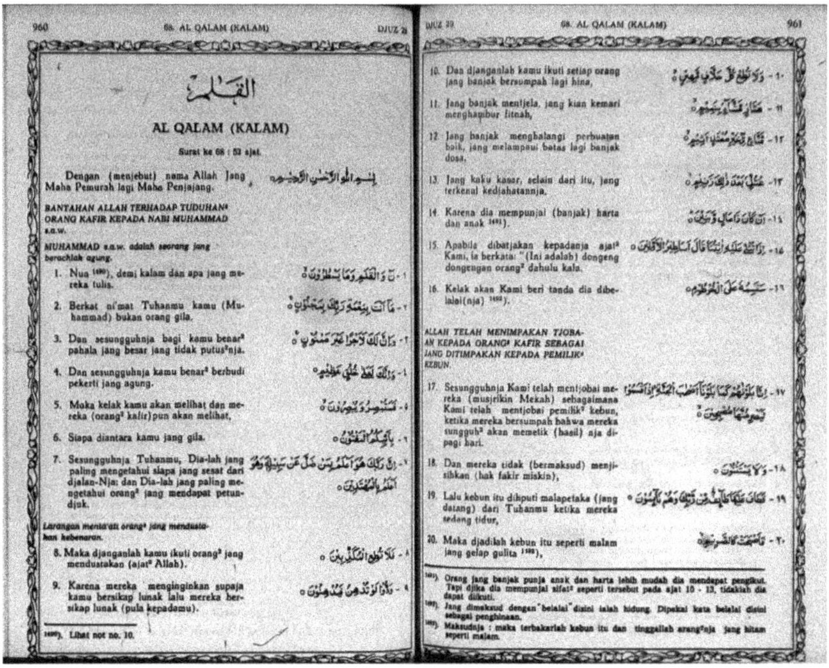
960 68. AL QALAM (KALAM) DJUZ 29

القلم

AL QALAM (KALAM)

Surat ke 68 : 52 ajat.

Dengan (menjebut) nama Allah Jang Maha Pemurah lagi Maha Penjajang.

BANTAHAN ALLAH TERHADAP TUDUHAN[2] ORANG KAFIR KEPADA NABI MUHAMMAD s.a.w.

MUHAMMAD s.a.w. adalah seorang jang berachlak agung.

1. Nun [1490]), demi kalam dan apa jang mereka tulis.
2. Berkat ni'mat Tuhanmu kamu (Muhammad) bukan orang gila.
3. Dan sesungguhnja bagi kamu benar[2] pahala jang besar jang tidak putus[2]nja.
4. Dan sesungguhnja kamu benar[2] berbudi pekerti jang agung.
5. Maka kelak kamu akan melihat dan mereka (orang[2] kafir)pun akan melihat,
6. Siapa diantara kamu jang gila.
7. Sesungguhnja Tuhanmu, Dia-lah jang paling mengetahui siapa jang sesat dari djalan-Nja: dan Dia-lah jang paling mengetahui orang[2] jang mendapat petundjuk.

Larangan menta'ati orang[2] jang mendustakan kebenaran.

8. Maka djanganlah kamu ikuti orang[2] jang mendustakan (ajat[2] Allah).
9. Karena mereka menginginkan supaja kamu bersikap lunak lalu mereka bersikap lunak (pula kepadamu).

[1490]). Lihat not no. 10.

DJUZ 29 68. AL QALAM (KALAM) 961

10. Dan djanganlah kamu ikuti setiap orang jang banjak bersumpah lagi hina,
11. Jang banjak mentjela, jang kian kemari menghambur fitnah,
12. Jang banjak menghalangi perbuatan baik, jang melampaui batas lagi banjak dosa,
13. Jang kaku kasar, selain dari itu, jang terkenal kedjahatannja,
14. Karena dia mempunjai (banjak) harta dan anak [1491]).
15. Apabila dibatjakan kepadanja ajat[2] Kami, ia berkata: "(Ini adalah) dongeng dongengan orang[2] dahulu kala.
16. Kelak akan Kami beri tanda dia dibelalai(nja) [1492]).

ALLAH TELAH MENIMPAKAN TJOBAAN KEPADA ORANG[2] KAFIR SEBAGAI JANG DITIMPAKAN KEPADA PEMILIK[2] KEBUN.

17. Sesungguhnja Kami telah mentjobai mereka (musjrikin Mekah) sebagaimana Kami telah mentjobai pemilik[2] kebun, ketika mereka bersumpah bahwa mereka sungguh[2] akan memetik (hasil) nja dipagi hari.
18. Dan mereka tidak (bermaksud) menjisihkan (hak fakir miskin),
19. Lalu kebun itu diliputi malapetaka (jang datang) dari Tuhanmu ketika mereka sedang tidur,
20. Maka djadilah kebun itu seperti malam jang gelap gulita [1493]),

[1491]). Orang jang banjak punja anak dan harta lebih mudah dia mendapat pengikut. Tapi djika dia mempunjai sifat[2] seperti tersebut pada ajat 10 - 13, tidaklah dia dapat diikuti.

[1492]). Jang dimaksud dengan "belalai" disini ialah hidung. Dipakai kata belalai disini sebagai penghinaan.

[1493]). Maksudnja : maka terbakarlah kebun itu dan tinggallah arang[2]nja jang hitam seperti malam.

Figure 1 The tabular layout of QT (first edition), my personal collection.

QT applies a tabular layout. Copies of the translation printed by MORA, the King Fahd Complex, and earlier private publishers also follow this format. The Qur'anic text and the translation are set separately, with the original Arabic text placed on the right-hand side and the translation on the left. Each verse, and its corresponding translation, are set individually, and sorted via a numbering mechanism. The uppermost line of each verse is at the same height as its translation. The translation text is usually longer than the source text, and consequently there are blank spaces between each verse of the Arabic text. Information deemed necessary in the rendering of certain words or phrases is provided in brackets or below the text in footnotes. At the start of every new *sūra*, the name of the *sūra* is written in both its Arabic and transliterated form, followed by the identification of the *sūra* number in the canonical sequence, and the number of verses in the *sūra*. Every opposite page is decorated with a simple floral frame. At the header of the page is the page number, the name of the *sūra* (written in transliteration) along with its translation in brackets, and the *juzʾ* identification number. The reading direction of the earlier edition is from left to right, probably expressing the primary relevance of the translated text to the reader over the Arabic. The edition printed by the King Fahd Complex, however, inverts the reading direction, thereby privileging the Arabic text.

By this time in the history of QT, private publishers have initiated a wide range of adjustments to the versions they print. Firstly, like the King Fahd Complex, some of them reverse the reading direction. A number of other individually authored translations, such as those by A. Hassan and Mahmud Yunus (1899–1982), have applied this format, and the publishers presumably thought that following this mainstream approach would have a broader appeal to readers. At some point, a particular copy printed in 1992 changed the layout completely to a gloss format (the identity of the publisher is however missing in the copy that I have obtained). In this new layout, every page is divided into two separate sections. The first section, the inner box, contains the running Qur'anic text. The translation occupies the other section, the remaining space around the inner box. This format essentially restores the Qur'anic text to its common traditional typesetting, as a continuous block of text, which makes the practice of continuous recitation easier by removing the distraction of blank spaces between each verse. The foreword of this 1992 copy reveals that it has been printed for the express purpose of memorization of the Qur'an by a particular yet unnamed *pesantren*. Some other publishers decided to combine this modern gloss format with the more classic interlinear layout. In these copies, while the translation text is situated around the box containing the Arabic text, a word-for-word translation is also included between the lines of the Arabic. This essentially means that the *mushaf* employs two kinds of translation. That situated around the text is usually QT, while the word-for-word interlinear translation is written by a translator appointed by the publisher.

I would suggest that these initiatives go beyond just modifying the layout of QT; these publishers have embedded the translation into the traditional shape of the *mushaf*. The initial form of the publication of QT, as produced by MORA, indicates that it was considered as completely distinct from the *mushaf*. In other words, they were effectively considered as belonging to separate genres that are printed with different orientations and for different target readerships; one is a

Qur'an translation and the other is the *mushaf* or the Arabic text of the Qur'an. However, in these, transformed versions, both genres merge, and what the reader is actually presented with is the Arabic *mushaf* with the translation attached as a complementary element.

Figure 2 The combination of gloss and interlinear layout from QT (third edition), the collection of Muhammad Dluha Luthfillah, CC-BY 4.0.

It is clear that technological advancements have enhanced the potential for printing the Qur'an and Qur'an translations. Private publishers are eager to demonstrate their creativity in producing different versions of the Qur'an. The use of a stylistic, luxurious design and cover can contribute to the technical and aesthetic value of the *mushaf* in terms of its material aspects: some editions are regarded as extremely precious and are presented as exclusive gifts or as part of a dowry, while others are merely used as ordinary instruments for recitation. However, developments in printing have affected more than the technical and aesthetic value of the various versions of QT made available by private publishers. Nowadays, there are huge marketing opportunities available for publishers who tailor their products to specific target customers. This has led to the production of versions of the *mushaf*—with QT embedded—aimed at specific readerships: men, women, teenagers, those wanting a classic Qur'an layout, those wanting luxurious, glamorous volumes, and those requiring a more minimalist product.[69] Some others have clear pedagogical motives, such as those using the aforementioned gloss and interlinear combination, or the 'Qur'an for Children,' which is filled with drawings and illustrations, or the 'Qur'an for Travellers,' the cover of which features a design in the shape of camping equipment. The design of the volume might also focus on particular interpretive, instructional, and theological values. For example, in the 'Qur'an for Women,' topical verses are highlighted in blocks of color. In other versions, recitation instructions, traditionally known as *tajwīd*, are depicted with colorful ornamentation. Or certain words, such the names of God, might be given a different color so as to provide a visual pointer reminding the reader of awareness of Him.[70] Some publishers go as far as slightly revising the actual text of the translation. In one case, for example, a particular version of QT retains the Arabic word *rabb* ('Lord') instead of using the translated word, *Tuhan*. In another instance, a publisher substituted the translation *teman setia* (loyal friends) with *pemimpin* (leaders) for *awliyāʾ* in Q 5:51.[71]

Online and Mobile App Versions

There are dozens of mobile applications available in Indonesia that are used for Islamic activities, including some that provide notification for prayers and *azan*, indicate the direction of the *qibla*, and, of course, provide a copy of the Qur'anic text along with recorded recitations from notable *qurrāʾ*, translations, and *tafsīr*. These apps have enjoyed great popularity, as indicated by the high number of downloads. In the face of the popularity of such apps, MORA eventually followed suit and, on 30 August 2016, launched their official online and mobile Qur'an app. The app integrates all of MORA's Qur'an related products, including the standardized *mushaf*, QT, *Al-Qur'an dan Tafsirnya*, *Tafsir Ringkas* and *Sabab al-Nuzul*, and it is anticipated that it will be developed further, for example by the addition of other texts such as *Tafsir Tematik* and

69 Akbar, 'Pencetakan Mushaf Al-Qur'an di Indonesia', p. 284.

70 Hamam Faizin, 'Colored-Text Qur'anic Mushaf in Modern Indonesia' (Jakarta, 2017).

71 I did not obtain this particular *mushaf* myself. This information comes from an interview with an LPMQ official, conducted on 15 August 2018.

Tafsir Ilmi. Since MORA has not yet produced their own recordings of Qur'an recitation, the app instead uses Mahmud Khalil al-Hushari's recordings.[72]

MORA's production of this app reflects an internal desire to increase people's interactions with its various Qur'anic and Islamic projects. Relying only on physical book editions for public engagement is a strategy with certain limitations. A single book might only integrate three Qur'anic products at most: the standardized *mushaf*, the translation, and the color-coded *tajwīd*. *Al-Qur'an dan Tafsirnya* and *Tafsir Ringkas*, on the other hand, have reached a much narrower readership due to their huge size. The online platform integrates all of MORA's Qur'anic projects in one place, and the strong potential for an increased audience is evident. The print edition has other shortcomings, for example, it is not so easy to carry around, and there are stricter concepts connected to the sacred nature of the holy book (for instance, many believe that one cannot touch the Qur'an unless one is sure about one's state of physical purity, and it cannot be taken into a lavatory, or put on the floor). An online platform overcomes these restrictions. In permitting greater mobility, the online and mobile platform also provides a user interface experience, connecting MORA's Qur'anic project with social media activity.

Conclusion

This chapter has provided a historical overview that will provide context for the following discussion. To sum up: there are four main editions of QT: the first edition (1965–70), the second edition (1989–90), the third edition (2002), and the fourth edition (2019). In addition to these main editions, there is also a Saudi edition and various translations of QT into Indonesian regional languages. This overview also addressed the fact that if one only looks at changes to the actual text of the translation,

72 Kompas Cyber Media, 'Kementerian Agama Resmi Luncurkan Aplikasi Al Quran Digital Pertama', *KOMPAS.com*, 2016, https://nasional.kompas.com/read/2016/08/30/22125031/kementerian.agama.resmi.luncurkan.aplikasi.al.quran.digital.pertama; 'Alquran Digital Kemenag Sudah Bisa Diunduh di Google Play Store', *Republika Online*, 2016, https://republika.co.id/berita/dunia-islam/islam-nusantara/16/08/31/ocriqt313-alquran-digital-kemenag-sudah-bisa-diunduh-di-google-play-store; 'Website Alquran Kementerian Agama', https://quran.kemenag.go.id/index.php/about.

this does not tell us the full history of QT. It is also essential to consider developments in orthography, and in the physical aspects of the translation such as its layout and format, and its script and binding, and integration with new media platforms. In terms of visual formulation and production, there are several forms of QT: three-volume and single-volume forms; versions applying Soewandi spelling, EYD spelling, and the formalized transliteration system; those that follow the tabular and gloss format; visual and stylistic aspects that are imposed on the translation by the Qur'an printing industry for marketing reasons; the book itself and the online mobile app platform.

The history of QT shows that it is a multifaceted work; the translation is the site of different interests for a number of parties. QT has consistently been subjected to critique on the part of Indonesian *ulama* for its interpretive value, as is evident from the recurring concerns about the translation that have been raised by the National Congress of the Ulama of the Qur'an. These criticisms have shaped the development of the translation. QT's readers have also contributed to changing the shape of the translation: they want a translation with a more stylish design, a smaller, more user-friendly size, at a lower price, and with a text that is more readable. LPMQ has granted these requests, but demand from readers has led to the industrialization of the Qur'an and its interpretation: in response the publication industry has re-presented QT in various forms, and with various different intentions. Last but not least, it is evident that in QT the political interests of two different political institutions, the Saudi and Indonesian governments, meet and sometimes collide. The Indonesian government's main priorities in its development of QT are to ensure that, on the one hand, it keeps pace with the developing language policies of the state and, on the other, that it adapts to innovations in printing and Internet technologies to maintain and expand its encounters with citizens. Both of these priorities reflect its overall concern with state involvement in religion, and with presenting itself as supportive to Muslim interests. In contrast, the involvement of the Saudi authorities is in part driven by their desire to promote a particular theological affiliation, and in part by their broader project of expanding the Qur'an's readership worldwide.

3. The Political Significance of *Al-Qur'an dan Terjemahnya*

One of the markers of the official privilege of *Al-Qur'an dan Terjemahnya* is the inclusion of several forewords provided by some of the highest figures in government. The first edition of QT incorporates a foreword by President Sukarno (1901–70) in the first volume, and by President Suharto (1921–2008) in the later two volumes. The first edition of QT also contains additional forewords not only by the Minister of Religious Affairs, who led the project, but also by the Chairman and Vice-Chairman of Majelis Permusyawaratan Rakyat Sementara (MPRS, Provisional People's Consultative Assembly) and the Minister of People's Welfare. The second volume of the first edition of QT also included a foreword by a former Minister of Religious Affairs. Suharto called a halt to the tradition of presidential forewords in the 1971 copy, but a foreword by the Minister of Religious Affairs has still been included in all later editions except (of course) the Saudi edition. All editions also include a foreword from the leader of the translation committee.

The paratextual elements of a translation are effectively spaces in which stakeholders are not bound by the confines of the source text, and can express anything they wish. The various government officials who have contributed to QT have revealed much in their respective forewords, from technical information on the production of QT, or the general policies of the government, to their personal political and ideological views. Given this, these forewords are critical to our understanding of the position of QT as a governmental project.

This chapter deals with the forewords to the various editions and copies of QT in order to situate the project of the official Qur'an translation in the broader context of the state's political development and to understand the role it plays in this. QT is an important national project

 https://doi.org/10.11647/OBP.0289.03

that has been entwined with the formal state bureaucracy on an ongoing basis throughout the three phases of post-independence Indonesian history—the Old Order, the New Order, and the Reformation Era. As mentioned above, the foreword is a space where the state, or to be more precise, the ruling government of the time, can interject its ideological input into QT, and, as we will see, those who provide them deploy a set of typical vocabularies in them. This chapter illustrates the ways in which these forewords are integral for understanding the history of the production of QT and demonstrates how, throughout the history of QT, the interests of each government are most apparent in the forewords, which record the political dynamics of the state during the Sukarno, Suharto, and post-Suharto periods. They each use specific vocabulary and language that the respective presidents typically used on official occasions: in other words, the ruling governments deploy the paratext of QT to bolster their own political and personal image. Additionally, the forewords illustrate one way that QT has played a public role that goes beyond its conventional aim of providing access to the text and meaning of the Qur'an for Indonesian Muslims.

Sukarno and the Ideologization of *Al-Qur'an dan Terjemahnya*

After prolonged colonization under Dutch rule, and a short-lived Japanese occupation, Indonesia eventually achieved independence in 1945, although it was only formally recognized by its former colonial masters in 1949. The lack of recognition from the Dutch in those four years was just one more problem Indonesia had to struggle to overcome, socially, militarily, and politically. In these early years, the new Republic of Indonesia faced many difficulties. The central government struggled to win the support and allegiance of regional powers, which in turn created obstacles on the path to unity. For the Dutch colonial authorities who returned to the region under the Netherlands Indies Civil Administration (NICA), intervention in these regional interests served as an entry point for their attempts to undermine the newly declared republic and to restore Dutch power in the country. They formed several federal states in cooperation with local elites in the outer lands and twice threatened the fledgling Indonesian state with military aggression, in July 1947 and December 1948. These interventions damaged the attempts by the central leadership in Jakarta to achieve a stable, unified state. In the 1950s, Indonesia was politically at its lowest ebb, with the government unable to achieve social order or a proper distribution of resources. This situation led to socio-political instability and recurring turmoil throughout the 1960s, as is evidenced by movements such as S.M. Kartosuwirjo (1949–62) in West Java, Kahar Muzakkar (1921–65) in South Sulawesi, Daud Beureu'eh (1896–1987) in Aceh, Pemerintah Revolusioner Republik Indonesia (PRRI, The Revolutionary Government of the Indonesian Republic) in Bukittinggi, and Permesta (Perjuangan Semesta Alam, the Universal Struggle in North Sulawesi.[1]

Negotiations with the Dutch and the federal states they had formed ended with the establishment of Republik Indonesia Serikat (RIS, The United Indonesian Republic) on 27 December 1949, after which the Republic of Indonesia existed as one of seven federal states within in the RIS. However, the RIS did not last long, and on 17 August 1950 all seven states agreed to become a unitary state once more, under the name of the Republic of Indonesia. In 1955, the newly formed republic held its first elections: one for parliament and a second round of elections for the provisional constituent assembly, whose duty it was to draft and approve the new constitution that would replace the temporary constitution which had been used since 1950. The election yielded a balanced share of representatives, particularly across the four biggest parties: the PNI (who won 22.2% of parliamentary seats), Masyumi (22.2%), the NU (17.5%), and the PKI (15.2%).[2]

This relatively balanced share of power made the meetings held by the Constitutional Assembly unproductive. Frustrating ideological disputes on the issue of the basis of the state substantially occupied the politicians' energy, reproducing the earlier debates that had taken place during the preparations for independence in the 1940s. The Islamic leaders of Masyumi and the NU parties recalled the enactment of Piagam Djakarta, while the secular parties associated Masyumi with

1 M. C. Ricklefs, *A History of Modern Indonesia* (New York: Palgrave Macmillan, 2008), pp. 249–71; Bakhtiar Effendy, *Islam dan Negara: Transformasi Gagasan dan Praktik Politik Islam di Indonesia*, trans. by Ihsan Ali-Fauzi and Rudy Harisyah Alam, Digital (Democracy Project, 2011), p. 54.

2 Ricklefs, p. 286.

Darul Islam movements and framed Pancasila as a 'partisan anti-Islamic slogan.' The constitutional assembly eventually reached an agreement on some issues that would ultimately be included in the constitution, yet on the fundamental issue of the basis of the state, its members were starkly at odds. They could not agree on whether Indonesia should become a Pancasila state or an Islamic state. Discussions rumbled on for almost two years without any resolution as none of the parties involved could gather the two thirds of the majority required for any decision to be approved.

In the meantime, Sukarno began his attempts to gain more influence. On 28 October 1956, he introduced his idea of what later was officially called *demokrasi terpimpin* (Guided Democracy). He devised a system of 'mutual cooperation' (*gotong royong*), according to which the cabinet would operate under an advisory council with representatives from functional groups (youth groups, urban laborers, agricultural laborers, religious groups, regional representatives, and so on) that would be led, or guided, by himself. The PNI and PKI declared their support, Masyumi voiced their disapproval, and the NU accepted the proposal whilst objecting to the communist faction on the council. The situation escalated, giving rise to the aforementioned Permesta and PRRI movements. Some of the leaders of Masyumi became involved in PRRI, and even continued to show sympathy to the movement after the dissolution of the party. This was unsurprising, because Masyumi was in constant opposition to any political developments that would bring the country closer to Sukarno's ideal. The NU, on the other hand, maintained an association with the President, and this only exacerbated the divide between the modernist and traditionalist Muslim factions. This bitter opposition on the part of Masyumi ended with its dissolution, and the imprisonment of those of its leaders who had been involved in the PRRI movement.[3]

Political developments, and the gridlock in the constitutional assembly, led to the idea of returning to the 1945 Constitution. This became a reality when, on 5 July 1959, President Sukarno issued a decree that dissolved the constituent assembly for their failure to achieve a consensus about

---

3 B. J. Boland, *The Struggle of Islam in Modern Indonesia* (Dordrecht: Springer Netherlands, 1971), pp. 88–104, https://doi.org/10.1007/978-94-017-4710-3; Ricklefs, pp. 282–306.

the foundation of the state, and re-enacted the 1945 Constitution. The decree turned what was a Liberal Democracy into a Guided Democracy. The parliamentary cabinet, which represented Liberal Democracy, was removed, and a new presidential cabinet was formed.[4] On 17 August 1959, in his annual speech, Sukarno introduced his *Manifesto Politik* (Manipol), a manifesto that addressed the unresolved issue of the three competing ideologies in the country. His response to this ideological uncertainty was a synthesis of *Nasionalisme* (nationalism), *Agama* (religion), and *Komunisme* (communism), abbreviated as Nasakom. In the same speech, Sukarno introduced another concept, Usdek, an acronym derived from the terms *kembali ke* [*U*]*UD 1945* (return to the 1945 Constitution), [*S*]*osialisme Indonesia* (Indonesian Socialism), [*D*]*emokrasi Terpimpin* (Guided Democracy), [*E*]*konomi Terpimpin* (Guided Economy), and [*K*]*epribadian Indonesia* (Indonesian Identity). Sukarno saw Manipol-Usdek as a new direction of governance and regarded Pancasila as the philosophy of the state, the essence of which was mutual cooperation (*gotong royong*) between the three most significant groups in Indonesia: the nationalists, the communists, and the Muslims. He underlined the idea that Pancasila represented the spirit of Nasakom, and to be Pancasilaist was to be Nasakomist.[5]

The genealogy of Sukarno's synthetic Nasakom ideology can be traced back to the emergence of mass political movements of Indonesia in the early twentieth century. In the first quarter of the century, Indonesia witnessed the emergence of various political movements, with three main ideological streams, that strove for the independence of Indonesian society, the right to self-governance and an end to Dutch colonialism. The first stream to emerge was Sarekat Islam (SI). Initially established as a trade organization (SDI, Sarekat Dagang Islam), SI was the first mass political movement that inclusively gathered together a diverse Muslim membership from a range of classes and geographical locations,

4 Moch. Nur Ichwan, 'Official Reform of Islam: State Islam and the Ministry of Religious Affairs in Contemporary Indonesia, 1966–2004' (unpublished doctoral dissertation, Tilburg University, 2006), p. 74, https://pure.uvt.nl/portal/en/publications/official-reform-of-islam(f07a60f1-bf55-4979-8ea1-bab6e45a42ac).html.

5 Eka Darmaputera, 'Pancasila and The Search for Identity and Modernity in Indonesian Society: A Cultural and Ethical Analysis' (unpublished doctoral dissertation, Boston Collegee, 1982), pp. 306–11.

in both urban and rural areas, including traders, urban laborers, *kyais* and *ulama, priyais,* and peasants. SI was successful because its founders realized that Islam could be a unifying ideology for otherwise diverse groups of people against the hegemonic Dutch colonialist powers. SI leaders, such as Agus Salim (1884–1954), and most importantly his pupil Muhammad Natsir (1908–93)—later an important leader of Masyumi—became keen proponents of the power of religion (specifically Islam) as an ideological basis for an independent Indonesia.

The second stream followed ideas of secular nationalism, and its foremost spokesperson was Sukarno. Sukarno believed that nationalism could be a unifying bond in the fight for an independent Indonesia. He defined nationalism as love of the homeland, and a sincere willingness to dedicate oneself to the homeland at the expense of narrow political interests. He also explained nationalism as the conviction and awareness of the people that they are united under one nation. On the issue of the relationship between religion and state, he insisted that nationalism should involve the separation of religion from state in its legal-formal format, but should not completely deny the role of religion in the state's political development. Natsir, Sukarno's greatest opponent, believed in the holistic nature of Islam and thus rejected the idea of separation between Islam and the state: for him, Islam and the state should be regarded as one, and he criticized Sukarno for placing too much store in nationalism. Independence and the state, for Natsir, were tools with which to achieve the ultimate goal of religion, which is submission to God.

In another political development, Marxism became appealing for a small but growing segment of Indonesian nationalists associated with Europa-Indonesian politics, namely the Nationale Indische Partij (NIP), which was affiliated with the leftish Indische Sociaal Democratische Vereeniging (ISDV), established by an ex-activist in a left-wing party in the Netherlands. The Europe-centric ideas they proposed created a barrier between them and much of the Indonesian population, which meant that they gained relatively little support, as a result of which they infiltrated the SI to gather more support. In 1920, the ISDV transformed into a fully-committed communist party, namely the PKI. This represents the third ideological stream.[6]

6 Effendy, pp. 69–105.

These three streams were in continuous competition for political significance in Indonesia. When Sukarno came up with Nasakom, he believed that these ideologies could be merged into one functional system of political governance, a Guided Democracy. When it came to *agama* (religion), Sukarno made political use of various Islamic slogans and commissioned various Islamic projects. In his speeches, he articulated Islamic slogans, for example calling on *Api Islam* (the fire of Islam), and infused other slogans, such as character and nation-building, or *mertjusuar* (lighthouse), with Islamic rhetoric. The use of such political rhetoric was prevalent during his last five years as president in all public addresses in which he mentioned Islam and the Qur'an, especially on Islamic commemoration days. In his presidential decree, he asserted that Piagam Djakarta, a declaration that Muslim leaders had fought for during debates in the constituent assembly,[7] was the spirit of the 1945 Constitution. Likewise, during the inauguration of K.H. Wahib Wahab (1918–86) as Minister of Religious Affairs in July 1959, Sukarno identified religion as one of the most significant principles of state life (*perikehidupan Negara*), and during the later inauguration of K.H. Saifuddin Zuhri (1919–86), who replaced K.H. Wahib Wahab, he acknowledged religion as an 'absolute element' (*unsur mutlak*) in the Indonesian Revolution and nation-building project.[8] He also repeatedly appropriated the Qur'an, hadiths, and segments from the Prophet Muhammad's biography, as in his explanation of the withdrawal of Indonesia from the United Nations due to growing tensions with Malaysia, where he connected this particular political decision to the politically motivated *hijra* of the Prophet Muhammad from Mecca to Medina.[9]

7 See Chapter One.

8 Ichwan, 'Official Reform of Islam: State Islam and the Ministry of Religious Affairs in Contemporary Indonesia, 1966–2004', pp. 74–75.

9 Sukarno compared his decision to withdraw Indonesia from the United Nations to Muhammad's *hijra*, the migration of the Prophet and his companions from Mecca to Medina in response to challenges they faced in Mecca. Sukarno stated that this migration was misinterpreted as a 'flight' by a number of Western scholars, including Snouck Hurgronje, Muir, Hartmann. Rejecting this viewpoint, he proposed that the *hijra* involved Muhammad and his followers dissociating themselves from their Meccan enemies rather than fleeing them. Using this concept, he proposed that his decision to withdraw Indonesia from United Nations membership be interpreted as a disassociation from the organization, implying that this political decision was influenced by the Prophet's example. Elsewhere, talking about Q. 110, he expressed

Api Islam was one of the most prominent concepts that Sukarno articulated during the Guided Democracy period that predated the New Order between 1959 and 1966. It was, in fact, one of Sukarno's primary slogans, which he used as a tool[10] to define and accentuate his ideology, but it also functioned to frame Sukarno's image as a leader of the Indonesian Muslim community. He even founded the *Jajasan Api Islam* (JAI, Fire of Islam Foundation) to spread his ideas. This foundation published several books that maintained his religious image and elaborated his vision with regards to issues such as revolution, history, politics, and law.[11]

This context enables us to understand the multifaceted significance of QT for Sukarno. Let us start with the more practical significance: the QT project was a vehicle through which he could realize his Nasakom

---

the belief that Indonesia had been lenient for long enough about the United Nations response to the tension between Indonesia and Malaysia. Soekarno, 'Inilah Kehidupan Islam di Indonesia: Tidak akan Terdjadi Demikian Dinegara-negara Lain' (Departemen Agama R.I, 1965), pp. 6–11.

10 Sukarno was a great orator. His language either in speeches or writing was dynamic and flexible, embellished with foreign or Javanese expressions. He used powerful words such as *menghantam* (strike), *menggempur* (smash), and provocative and driving phrases such as *jiwa revolusi* (the soul of the revolution), *negara mulia* (the noble state), etc. See James Sneddon, *The Indonesian Language: Its History and Role in Modern Society* (Sydney: UNSW Press, 2003), p. 144.

11 The books include Peran Agama Islam dalam Revolusi Indonesia (The Role of Islam in the Revolution of Indonesia), Kata-kata Penumpas Menentang Imperialisme Kolonialisme Jang Selalu Dipakai Bung Karno (Brother Sukarno's Crushing Arguments against Imperialism-Colonialism), Amnesti Abolisi Ditinjau dari Adjaran Nabi Muhammad S.A.W (The Abolition of Amnesty from the Perspective of the Teachings of the Prophet Muhammad pbuh), Menggali Api Revolusi dari 11 Amanat Bung Karno (Excavating the Fire of Revolution from Eleven Mandates of Brother Sukarno), Bung Karno Mencari dan Menemukan Tuhan (Brother Sukarno Seeks and Finds God). All of these works were compiled by Achmad Notosoetarjo, one of the NU leaders and the co-founder of Jajasan Api Islam alongside Saifuddin Zuhri (1919–86) and Idham Khalid (1921–2010), who were also members of the NU leadership. Federspiel mentions another book written by the very same figure, entitled Menggali Api Islam (Excavating the Fire of Islam). Achmad Notosoetardjo, *Peranan Agama Islam dalam Revolusi Indonesia* (Jakarta: Lembaga Penggali dan Penghimpun Sedjarah Revolusi - Endang - Pemuda, 1963); Achmad Notosoetardjo, *Kata-Kata Penumpas Menentang Imperialisme Kolonialisme Jang Selalu Dipakai Bung Karno* (Jakarta: Lembaga Penggali dan Penghimpun Sedjarah Revolusi - Endang - Pemuda, 1963); Achmad Notosoetardjo, *Amnesti Abolisi Ditinjau Dari Adjaran Nabi Muhammad S.A.W.* (Jakarta: Jajasan Pemuda, 1961); Achmad Notosoetardjo, *Menggali Api Revolusi Dari 11 Amanat Bung Karno* (Jakarta: Lembaga Penggali dan Penghimpun Sedjarah Revolusi - Endang - Pemuda, 1962); Achmad Notosoetardjo, *Bung Karno Mencari dan Menemukan Tuhan* (Jakarta: Jajasan Pemuda, 1963); Howard. M. Federspiel, p. 22.

ideology, first of all, in terms of *agama* (religion). Yet, the QT project was not exclusively about religion (*agama*). Instead, it was also closely connected to *nasionalisme* (nationalism), because of the use of the Indonesian national language, an aspect which will be the focus of the next section of this chapter. Although I will not dwell on this aspect here, it is imperative to mention that Sukarno had learned that unitary language could be a critical element in the rise of nationalism from his activism in PNI and his involvement in youth organizations in the 1920s, and was one of a number of public figures who encouraged fellow activists to write and make public statements in the Malay language in the early twentieth century.[12] In 1928, Malay was named the 'Indonesian language' as part of the Second Youth Pledge made by young Indonesian nationalists, and eventually became the official language of the state following the independence of the Republic of Indonesia. Against this backdrop, the translation of the holy scriptures into the Indonesian language was important because it would lead to the development of a religious discourse in the national language. Thus, the QT project for Sukarno integrated *agama* (religion) with *nasionalisme* (nationalism), two axes of the Nasakom ideology. The mandate of Majelis Permusyawaratan Rakyat Sementara (MPRS, Provisional People's Consultative Assembly) to translate the holy scriptures of religions into the national language fused two of three essential elements of Sukarno's synthetic ideology, namely the official language of the state for nationalism and the holy scripture for religion.

All of Sukarno's Islamic projects, including QT, were designed to win support and confidence from Muslims for his Guided Democracy and Nasakom ideologies. The Masyumi Party was unequivocally opposed to Sukarno, and so he turned his attention to the NU, which took a more flexible view of Nasakom and Guided Democracy. The NU became an integral part of Sukarno's government and its members assumed the highest positions in MORA. Sukarno's attempt to win the confidence of Muslims through this strategy was a reasonable maneuver, particularly after the tensions that had arisen following the dissolution of the Masyumi Party and the arrest of a number of influential Muslim figures, including Natsir and Hamka (1908–81), the famous author, poet, activist,

12 Sneddon, pp. 97–102.

and *ulama.*[13] The attempt to heal the divisions this created in Indonesian society lay behind Sukarno's decisions to build the Istiqlal Mosque, transform the existing Islamic higher education institutes into state-run universities, and of course, initiate the official Qur'an translation of the state. The MPRS Mandate No. II/MPRS/1960, which originally set out government policy on the translation of religious scriptures had only included the Bible, Weda, and Wiharma.[14] However, as Sukarno had had no conflict with the religious leaders of other religions, only Islam, government-approved translations of scriptures other than the Qur'an ever actually materialized.

The part played by QT in establishing Sukarno's image as a Muslim leader was significant. As I have already mentioned, Sukarno set out to frame himself as a Muslim leader through his speeches and publications. The biographical *Bung Karno Mencari dan Menemukan Tuhan* (*Brother Sukarno Seeks and Finds God*) might be the most articulate example of this. It describes Sukarno's childhood days, his effort to make sense of the concepts of religion and God, his reflections on God, Muhammad's life, the Qur'an, and mosques and their contemporary relevance, as well as his spiritual experiences of worshipping, meeting (*bertemu*) and speaking with (*bercakap-cakap*) God. Copies of the letters he wrote when he was in exile in Ende are also included. The book was quasi-sacred as it opened with his prayers (*Permohonan Bung Karno Kepada Allah*), *Sūrat al-Fātiḥa* (the first sura of the Qur'an), and *āyat al-kursī* (the Throne verse, Q 2:255). The significance of this book for Sukarno's image as a religious leader is perfectly reflected by a leaflet discovered within a collection of the Arnold-Bergsträsser-Institute Library in Freiburg, which reveals that the book had been advocated for use as one of the primary textbooks for Islamic courses in universities.

---

13 *Ulama* is an Indonesian word derived from Arabic. In its original Arabic term, it is a plural form of *ʿālīm*. Indonesian also adopted *alim* as a lexical unit, nevertheless, Indonesian speakers do not treat this word as a singular form of *ulama* and it does not have the same semantic connotation as *ulama*. In everyday colloquial, *alim* refers more to one being pious and less to one being knowledgeable. It works more as an adjective. *Ulama*, on the other hand, is an epithet referring to the recognition of the public of one's expertise in Islam, and the word is used both for singular and plural context. That is why as an individual Hamka is also recognized as an *ulama*.

14 M.P.R.S and Departemen Penerangan, *Ringkasan Ketetapan Madjelis Permusjawaratan Rakjat Sementara-Republik Indonesia No. I dan II/MPRS/1960* (M.P.R.S dan Departemen Penerangan, 1961), p. 224.

> *Dan pada bulan Juli 1963 Seminar Pendidikan Agama Islam pada Perguruan Tinggi di Djogja telah memutuskan bahwa buku ini dianjurkan untuk dipakai dalam memberikan pendidikan agama Islam kepada mahasiswa bahkan diletakkan ia pada daftar yang teratas sekali.*
>
> [And on July 1963, a Conference of Islamic High Education in Yogyakarta has decided to encourage the use of the book as a textbook for students; as a matter of fact, this should be regarded as a priority.]

I would argue that QT played a part in this image construction, because Sukarno wanted himself to be visibly associated with the translation. As I have already posited, this is perhaps why the first edition was published in three different volumes; Sukarno needed an immediate, tangible product. In addition, he made sure to introduce the QT translation project during a speech given when he was being awarded an honorary degree from the Muhammadiyah University in Jakarta on 3 August 1965, a couple of weeks before the supposed official launch of the project.[15] He then strengthened his association with QT by writing a foreword for the translation, and his *Api Islam* slogan is mentioned in the introduction. However, the most important reason to assume that Sukarno deliberately set out to create a personal association between himself and the QT project is the fact that, if he had merely wanted to provide Indonesian Muslims with a Qur'an translation, he could have selected one of the Qur'an translations already available at that time for mass publication. Sukarno seemed to be seeking a Qur'an translation which could be credited back to the state rather than to any individual translators. This explains why he started the project from scratch, why he felt the need to provide a foreword in his name for the translation, and why he officially launched the translation on the same day as the commemoration of Indonesian independence.

Beyond these practical interests, Sukarno conceived the project of QT in order to promote and elaborate on his own personal ideology. Sukarno had a progressive view of Islam and the Qur'an. He was interested in the new world, and his interpretation of Islam did not favor the idealization and glorification of the past. He felt (perhaps hyperbolically) that Islamic civilization had been left behind by a thousand years, and was unable to respond to the empirical challenges raised by the modern

15 Boland, p. 131.

world. Islam was in need of a fresh perspective, of being reinvented as a substantial and progressive Islam instead of a formal, traditional, text-based Islam. He saw the Qur'an as a revolutionary scripture which had, during its history, inspired many kinds of revolution that encompassed every aspect of human civilization, and it was this revolutionary nature of the Qur'an that he conceptualized as *Api Islam.*[16] The following is an excerpt from his *Nuzul al-Qur'an* speech, delivered on 6 March 1961, where he explained the conceptual links between Qur'an, revolution, and *Api Islam:*

> *Kitab ini, yang telah mengadakan revolusi maha hebat di dalam peri kehidupan manusia, bukan saja peri kehidupan manusia di Arabia, tetapi peri kehidupan manusia di permukaan bumi ini.*
>
> [...] *Qur'an mendatangkan revolusi ekonomi... Qur'an mendatangkan revolusi yang mengenai hubungan manusia dengan manusia, dus revolusi sosial. Qur'an mendatangkan revolusi yang mengadakan perubahan yang mutlak, membentuk manusia baru. Qur'an mendatangkan revolusi moral, moral yang meliputi seluruh dunia.*
>
> *Maka sebaiknya saudara-saudara, kita berusaha untuk mengerti sedalam-dalamnya akan isi, semangat, jiwa, kehendak daripada Qur'an ini. Inilah yang tempo hari saya namakan dengan perkataan Api Islam. Siapa yang bisa memegang atau menangkap Api Islam, dialah yang sebenarnya mukmin sejati.*[17]

> [This scripture has created a superb revolution in the lives of human beings, not only the lives of those in the Arabian [Peninsula] but rather of every human being across the world.
>
> [...] The Qur'an has led to economic revolution [...] The Qur'an has led to a revolution in the relationship between people and [other] people, thus a social revolution. The Qur'an has enabled a revolution that resulted in a total change, forming new human beings. The Qur'an has led to a moral revolution, a morality that encompasses the entire world.
>
> Therefore, ladies and gentlemen, we need to strive to understand as deeply as possible the content, the spirit, the soul, and the purpose of the Qur'an. This is what I have referred to previously using the term *Api Islam* (the fire of Islam). Whoever holds or catches *Api Islam* becomes a true believer.]

Against this backdrop, this state-produced Qur'an translation was intended to provide Indonesians with the ethical and spiritual spark that lay at the source of Sukarno's revolution. Sukarno believed that the way

16 Boland, pp. 125–26; Effendy, pp. 86–90.
17 Soekarno, 'Alqurän Membentuk Manusia Baru', pp. 10–13.

to make Islam the foundation of the state was not through formalistic notions of Islamic jurisprudence, but through Muslim representation in democracy.[18] However, democracy, or Guided Democracy, fueled by the fire of Islam, would only be achievable when Muslim representatives embraced the Qur'an. While access to the Arabic Qur'an was limited to one segment of Indonesian Muslims, i.e., the traditionally trained intellectuals (*ulama*), QT would improve its accessibility for all. Through QT, Sukarno expected Indonesian Muslims to embrace the Qur'an in order to achieve his revolution. It is for this reason that, in his foreword to the first volume of the first edition of QT, Sukarno does not forget to mention his *Api Islam* slogan:

> *Di dalam suasana semakin meningkatnya taraf revolusi dan Nation & Character-Building kita yang kian terkonsolidasikan, maka terbitnya terjemahan Kitab Suci Al-Qur'an merupakan sumbangan amat besar bagi seluruh lapisan rakyat kita* [...] *karena dengan kitab ini kita semua memperoleh kesempatan lebih besar untuk lebih memahami isi dan makna Al-Qur'an* [...] *bahwa hanya jikalau umat Islam setia menjalankan isi seluruh dari Al-Qur'an, pasti mereka akan mencapai puncak-puncak kejayaan lahir batin.*
>
> *Saya tidak pernah bosan-bosan untuk selalu mengajurkan: Ayo gali dan sebar-sebarkan terus Api Islam! Justru Al-Qur'an adalah satu-satunya sumber paling hebat dan dahsyat daripada Api Islam.*
>
> [During a time of increasing revolutionary feeling, and the more consolidated our Nation & Character Building became, the publication of the translation of the holy scripture Al-Qur'an is a profound endowment to the whole of our people [...] for with this translation we all have a greater opportunity to understand the content and the meaning of the Qur'an [...] Only when Muslims fully implement the teachings of the Qur'an will they surely achieve the summit of physical and mental triumph.
>
> I tirelessly encourage [you]: come, elaborate and share the spirit of the Fire of Islam! Indeed, the Qur'an is the sole and ultimate source of the Fire of Islam.][19]

The foreword makes it quite clear that the QT project formed part of Sukarno's plan to define the nature of his revolutionary nation-building project during the Guided Democracy period. He makes the Qur'an the spiritual and ethical basis for his Nasakom ideology, and an

18 Effendy, p. 86.
19 Departemen Agama Republik Indonesia, i, p. iii.

understanding of its full meaning and revolutionary ideas is essential for his synthetic ideology. The Qur'an, he suggests, is the fundamental source of *Api Islam,* and only through knowledge of it can the revolution achieve its full potential.

I would argue that QT's status as a tool through which Sukarno elaborated his ideology means that it was most definitely an ideological project, even if an explicitly modernist-leaning view of Islam and interpretation of the text in the first volume of QT that was produced under his administration is not dominant. This reflects the fact that QT is a composite of both modernist and traditionalist views of the Qur'an. Nevertheless, as previously stated, the very existence of QT and the motivation behind its production symbolize Sukarno's modernist tendencies, even though the officials actually heading the project were traditionalists. When he introduced QT while receiving his honorary degree, Sukarno spoke of it in terms that associated it with reason, a great concern of the modernists. Likewise, Idham Chalid (1921–2010), the Vice-Chairman of MPRS, also emphasized this association of the Qur'an with rationality in his foreword. Thus, the ideological presence of modernism in the actual translation itself may not be as significant as it is in the paratextual elements of QT (most notably Sukarno's foreword). Nevertheless, one may speculate that, should Sukarno have been in power for longer, more tangible ideological nuances could have been written into the translation itself—a situation that however did not manifest due to the very different attitude of his successor, Suharto.

Suharto and the De-ideologization of *Al-Qur'an dan Terjemahnya*

Sukarno was not able to maintain the support of the Muslim community[20] and eventually lost his power after a bloody incident commonly referred to as the 30 September Movement (G30S/Gestapu). He was succeeded by Suharto and his New Order regime: on 12 March 1967, the MPRS withdrew Sukarno's presidency and named Suharto as his successor. As soon as Suharto took control, he exerted his power to build a sense

20 For the change of Muslim organisations' political stance, see Steven Drakeley, 'Indonesia's Muslim Organisations and the Overthrow of Sukarno', *Studia Islamika*, 21.2 (2014), 197–232, https://doi.org/10.15408/sdi.v21i2.1039.

of political stability by removing traces of Sukarno's government across the country. He also sought to eradicate Sukarno's ideological legacy by discharging his loyalist supporters from the government. 'Desukarnoization', as some scholars have called it,[21] was carried out by various means. One was the allegation that Sukarno was involved in the violent coup of G30S/PKI. The New Order regime blamed Sukarno for the political instability and chaos of his Nasakom ideology, notably for its inclination to communism, which was described as a 'deviation from Pancasila, the state ideology, and the 1945 Constitution.'[22] After the 1965 coup, based on MPRS Decree No. 25/1966, the New Order regime labeled communism as identical to atheism and categorized it as the direct opposite of Pancasila. MPRS Decree No. 27/1966, on religious instruction in public schools, demanded that religious education should be provided in schools at every level, and Decree No. 34/1967 banned all works which mentioned Manipol (Sukarno's political manifesto). The PKI, along with its affiliated organizations, was also dissolved, and the PNI, with which Sukarno's loyalists were affiliated, was annulled. Books promoting communist ideas were prohibited. To justify this dissolution the New Order regime claimed that the PKI had betrayed the state by attempting to change the state Pancasila ideology.[23]

Muslim activists' contribution to the rise of Suharto gave them hope that their political aspirations would be revived, and ex-Masyumi leaders expected Suharto to restore the party as compensation for their role in dissolving the Indonesian Communist Party (PKI). However, Suharto was enormously concerned with political stability and exercised close surveillance of political activism, both when it came to leftist ideology (then called *ekstrim kiri*, the extreme left) and to Islamist ideology

21 Such as Cornelis Lay, as in Cornelis Lay, 'Pancasila, Soekarno, dan Orde Baru', *Prisma*, 2013, 43–61 (p. 45).

22 See Suharto's foreword for the second volume of QT the first edition: Departemen Agama Republik Indonesia, *Al-Quräan dan Terdjemahnja*, 3 vols (Jakarta: Jamunu', 1967), ii.

23 Faisal Ismail, 'Islam, Politics, and Ideology in Indonesia: A Study of The Process of Muslim Acceptance of the Pancasila' (unpublished doctoral dissertation, McGill University, 1995), p. 114; R. William Liddle, 'The Islamic Turn in Indonesia: A Political Explanation', *The Journal of Asian Studies*, 55.3 (1996), 613–34 (p. 621), https://doi.org/10.2307/2646448; Lay, pp. 44–45; Ahmad Munjid, 'Building A Shared Home: Investigating The Intellectual Legacy of The Key Thinkers of Inter-Religious Dialogue in Indonesia' (unpublished doctoral dissertation, The Temple University Graduate Board, 2014), pp. 15–22.

(then named *ekstrim kanan*, the extreme right). With regards to Islamic movements, the government classified these in three types: those which were dangerous to Pancasila, those which were apolitical but potentially helpful to Pancasila, and those which were supportive of Pancasila. This categorization essentially relied on a binary division between the idea of Islam as a potential political force and the idea of Islam as a personal, spiritual endeavour. The New Order government opposed the former and supported the latter.

Suharto introduced a state policy of developmentalism. As far as Islam and Muslims were concerned, the New Order government opened up opportunities for non-partisan Islam—the last two of the three types outlined above—to play a role in government as long as it accorded with its developmentalist objectives. For example, the modernist-leaning Abdul Mukti Ali (1923–2004), the Minister of Religion from 1971–78, and Harun Nasution (1919–98), the Rector of IAIN Syarif Hidayatullah Jakarta from 1973–84, designed a radical reorientation of the Islamic education system in order to provide future Muslim intellectuals and technocrats who, it was expected, would contribute to the economic development of the state.[24] As for Islam's potential as a political force, MORA was charged with constraining Islamist demands for the restoration of the 1945 Jakarta Charter, which were considered disruptive to both the government's developmentalist agenda and Pancasila. Any discussion on the re-enactment of the Jakarta Charter was forbidden and, for the very same reason, demands for the restoration of the Masyumi Party were thwarted. Instead, the various Islamic political parties were merged into a single party, the Partai Persatuan Pembangunan (PPP, United Development Party), which was rebranded as a secular party. Additionally, in 1984, all political parties and civil organizations were asked to make Pancasila their sole ideological basis (*asas tunggal*).[25] Islamist groups were astonished to once again find their political aspirations thwarted, as they were forced into a corner and prevented from exerting any influence on the political and ideological agenda.

---

24 Ichwan, 'Official Reform of Islam: State Islam and the Ministry of Religious Affairs in Contemporary Indonesia, 1966–2004', p. 105; Liddle, pp. 621–22; Lay, p. 57; Kersten, *Islam in Indonesia: The Contest for Society, Ideas and Values*, p. 37.

25 Burhani, xvi, p. 31.

In short, political stability and economic developmentalism formed the basis of Suharto's regime. Desukarnoization, i.e., Suharto's effort to erase all traces of his predecessor, was a part of this policy, and further defined the trajectory of the QT project under Suharto. Suharto's desukarnoization inevitably had an impact on the Qur'an translation project. As in other fields, Suharto obliterated all traces of Sukarno within QT. Suharto replaced Sukarno's foreword with his own, in which he set out his political ideology. The following paragraph, quoted from his foreword to the second volume of the first edition of QT, reflects these ideas:

> *Penerbitan ulangan cetakan kedua*[26] *yang bertepatan pada ulang tahun kemerdekaan kita yang ke-XXII, yaitu pada masa konsolidasi Orde Baru ini sangat penting artinya, untuk menguatkan kembali landasan-landasan mental/ spiritual/keagamaan kita yang hampir saja dihancurkan oleh Orde Lama dan kaum atheis G-30-S/PKI.*
>
> [The second publication, which coincides with the XXIInd anniversary of our Independence Day, which is in the consolidation period of the New Order, has an essential relevance in terms of re-enhancing our mental/ spiritual/religious foundations, which have almost been decimated by the Old Order and the atheist G-30-S/PKI people.]

This short paragraph plainly sets out Suharto's intention to remove all traces of Sukarno. First of all, he clearly underscores the difference between them using new terminology, labeling his period as the New Order and his predecessors' as the Old Order. Both of these labels were consciously designed to distinguish his government from the regime that supposedly deviated from Pancasila and the 1965 Constitution.

26 I found two slightly different versions of this part of the foreword in two different copies of the second volume of QT's first edition. The above is the version I obtained from a microfilm in the library of the University of Leiden. The hard copy I found a couple of years later calls itself *'Penerbitan ulangan cetakan kedua jilid ke satu'* (the second publication of the first volume). It is a curiosity that this foreword mentions 'the first volume', even though it was printed in the second volume. Even more curious is the fact that the first volume that I obtained accompanying this particular copy does not include Sukarno's original foreword which was present in the copy of the library of the University of Leiden. One can speculate that this foreword was intended as a replacement for Sukarno's original preface to the first volume, a line of argument I propose in this section. Yet, this does not seem convincing, for the forewords by Idham Chalid and Saifuddin Zuhri remain. I cannot at this point propose any further hypothesis for this finding, which may merely be the result of human error.

Secondly, he describes the Old Order as the cause of political instability and atheism, which he equated with communism.

Suharto's desukarnoization of QT is also made implicit in the one-volume first edition that was published in 1971. In this edition, even Suharto's foreword has been removed, and a new foreword inserted, from the pen of the head of the Yayasan Penyelenggara Penterjemah/Pentafsir Al-Qur'an (YPPA, The Foundation of the Organizing Committee for Translating/Interpreting the Qur'an),[27] R.H.A. Soenarjo (1908–98). In this foreword, Soenarjo acknowledges the transformation of the Lembaga Penyelenggara Penterjemah Kitab Suci Al-Qur'an (LPPKSA, The Organizing Committee for the Translation of the Holy Qur'an) into YPPA, a change which was mentioned in the previous publication of QT that went back to the 26/1967 Ministerial Decree. However, he fails to mention the initial attempt to produce an Indonesian Qur'an translation in the early 1960s, which was recorded in his foreword in the earlier QT. Even though Suharto chose to refrain from writing a foreword in which he articulately condemned the Old Order, I contend that Soenarjo's 1971 foreword was very effective in suppressing Sukarno's impact on QT; his foreword, which was consistently reproduced in every publication of QT during the New Order period, gives a misleading impression of the history of QT by mentioning only the previous publication dates of 1967 and 1971. This successfully created the idea that QT was first produced as late as 1967, i.e., during the first year of Suharto's administration, leading readers to forget about Sukarno's role in the QT project. In fact, the success of this strategy can be seen in the fact that even academics such as R.M. Feener and Howard Federspiel have been misled.[28]

---

27 In 1967, Badan Penyelenggara Penterjemah Al-Quräan was transformed into a foundation by the Ministry of Religious Affairs Decree on March 14, 1967, No. 26/1967. The information on this reformation was presented by Soenarjo in his foreword to the second volume of the first edition of QT.

28 Moch. Nur Ichwan, 'Negara, Kitab Suci dan Politik: Terjemahan Resmi Al-Qur'an di Indonesia', in *Sadur Sejarah Terjemahan di Indonesia dan Malaysia*, ed. by Henri Chambert-Loir (Jakarta: Kepustakaan Populer Gramedia, 2009), pp. 417–33 (p. 419); R. Michael Feener, 'Southeast Asian Qurʾānic Literature', ed. by Jane Dammen McAuliffe, *Encyclopaedia of the Qurʾān* (Leiden; Boston; Köln: Brill, 2006), 98–101 (p. 100), http://referenceworks.brillonline.com/entries/encyclopaedia-of-the-quran/southeast-asian-quranic-literature-EQCOM_00190; R. Michael Feener, 'Notes Towards the History of Qur'anic Exegesis in Southeast Asia', *Studia Islamika*, 5.3 (1998), p. 63, https://doi.org/10.15408/sdi.v5i3.739; Federspiel, p. 64.

One may, then, pose the following question: if Suharto wanted to obliterate traces of Sukarno in every field, why did he not just terminate the production of QT altogether, given that Sukarno's footprints were all over the project? It is true, as I have observed, that Sukarno built this project from scratch and, in the process, infused it with his own ideological views on Islam and the direction of the state, which was what Suharto wanted to obliterate. However, Suharto's depoliticization project allowed for a non-political Islamic agenda, and among Suharto's policies during this early period was the 'promotion of personal piety and opposition to the politicization of religion.' As Edward Aspinall puts it, the New Order government only approved purely religious activities and allowed accommodationist leaders to conduct them.[29] The fact that he allowed the QT project to continue implies that Suharto considered the translation of the Qur'an a purely religious and unideological program and was of the opinion that it did not have any potential to disrupt his development agenda or the Pancasila state. In fact, A.H. Nasution (1918–2000), the Chairman of MPRS, in his foreword to the third volume of QT, is the first to directly associate QT with MPRS Decree No. 27/1966, which demands that religious education be provided in schools at every level. Thus, it is reasonable to conclude that Suharto saw no need to terminate the QT project, and it is this idea that is most likely behind his decision to no longer contribute his own foreword to QT. Moreover, Suharto's project of de-ideologization required balanced articulation, and the production of QT could have benefited him in this regard. QT—along with other projects such as the organization of a national competition for recitation of the Qur'an known as MTQ (*Musabaqah Tilawatil Qur'an*)[30]—provided the regime with a platform for balanced discourse and rehabilitated Suharto's image as a leader of Muslims. In fact, the New Order government included the QT project in their developmentalist agenda, *Pelita*, and we find mention of *Pelita* in the forewords to the second and third volumes of the first edition of QT. It is clear from this alone that the QT project was regarded by Suharto's government as a part of their development plan.

---

29 Edward Aspinall, *Opposing Suharto: Compromise, Resistance, and Regime Change in Indonesia*, Contemporary Issues in Asia and the Pacific (California: Stanford University Press, 2005), p. 39.

30 Anne K. Rasmussen, *Women, the Recited Qur'an, and Islamic Music in Indonesia* (Berkeley: University of California Press, 2010), p. 157.

The Post-Suharto Period:

In Defense of the Ministry of Religious Affairs

The overthrow of Suharto's three-decade long authoritarian regime in 1998 was followed by the *era reformasi* (reformation era), and over the next two decades Indonesia would have no less than five presidents; the short-lived B.J. Habibie (1936–2019), the last vice president under Suharto (1998–99); Abdurrahman Wahid (1940–2009), an NU leader, who represented the central axis (*poros tengah*) of Islamic parties (1999–2001); Megawati Sukarno Putri (b. 1947), a daughter of the first president of Indonesia who replaced the impeached Gus Dur (2001–04); Susilo Bambang Yudhoyono (b. 1949), a high-ranking general during the New Order period (2004–14); and Joko Widodo (b. 1961), an entrepreneur who became a pupil of Megawati, who continued his second period of presidency from 2019–24. The *era reformasi* started with growing hopes and optimism that the state would finally be able to cure itself after thirty years under an authoritarian regime. The process of deconstructing Suharto's policies began, starting with the dissolution of Badan Pembina Pendidikan Pelaksanaan Pedoman Penghayatan dan Pengamalan Pancasila (BP7, The Supervisory Body for Implementation of Guidance for Comprehension and Practice of Pancasila), a body responsible for state propaganda initiatives and for the introduction of laws on issues such as local autonomy, freedom of the press, and human rights. However, the euphoric early years of this political phase were characterized by political instability and economic uncertainty. This period has been aptly described by an Indonesian historian, Taufik Abdullah as follows:

> With the fall of Suharto, 'the era reformasi' was supposed to have begun. All errors should be rectified, political mistakes corrected, and the once imagined Indonesia to be re-constructed. It was also, however, the time of democratic euphoria when all the hitherto hidden ideas and unstated dreams and prejudices made their appearances. When the hidden faces and ideas had made themselves prominent, Indonesia soon found itself in the crisis of mutual trust. Signs of social disruption showed their ugly faces in several regions. Different types of vigilante groups came forward to attack and—as they claimed—to fix whatever they consider immoral

> and improper in society. Suddenly Indonesia found itself as if it has already entered into a period of a fragmented society.[31]

The *Reformasi* enabled the resurgence of democracy and the promise of good governance, the end of corruption, public transparency, and increased individual freedom. These increased personal and political freedoms, however, also meant the freedom to reconsider the philosophy of the state and the Jakarta Charter. At a grassroots level, this eventually led to a growing number of vigilante groups, as well as the rise of conservative and militant Islamic movements that rejected the legitimacy of the current nation-state. Having been continuously suppressed during the New Order period, these Islamic political groups benefited greatly from the fall of the regime and the change to a more open society. Calls for the establishment of sharia law, and even an Islamic state, were revived.[32] At the same time, the phenomenon of Islamic terrorism was on the rise around the globe, as was marked by the worsening situation in a number of countries in the Middle East, and—of course—by 9/11, and the effects of this phenomenon were also felt in Indonesia.[33] Ethnic and religious conflicts arose, and there were four major Islamist terrorist attacks between 2002 and 2005 in Bali and Jakarta.[34]

Despite the different approaches of the *Reformasi* governments in dealing with Islamic militant movements,[35] Islamic moderation was one of the critical discourses in the country at the time. On the one hand, the

---

31 Taufik Abdullah, 'Islam, State and Society in Democratizing Indonesia: An Historical Reflection', *Studia Islamika; Vol 18, No 2 (2011): Studia Islamika*, 2014, pp. 216–17, http://journal.uinjkt.ac.id/index.php/studia islamika/article/view/432/285.

32 Martin van Bruinessen suggests that radical Muslim movements in contemporary Indonesia are rooted partly in indigenous Muslim political movements, such as Darul Islam and Masyumi in the 1940s. Martin van Bruinessen, 'Genealogies of Islamic Radicalism in Post-Suharto Indonesia,' *South East Asia Research* 10.2 (2002), 117–54.

33 The cyber-space is one medium through which the spread of Islamic fundamentalist ideas becomes effective. Birgit Bräuchler, 'Islamic Radicalism Online: The Moluccan Mission of the Laskar Jihad in Cyberspace.,' *Australian Journal of Anthropology* 15.3 (December 2004), 267–85.

34 Ichwan, 'Official Reform of Islam: State Islam and the Ministry of Religious Affairs in Contemporary Indonesia, 1966–2004', p. 224; Zachary Abuza, *Political Islam and Violence in Indonesia* (London, New York: Routledge, 2007), p. 5.

35 van Bruinessen, 'Genealogies of Islamic Radicalism in Post-Suharto Indonesia', pp. 118–19.

ruling government took the necessary measures to protect the nation from turbulence. Thus, for example, Megawati was the first president of a Muslim-majority country to openly support the US war on terrorism. Furthermore, she also issued Governmental Regulation in Lieu of Statute No. 1/2002 on War against Terrorist Crimes, and instructed the Coordinating State Minister of Politics and Security Affairs to implement it. On the other hand, religious moderation was pursued through Pancasila. Despite a shift in its attitude, at that time Majelis Ulama Indonesia (MUI, Indonesian Ulama Council) maintained its moderate stance, as indicated by its rejection of radicalism and terrorism and its acceptance of the Indonesian state, democracy, and Pancasila. The NU and Muhammadiyah played a similar, significant role in defining Islam for the majority of Muslim citizens in the country.

One of the most influential Islamist movements that emerged in the aftermath of the fall of Suharto was Majelis Mujahidin Indonesia (MMI, The Council of Indonesian Warriors). Established on 8 August 2000 at a conference held in Yogyakarta, the MMI was originally envisaged as an umbrella organization that would gather together various Islamist groups and individuals with the aim of establishing an Islamic state. The conference appointed Abu Bakar Ba'asyir (b. 1938), a great proponent of Darul Islam who allegedly has connections with al-Qaeda,[36] as their first chief, and Muhammad Thalib (b. 1948) as his deputy. Most importantly, the conference also defined the direction of the organization, setting out establishing sharia, *imāma* (political leadership), and jihad as their ultimate goals.[37] In 2008, Abu Bakar Ba'asyir decided to leave the MMI, due to issues surrounding his succession, and established the Jama'ah Ansharut Tauhid (JAT) with a group of loyal followers. He was replaced as leader of the MMI by Muhammad Thalib, who held the position until his resignation in 2012.[38]

36 Ichwan, 'Official Reform of Islam: State Islam and the Ministry of Religious Affairs in Contemporary Indonesia, 1966–2004', pp. 226–27; Ichwan, 'Towards a Puritanical Moderate Islam: The Majelis Ulama Indonesia and the Politics of Religious Orthodoxy', pp. 63–70.

37 Muhammad Thalib and others, *Panduan Daurah Syar'iyyah untuk Penegakan Syari'at Islam* (Yogyakarta: Markas Majelis Mujahidin Pusat, 2010).

38 Mohamad Yahya, 'Analisis Genetik-Objektif atas Al-Qur'an Karim: Tarjamah Tafsiriyyah Karya Muhammad Thalib' (unpublished master's thesis, State Islamic University Sunan Kalijaga, 2012), pp. 128–31.

Muhammad Thalib is a reformist adherent who prefers to base his ideology directly in the Qur'an and hadith, and who fights for the implementation of sharia law in Indonesia. According to him, the complete implementation of sharia law at both the societal and political level is the essence of *tawḥīd*. Accordingly, he is an adversary of Pancasila, which he frames as a conspiracy theory. He believes that Sukarno derived Pancasila from freemasonry and secularism and that these ideas can be traced back eventually to Jewish anti-Islamic ideas. Additionally, he takes a hostile view of Judaism and Christianity and disapproves of the Ahmadiyya and Shīᶜism.[39]

In 2010, Muhammad Thalib publicly criticized QT, focusing on three main issues. First, he was concerned with the number of what he viewed as interpretive mistakes he had found in QT. In an interview reported in a magazine called *Gatra*, on 8 September 2010, he stated that his research, undertaken over ten years, had revealed that QT contained 1,000 mistakes, 100 of which he would discuss in a forthcoming book. In Thalib's view, QT contains numerous errors from the perspective of theology (*akidah*), logic, the structure of the Arabic language, and sharia. It is indecisive, unclear, ambiguous, and has the potential to mislead readers. He asserted that the mistakes were so disastrous that MORA should withdraw it from distribution in order to undertake a thorough revision.[40] The book he mentioned during his interview, *Koreksi Tarjamah Harfiyah Al-Qur'an Kemenag RI: Tinjauan Aqidah, Syariᶜah, Muᶜamalah, Iqtishadiyah* (Correction of the Literal Qur'an Translation of the Ministry of Religious Affairs of the Republic Indonesia: A Review of Faith, Law, Social, and Economic Verses), made its first appearance in November 2011, and in it he actually discusses 170 'errors' rather than 100. (Interestingly, only a year after the interview, the number of mistakes he claimed to have found in QT significantly increased to 3,400!) His criticism is harsh, and he describes QT in pejorative terms, saying *'ajaran kitab suci Al-Qur'an ternodai akibat adanya salah terjemah yang jumlahnya sangat banyak'* ('the teaching of the Holy Qur'an is tarnished (*ternodai*)

39 Munirul Ikhwan, 'Challenging the State: Exegetical Translation in Opposition to the Official Religious Discourse of the Indonesian State', *Journal of Qur'anic Studies*, 17.3 (2015), 157–121 (p. 136), https://doi.org/10.3366/jqs.2015.0214; Yahya, pp. 116–21.

40 Herry Mohammad, 'Alih Bahasa Mengungkap Makna', *Majalah Gatra*, 8 September 2010, pp. 78–79.

by the existence of numerous mistakes').[41] An MMI colleague of Thalib's Irfan S. Awwas provided the foreword for *Koreksi Tarjamah Harfiyah Al-Qur'an*, in which he likewise argues that QT has long been a source of errors in religious thought and practice in Indonesia, as it leaves the reader with uncertainties and confusion on the meaning of verses, provides misleading explanations about Islamic teaching, and even encourages terrorism, liberalism, and religious pluralism.[42]

Muhammad Thalib's second concern relates to the translation methodology used in QT. On 29 September 2010, he wrote an essay, again in *Gatra*, with the title 'Tarjamah Harfiyah Mengundang Masalah' ('Literal Translation Creates Problems'). In this, he asserts that the interpretive mistakes of QT are rooted in the use of 'literal translation' (*tarjama ḥarfiyya*) by the committee. He suggests that literal translation is forbidden (*haram*), on the basis of a legal opinion (*fatwa*) issued by Saudi authorities on 26 June 2005. According to Thalib, the only permissible method to use when translating the Qur'an is 'interpretive translation' (*al-tarjama al-tafsīriya*),[43] the method he used in his own *Al-Qur'an Karim Tarjamah Tafsiriyah* (The Noble Qur'an: An Interpretive Translation), which made its first appearance in 2011.

Thalib's objections, on the surface, specifically relate to QT, however the form his attacks on it took indicate that there may well have been other motives at work in the background, namely an attempt to further the agenda of the increasingly influential MMI. Thalib did not just criticize the methodology used in QT and its reading of many of the Qur'anic verses, he went so far as to demand that the government withdraw QT from the market. He also demanded that the government apologize for having provided an incorrect translation of the Qur'an over the last several decades. Moreover, the MMI attempted to negotiate with the King Fahd Complex, to discourage them from publishing QT and replace it with Thalib's own translation.[44] Seen from this broader

41 Thalib, *Koreksi Tarjamah Harfiyah Al-Qur'an Kemenag RI: Tinjauan Aqidah, Syariah, Mu'amalah, Iqtishadiyah*, p. 9.

42 Irfan S Awwas, 'Kontroversi Tarjamah Harfiyah', in *Koreksi Tarjamah Harfiyah Al-Qur'an Kemenag RI: Tinjauan Aqidah, Syariah, Mu'amalah, Iqtishadiyah*, by Muhammad Thalib (Yogyakarta: Ma'had An-Nabawy, 2011), pp. 11–22 (pp. 23–26).

43 Muhammad Thalib, 'Tarjamah Harfiyah Mengundang Masalah', *Majalah Gatra*, 29 September 2010, p. 36.

44 Muhammad Thalib, *Tarjamah Tafsiriyah: Memahami Makna Al-Qur'an Lebih Mudah, Cepat dan Tepat* (Yogyakarta: Ma'had An-Nabawy, 2011), p. x; Yahya, p. 142.

perspective, it is reasonable to conclude that Thalib's criticism of QT was part of a wider strategy that sought to delegitimize QT, the Ministry of Religious Affairs, the state, and the hegemonic religious discourse of the country.[45]

In addition to their general criticism of QT, a particular incident that took place in 2011 gave Muhammad Thalib and Irfan S. Awwas the opportunity for more focused criticism. On 15 April 2011, a suicide bomber attacked a mosque located in a police compound in Cirebon, West Java. Focusing on Qur'anic verses relating to war, Thalib and Awwas asserted that QT had been the source of inspiration for this terrorist attack. According to Irfan S. Awwas, the translations in QT of a number of relevant verses, for example Q 2:191, Q 9:5, and Q 29:6, were dangerous, because they could be said to create an incentive to kill people at anytime, anywhere.[46] The suicide bombing gave the MMI the chance to rehabilitate their reputation as a supposed radical and fundamentalist organization, by alleging that it was the state itself that had created terrorist ideology, and not religious organizations such as themselves. At a more prosaic level, it seems that the political furor surrounding this incident allowed the MMI to promote Thalib's translation even more.

In response to Thalib's criticism, Muhammad Shohib, then the director of Lajnah Pentashihan Mushaf Al-Qur'an (LPMQ, The Qur'anic Text Review Board), argued that QT is a collective work, and differences in rendering between one translation and another are common and inevitable. Muchlis M. Hanafi, then a member of the *Dewan Pakar* (Expert Committee) of the LPMQ and a member of the translation committee, said, '[i]f they say there are 1,000 mistakes in the MORA translation, I will find 2,000 mistakes in their commentary.'[47] Hanafi also wrote a response in *Gatra*, in which he pointed out that no translation could fully capture the range of nuance and meaning of the Qur'an, but that this did not mean that it could not be translated literally in some parts.

In 2011, Muchlis M. Hanafi published a second response, this time in an academic journal published by the LPMQ, *SUHUF: Jurnal Pengkajian*

45 Ikhwan, pp. 136; 155.
46 Irfan S Awwas, 'Ideologi Teroris dalam Terjemah Qur'an Depag', *Majalah Gatra*, 27 April 2011, pp. 26–27.
47 Mohammad, p. 78.

Al-Qur'an dan Budaya, in which he built on what he had previously written in his article for *Gatra*. He argued that, on the basis of Soenarjo's concept of *tarjama ḥarfiyya,* QT clearly could not be included in the category of translation that is forbidden by Muslims scholars, i.e., it did not seek to produce a new form of the Qur'an as a substitute for the original Arabic text. He insisted that the translation of the Qur'an was the work of human beings, and could by no means compete with the divinely authored scripture. It is owing to this belief that the committee felt the need to constantly revise and improve the translation, which had so far led to two full revisions of QT. The very fact of this revision process clearly demonstrated that what the committee did was transport *the meaning* of the Qur'an into the Indonesian language, rather than seek to replace the Qur'an. Additionally, Hanafi argued that despite the divine status of the Qur'an and the discrepancies between the grammatical structures of Arabic and Indonesian, many Qur'anic verses were open to literal translation. Referring to a theory proposed by al-Shātibī (d. 1388), which divides the meaning of the Qur'an into *al-dalāla al-aṣliyya* (the primary meaning) and *al-dalāla al-tabīᶜa* (the consecutive meaning), he suggested that the verses classified into the primary meaning can be rendered into other languages literally. This method, Hanafi suggested, is compatible with the views of many pre-eminent Muslim scholars, such as Ibn Qutayba (d. 889) and the contemporary *ulama* Muḥammad Musṭafā al-Marāghi (d. 1952). Additionally, Hanafi argued, as Soenarjo had already indicated, that literal translation was not the only approach used by the QT translation committee: additional information was provided either in brackets and/or in footnotes when a literal translation alone was not comprehensible, and this was evidence of interpretive translation. To support his argument further, Hanafi also pointed out that the same method had essentially been employed by other translators in Indonesia, such as Ahmad Hassan (1887–1958) and Hasbi Ash-Shiddieqy (1904–75).[48] It appears that Thalib's criticism greatly concerned the LPMQ because they repeated this argument on many occasions, as recently as the preface to the fourth edition of QT.

48 Muchlis Muhammad Hanafi, 'Problematika Terjemahan Al-Qur'an Studi pada Beberapa Penerbitan Al-Qur'an dan Kasus Kontemporer', *SUHUF Jurnal Pengkajian Al-Qur'an dan Budaya*, 4.2 (2011), 169–95, https://doi.org/10.22548/shf.v4i2.53.

Despite such repudiations of criticism of QT, it seems that these responses were not thought to be sufficient, primarily because the MMI and Thalib pointed their fingers not only at issues with the translation but also at MORA and the state. When criticism from the MMI and their allies escalated into a nationwide controversy thanks to the 2011 suicide bombing, the response of MORA as well as other stakeholders intensified. Muchlis M. Hanafi, Sarlito Wirawan Sarwono from BNPT (Badan National Penanggulangan Terorisme, National Body of Eradication of Terrorism), Masdar Farid Mas'udi from NU, and Ahsin Sakho Muhammad from IIQ (Institut Ilmu Al-Qur'an, the Institute of the Qur'anic Science) all dismissed Thalib and Irfan's accusations. However, the temperature soon cooled, and in spite of the polemics involved, the LPMQ has allowed Thalib to publish and distribute his MMI translation as long as its Arabic Qur'anic text is submitted to the LPMQ for *taṣḥīḥ*. The cooling of the debate was probably connected with the ongoing internal differences within the MMI that led Thalib to resign from the MMI leadership.[49] Nevertheless, the MMI has continued to print Thalib's translation, although as far as marketing is concerned, it cannot compete with QT.

The Expansion of the QT Project

During the current administration led by Joko Widodo, who was elected in 2014, moderate Islamic discourse has been articulated through the concept of *Islam Nusantara* (archipelagic Islam), predominantly by the NU. This concept underlines the need for harmonious relations between Islam, local wisdom and culture, and the state, along with the philosophy of Pancasila. It is sensitive to the sociology of Muslims in the region and is frequently described as reflecting the living values and practices of Muslims in Indonesia.[50] The proponents of *Islam Nusantara* believe that the relatively peaceful experience of Indonesian Islam and its capability to adopt and adapt to democracy will maintain Islam as *raḥmatan li 'l-ᶜālamīn* (a mercy upon the worlds) amidst the crises

49 Herry Mohammad, Ade Faisal Alami, and Arif Koes Hernawan, 'Mundur Bukan karena Uzur', *Majalah Gatra*, 11 July 2012, pp. 90–91.

50 Ma'ruf Amin, 'Khittah Islam Nusantara', *Kompas* (Jakarta, Agustus 2015).

and conflicts taking place in Islamic countries that are stimulated by fanaticism and sectarian tendencies.

Apart from the criticisms levelled against QT by Muhammad Thalib, there were no noticeable innovations in the QT project during the post-Suharto period until 2011, when the project was extended to include the translation of the Qur'an into Indonesian regional languages. While this demonstrated a growing awareness of the need to preserve local languages (the specific topic of the next subsection), it is worth mentioning that the project went entirely unnoticed for six years until 2017, when Jokowi's administration openly introduced it to the public. For the first time, it made headlines in several news outlets and was nationally acknowledged. The official introduction of the project was, however, part of the state's promotion of *Islam Nusantara*, as was clearly articulated by Lukman Hakim Syaifuddin, the Minister of Religious Affairs, in a foreword incorporated into all of the various translations published in 2016. According to Syaifuddin, the underlying motivation for the project to translate QT into regional languages was '*Mendorong dan Memperkuat konsep dan praktek* (*sic.*) *Islam Nusantara dalam bingkai Negara Kesatuan Republik Indonesia*' (to encourage and strengthen the concept and implementation of Islam Nusantara within the framework of the unitary state of the Republic of Indonesia).

However, the articulation of *Islam Nusantara* in the various QT translations into regional languages goes beyond the preservation of regional languages. The association of the project with *Islam Nusantara* can be seen as a political move to enforce the concept of *Islam Nusantara* itself, which was officially introduced during the 2015 annual NU conference, and has become the guiding concept of NU ever since. The project of translating QT into regional languages suggests a harmonizing of Islam with local particularities, and the introduction of *Islam Nusantara* into the project in turn raises the profile of this new concept, a necessary step in the early stages of the implementation of *Islam Nusantara* when it was a relatively new idea, especially in the public sphere.

Since *Islam Nusantara* is a relatively newly introduced term, it makes sense that its proponents would attempt to empower the idea through various approaches, such as including it in the names of universities, publishing on it, and organizing conferences and workshops to discuss it, and, in an extension of this logic, by introducing it into the QT project. The term *Islam Nusantara* has swiftly become ubiquitous in the public sphere and, in the academic sphere, many scholars immediately celebrated the term within their writings.[51] For example, two books on the subject were published shortly after the NU's 2015 conference: *Nasionalisme dan Islam Nusantara*,[52] and *Islam Nusantara: Dari Ushul Fiqh hingga Paham Kebangsaan*,[53] and many others have since followed. These approaches are critical because, for ordinary people, *Islam Nusantara* sounds strange and suspiciously deviant from orthodox Islam, especially after the controversy of the Qur'anic recitation for the commemoration of *Isra᾽ Miᶜrāj* held in Indonesia State's Palace on 5 May 2015 which was undertaken using a Javanese melody. The recitation met with a harsh response from some quarters of the public, and particularly from hardline figures such as Muhammad Rizieq Syihab, the leader of Front Pembela Islam (FPI, The Islamic Defender Front), who vociferously condemned the recitation as an act of the *dajjal*,[54] and the palace where it was recited as the palace of *Iblis* (Satan), with the result that this version

51 Unlike Indonesian scholars, however, Southeast Asian Islam or Malay-Indonesian Islam remain the terms used by international scholars of Indonesian Islam, even in their Southeast Asian neighbour, Singapore, as evidenced in the recently published book by Aljunied Khairudin, *Muslim Cosmopolitanism: Southeast Asian Islam in Comparative Perspective* (Edinburgh: Edinburgh University Press, 2017). Azyumardi Azra, an Indonesian historian, uses the term *Islam Nusantara* in an Indonesian edition of his book, while the English edition uses 'Indonesian Islam'. In the field of *tafsīr*, scholars from Malaysia and Indonesia use the term *tafsir Nusantara* to refer to the history of *tafsīr* in the Malay-Indonesian region. International scholarship prefers to use the more widely recognized term 'Malay-Indonesia.' See Azra, 'Islamic Reform in Southeast Asia: Assimilations, Continuity and Change'; Azyumardi Azra, *Islam Nusantara: Jaringan Global dan Lokal* [*Historical Islam: Indonesian Islam in Global and Local Perspective*], trans. by Iding Rosyidin Hasan (Bandung: Mizan, 2002); *The Qur'an in the Malay-Indonesian World: Context and Interpretation*, ed. by Majid Daneshgar, Peter G. Riddell, and Andrew Rippin (London, New York: Routledge, 2016); Riddell, *Malay Court Religion, Culture and Language: Interpreting the Qur'ān in 17th Century Aceh*; Fadhli Lukman, 'Telaah Historiografi Tafsir Indonesia: Analisis Makna Konseptual Terminologi Tafsir Nusantara', *SUHUF Jurnal Pengkajian Al-Qur'an dan Budaya*, 14.1 (2021).

52 *Nasionalisme dan Islam Nusantara*, ed. by Abdullah Ubaid and Bakir (Jakarta: Kompas, 2015).

53 *Islam Nusantra: Dari Ushul Fiqh Hingga Paham Kebangsaan*, ed. by Akhmad Sahal and Munawir Aziz (Bandung: Mizan, 2015).

54 The *dajjal* is an eschatological figure in Islam, who is believed to come before the Day of Judgement. It is described as a figure who will bring the world calamity greater than any calamity that has ever existed.

of the recitation has never been heard on an official occasion at the State Palace again.[55]

The introduction of *Islam Nusantara* into QT and its regional language translations is also evidence of the NU's intimacy with the regime in power. In fact, politically, both the state as an institution, and Jokowi as the President, need *Islam Nusantara* because it lies at the heart of the harmonious relationship between Islam, local wisdom and culture, and the state and its Pancasila philosophy.[56] The concept is reinforced to promote the continuation of a moderate form of Islam in the face of the growing transnational radical Islamist movement, which is considered a threat to both the authority of the state and Pancasila. *Islam Nusantara* provides a counterargument to those who claim that nationalism is not justified according to Islam, and who forbid people to respect the national flag during the Independence Day ceremony. Additionally, the current president Jokowi needs to maintain his image by fulfilling the needs of Muslims, to counteract the consistent denunciations of him as a communist or an un-Islamic figure by his political opponents. To this end, Jokowi has gained and secured the support of the NU, who then became clear supporters of him.[57] In this context, the Ministry of Religious Affairs seemingly played a similarly critical role during the Jokowi administration as it did during the New Order[58] by commissioning projects associated with *Islam Nusantara* such as the

55 Although the state refrains from using Qur'an recitation to a Javanese melody on official Islamic occasions held at the State Palace, this method of recitation has become familiar in some other places, such as in the State Islamic University Sunan Kalijaga Yogyakarta.

56 Said Agil Siroj, 'Mendahulukan Cinta Tanah Air', in *Nasionalisme dan Islam Nusantara*, ed. by Abdullah Ubaid and Bakir (Jakarta: Kompas, 2015).

57 A number of the NU elites have publicly declared their support, and the Minister of Religious Affairs, Lukman Hakim Syaifuddin, is an NU affiliate. It was in this regime that *Hari Santri* (the Santri Day) began to be celebrated as a national holiday to commemorate the *resolusi jihad* (*jihad* resolution) issued by the NU's most charismatic figure, K.H. Hasyim Asy'ari, to empower the spirit of Indonesian Muslims in the struggle against their Dutch colonizers.

58 Ichwan suggests that 'Suharto's politics of Islam would not have been able to succeed without the contribution of this ministry in such various fields of Islamic affairs, such as education, law and the courts, charity, and pilgrimage (hajj).' Ichwan, 'Official Reform of Islam: State Islam and the Ministry of Religious Affairs in Contemporary Indonesia, 1966–2004', p. 13.

writing of *Tafsir Kebangsaan*,[59] establishing the Study Centre of Islam *Nusantara*, and developing *Islam Nusantara* departments in universities. Against this background, the introduction of ideas pertaining to *Islam Nusantara* into regional language translations of QT is not surprising.

Al-Qur'an dan Terjemahnya and the State's Preoccupation with Language

Ideological issues are not the only input from the various Indonesian government regimes to be found in the paratext of QT. As I have mentioned previously, the state's ambition to enhance the status and use of the Indonesian national language was another motivation for the production of this translation. The first edition of QT aimed to normalize the use of Indonesian with romanized script as the language of Islamic scholarship, and the most recent (fourth) edition of QT addresses the expansion of the Indonesian lexicon. In a similar vein, the various editions of QT in regional languages are intended as a vehicle for the preservation of local languages. All of these are best understood in the context of the emergence and growth of Indonesian with Roman orthography as the official national language and the shift in policy with regard to regional languages.

Bahasa Indonesia, the national language of the modern state of Indonesia, is a relatively new language. It is derived from Malay, the language of trade and education that became predominant during the Dutch colonial period. Until the first quarter of the twentieth century, Indonesian simply did not exist and, although Malay was commonly used, there was no 'national' Indonesian language at this stage. The increasing use of Malay, and the subsequent transition from Malay to Indonesian, was triggered by the growth of popular literature produced in Malay and the birth of Indonesian nationalism. In 1908, the Dutch colonial force established the *Commissie voorde Volkslectuur* (the Committee of Popular Literature, renamed *Balai Pustaka*, i.e., 'Publishing House' in 1917) which produced Malay reading materials for both educational purposes and light reading. A few decades earlier, newspapers written

59 'PTIQ Jakarta Gagas Tafsir Kebangsaan – INSTITUT PTIQ JAKARTA', 2018, https://ptiq.ac.id/2018/03/05/ptiq-jakarta-gagas-tafsir-kebangsaan/.

in Malay began to appear, such as *Surat Kabar Bahasa Melaijoe* (The Malay Language Newspaper), *Bintang Oetara* (The Northern Star), and *Melayu Luar* (Outsiders' Malay). Newspaper publications soon came to contribute a great deal to the growth of nationalism, especially amongst young intellectuals, including those who had gone through the Dutch education system in the Netherlands. One of the turning points in this process was the birth of the periodical *Bintang Hindia* (The Indies Star), which first appeared in 1902, and which promoted nationalism amongst the Indonesian youth who spoke Malay. They began to use Malay in their speeches and writing, although they also adopted Dutch, especially in their private conversations. In 1926, Jong Java (The Yong Javanese), the largest youth organization, encouraged the use of Malay, and acknowledged it as their official language the following year. In 1927, Sukarno formed the Jong Indonesie (The Young Indonesian), using a Dutch phrase, but soon renamed it Pemuda Indonesia (The Indonesian Youth), using a Malay phrase, to promote the virtues of the Malay language. Malay became the dominant language of the nationalist movement and soon enough found itself, alongside Javanese, as one of the two languages put forward to become the unifying language of a future independent state during the first Youth Congress, held between 30 April and 2 May 1926. During the second Youth Congress on 27–28 October 1928, Malay won out over Javanese, and was officially recognized as the new *Bahasa Indonesia* and became the unifying language with the issuance of the Youth Pledge (*Sumpah Pemuda*). This promised, among other things, 'to uphold the language of unity, the Indonesian language' (*'Menjunjung bahasa persatuan, Bahasa Indonesia'*).[60]

The Youth Pledge was a starting point for a move to implement the new official Indonesian language across the country. From this point, the newly-born language held a symbolic function, namely to unify the mixed ethnicities and languages of those people who had resided under the Dutch colonizers in order to establish a future state of Indonesia, this being the Youth Pledge's main aim. However, despite the unanimity with regards to the unifying role of the new national language in the pledge itself, this was not a clear-cut turning point in the popularity of Indonesian. Dutch continued to play a critical role as

60 Sneddon, pp. 89–102.

the language of administration, and was the language of choice for the upper-class population. On the other hand, regional languages were still prevalent, particularly amongst lower-class communities. This state of affairs continued until the occupation of the Dutch Indies by the Japanese in 1942, which effectively reduced the influence of Dutch in the region when the Japanese banned its use. '[The] Indonesian language overnight achieved the de facto status of official language'[61] for the simple reason that there was no other alternative: it would have been logistically utterly impossible to implement Japanese as the official language. The Indonesian declaration of independence in 1945 then established the cultivation of Indonesian as a national language as one of the central projects of the state.[62] Indonesian has since become the primary language in the literary culture of Indonesia. It is employed at official government events and in the mass media, in education, and in official publications.

The consolidation of Indonesian as the national language is also connected with the decline of the *Jawi* script, which was adapted from the Arabic script following the spread of Islam in Southeast Asia. As well as being used for Malay, *Jawi* script was used in other languages in the region, such as Acehnese, Sundanese, and Bugis/Makassar. Each language adapted the script to their own system with its own peculiarities, and these were given different names, such as *Pegon* in Javanese, and *Sérang* in Bugis.[63] The early Muslim kingdoms in the archipelago supported the use of the script by employing it in education, administration, trade, and diplomacy, and it had been dominant since the fifteenth century. Islamic religious writings were produced in *Jawi* and it continued to be hegemonic in the academic sphere for six centuries, as most Islamic scholars used it for scholarly purposes or for pedagogical reasons. Kevin W. Fogg points out that, throughout the 1920s, Indonesian Muslims, especially from the lower classes, were

61 Sneddon, p. 9.

62 Junaiyah H. Matanggui, *Bahasa Indonesia Serba Sekilas* (Jakarta: Indra Press, 1984), pp. 22–23; Sneddon, pp. 9; 111; Kevin W. Fogg, 'The Standardisation of the Indonesian Language and Its Consequence for Islamic Communities', *Journal of Southeast Asian Studies*, 46.1 (2015), 86–110 (p. 88), https://doi.org/doi:10.1017/S0022463414000629.

63 Annabel Teh Gallop and others, 'A Jawi Sourcebook for the Study of Malay Palaeography and Orthograpy', *Indonesia and the Malay World*, 43.125 (2015), 13–171, https://doi.org/10.1080/13639811.2015.1008253.

more familiar with *Jawi* Malay than romanized Malay. In the first half of the twentieth century of West Sumatera, he suggests, most of the religious debates between the reformist and traditionalist Muslims were conducted in the *Jawi* script.[64]

Ichwan likewise points out that 'the rise and decline of *Jawi* Qur'anic works in Indonesia has been very much influenced by the politics of language and script introduced by the ruler(s)—Muslim sultanates, colonial administration, and post-colonial government on the one hand and by the interest of reading communities, on the other hand.'[65] It is certainly true that, during the colonial period, the Dutch introduced the Roman alphabet into the region, and this eventually influenced a growing number of Indonesian Muslim intellectuals. Therefore, the hegemony of *Jawi* in Islamic texts began to decline, with Qur'anic exegesis, as Ichwan suggests, bearing the brunt of the damage. According to Kevin Fogg, A. Hassan's *al-Burhan* (published in 1928) was the first Islamic text to become popular in romanised Indonesian. His works appealed to a Dutch-educated Muslim readership, including future leaders such as Kasman Singodimedjo (1904–82), Kartosuwirjo (1949–62), Abu Hanifah (1906–80), and Muhammad Natsir.[66]

The post-colonial Indonesian authorities supported the introduction of the Latin alphabet by the Dutch, and it appears that Muslim reformists and emerging intellectuals benefited the most from its adoption. Fogg points out that Abu Hanifah, one of the Masyumi leaders, a Dutch-educated medical doctor, and the Minister of Education in the 1950 RIS (*Republik Indonesia Serikat*, Republic of the United States of Indonesia), describes his familiarity with the Roman alphabet and its significance for his comprehension of Islam and the Prophet Muhammad as follows: 'It may sound strange, but many intellectuals had their knowledge of Mohammad and Islam from books written by European scholars and orientalists. I myself learned much about Mohammad's life from a

64 Ichwan, 'The End of Jawi Islamic Scholarship? Kitab Jawi, Qur'anic Exegesis, and Politics in Indonesia', p. 83; Fogg, 'The Standardisation of the Indonesian Language and Its Consequence for Islamic Communities', p. 90.

65 Ichwan, 'The End of Jawi Islamic Scholarship? Kitab Jawi, Qur'anic Exegesis, and Politics in Indonesia', pp. 83–84.

66 Fogg, 'The Standardisation of the Indonesian Language and Its Consequence for Islamic Communities', p. 91–92.

book by the German Professor Hartmann.'[67] On the other hand, many traditionalist Muslims were unfamiliar with the Latin alphabet, such as Muhammad Zainuddin Abdul Madjid (1908–97), the founder of Nahdatul Watan, Sayyid Idrus al-Jufri (1892–1969), the founder of Al-Khairat organization in Central Sulawesi, and Gurutta Haji Ahmad Bone (1885–1972) in South Sulawesi. This has led Fogg to point out that the Masyumi leadership were more comfortable with the Roman alphabet than the Arabic script, while traditionalist Muslims, on the other hand, had become peripheral. Those who were solely familiar with the Arabic script and not with Roman characters were deemed illiterate in the modern state.[68]

When it comes to QT, it is imperative to mention Idham Chalid, the Vice-Chairman of MPRS who wrote a foreword for the first volume of the first edition of QT in which he made the following assertion:

> *Jangan dikira, bahwa adanya terjemahan Al-Qur'an dalam bahasa Indonesia ini hanya akan menolong orang-orang yang tidak mengerti bahasa Arab saja, untuk mengetahui dan mempelajari kandungan Kitab Suci itu, tetapi juga akan memberi manfaat kepada orang-orang yang sudah mengerti bahasa Arab, tetapi tidak begitu biasa dengan bahasa Indonesia yang baik dengan susunannya yang indah.*
>
> [Do not think that the existence of the translation of the Qur'an in the Indonesian language will only help those who do not comprehend the Arabic language alone, [so that] they can understand the content of this Holy Scripture. It will [also] benefit those who understand Arabic but have not been familiarized with a well and beautifully structured *Bahasa Indonesia*.]

Within the above context, this statement conveys a number of significant points. First, QT was intended to provide those Indonesian Muslims with no competence in Arabic and Islamic intellectual tradition with an accessible interpretation of the Qur'an. That was its initial aim, as has been frequently mentioned. QT allowed Indonesian lay Muslims to understand the Qur'an, and this was the ideological motive behind Sukarno's support for the project. According to him, only with this

67 Kevin W. Fogg, 'The Fate of Muslim Nationalism in Independent Indonesia' (unpublished doctoral dissertation, Yale University, 2012), p. 253.

68 Fogg, 'The Standardisation of the Indonesian Language and Its Consequence for Islamic Communities', p. 95.

comprehension would *Api Islam* take hold and enable progress in nation-building. Secondly, this foreword contributed to a nationalist ideology, given that since the Youth Pledge in 1928 language was viewed as one of the primary means by which to reinforce nationalism. Thirdly, and most importantly in this context, the translation of the Qur'an into the Indonesian language was intended to unify Muslims through the use of one language, the official language of the state, written with Roman script. While the reformists and the new intellectuals were already long accustomed to Indonesian and the Latin script, this new system was strange for the traditionalists. As the quote cited above from Idham Chalid's foreword to QT points out, the translation was also intended to benefit those who were familiar with the Arabic language but not with 'well and beautifully structured Bahasa Indonesia.' To further this end, Sukarno established state-run Islamic higher-education institutions as centers of Muslim scholarship operating in Indonesian and dictated that they must produce religious literature in the official language.[69] Through both QT and Islamic higher-education institutions, the state aimed to establish Indonesian as the language of Islamic scholarship.

In addition to this, the fourth edition of QT provides the first acknowledgment of the official involvement of the BPPB, the department responsible for language planning under the Ministry of Education, which supplied its own experts to contribute to the revision. The BPPB officials became members of the editorial team during this third revision process, with the responsibility of overseeing the translation in terms of the structure of the Indonesian language used in the target text.[70] In other words, they played the same role they usually do in the formulation of state documents such as the constitution and legislative texts, which is to make sure that they are appropriately written in well-structured Indonesian with formal diction (*kata baku*). However, their presence was part of a reciprocal process: not only were they supposed to improve the editorial quality of the translation, but they were also responsible for expanding the Indonesian lexicon. If they found no

69 Federspiel, p. 22; Greg Barton, 'Indonesia's Nurcholish Madjid and Abdurrahman Wahid as Intellectual 'Ulama': The Meeting of Islamic Traditionalism and Modernism in Neo-Modernist Thought', *Studia Islamika*, 4.1 (1997), 30–81 (p. 42), http://dx.doi.org/10.15408/sdi.v4i1.786.

70 Lajnah Pentashihan Mushaf Al-Qur'an, 'Panduan Kajian Revisi Al-Qur'an dan Terjemahnya Kementrian Agama Tahun 2016'.

equivalent Indonesian term for a particular Qur'anic word with the potential to be widely used in daily conversation, they were asked to list the word for inclusion as a prospective part of the Indonesian vocabulary. At one point, during a presentation given as part of a public consultation, Muchlis M. Hanafi stated that, at the time the team had reached the second *juzʾ* of the Qur'an, twenty-seven words had been listed for inclusion in the next edition of the KBBI,[71] while during an interview I conducted in early 2017, Sriyanto, an expert from the BPPB, mentioned that they had listed approximately sixty words.

Government interest in the preservation of local languages began during the *Reformasi,* in the aftermath of the fall of Suharto in 1998. In comparison to other countries in the Asia-Pacific region, Indonesia has a massive number of languages whose exact total is impossible to determine.[72] The recognition of Indonesian as a national language by the post-colonial government of Indonesia had been intended to forge a sense of national unity, and successive governments have continued to recognize Indonesian as the primary literary language and the parameter by which citizens were to be acknowledged as literate or illiterate. Consequently, the number of people speaking Indonesian has significantly increased year by year. However, this popularity has inevitably led to a decline in the use of regional languages, especially in urban areas. Although the constitution mandates that the government promote local languages as part of the cultural wealth of the nation, prior to the Reformation Era concern for regional languages had been minuscule, particularly during Suharto's presidency. His concentration upon the unity of Indonesia was at the expense of local concerns. Since the beginning of the Reformation Era in 1998, concerns about

---

71 Personal interview on 14 February 2018.

72 The varying criteria employed by several researchers have led to this uncertainty; one study reveals that Indonesia has roughly 550 languages, and another researcher even claims that there are a total number of 714 languages. A further problem was the equivocal framing of the question in the census. The term 'Indonesia' is not defined in the 1971 census, and nor are the particular people who lived in the areas where a local form of Malay was spoken, in order to judge whether they speak Indonesian or their local form of Malay. Additionally, the census did not indicate the level of linguistic competence. Hein Steinhauer, 'The Indonesian Language Situation and Linguistics; Prospects and Possibilities', *Bijdragen Tot de Taal-, Land- En Volkenkunde / Journal of the Humanities and Social Sciences of Southeast Asia*, 150.4 (1994), 755–84, https://doi.org/10.1163/22134379-90003070; Sneddon, pp. 199–203.

local autonomy have increasingly been raised, and the fate of regional languages has attracted more attention than it used to.[73] Hence, in the foreword to the various translations of the Qur'an into regional languages that launched the *Penerjemahan Al-Qur'an ke dalam Bahasa Daerah* (the Translation of the Qur'an into Indonesian Regional Languages) project in 2011, it is clearly stated that the objectives of these translations are to maintain the heritage of the nation (*pengelolaan kekayaan bangsa*), to preserve regional cultures (*pelestarian budaya daerah*), and to serve the religious interests of Muslims (*pelayanan keagamaan*). It is clear from this that MORA believes that one way to effectively conserve regional languages is through the translation of the Qur'an. They also believe that the translation of the Qur'an into regional languages will bring Muslim speakers closer to the teachings of the Qur'an.[74] The importance MORA attributes to this ambitious initiative can be seen in the fact that, since the project began in 2011, translations into some twenty languages have so far been published.[75]

Conclusion

This chapter has discussed how the various forewords to QT indicate that its production over the course of its history has been bound to various political interests. The interpretive dimension of the translation will be the focus of the forthcoming chapters. However, at this point, it is clear that the production of the paratextual aspects of QT already indicates that the project is a means for the Indonesian government to signal their power. In a state inhabited mostly by Muslims, the production of a translation of the primary text of Islamic civilization is a recognizable

73 Sneddon, p. 209.

74 My personal interview with an official of the division of Research and Development of Literature and Religious Treasures (Puslitbang Lektur dan Khazanah Keagamaan), Yasin, on 13 August 2018.

75 The foreword by Choirul Fuad Yusuf, the head of the Division of Research and Development of Literature and Religious Treasures (Puslitbang Lektur dan Khazanah Keagamaan) for the editions of *Al-Qur'an dan Terjemahnya* in regional languages published in 2015, mentions nine languages. During my personal interview with the head of the division, Muhammad Zain (Choirul Fuad Yusuf's successor), on 10 August 2018, added some more languages, mentioning that there had been seventeen regional languages, and that there were five more in progress. Yusuf, pp. vii–viii.

project through which state interests may be deployed, either with the aim of serving Muslims' religious interests or as a tool to establish the image of the ruling government as supportive of Muslim interests.

Additionally, it has become clear that because the forewords are free from the restrictions of the Qur'anic text and fall outside the traditional remit of the *ulama* or the *tafsīr* tradition, they have provided successive ruling governments with a space to freely elaborate on their ideas and ideological visions of themselves or the state. For this reason, each ruling government has consistently made their presence felt through the adoption of ideological vocabulary in them, in order to highlight the desired political stance of the state. It would be no wonder, then, if the forewords to QT were more political than the text of the translation itself.

The production of the first version of QT, I contend, had more to do with Sukarno's personal ambitions and political agenda than any other motive, such as performing a religious service for Indonesia's Muslim citizens. It was very much connected to his idea of *Nasakom*, his effort to win Muslims' support, and his desire to promulgate an image for himself as a religious leader. That is why official translations of other religions' scriptures were never conducted under his regime. Suharto, in contrast, cleansed the project of ideology and made it 'purely religious', thereby aligning it with the concept of an 'apolitical Islam'. Over the three decades of the New Order, the purely religious, unideological, and apolitical QT has become the norm, and that is how the project has continued until recently. In the aftermath of the fall of Suharto, the QT project has been faced with the re-emergence of a kind of Islamism that questions the authority of MORA, and also the state. QT has become a gateway for such movements to attack both the ministry and the government, as can be seen in the critiques aimed at it by figures such as Muhammad Thalib and the MMI. In the face of this situation, it became necessary to defend the QT project, as a gesture to defend both MORA and the state. Jokowi's administration has gone further, and bought more fully into the idea of achieving a state-supported, moderate Islam through the expansion of the project to include regional languages, in line with the idea of indigenizing Islam or, as it has recently been called, *Islam Nusantara*.

Last but not least, the QT project accords with other governmental policies concerning language development. QT was initially intended not only for readers with no Arabic competency, but also for those who understood Arabic but were relatively distant from Indonesian and its development as the official language of the state. In other words, the translation of the Qur'an served as a tool to make the Indonesian language the modern language of Islamic scholarship. However, more recently, by expanding the range of the project through the inclusion of regional languages, QT has also become a significant instrument for the preservation of regional languages across the country.

4. The Hermeneutical Production

After a historical survey of the development of *Al-Qur'an dan Terjemahnya*, this chapter will consider QT at the micro level, in terms of the hermeneutical processes that underpin the translation decisions made by the committee. The most obvious issue when it comes to the hermeneutic processes at work in the production of QT is that this work has been coordinated by a particular institution, and is thus a collective-collegial product. That is, it is the product not of an individual author, but of a group of scholars working together. This characteristic has influenced many aspects of the hermeneutical processes at work in QT, including the distinctive form of authority and the hermeneutical assumptions behind the translation, such as theoretical perspectives on Qur'an translation and the practical relationship between the Qur'an and *tafsīr*, as well as the selection and hierarchy of sources used. This chapter shows that all of these considerations play an important role in defining the modern Qur'an translation as one genre of literary reception of the Qur'an. In doing so, it elaborates on several sub-topics. It discusses the ways in which the individual inquiries of the various committee members fed into the collective translation process, and the consequences this had for the target text. It also analyses the interpretive decisions of the translation committee and puts them into conversation with their views on the genre of Qur'an translation so as to gain a sense of the committee's understanding of the relationship between the Qur'anic text, the *tafsīr* tradition and translators. This chapter also puts the hermeneutical production of QT in conversation with the general *tafsīr* trends in Indonesia through analysis of the sources it uses and references, its place within the Indonesian history of exegetical sources, and its transregional networks. In doing so, I consider the bibliographies of all editions of QT, the occasional presence of exegetical authorities and their works in the footnotes, and some worksheets from the committee's

 https://doi.org/10.11647/OBP.0289.04

investigation and revision of the translation for the fourth edition. I also consider those authorities and works raised during the plenary sessions of the committee in which I was able to participate. Finally, I consider the information available in other works published by the individual committee members, as well as their biographies.

The General Structure of *Al-Qur'an dan Terjemahnya*

The first edition of QT includes a lengthy introduction that provides information on several basic topics relating to Islam, the Qur'an and the Prophet Muhammad. When it comes to the Qur'an, these topics include the history of the Qur'an and *tafsīr*, the history of the translation of the Qur'an, the major themes of the Qur'an, the Qur'an as a miracle, the Qur'an and the Islamic sciences, and the merits of Qur'an recitation. As for Muhammad, the Introduction elaborates on his biography and his socio-religious roles. We know that the introduction was written by the committee members from Yogyakarta, but there is no specific confirmation of who wrote particular sections, other than the fact that in his biography R.H.A. Soenarjo (1908–98) is reported to have written the section on major themes of the Qur'an, which discusses the principles of *imān* (belief) and *islām*, for which he drew on Soedewo's (1906–71) *De Heilege Qoeran* (1934).[1] The rest of the introduction seems to rely on traditional Islamic accounts of the Qur'an, its history, its merit, its miraculous nature, and the history of the *tafsīr* genre. It also briefly recounts the history of the translations of the Qur'an (classified into Western and non-Western languages) as recounted in modern sources. Additionally, as mentioned in the previous chapter, the introduction drew on Mirza Bashir-ud-din Mahmud Ahmad's *The Introduction to the Study of the Holy Quran* for one sub-section on the history of Muhammad and arguments outlining the necessity for the revelation of the Qur'an.

In addition to this lengthy general introduction, a concise introduction and summary preface each *sūra*. To avoid confusion, I call the former 'the Introduction,' and the latter 'the *sūra* prologue.' The *sūra* prologue contains basic information about the *sūra* as is typically

1 Machasin, 'Prof. Mr. R.H.A Soenarjo', in *Lima Tokoh IAIN Sunan Kalijaga Yogyakarta*, ed. by Muhammad Damami (Yogyakarta: Pusat Penelitian IAIN Sunan Kalijaga, 2000), pp. 71–102 (p. 96).

presented in Qur'an commentaries, such as issues around the name of the *sūra*, the number of verses, its macro-historical context (whether it is Meccan or Medinan), and the specific character of the *sūra*. The *sūra* prologue also explains the main messages (*pokok-pokok isi*) of each *sūra*, which are commonly divided into four categories: *keimanan* (faith), *hukum-hukum* (laws), *kisah-kisah* (stories), and *lain-lain* (miscellaneous). The *sūra* prologue is typical of the *tafsīr* tradition as many Qur'an commentaries—such as the pre-modern works by Ibn Kathīr (d. 1372) and al-Zamakhsharī (d. 538/1144), and the modern *tafsīr* by al-Marāghī (1881–1945)—provide the same kind of basic information at the beginning of each new *sūra*. QT also provides epilogues that serve as the conclusion of each *sūra* and connect it to the next *sūra*.

Turning to the main part of the translation, the actual target text, most editions of QT divide each *sūra* into successive thematic blocks. The *sūra* is divided into several themes, marked with different headings, which are then further broken down into a number of smaller subthemes. This thematization features in the first, second, Saudi, and fourth editions. QT tends to use this feature to explain the *sūra* as working to convey a structured body of messages, the summary of which is indicated in the *sūra* prologue and/or epilogue. It is evident from textual similarities that the thematization in the first edition is drawn from *Tafsīr al-wāḍiḥ* by Muḥammad Maḥmūd Hijazī (1914–72). The second and Saudi editions retain this aspect of the text verbatim, whilst the third edition removes it, and the fourth edition reprises it with slight modifications.

The Saudi edition printed in recent years differs from the others in that it provides its own introduction, which is much shorter than that of the first edition. The Saudi introduction is an entirely re-written account that provides basic information about the Qur'an, ranging from the definition of the word '*Qurʾān*', its names and attributes, the history of the revelation, the writing and compilation of the codex, to the merits of learning the Qur'an and the concept of Qur'anic inimitability (*iʿjāz al-qurʾān*), and issues relating to the interpretation and translation of the Qur'an and the correct way to undertake these. The main references for this section include Qur'an commentaries such as the *Jāmiʿ al-bayān ʿan taʾwīl āy al-qurʾān* by al-Ṭabarī (d. 311/923), and canonical *hadīth* compilations such as *al-Burhān fī ʿulūm al-qurʾān* by al-Zarkashī (1344–92), *Muqaddima fī uṣūl al-tafsīr* and *Majmūʿ al-fatāwā* by Ibn Taymiya, and *al-Tafsīr wa al-mufassirūn* by Husein al-Dhahabī (1915–77). Effectively, this introduction removes all traces of material about the historical accounts and major themes of the Qur'an included in the introduction to the first edition that are written from a modernist Ahmadiyya outlook.

With the aim of producing a shorter work, all the above features—the introduction, the *sūra* prologue and epilogue, and the thematization blocks—are removed from the third edition. The translation itself is also more concise, and the number of footnotes is reduced. In this edition, the beginning of the *sūra* is marked only with a heading indicating its name, both in Arabic script and in Indonesian transliteration, information on whether the *sūra* is Meccan or Medinan, and the number of the *sūra* according to the canonical order. The editions printed by private publishers typically apply a simpler method, providing only the name of the *sūra* (sometimes with its meaning) and removing all other details. As for the fourth edition, it reintroduces the thematization blocks, but not the other features.

As indicated by the committee for the first edition, the main text is preferably translated literally. In cases where the results of a literal translation would be incomprehensible, the committee provides more explanation in parentheses or footnotes. This method gives parentheses and footnotes an integral role in QT, and these are maintained in all later editions. The committee primarily uses parentheses to accommodate a wide variety of interpretive interpolations or to add words to create an idiomatic sentence in the target language. They may also be used to provide a view from a specific Qur'an commentary, clarifications of Qur'anic metaphors, or to include additional words so as to create an idiomatic sentence in the target text. It should be noted, however, that not all additional words are written in parentheses. Even a cursory reading of QT reveals many instances in which words that are additions with their own interpretive motives occur in the main text rather than in parentheses.

The footnotes in QT are essentially an extended space in which the committee can further explore those specific issues they deem necessary: they are not intended as a space for a genuine commentary. There is a translation format, used by authors such as Mahmud Yunus (1899–1982) and Kasim Bakry (1907–64) et al., in which, essentially, two products are presented in one work: a translation written alongside the original Arabic text, and a very short commentary written in the footnotes. This is not the case for QT, in which the committee uses footnotes on an ad hoc basis to provide additional information they think is important for a specific interpretive instance. They provide different kinds of information, such as clarifications of key terms, explanations for metaphorical phrases, information on the intratextuality of the Qur'an, details about narrative interpretation, different interpretive opinions, the historical context of a particular verse, or occasionally a designation of a Qur'anic prayer (*du*ᶜ*ā*) composition in the main text of the verse which is left untranslated.

The footnotes in Q 1 (*al-Fātiḥa*) serve as a good example of the approach in QT as they are indicative of the various kinds of information provided. In almost all Qur'an commentaries, the authors give special attention to this particular *sūra,* and QT is no exception. QT uses footnotes to explain a number of key words, such as *ḥamd* (praise), *rabb* (Lord), *mālik* (king, master) and *yawm al-dīn* (the Day of Judgement). The footnotes on this *sūra* include philological analysis, such as a clarification that *na*ᶜ*budu* (we worship) is from the same root as ᶜ*ibādā* (worship), or that *ihdinā* (show us, lead us or guide us) is derived from *hidāya* (guidance); explanations of theological principles, as in the clarification of the words *allāh, rabb, al-raḥmān, al-raḥīm,* and *al-ḥamd;* legal opinions, such as an encouragement to start every deed by reciting the *basmala;* and explanations on eschatology, as in its gloss on the phrase *mālik al-yawm al-dīn* (King of the Day of Judgement). That the footnotes provide so much explanation for this verse is understandable, because *sūrat al-Fatiḥa* is believed to be a concise summary of all teachings of the Qur'an. Another reason for such extensive explanation could be that it is the first *sūra* of the Qur'an, which might also have influenced the authors to elaborate further on it than others. In this light, it may be relevant that the committee also provides more footnotes for Q 2 (*al-Baqara*) than other, later *sūras*. Nevertheless, in order to produce a shorter work, the third edition of QT significantly reduces the quantity of explanatory footnotes.

The Development of the Collaborative Translation Process

The hermeneutical production of QT has developed from quite a disorganized set of procedures to a more systematically structured process. For the first edition, Soenarjo indicates in his preface that the team was divided into two groups, the Jakarta and Yogyakarta groups. The Jakarta board wrote a lengthy introduction to the translation and the Yogyakarta board shared the responsibility for the translation of the first ten *juz᾽* of the Qur'an. There is no information about the working plan of the committee for the other two volumes of this edition, but it seems likely that they followed the same procedures and all members were assigned a fair share of initial translational duties for the other twenty *juz᾽*. After this initial step, as Soenarjo writes, the work of each team was subject to assessment by the other as they exchanged their translations for evaluation. Next, both teams gathered for a plenary meeting, during which they discussed the result of their respective evaluations. Once they had reached a consensus, they moved on to the next step, authorization. For the first edition, the necessary approval and authorization was the responsibility of the Minister of Religious Affairs.

However, in reality, the project did not strictly follow these steps because the sub-groups allegedly never actually organized the plenary session in which to synchronize their works.[2] This would explain why there are a great deal of inconsistencies in the translation in this edition. For example, this edition translates *alam taᶜlam* (Do you not know) as *'tiadakah kamu mengetahui'* in Q 2:106–107, *'tidakkah kamu tahu'* in Q 5:40, and *'tidakkah kamu ketahui'* in Q 12:80. One other example is the translation of the interjection *uffin* as *'Tjis'* in Q 46:17, *'ah'* in Q 17:23, and *'ah (tjelakalah)'* in Q 21:67. Of course, there are countless other examples, but the selection of these two examples is significant because these inconsistencies are technical and do not suggest any hermeneutical problem whatsoever, yet the first edition of QT fails to unify them. Accordingly, instead of being a truly collective work, it is not farfetched to suggest that the first edition of QT is a composite of separate individual works that were never fully synchronized.

The second and Saudi editions came into existence through the collaboration of two committees, one from MORA and the other from the Saudi government. As mentioned in the previous chapter, each committee conducted their own examination of the first edition of QT, and it is reported that they organized as few as three plenary sessions.[3]

2 Hamam Faizin, *Sejarah Penerjemahan Al-Quran di Indonesia* (Ciputat: Gaung Persada, 2022), p. 147.

3 Faizin, *Sejarah Penerjemahan Al-Quran di Indonesia*, p. 165.

The result of this collaboration was published both in Saudi Arabia, by the King Fahd Complex, and in Indonesia, primarily by the Qur'an printing industry. The edition printed by King Fahd Complex received a further review from King Fahd Complex's officials before it was launched into mass production.

The third edition proceeded more gradually but essentially followed a similar process: the project began with individual investigations which proceeded into regular plenary meetings. Yet a significant improvement took place in the production of the fourth edition. The translation committee for this edition extended their focus to include specialists in the Indonesian language. Accordingly, the committee consisted of two sub-groups with two different tasks: *tim substansi* (lit. 'the team of substance') and *tim redaksi* (lit. 'the editorial team'). The former consisted of a group of scholars and *ulama* whose expertise included *tafsīr* and Islamic disciplines, while the latter consisted of individuals from Badan Pengembangan dan Pembinaan Bahasa (BPPB, The Language Cultivation and Development Agency), a unit responsible for language planning under the Ministry of Education. While the first sub-group was responsible for the interpretive aspects of QT, the second was tasked with ensuring that the target text was written in an idiomatic and well-structured *Bahasa Indonesia*.

There was one other sub-group that played an important role in the translation process during the production of this fourth edition. The members of this group were employees of the Lajnah Pentashihan Mushaf Al-Qur'an (LPMQ, The Qur'anic Text Review Board)—civil servants working under the Ministry of Religious Affairs—who were essentially responsible for organizing meetings and handling administrative tasks. This basic duty might at first sound like a supporting role that simply ensured the smooth progress of the translation but was not an integral part of the team. However, they also became involved in discussions and contributed to the outcome of the translation. This group was mainly concerned with problems of consistency in comparison with the earlier editions, and for this reason, they will be referred to as 'the consistency team' throughout this section.

The third revision project was taking place at the time I was undertaking this study, which meant that I was able to observe the revision process for this edition closely. As was the case with the earlier editions, each translator first conducted an individual translation of a specific section of the Qur'an. To make sure that the result would be an upgraded version of the previous edition, their initial translation was based on the previous edition of QT. In other words, the committee's first duty was to assess the existing translation and revise it where they felt necessary. They worked on worksheets comprising a table with four rows. The first row featured the text of the Qur'an and *sūra* and verse identification. The second and third rows provided the translation from the previous edition and the suggested revision respectively, and the final row contained the explanation or argument for the proposed revision. The editorial team also worked on a similar worksheet; however, their task was to assess the editorial quality of the previous edition and whether the output of the translation was idiomatic.

During the next phase, the teams regularly gathered in monthly plenary meetings. They would spend two or three days discussing the outcomes of individual inquiries to conclude the final output of the translation. In this phase, the consistency team recorded the meeting. They worked with a second worksheet, which also contained four rows: the first row contained the existing translation, the second and third rows contained the suggested new translations by individual translators along with their complementary explanations, and the fourth row contained the final translation agreed upon by the committee. During these meetings, the members of the committee would alternately read their assessments and recommendations, and after that the discussion would begin. The level of intensity of discussions varied, depending on the sorts of problems a given verse contained. While the discussions were mostly about the content of the translation, this did not mean that the participants had vastly different opinions on the meaning of a certain phrase or verse. The debates mostly centered on different views regarding the precision of a translation, rather than firm contradictions. Editorial aspects also generated lengthy discussions on many occasions, and the editorial team was heavily involved in these. One of the consistency team's jobs was to make sure that the committee did not spend time discussing similar verses, phrases, or keywords over and over again, and to ensured that the upcoming translation would be more consistent in the rendering of similar or repeated phrases than previous editions. They kept an ongoing list, which was frequently referred to, of particular verses or phrases which could be translated identically as a reminder should an identical verse, phrase, or keyword recur later on. Once a decision was made on a given verse, and the translation was decided, one member of the team would read it aloud so that everybody could hear how it sounded.

Collaboration is one of the primary features of QT. It is the product of a team, as opposed to an individual. This type of collaborative approach is not regarded as peculiar in Indonesian Islamic scholarship. For example, Hasbi Ash-Shiddieqy (1904–75), who was a member of the QT translation committee, called for collective *ijtihād* (independent reasoning) to reformulate the national *madhhab* (school of Islamic law), arguing that the Majelis Ulama Indonesia (MUI, Indonesian Ulama Council) should only issue a *fatwa* after achieving consensus on a given subject among its members.[4] In 2004, the Kelompok Kerja Pengarusutamaan Gender (Pokja PUG, The Working Group for Gender Mainstreaming), led by Siti Musdah Mulia, aimed to formulate a more grounded family law via the Counter Legal Draft (CLD), through a collective enterprise that they named Ijtihad Jama'i Forum (The Forum of Collective Independent Reasoning).[5] When it comes to *tafsīr*, the Muhammadiyah published two works, *Tafsir Tanwir* (The Enlightenment Commentary) and *Tafsir Tematik Al-Qur'an tentang Hubungan Sosial Antarumat Beragama* (Thematic Commentary on the Qur'an about Social Relations between Religious Believers), both of which were written by a group working in collaboration.

The collective nature of QT has certain consequences. First, the project is intended to politically represent various religious views, which is accomplished through the selection of committee members from different religious organizations, such as the NU, the Muhammadiyah, and Persis. Another facet of this can be seen in the fact that the committee is composed of experts affiliated with a combination of Islamic higher education institutes, *pesantren*, and the MUI, all of whom have a different religious education and background. Some of the committee members hold positions in several of these organizations/institutes. Furthermore,

4 Syafiq Hasyim, 'The Council of Indonesian Ulama (Majelis Ulama Indonesia, MUI) and Religious Freedom', in *Les Notes de l'Irasec n'12—Irasec's Discussion Papers #12* (Bangkok: IRASEC, 2011), p. 10.

5 Moch. Nur Ichwan, 'Official Reform of Islam: State Islam and the Ministry of Religious Affairs in Contemporary Indonesia, 1966–2004' (unpublished doctoral dissertation, Tilburg University, 2006), p. 257, https://pure.uvt.nl/portal/en/publications/official-reform-of-islam(f07a60f1-bf55-4979-8ea1-bab6e45a42ac).html.

this notion of representation can also be observed in the *Konsultasi Publik* (Public Consultations), a series of conferences held by the LPMQ to collect interpretive suggestions for the third revision of QT in 2016–19. These conferences targeted a wide variety of institutions and included academics, *ulama*, the MUI, mass Muslim organizations, and members of *pesantren* communities.

Second, it is also apparent that the idea of collective authorship is rooted in the concept of conformity, which works, to some extent, along the lines of *ijmāᶜ* (consensus). Islamic jurisprudence recognizes *ijmāᶜ* as a source of law, second to the Qur'an and *sunna*. Essentially, *ijmāᶜ* is applied in situations where the Qur'an and Sunnah do not provide an explanation.[6] In his explanation of encyclopaedic *tafsīr*, Walid Saleh suggests that the doctrine of *ijmāᶜ* made way for the polyvalent nature of the classical commentary.[7] This situation is reversed in QT: in this translation, *ijmāᶜ* becomes a method through which to decide which interpretive opinion on a particular term in the Qur'an is considered the most cogent or compatible. In this context, 'most cogent' refers to the interpretation that is considered most valid out of the various interpretive opinions provided by *the tafsīr* tradition, while the notion of 'compatibility' relates to the attempt to determine which interpretation is most appropriate for a given context. Thus, when seeking 'compatibility', the translator transmits a Qur'anic message into the Indonesian language with consideration for the particularities of Indonesia's social and historical context. This approach conforms to the idea of 'Indonesizing Islam' first promoted by Hasbi Ash-Shiddieqy in his proposal for a national *madhhab* through the doctrine of *ijmāᶜ*. He suggested that Islamic law deduced from the classical *fiqh* should be reviewed and reformed, and that the reform process should be undertaken on a collective basis, so as to comply with the principles of *ijmāᶜ*.[8] The collaboratively-authored *tafsīr* works produced by the Muhammadiyah mentioned above likewise assert that they are a product of the collective *ijtihād* that reflects the view of the institution it represents. When it comes to QT, the collectively determined interpretation that can be found in its pages

6 Fakhr al-Dīn al-Rāzī, *Mafātīḥ al-ghayb*, 32 vols (Beirut: Dār al-Fikr, 1981), x, p. 148.

7 Saleh, *The Formation of The Classical Tafsīr Tradition: The Qur'ān Commentary of al-Thaᶜlabī (d. 427/1035)* (Leiden; Boston: Brill, 2004), pp. 17–18.

8 R. Michael Feener, 'Indonesian Movements for the Creation of a "National Madhhab"', *Islamic Law & Society*, 9.1 (2002), 83–115 (p. 100).

therefore represents the *ijmāᶜ* of the state which, accordingly, in this context is connected to contextualization and conformity.

Consensus on the interpretation of the Qur'anic verses was, however, not always achieved. Of course, there were interpretive cases that for a variety of reasons did not end in actual consensus between the committee. The issue of the attributes of God is a good example. The joint committee of the 1989 revision faced difficulties in arriving at a shared understanding of the word *nafsah* in Q 3:28. Some committee members from the LPMQ found it inappropriate to translate the word literally as *'diri'* ('the self') as this imposes an anthropomorphic idea onto God. For this reason, they proposed interpreting it metaphorically with the word *'siksa'* ('chastisement'). The committee members from the King Fahd Complex, however, insisted on translating it literally. As a result, the final translation was a combination, *'diri* [*siksa*]*-Nya'* ('Himself [His chastisement])'. What is significant in this context is that it illustrates one strategy used by the translation team to resolve the interpretive disagreements: accommodating all the options raised in the discussion. While this particular case shows that the options were written in the main body of the translation, we also find frequent instances where alternative readings are added in footnotes. Another frequent strategy used to resolve disputes is to simply write the debates out of the text. We can see this, for example, in the cases of Q 1:6 and Q 4:3, where the fourth edition eventually removes contested ideas previously included in footnotes.[9]

These cases emphasize that the idea of conformity in many instances is reinforced by the genre of Qur'an translation, and is made possible by the way the committee understands the boundaries of translation as a genre. Whenever the committee would engage in a lively discussion of a particular case, it often ended in a decision for a literal translation. During the plenary session of the 2016–19 revision, the committee often raised the idea that they should opt for literal translation, and omit any discussion or debates about the chosen interpretation, on the assumption (or expectation) that should readers want to know more, they could seek elaboration in *tafsīr*. Thus, conceptions about the actual genre of the translation itself provided a solution for the issue of how to approach the debates over meaning within the translation team, but

9 For more on this, see Chapter Six.

at the same time, this solution says a lot about how the team conceived of Qur'an translation, i.e. as a sub-genre within the *tafsīr* tradition that cannot be isolated from *tafsīr.*

The most important consequence of the collective nature of QT for this study is that it introduces a somewhat paradoxical form of authority to the translation. Mukhlis M. Hanafi, the current director of the LPMQ, has expressed his opinion that the interpretive authority of QT goes back to the Indonesian *ulama*, not the state, because MORA is only the facilitator of the QT project. His statement reflects the fact that the experts of which the translation committee is comprised are not necessarily MORA employees. Instead, they were invited to undertake the translation because of their expertise in their respective fields. Although some of them are employed in various bodies or institutions run by MORA, for example as teaching staff in Islamic higher education institutes, their presence in the committee is essentially due to their expertise rather than their status as MORA employees. Furthermore, at the end of the process, their work was brought forward to the National Congress of the Ulama of the Qur'an for approval, rather than being signed off by MORA (with the exception of the first edition). Only following their scrutiny and with their approval was the translation be published.[10]

Because of the hermeneutical process of collective authorship and consensus that underpins the production of QT, it is considered to have an authority that goes far beyond the individual intellectual authority of a scholar. Qur'an commentary, and indeed Qur'an translation, is essentially an intellectual pursuit, for which credit is attributed to the authors. However, the collective or collaborative authorship of QT requires an assemblage of several sources from a number of authors, and these fuse together to convey a higher form of authority. This is especially the case when individual contributions within the translation can no longer be identified.[11] This situation is the result of the three steps

10 Personal interview with Muchlis M. Hanafi. For the fourth edition, the national congress was held on two separate occasions: on the first occasion, 25–27 September 2018, the review addressed the first twenty *juz'* of the Qur'an, while the remaining ten *juz'* were reviewed on 8–11 July 2019.

11 Gusmian observes a similar situation with the collective *tafsīr* of Muhammadiyah. See Islah Gusmian, *Khazanah Tafsir Indonesia: dari Hermeneutika hingga Ideologi* (Yogyakarta: LKiS, 2013), p. 177.

introduced in the production of QT. The list of translator names—which was provided in the first, second, and Saudi editions but was no longer included in the third edition, except in those copies printed by MORA—simply acknowledges their service rather than recognizing their specific intellectual contribution. Likewise, the Qur'an printing industry does not attribute the translation to the translators themselves, presenting it instead as a 'publication of the Ministry of Religious Affairs.' Accordingly, the intellectual authority of QT shifts from an individual to an institutional authority (this argument will be further elaborated in the case study in Chapter Seven). It is also worth noting that, at this point, we are witnessing an ambivalent notion of authority in QT. While the LPMQ states that the authority of QT lies with the *ulama* instead of the state, the Qur'an industry assigns it to MORA, i.e., the state.

There is another aspect to the idea of conformity that gives further shape to the state's authority in QT. This does not lie in the fact that the state closely supervises and controls the output of the translation so that it conforms to a so-called standard religious discourse, a point that will be exclusively discussed in Chapters Five and Six. Rather it lies in the fact that the state maintains its supervision over the content of QT simply by giving the *ulama* full interpretive authority over the translation, knowing that, as the loyal followers of the main Sunnī stream of Islam, they will adopt certain theological positions. This explains why the committee members do not include progressive and controversial names who are interested in using new approaches and challenging mainstream Qur'an commentaries. Thus, individuals such as Moqsith Ghazali, Musdah Mulia, or K.H. Husein Muhammad were not assigned to the committee, even though they are involved in other MORA projects. Having said that, MORA does, of course, impose certain interpretive restrictions on the translation committee. For example, a document entitled 'Panduan Revisi Terjemah' (Guidelines for Revision of the Translation) conveys, inter alia, that the committee should refer to the interpretive opinion supported by the *jumhur* (majority) of exegetes, and that special attention should be directed towards those verses with the potential to incite discrimination (SARA[12]), such as the

12 SARA is not a word, but an acronym from *Suku* (tribe), *Agama* (religion) *dan Ras* (race), which refers to a conceptualization of discrimination in Indonesia.

verse mentioning *qitāl* (killing).[13] Although these guidelines were only issued during the preparation of the fourth edition, the same idea has essentially been applied in previous editions too, as evidenced by the fact that the previous editions of QT essentially only reflect the interpretive range found in widely approved Sunnī commentaries.

At this point, I argue that the assembly of the QT team and the production process are both motivated by the state's desire to ensure that the translation will further its own interests. On the one hand, the state asserts its authority by giving full interpretive control to the large *ulama* community so the work cannot be identified as the intellectual output of a certain individual. On the other, the selection of committee members favors those who are faithful to the mainstream intellectual legacy of Islam, to ensure that the translation reaches a wide readership and complies with the broadest outlook on Islamic teachings, with no unconventional readings of the scripture.

Methodology

QT provides short hermeneutical expositions at the beginning of some of its editions. In the first edition, the head of the committee, Soenarjo, explains that the work first seeks to follow the literal method of translation but, for those cases in which this method fails to provide a comprehensible rendition of the source text, the committee opts for further explanation presented either in parentheses or footnotes. This methodological note is, however, very brief and, as is the case with the introductions to many Qur'an commentaries, explains very little about the complicated hermeneutical processes actually involved in interpreting the Qur'anic text.[14] Yet, it does not fail to mention an established truism of Qur'an translation: that in comparison to the Arabic Qur'an, any translation will always be inadequate and lose something of the original. Accordingly, any translation, no matter the effort put in by the translator, will never provide an exhaustive

13 Lajnah Pentashihan Mushaf Al-Qur'an, 'Panduan Kajian Revisi Al-Qur'an Dan Terjemahnya Kementrian Agama Tahun 2016'.

14 Johanna Pink, 'Classical Qur'anic Hermeneutics', in *The Oxford Handbook of Qur'anic Studies*, ed. by Mustafa Shah and M. A. S. Abdel Haleem (Oxford: Oxford University Press, 2020), pp. 818–31 (p. 818).

account of the Qur'an's meaning. It should be noted that at this point Soenarjo is not concerned with the issue of substitution, i.e., of whether the translation is intended as a replacement for the Arabic Qur'an, a subject that is addressed in the Saudi edition which explicitly denies that this is the aim of the translators. The Saudi edition of QT follows the assumption that because of its divine nature the Qur'an can never be 'translated,' and that one can only reveal its meaning. Hence, despite the fact that this edition bears the original title *Al-Qur'an dan Terjemahnya,* the section in the preface that explains its view on translation is given the heading *Penerjemahan Makna Al-Qur'an al-Karim* (the translation of the meaning of the holy Qur'an), and the parallel Arabic title for the work is *'al-Qurʾān al-karīm wa tarjamat maʿānīh ilā al-lughat al-indūnīsī'* ('the holy Qur'an and the translation of its meaning into the Indonesian language').

Both the first and the Saudi editions are united in their emphasis on the impossibility of rendering the qualities of the original Arabic Qur'an into another language due to its divine status. However, they are not on the same page over the issue of precisely what the Qur'an's divine status means in terms of the possibility of translating it. Soenarjo's preface is concerned with the limited possibilities of equivalence and issues of readability/understandability of the translation for target readers. He implies that literal translation is possible but that in complicated cases it can result in an incomprehensible (*tidak dimengerti*) target text, in which case a strategy of paraphrasing should be adopted. This position rests on a rather flexible stance when it comes to the untranslatability of the Qur'an, namely that the Qur'an can be translated despite the fact that no attempt to translate it will ever be exhaustive. In contrast, the Saudi edition adopts a more doctrinal approach to the issue of Qur'anic inimitability: the notion that the Qur'an cannot be translated. However, because of the necessity for Qur'an translations, some scholars, such as al-Dhahabī,[15] one of the sources referenced in the Saudi edition, reached a solution to the issue of Qur'anic untranslatability by adopting a middle ground, according to which, although the Qur'an itself is untranslatable, it is possible to translate its meaning.

15 Muḥammad Ḥusain al-Dhahabī, *Al-Tafsīr wa al-mufassirūn*, 3 vols (Cairo: Maktaba Wahba, 2004), i, p. 19.

The third edition has little to say on the issue, except that the translation is not a duplicate of the Qur'an, as is stated in the preface by the Minister of Religion, Said Agil Husin Al Munawar. The fourth edition provides a relatively more elaborate exposition, although it is still too short to be deemed a comprehensive methodological account. Unlike the earlier editions which are grounded in the theological views posited in *ᶜulūm al-Qurʾān* literature,[16] the fourth edition uses terminology from Western translation theory, although no Western theorists are mentioned by name. For the first time, QT indicates that it basically prefers foreignization and aims to provide a faithful translation both in the content and the form of the source language. With regards to the issue of whether the Qur'an can or cannot be translated, this edition conveys the view that some parts of the Qur'an are subject to literal translation, while others are not. The opinions expressed here match those in an article written by the head of the committee, Muchlis M. Hanafi, in which he discussed the methodological issues posed by Qur'an translation, and put forward a similar proposition. Drawing on the ideas of pre-modern scholars such as al-Jurjānī (1009–78) and al-Shātibī (d. 1388), and the modern Azharite al-Marāghī (1881–1945), as well as his mentor Quraish Shihab, Hanafi suggests that one layer of the Qur'an's language can be translated literally, but there is another that cannot. Of course, he does not forget to insist that the translation is not a replacement for the Arabic Qur'an.[17]

Now let us turn to the actual work of the translation to see what this theoretical exposition means for its actual application, beginning with this particular case, Q 5:48:

وَأَنزَلۡنَآ إِلَيۡكَ ٱلۡكِتَٰبَ بِٱلۡحَقِّ مُصَدِّقٗا لِّمَا بَيۡنَ يَدَيۡهِ مِنَ ٱلۡكِتَٰبِ وَمُهَيۡمِنًا عَلَيۡهِۖ

'We sent to you the book with the truth, confirming the scriptures that came before it, and *muhaymin* over it.

16 Fadhli Lukman, 'Studi Kritis atas Teori Tarjamah Al-Qur'an dalam 'Ulūm al-Qur'ān', *Al-A'raf: Jurnal Pemikiran Islam dan Filsafat*, 13.2 (2016), 167–90.

17 Muchlis Muhammad Hanafi, 'Problematika Terjemahan Al-Qur'an Studi pada Beberapa Penerbitan Al-Qur'an dan Kasus Kontemporer', *SUHUF Jurnal Pengkajian Al-Qur'an dan Budaya*, 4.2 (2011), 169–95, https://doi.org/10.22548/shf.v4i2.53.

First edition	*Dan Kami telah turunkan kepadamu Kitab Al Qurään dengan membawa kebenaran, membenarkan apa jang sebelumnja, jaitu Kitab-kitab (jang diturunkan sebelumnja) dan batu udjian terhadap Kitab-kitab jang lain itu.* [And We sent to you the book Qur'an with carrying truth, confirming what came before, namely the books (that were sent previously), and [as a] measuring rock over those other books]
Third edition	*Dan Kami telah menurunkan Kitab (Al-Qur'an) kepadamu (Muhammad) dengan membawa kebenaran, yang membenarkan kitab-kitab yang diturunkan sebelumnya dan menjaganya* [And We sent the book (the Qur'an) to you (Muhammad) with carrying truth, which confirms the books sent previously and preserves them]
Fourth edition	*Kami telah menurunkan kitab suci (Al-Qur'an) kepadamu (Nabi Muhammad) dengan (membawa) kebenaran sebagai pembenar kitab-kitab yang diturunkan sebelumnya dan sebagai penjaganya (acuan kebenaran terhadapnya).* [We sent the scripture (the Qur'an) to you (Prophet Muhammad) with (carrying) truth, as the confirmer of what was sent previously and as an arbiter of truth for them)

From the point of view of content, these translations share the same message. God tells Muhammad that He sent him the Book/scripture with truth, and it has a particular role in relation to its earlier counterparts, which is represented as *muṣaddiq* and *muhaymin*. *Muṣaddiq* is straightforward to translate, meaning 'one who confirms or approves'. Hence, the statement that the Qur'an is *muṣaddiq* over earlier scriptures means that it approves them. Qur'an commentaries provide several meanings for *muhaymin*, but the issue is not that complicated. It is mostly interpreted as meaning *amīn* (one who keeps something safe), *shahīd* (a witness), *ḥāfiẓ* (one who preserves or keeps something), and/or *ḥākim* (a judge). In his *tafsīr* Ibn Kathīr gives all these words and suggests that the range of meaning of *muhaymin* encompasses all of them. The general idea is thus that the Qur'an, as the last scripture revealed to the last messenger, plays a role in maintaining and perpetuating the scriptural tradition.[18] The word also implies an apologetic stance towards those scriptures, indicating that the Qur'an is a measure by which to judge the validity of their content. Those which are approved by the Qur'an are considered truth, whereas those which deviate from the Qur'an are a corruption (*taḥrīf*).[19]

Yet, the translations of Q 5:48 provided in the various different editions of QT differ in many ways. The rendition given in the first edition is lengthy, and adds much to the text. Indeed, the wording of the verse in the original Arabic is extremely compact, which unsurprisingly raises problems for translators, even though it does not entail complicated interpretive issues—and this is most probably the exact reason that it is rendered so differently in the different editions. Many words not mentioned in the source text occur in the translation. *Al-Kitāb* is translated as '*Kitab*' ('book') but with the addition of '*Al Quräan*' (using the old spelling system) to give '*Kitab Al Quräan*' ('the book Qur'an'). This is most probably to explicate the discursive shift from the previous verses which had talked about *al-tawrāt* (the Torah) and *al-injīl* (the Gospels)[20] to the Qur'an, which is the main subject of this verse. The translators somehow find it necessary to add the word '*membawa*' ('carrying') to their translation of the phrase *bi l-ḥaqq* (lit. 'with the truth') to give '*dengan membawa kebenaran*' ('with carrying truth'), an addition without which readers would arguably still understand the sense.

The following phrse, *muṣaddiqan limā bayna yadayhi min al-kitāb* (lit. 'as a conformation of the book(s) that came before it') is rendered as '*membenarkan apa jang sebelumnja, jaitu Kitab-kitab (jang diturunkan sebelumnja)*' ('confirming what came before, namely the books [that were sent previously]'). It is apparent from this rendering that there

18 ᶜImād al-Dīn Abū al-Fidāᵓ Ismāᶜīl Ibn Kathīr, *Al-Tafsīr al-qurᵓān al-ᶜaẓīm*, 15 vols (Giza: Muᵓassasa Qurṭuba, 2000), iv, pp. 244–45.

19 *Tafsīr Al-Muyassar* (Medina: Mujammaᶜ al-Malik Fahd li Ṭibāᶜāt al-Muṣḥaf al-Sharīf, 2008), p. 116; Royal Aal al-Bayt Institute for Islamic Thought, 'Tafsīr Al-Muntakhab Fī Tafsīr al-Qurᵓān al-Karīm / Lajna al-qurᵓān wa al-sunna Sūrat al-Māᵓida 48', *Altafsir.Com*, https://www.altafsir.com/Tafasir.asp?tMadhNo=9&tTafsirNo=65&tSoraNo=5&tAyahNo=48&tDisplay=yes&UserProfile=0&LanguageId=1.

20 Q 5:46–47: 'We sent Jesus, son of Mary, in their footsteps, to confirm the Torah that had been sent before him: We gave him the Gospel with guidance, light, and confirmation of the Torah already revealed—a guide and lesson for those who take heed of God. And let the People of the Gospel judge by what Allah has revealed therein. And whoever does not judge by what Allah has revealed—then it is those who are defiantly disobedient.'

is an additional phrase *'jang diturunkan sebelumnja'* ('that were sent previously'), now in parenthesis, appended to their translation of *min al-kitāb*, effectively repeating the idea of *bayn yadayhi* that was rendered as *'apa yang sebelumnya* ('what came before'). While it seems unnecessary, this addition is an emphasis that the two *kitābs* mentioned in this verse have different meanings: while the first means 'the Qur'an', the second means 'the earlier scriptures'. Furthermore, it adapts *muhaymin* (criterion, final authority, guardian) into a local concept, *'batu udjian'* (lit. 'measuring rock'). The pronoun *hi* in *muhaymin ᶜalayhi* is rendered as a referent to the second *al-kitāb*, rather than as a pronoun as in the source text. However, not only is the referent of the pronoun made explicit, the committee adds *'jang lain itu'* ('those others') in it, to give in full the rendering *'terhadap Kitab-kitab jang lain itu'* ('over those other books') where the Arabic source text gives a simple *ᶜalayhi*. Again, this addition is most probably to emphasize what the word *kitāb* denotes in this instance. In addition to all of those additions, the committee understandably refrains from literal translation of the phrase *bayna yadayhi*, the result of which would have generated an unidiomatic and incomprehensible sentence in the target language (*'di antara kedua tangannya'*; 'between his two hands').

There is no change to this translation in the second and Saudi editions, except for the spelling. The third edition maintains a similar translation strategy, yet it is relatively closer to the source text, and is hence the most faithful translation. In this version, each word in the target text stands in the corresponding position to the relevant word in the source text. It also removes the many additions introduced in the first edition; this reflects the fact that, as mentioned above, one of the primary ideas behind the production of the third edition was to make a shorter translation.

The first part of the clause, *wa anzalnā ilayka al-kitāb bi 'l-ḥaqq* (lit. 'and We sent to you the book with the truth'), is rendered almost identically to the previous edition, except that the third edition adds Muhammad's name after *anzalnā ilayka* ('We have sent you') in parentheses to account for the pronoun *ka* (you) in *ilayka*. This addition is similar to the addition of *'Al-Qur'an'* following *al-kitāb* at the beginning of the verse. This edition also shows a tendency to produce a more idiomatic translation output. In previous editions, the phrase *anzalnā ilayka al-kitāb* was translated as *'Kami turunkan kepadamu kitab'* ('We sent to you the scripture'). However, a more idiomatic Indonesian structure would refrain from placing adverbs between verbs and objects; the object should be directly after the verb. As a result, this edition renders it *'Kami turunkan Kitab (Al-Qur'an) kepadamu (Muhammad)'* ('We sent the scripture [the Qur'an] to you [Muhammad]'), a sentence that slightly deviates from the original structure in Arabic. When it comes to the phrase *muṣaddiqan limā bayna yadayhi min al-kitāb* ('confirming the scriptures that came before it'), this edition abandons the redundancy of the previous editions' translation and follows the idiomatic structure of the Indonesian language—*'yang membenarkan kitab-kitab yang diturunkan sebelumnya'* ('which confirms the scriptures sent earlier'). A further shift is seen in the choice of word to translate *muhaymin*. The third edition refrains from using the local adaptation *'batu udjian'*, which has become an archaic idiom, for this word. Instead, this edition opts for *'menjaga'* ('[to] keep', '[to] preserve'), most probably because *muhaymin* has been interpreted as meaning, among other things, *amīn* ('one who keeps something safe'), or *ḥāfiẓ* ('one who preserves or keeps something') in the *tafsīr* tradition. This shows a shift from adaptation to semantic translation. Nevertheless, from the *tafsīr* point of view, the rendering, in this case, shifts from one potential meaning for *muhaymin* to another that is outlined in Qur'an commentaries. Finally, in this edition, *ᶜalayhi* is translated simply as *'nya'* ('it'/'them'), meaning that *muhayminan ᶜalayhi* is simply translated as *'menjaganya'* ('[which] preserves them').

The shift towards a more idiomatic Indonesian structure shown in the third edition is taken even further in the fourth edition, where it goes in the opposite direction from the theoretical exposition provided in the preface. This fourth edition retains the transposition of adverbs as in the third edition. However, unlike the third editions, there is no conjunction *'dan'* ('and') at the beginning of the translation of this verse, which stands for *wa* ('and') in the source text. This reflects the fact that this usage is prevalent in Arabic, but not idiomatic in Indonesian, and hence the committee agreed to remove the conjunction whenever it is used at the start of a verse, as long as in the original Arabic it does not denote a connection between the following clause and the final clause of the preceding verse. Because this is a translation decision that reflects Indonesian language usage, it seems likely that representation from the

BPPB is probably the reason behind this decision. Nevertheless, I am aware that not every member of the committee personally agreed with this decision. To my knowledge, at least one of them was concerned with this removal due to their conviction that every word and letter in the Qur'an has a particular meaning and function.

The shift from rendering *muṣaddiqan* as *'yang membenarkan'* ('which confirms') in the third edition to *'sebagai pembenar'* ('as the confirmer') in the fourth edition and from rendering *muhayminan* as *'menjaga'* ('[to] keep', '[to] preserve') to *'sebagai penjaga'* ('as the keeper') in these editions is motivated by an Arabic grammatical consideration. The shifts are related to the emphasis on the grammatical function of the original Arabic words. *Muṣaddiqan* and *muhayminan* are grammatically speaking *ḥāl* accusatives, and the corresponding semantic function in the Indonesian language is better represented by *'sebagai'* (as) and the noun *'pembenar/penjaga'* ('confirmer/keeper'), instead of *'yang membenarkan/ menjaga'* ('which confirms/preserves').

The fourth edition also introduces another shift in the way it renders the word *muhaymin*. As mentioned above, the shift from *'batu udjian'* ('the measuring rock') to *'menjaga'* ('[to] keep') in the third edition, from one point of view, is a shift to semantic translation, while from another point of view it demonstrates an interpretive shift from one option to another. But, by opting for this particular wording in Indonesian, the third edition refrains from taking an explicit theological stance over the issue of the Qur'an's relationship to previous scriptures. The translation committee for the fourth edition, not happy with merely translating this as *'penjaga'* ('the keeper'), decided to add an explanation in parenthesis, *'acuan kebenaran terhadapnya'* (lit. 'an arbiter of truth for them'). The phrase chosen here, *'acuan kebenaran'*, conveys a relatively similar concept to *'batu udjian'*, the wording that appeared in the first edition. Yet, it should be noted that neither *'batu udjian'* ('measuring rock') nor *'acuan kebenaran'* ('arbiter of truth') can be described as synonyms for *'menjaga'/'penjaga'* ('[to] keep'/'the keeper'). Instead, *'batu udjian'/'acuan kebenaran'* on the one hand, and *'menjaga'/'penjaga'* on the other, represent two different interpretive options provided by the Qur'an commentaries, from which the committee makes a selection. The committee for the first edition preferred the first option, while that of the third edition preferred the latter, and the committee for the fourth edition, instead of making a selection, preferred to suggest a combination of all options.

Translating words such as *anzalnā* ('we sent'), *ilayka* ('to you'), or *al-ḥāqq* ('truth') is quite straightforward because they have literal equivalents in the Indonesian language and do not generate hermeneutical problems or hold specific sectarian, theological, legal, or eschatological significance. The word *muhaymin* is, however, different. It has no natural equivalent in the Indonesian language, and holds a specific theological significance, as it conveys the idea of the Qur'an as the scripture that defines the truth of previous scriptures. Such cases require an approach that falls somewhere between translation and *tafsīr*. Whereas for straightforward words the committee can simply rely on their knowledge of Arabic, when it comes to words that raise specific hermeneutical issues, recourse to *tafsīr* is almost inevitable. It is in such cases that we can see the boundaries between Qur'an translation and *tafsīr* melt in to one another.

The explicit presence of *tafsīr* in QT is, of course, most often found in the presence of untranslated words. A large number of Qur'anic words are left untranslated in QT, either because they do not have Indonesian equivalents or because they have become recognizable as technical terms in the Islamic intellectual disciplines. For such words, interpretive exposition is inevitable, and is presented either in parenthesis or in footnotes, as with, for example *khalīfa* (Q 2:30), *al-ṭaghūt* (Q 2:256), *al-kursī* (Q 2:255), *khamr* (Q 2:219), *muḥkamāt* and *mutashābihāt* (Q 3:7), and *fitna* (Q 3:7), as well as many others. Furthermore, many words are also translated with an interpretive angle. The way that a number of key words in Q 1 are treated provides sufficient evidence for this: nine key words are accompanied by an additional explanation in a footnote in the first edition of QT, even though they are also all translated into Indonesian.

The provision of further explanation is a strategy commonly used in translating scripture. Many words cannot be translated, or their translation is considered inadequate for explaining their original concepts, which is why additional exegetical interpolations are presented alongside the translation. Yet, the intervention of *tafsīr* in QT is much more nuanced than mere addition. Let us take another example to illustrate more about this kind of interpretive intervention. Q 55:27

contains a phrase, *wajh rabbika* (lit. 'the face of your Lord'), that raises a theological problem. There is a longstanding theological dispute over whether the word *wajh* literally denotes the physical face or should be read figuratively as referring to something else. Fakhr al-Dīn al-Rāzī (d. 1210) is one of many exegetes concerned about this issue, and it is thus not surprising that he opens his interpretation of this verse with a theological discussion. He argues that the word *wajh* in this verse refers to the *ḥaqīqa* ('essence') or *dhāt* ('self') of God and cannot denote a physical face, because the latter would assign God a physical materiality which is, for him, theologically unacceptable.[21] This line of interpretation shows that the understanding of *wajh* as 'the self' and as a physical face stand in stark contrast. Apart from this theological matter, the word used for 'face' is basically a simple one, lexically speaking, in both Arabic and Indonesian. *Wajh* can be rendered as either '*wajah*' or '*muka*' in Indonesian, and a literal translation would be '*wajah Tuhanmu*' ('the face of your God'). If the committee's concern lay merely with translating the words of the source text literally, this verse would not cause any problems whatsoever. Yet, when it comes to this theological problem, the shifts between the way it is rendered in the various editions of QT indicate that that is not the case.

At first glance, the first edition of QT translates *wajh rabbika* figuratively, as '*Dzat Tuhanmu*' ('the self of your God'). The second, Saudi, and third editions go with a literal translation '*Wajah Tuhanmu*' ('the face of your God'), whereas the fourth edition combines both and gives the reader '*wajah* (*zat*) *Tuhanmu*' ('the face [self] of your God'). These changes reflect the different translation strategies followed by the committee, and they reflect hermeneutical problems at work in the interpretation of the source text.[22] The above-mentioned theological problem understandably leads to two different ways of translating the word *wajh*, one figurative, as in the first edition, and the other literal, as in the second, Saudi, and third editions. It makes sense to take an approach that combines both strategies, as the fourth edition does. However, the different translation

21 Fakhr al-Dīn al-Rāzī, *Mafātīḥ al-ghayb*, 32 vols (Beirut: Dār al-Fikr, 1981), xxix, p. 106.

22 Bariq Al-Husain, 'The Translation of Mutashaabih, Ambiguous, and Muḥkam Quranic Verses: A Contrastive Study' (unpublished doctoral dissertation, Western Sydney University, 2018), pp. 126–31.

strategies themselves do not give a complete picture of the underlying methodological dynamic behind these different renderings.

Closer examination of the first edition is crucial at this point. It is only partly accurate to categorize the rendering of *wajh* as *'dzat'* as a figurative translation. It is important to know that *'dzat'* is written using transliteration, which means that it is perceived by the translator as a foreign Arabic word (in its original Arabic: *dhāt*), instead of an Indonesian one. Hence, the first edition of QT effectively translates the Arabic, Qur'anic word, *wajh*, using another Arabic word, *dhāt*. Many classical Arabic Qur'an commentaries interpret this word as *dhāt*, and knowing this we can certainly say that commentaries such as those by al-Jalālayn or al-Rāzī have shaped the committee's translation decisions here, as both use the term *dhāt* in their interpretation of *wajh*. Thus, we can see here an explicit intervention of *tafsīr* into a work of Qur'an translation. Instead of translating *wajh* literally or looking for an Indonesian word to represent the figurative idea of *wajh*, the first edition of QT directly brings up a text from *tafsīr* into the translation, replacing the Qur'anic word in question.

With their very different decision to translate the word *wajh rabbik* as *'wajah Tuhan-Mu'* ('the face of your God'), the second and Saudi editions seem to translate instead of merely surrendering to *tafsīr*. Yet, again, there is much more going on under the surface. The change in the second and the Saudi editions may have something to do with the involvement of the King Fahd Complex in the revision process. As indicated in the previous chapter, the King Fahd Complex promotes specific theological interests in their translation projects, and figurative interpretation is one of their areas of concern.[23] Their stance is clearly visible in *al-Tafsīr al-Muyassar*, a concise *tafsīr* published by the King Fahd Complex and intended as a guideline for translating the Qur'an, which justifies the literal understanding of the word *wajh*.[24] This commentary is also one of the references used by the QT team. Hafizh Dasuki, the head of the committee for the second and Saudi editions, reveals that there were intense discussions between committee members with regards

23 Ziauddin Sardar, *Reading the Qur'an: The Contemporary Relevance of the Sacred Text of Islam* (Oxford: Oxford University Press, 2011), p. 47.

24 Nukhbat al-ᶜUlamāᵓ al-Tafsīr, *Tafsīr Al-Muyassar* (Medina: Mujammaᶜ al-Malik Fahd li Ṭibāᶜāt al-Muṣḥaf al-Sharīf, 2008), p. 532.

to this and other 'anthropomorphic' verses, and in the end, they had to compromise.[25] The word they choose to use, *'wajah'*, may not be an Arabic word borrowed and written in transliteration like *dzat*. But let us not forget that the second and Saudi editions on the one hand, and the first edition on the other, are concerned with the same theological issue, and the choice made in the second and Saudi editions is in this regard no less interpretive than the first edition. This is also the case when it comes to the choice of *zat*, which is used in the fourth edition. In this edition, the word *zat* is perceived as an Indonesian word, but let us not forget that it is actually a loanword rooted in an Arabic word[26] that still has a specific theological significance when associated with God, as it is here. Not happy with an interpretation that would fall somewhere between the two axes, the translation team working on the fourth edition covered both bases and presented both interpretations.

One more observation needs to be made about the choice to use *zat* in the fourth edition. One might assume that *'wajah'* in the second, Saudi, and third editions and *'zat'* in the fourth edition are both direct translations of the Qur'anic word *wajh*. However, *wajah* and *zat* are in fact two different Indonesian words with completely different meanings that represent different forms of semantic relationship with the original Arabic *wajh*. This does not detract, however, from the fact that they both reflect the views provided in the *tafsīr* tradition that were selected by the translators in QT. This is an example of what I have above called the 'intervention' of *tafsīr* in Qur'an translation. Thus, while the translation of *wajh* to *'dzat'* may denote the explicit presence of *tafsīr* in the target text, when it comes to the translation of *wajh* to the Indonesian word *'zat'*, the influence of the word *dzat* (that is, the Arabic loan word used in *tafsīr*) is still at work. In other words, *'zat'* in the fourth edition is not necessarily a translation of *wajh* in the verse, but a translation of *dhāt* taken from Qur'an commentaries. Accordingly, in the use of *'wajah'*, *'zat'*, and a large number of other words, even in undisputed cases, *tafsīr* might not be explicitly mentioned in the translation, but it is present in the background. Other examples can be seen in the translations of

25 Sadhewo S and Hartoyo W.H., 'Quran Yang Terpelihara', *Majalah Tempo*, 25 April 1992, p. 77.

26 Badan Pengembangan dan Pembinaan Bahasa, 'Zat', *KBBI Daring*, 2016, https://kbbi.kemdikbud.go.id/entri/zat.

ẓālika (lit. 'that') in Q 2:1 as *'ini'* ('this') instead of *'itu'* ('that'), of *ṣadaqa* in Q 9:60 as *'zakat'*, of *al-dīn* in Q 2:256 as *'agama (Islam)'*, of *al-nūr* in Q 2:257 as *'cahaya (iman)'*, or in the addition of *'orang-orang munafik'* for *yaᶜtadhirūna* in Q 9:94, and many more. This phenomenon suggests that the theoretical influence of *tafsīr* in QT is much greater than is visible in the actual text of the translation.

Zadeh and Pink have argued for the limited relevance of contemporary theories of scriptural translation in explaining the complicated and dynamic history of Qur'an translation. Examination of pre-modern Persian interlinear Qur'an translations, Zadeh suggests, makes it clear that the perception that there is a dichotomy between literal and paraphrastic translation has little value when it comes to understanding the complexities of Qur'an translation in history, a suggestion that also undermines the (doctrinal) assumption that a Qur'an translation is necessarily intended as substitutive of the original text.[27] In her discussion of Qur'an translations into Javanese, Pink suggests that the oral origin of these translations and their functions in the teaching context 'result in a higher visibility of the translator who appears as a religious authority in his own right.'[28] QT does not conform to the interlinear format of traditional Javanese Qur'an translations, is not of oral origin, and is not designed for a teaching context, but this does not mean that the actual process of translation does not require a nuanced exploration that goes beyond the identification of techniques and methods, degree of accuracy to the source text, readability, and doctrinal acceptability, and kinds of equivalence so as to reveal the complicated variables at play in the production of QT.

To begin with, QT is a translation that conforms to our modern understanding of the genre. It essentially follows the structure and semantic content of the source text, and in all editions the committee claims that they privilege the source text over all other considerations. In other words, despite the existence of specific literary features in the individual verses of the Qur'an, and semantic and grammatical

---

27 Travis Zadeh, *The Vernacular Qur'an: Translation and the Rise of Persian Exegesis* (New York: Oxford University Press, 2012), pp. 15–16.

28 Johanna Pink, 'The "Kyai's" Voice and the Arabic Qur'an; Translation, Orality, and Print in Modern Java', *Wacana*, 21.3 (2020), 329–59, https://doi.org/10.17510/wacana.v21i3.948.

discrepancies between Arabic and Indonesian, both aspects of the source text which require some level of translatorial intervention, the translators were committed to keeping their translation as close to the source text as possible. However, when it comes to translating the Qur'an, what exactly *is* the source text? When it comes to QT, it is clear that the translators are not just translating the Qur'anic text in isolation: they are actually always engaging in two interpretive processes simultaneously, namely *tafsīr* and translation. We can also see that the *tafsīr* tradition does not just help to fashion the interpretive choices of the translators, but also has an actual presence in the translation outcome. At this point, I argue that the role of *tafsīr* in Qur'an translation may be to function as a substitute source text. Thus, in order to understand the dynamic behind the translation decisions made by the QT teams, one needs to situate the translation within the long history of the *tafsīr* tradition, with which it is always in dialogue. While prevailing translation theories recognize the agency of both source text and translators, QT demonstrates that, in the case of Qur'an translation, *tafsīr* also plays a critical role, to the extent that excluding it from our analysis would add little to our understanding of the genre.

The notion that QT is a source text-oriented translation is further challenged by factors relating to the government's agenda for the development of the Indonesian language. While the translators sought to be faithful to the Arabic Qur'an, the BPPB team that joined the project for the fourth edition were concerned with 'improving' the Indonesian language used in QT. Their intervention in the target text resulted in features such as the removal of *dan* from the start of verses, and a large amount of transposition, due to their commitment to producing a translation that followed the idiomatic structure of the Indonesian language.[29] On another front, there are also issues pertaining to the foreignization and domesticization of words such as *salat, zakat, zalim, kafir,* and *syirk* in QT. One cannot see the inclusion of these in the text

---

29 A recent study using translation methodologies as the framework for analysis found that focusing on the opening verses of a number of *sūras* comes to a similar conclusion. See M. Fahri Andrianto, M.R. Nababan, and Eva Farhah, 'The Impact of Translation Techniques on Translation Methods of Qur'an Translation of Indonesian Ministry of Religion on Fawatih Al-Suwar', *International Journal of Linguistics, Literature and Translation*, 4.6 (2021), 291–98, https://doi.org/10.32996/ijllt.2021.4.6.34.

of QT as indicative of the committee's retention of foreign elements in the translation, since those words are well established as loan words, and were used by Indonesians long before the production of QT. Yet, it is similarly problematic to ignore the connotative significance that their Qur'anic origin and context gives them. This situation becomes more complicated when one takes into account the fact that one of the tasks assigned to the BPPB team working on the fourth edition was to expand the Indonesian lexicon by locating new Arabic loan words to be incorporated into Indonesian, which is why this edition treats a range of Arabic words (for example *sabiin, baitulmaqdis, bani israil,*and *ruhulkudus*) as 'new' Indonesian words. What are we to make of those cases in which the committee retains an original word from the Qur'an in the translation, while at the same time the BPPB members include it in the Indonesian dictionary, thereby making it an official Indonesian word? This creates a dichotomy that raises some obvious problems for anyone seeking to assess the extent to which QT can be said to be source-text and target-text oriented.

Thus, the committee's statement that QT is a source text-oriented translation reflects more about their perception of what qualifies as Qur'an translation than it does about the actual dynamics of the translation process. In their opinion, Qur'an translation should stay close to the original text and is a body of literature distinct from *tafsīr.* When discussing the best translation for a phrase in the fourth edition, the committee often ended up opting for a relatively word-for-word translation without adding further explanation, assuming that this was the function of *tafsīr*, notably in the form of the official MORA commentary, *Al-Qur'an dan Tafsirnya*. However, it is also evident from the above analysis that the translation process attests to the entrenched presence of *tafsīr* in the translation. The demonstrable role of *tafsīr* in the hermeneutical processes at work in QT, either in the background or at a very apparent surface level, is actually a manifestation of what scholars have termed *tarjamat maᶜānī al-Qur'ān* ('the translation of the meanings of the Qur'an'). On this basis, I would argue that, first, all modern Qur'an translations, whether they claim to be literal translations or not, can actually be traced genealogically to the *tafsīr* tradition, and second, any Qur'an translation is a composite text, formed of both the Qur'an and *tafsīr*: *tafsīr* serves as an intermediary text, or a companion source text, alongside the actual text of the Qur'an.

The Legacy of the *Gandul* Method

QT also carries traces of a particularly Indonesian system of traditional Islamic education, in the form of a grammatically-oriented oral translation methodology that was developed in the pedagogical setting of the *pesantren*, known as *makna gandul* (lit. 'hanging meaning'). This methodology was widely used for translating Arabic texts in a number of regions in the Malay-Indonesian peninsula, yet has persisted more in Java than in other areas. When written in a text, it takes the form of an interlinear translation accompanying the original Arabic source text.[30] Ibnu Burdah has described it, in Arabic, as *al-tarjama al-waẓīfiyya al-muᶜjamiyya al-muᶜallaqa* ('hanging, lexical, functional translation'),[31] a description that concisely explains the nature of this translation approach. The *makna gandul* approach to translation is concerned not only with transferring the message of an Arabic text into the target language, but also with identifying the grammatical function of each word and correlating this function with the meaning presented in the target text. In practice, a teacher reads the Arabic text, translates and explains it, and the students make notes in between the lines of the copies at their disposal. The grammatical function of the word in the source text, and each corresponding word in the target language, are indicated by fixed formulas. The word *gandul* ('hanging') literally indicates the space between the two lines of the Arabic source text where the translation and the formulas for its various grammatical functions are written, literally hanging down from the line of the original Arabic text. This makes for a text that is dense on the page,[32] producing a similar layout

30 Ronit Ricci, 'Reading between the Lines: A World of Interlinear Translation', *Journal of World Literature*, 1.1 (2016), 68–80, https://doi.org/10.1163/24056480-00101008.

31 Ibnu Burdah, 'Ṭarīqa al-tarjama al-waẓīfiyya al-muᶜjama al-muᶜallaqa: taṣawwur ᶜām wa al-baḥth al-tārikhiy ᶜanhā', *Journal of Indonesian Islam*, 5.2 (2011), 353–76 (p. 354), http://dx.doi.org/10.15642/JIIS.2011.5.2.353-377.

32 Nur Ahmad, 'Sejarah Makna Kitab Gandul dalam Tradisi Pesantren', *alif.id*, 2018, https://alif.id/read/nur-ahmad/sejarah-makna-kitab-gandul-dalam-tradisi-pesantren-b212819p/.

to the interlinear translation format that was widespread in pre-modern Qur'an translations.[33] Later, this essentially oral pedagogical tool was adopted as a format for printed commentaries on the Qur'an, and some Javanese Qur'an translations combined it with the gloss format.[34]

The intention of this type of translation is to achieve a clear and precise understanding of the meaning of the text from the perspective of its source language. As a consequence of its attentiveness to Arabic grammatical issues, *gandul* translation tolerates linguistic flaws in its target language; in fact, it does not prioritize producing a meaningful sentence in the target language. In a *gandul* translation, the translator has two duties: to indicate equivalent words and synonyms in the target language and to indicate the Arabic grammatical features of the source text using specific technical terms. Each term represents a particular grammatical function, for example, *utawi* for *mubtadaʾ* (the subject of a nominal sentence), *iku* for *khabar* (the predicate of a nominal sentence), *hale* for *ḥāl* (*ḥāl* accusative), *sopo* for *fāʿil* (the subject of a verb), *ing* for *naʿt* (adjective). The simple phrase *Allāhu aḥad*, for example, would normally be translated as '*Allah itu satu*' ('Allah is one') in a simple, literal translation into Indonesian. However, using the *gandul* method, it becomes '*Allāhu aḥad*': '*Allah, utawi Allah, aḥad, iku satu*'. When it comes to complex phrases, and those for which there are numerous grammatical possibilities, the grammatical terminology is used to indicate why the teacher/translator decides to read the text the way he does. In other words, the *gandul* methodology prioritizes foreignization. When one translates an Arabic text with the *gandul* method, one does so with Arabic linguistic rules in mind, and puts the grammar of the target language aside. The output of the translation is 'forced to the utmost extent to comply with the structure of Arabic as the source language.'[35] This means that this method is too complicated for those who do not comprehend Arabic grammar to follow.

---

33 Johanna Pink, 'Form Follows Function: Notes on the Arrangement of Texts in Printed Qur'an Translations', *Journal of Qur'anic Studies*, 19.1 (2017), 143–54, https://doi.org/10.3366/jqs.2017.0274; Zadeh, p. 16.

34 Pink, 'The "Kyai's" Voice and the Arabic Qur'an; Translation, Orality, and Print in Modern Java', p. 340.

35 Burdah, p. 357.

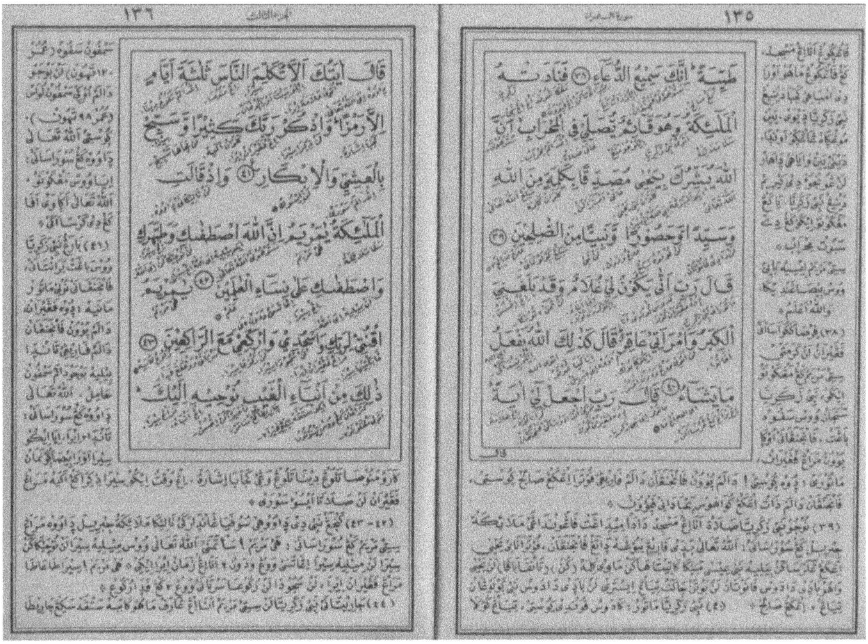

Figure 3 The printed version of a manuscript of translation undertaken using the *gandul* method. The commentary flows around the inner box that contains the Qur'anic text and its interlinear translation, the collection of Muhammad Dluha Luthfillah, CC-BY 4.0.

QT does not explicate the grammatical function of the Arabic Qur'an in the target text as much as the traditional *gandul* translation does. Nevertheless, there is ample evidence that QT, especially in its earlier editions, was influenced by this traditional approach to translation. Its legacy can be seen, for example, in the explication of the referents of pronouns, articles, or certain words in QT.

A simple example of the explication of pronoun referents is found in Q 9:105: *wa qul iᶜmalū fasayara 'llāh ᶜamalakum...* ('Say [Prophet], "Take action! God will see your action..."'; '*Dan katakanlah: 'Bekerdjalah kamu, lalu Allah akan melihat perkedjaanmu itu'*'). The word *iᶜmalū* ('Take action!'; 'Work!') is translated as '*bekerjalah kamu*' in all but the fourth edition of QT. *Iᶜmalū* is an imperative form of the verb (*fiᶜl amr*). English and the Indonesian language share a common characteristic with regard to the linguistic structure of the imperative: the subject of this verb is not mentioned explicitly in the sentence. With this in mind, Abdullah Yusuf Ali, Arberry, and Abdel Haleem do not feel the need to state the subject—rather than rendering it as, for example, 'You (pl.) work!' they translate it as, respectively: And say: 'Work (righteousness): soon will Allah observe your work;' Say [Prophet], 'Take action! God will see your actions;' Say: 'Work; and God will surely see your work'. Although Indonesian has the same grammatical rule, all editions of QT except the latest prefer to bring the subject into the target text as, according to the *gandul* method, including the subject of a verb is a must. Of course, there are inconsistencies, and these probably reflect the different decisions taken by different individuals within the committee when translating a certain verse.

Q 2:4 is also worth examination in this context. The phrase *alladhīna yuʾminūna bimā unzila ilayka* ('those who believe in what has been sent down to you') in the first edition is translated as *'dan mereka yang beriman kepada Kitab (Al-Qur'an) yang telah diturunkan kepadamu'.* What matters here is that the Arabic word *mā* ('what') is translated as *'Kitab (Al-Qur'an)'*, thereby changing the text to read 'and those who believe in the Book (the Qur'an) that has been sent down to you'. There are three possible underlying factors influencing the translators' decision here. The first is that the committee is simply relying on an interpretation provided by one or more Qur'an commentaries, as discussed in the previous section of this chapter. In this context, *al-Jalālayn,* one of the most popular *tafsīr* works in Indonesia, for example, explicitly states that the phrase *mā unzilā ilayka* refers to the Qur'an. The second factor relates to the context of the verse itself: on the basis that the 'thing' in question is described as having been sent down to Muhammad, it is clear from the context that the verse is talking about the Qur'an. The third factor relates to the *gandul* method, according to which when translators encounter the word *mā* they are obliged to identify what is being referred to. To do so, they have to go back to the previous section of the text to look for the potential referent. In this case, *mā* refers to the word *kitāb* mentioned in the second verse. The fact that the translators' choice here was guided at least partially by the *gandul* approach is indicated by the fact that, should they have only been influenced by the first and second perspectives, one would logically expect them to translate *mā* with *'Al-Qur'an'*, rather than *'Kitab'*, which they then had to further explicate by adding in *'al-Qur'an'* in parentheses. If they were only guided by the textual context and interpretations provided by Qur'an commentaries, the choice to render *ma* as *'Al-Qur'an'* alone, to give *'Dan mereka yang beriman kepada Al-Qur'an yang telah diturunkan kepadamu'*, would have been sufficient. However, the translators appear to have chosen to prioritize the word *'Kitab'* in their translation based on the *gandul* method, on the basis that the word *mā* refers back to the usage of *kitab* two verses earlier.

Another example of the impact of the *gandul* method on the team's hermeneutical apparatus can be seen through the addition of the word *'hanya'* ('only') to the translations of Q 1:5 (*Iyyāka naᶜbudu wa iyyāka nastaᶜīn;* 'it is You we worship; it is You we ask for help') and Q 9:51 (*wa ᶜalā 'llāhi falyatawakkali l-muᵓminūn;* 'let the believers put their trust in God') in all editions of QT. In the original Arabic, both phrases share a common grammatical structure according to which a lexical item that, under the normal rules of Arabic grammar, one would expect to be at the end of the phrase, is brought forward to the beginning. In the first case, Q 1:5, *iyyāka* is the direct object of *naᶜbudu*. According to Arabic norms, the common grammatical structure is to put the subject and verb before the object, but in this example, the object is at the beginning. Rather than the expected *naᶜbuduka* ('we worship You'), the word order is reversed to read 'You we worship'. In the second case, *ᶜala 'llāhi* ('and in God') is a compound phrase composed of a preposition (*jār*) and its dependent genitive noun (*majrūr*) which one would, as in the previous example, expect to follow the verb and subject. Again, the expected word order is reversed so that the verb *falyatawakkal* comes later, giving 'In God, let the believers put their trust' as opposed to 'Let the believers put their trust in God'. In terms of Arabic grammar, this composition grammatically implies a meaning of limitation (*al-ḥaṣr*), and it is this implied meaning that the committee chooses to explicate by adding the word *hanya* in to their translations of these verses. Accordingly, instead of *'Kepada Engkau lah kami menyembah'* ('it is You we worship'), the committee provides *'Hanya kepada Engkau lah kami menyembah'* ('It is only You we worship').

The influence of the *gandul* method seems to gradually decline from one edition to the next. This is not because this way of translating and understanding the Arabic text of the Qur'an has died out, nor because the later QT translation committees have increasingly consisted of individuals with less familiarity with the method. In fact, this method was often referenced in the discussions that took place during the plenary sessions to review the revisions to the fourth edition. The reduced influence of the *gandul* methodology in QT is rather primarily a result of the ambition to produce a more idiomatic target text. This process begins in earnest in the third edition, and the fourth edition, in no small part due to the inclusion of the BPPB team, further reduces—except in minor cases—the impact of the *gandul* method on the translation. The preface to the fourth edition explicitly states that the translation has prioritized following the accepted linguistic structures of modern Indonesian wherever possible. Only if this would lead to misunderstandings of the original Arabic was the Indonesian structure sacrificed in favor of the grammatical and linguistic structures of the source text.[36]

The Sources Consulted by the Translation Teams

The bibliography in the first edition lists twenty-five sources, with a twenty-sixth listing for 'miscellaneous.' These sources can be divided into six categories: Arabic commentaries, Indonesian commentaries/translations, non-Arabic and non-Indonesian translations, Qur'an concordances and indexes, Arabic dictionaries, and Indonesian dictionaries. There are thirteen Arabic commentaries, four Indonesian commentaries, four non-Arabic and non-Indonesian translations, one Qur'anic index, one Arabic dictionary, and two Indonesian dictionaries. The categories of the sources are listed in groups, yet without a heading for each category, and the titles are sorted randomly—the listing does not follow alphabetical or chronological order. Additionally, full bibliographic information is not provided; only the titles and the authors of the works are given. This means that there is no indication as to which editions of these sources the team referred to.

The sources listed in the bibliography of the second edition are much more extensive: a total of fifty-five books are listed, and are divided into nine different categories. In addition to the earlier six categories, this edition adds *ᶜulūm al-Qurʾān* literature, canonical *ḥadīth* compilations, and the *sīra nabawiyya* ('Biography of the Prophet'). The bibliography comprises twenty-nine Arabic commentaries, three

36 Departemen Agama Republik Indonesia, *Al-Qur'an dan Terjemahannya* (Jakarta: Lajnah Pentashihan Mushaf Al-Qur'an, 2019), p. vi.

Indonesian commentary/translations, two non-Arabic and non-Indonesian translations (this is the last edition to include translations in this category in languages other than English), twelve *ᶜulūm al-Qurᵓān* works, two *ḥadīth* compilations, three *sīras*, two Qur'anic Indexes, and one Arabic and one Indonesian dictionary. As well as including more sources, the bibliographic details are provided in a more professional manner: works are listed in alphabetical order and almost all the necessary bibliographic details are included. The year of publication is omitted for a number of Arabic works, but this may reflect the fact that it is not unusual for Arabic books to be published without including this information. The Saudi edition essentially shares the same bibliography; the only difference is that the introduction to the later copies of the Saudi edition includes several entries for works by Ibn Taymiyya.

The third edition expands the bibliography further, so that it now comprises sixty-four works, classified into the same nine categories as the previous edition. This edition introduces five additional Arabic commentaries, three additional *ᶜulūm al-Qurᵓān* works, one additional Indonesian commentary, and a different Indonesian dictionary that replaces the one used in the second edition. The sources for *ḥadīth, sīra* literature, English translations, Qur'anic index, and Arabic dictionaries are identical to those in the previous edition. Finally, the bibliography of the fourth edition lists fifty-two works, grouped only into seven categories. There are no *sīra* works listed in this bibliography, nor any Indonesian dictionaries, presumably due to the involvement of the BPPB team, who were in the process of writing an Indonesian dictionary themselves. All in all, this edition comprises twenty-nine Arabic commentaries, eleven *ᶜulūm al-Qurᵓān* works, three *ḥadīth* compilations, four Indonesian commentary/translations, two English translations, two Qur'anic indexes, and one Arabic dictionary.

There is a high probability that not all of the sources consulted by the committee are listed in the bibliographies in the various editions. That is particularly evident in the case of the fourth edition, for which some of the references brought up in the translation team meetings are not present in the list. The worksheets produced by one of the committee members, for example, indicates that he relied heavily on al-Māwardī's (d. 1058) *al-Nukat wa al-ᶜuyūn*, yet it is not included in the bibliography. Another member of the committee would bring a number of English translations in to every meeting, but there are only two works of this category listed. Likewise, Quraish Shihab's *Al-Qur'an dan Maknanya* was widely consulted during meetings, but the bibliography only lists his *Tafsir Al-Misbah,* not *Al-Qur'an dan Maknanya.*

It is hard to achieve a complete picture of the role played by individual sources in QT, mainly because the translation is the work of several individuals who might have had differing personal preferences. However, this does mean that it is not possible to get a rough idea of the most important sources. Sometimes works are mentioned in the footnotes, especially in the first edition, whose footnotes are relatively more elaborate than those in following editions. As mentioned, the thematic blocks of QT follow the scheme used in Muḥammad Maḥmūd Hijazī's *Tafsīr al-wāḍiḥ*. This commentary is consistently listed in all editions, although the third edition does not use his thematization (it is however reinstated in the fourth edition). It is uncertain at this point whether copies of the fourth edition published by the Qur'an printing industry will also opt to re-implement this feature. Further to these sources, as mentioned in the previous chapter, Soenarjo has indicated that he referred to Soedewo's *De Heilige Qoeran* for a segment of his introduction. He also mentions George Sale, but it is not clear what the actual influence of Sale's translation might be in QT. From what I was able to observe of the production of the fourth edition, a number of other individual sources were consulted, but this completely depended on the personal preference of the translators. As with the third edition, the worksheets produced by the individual translators, which recorded their personal research and revisions,[37] might mention one or more commentaries that they had chosen to consult. It is likely that this is also equally true of earlier editions. For example, Hasbi Ash-Shiddieqy, one of the translators for the first edition, who drew on *Tafsīr al-Marāghī* for his personal commentary, *An-Nur,* might very well have used this commentary when he was working on QT.

The bibliographies illustrate the translators' heavy reliance on Arabic Qur'an commentaries, which constitute by far the largest category of sources. It is also evident that almost all the sources are Sunnī. Al-Zamakhsharī's *al-Kashshāf ʿan ḥaqāʾiq ghawāmiḍ al-tanzīl wa ʿuyūn*

37 I have been able to obtain the worksheets produced by the committee members of the fourth edition for both *Sūrat al-Baqara* and *Sūrat Āl Imrān*.

al-aqāwīl fī wujūh al-taʾwīl, a commentary with *Muʿtazilī* tendencies, is an exception to this rule that is consistently included in all editions. Curiously, the introduction does not perceive *al-Kashshāf* as a *Muʿtazilī* commentary, listing it instead as one of the commentaries dating to the so-called *mutaʾakhkhirīn* period (in the fourth to twelfth centuries) and not as a *Muʿtazilī* commentary.[38] However, the use of *al-Kashshāf* in Sunnī circles is not new. Due to its philological and rhetorical value, *al-Kashshāf* has long been at the center of Sunnī *tafsīr* scholarship.[39] Further to this, Ahmadiyya and Shīʿī literature appears inconsistently across the editions of the work. The first edition sees the presence of three Ahmadiyya translations: the English translations by Maulana Muhammad Ali (1874–1951) and Maulvi Sher Ali (1875–1947), and a Dutch translation of Muhammad Ali's *The Holy Qur'an* written by Soedewo. Ahmadiyya Qur'an translations played a significant role in Indonesia, from the first half of the twentieth century until several decades after Indonesian Independence,[40] and the inclusion of these literatures in the first edition of QT attests to their influence. However, these works are erased from following editions, in which they have no presence at all. As for the Shīʿī commentaries, the second edition includes the *Majmaʿ al-bayān fī tafsīr al-qurʾān* of al-Ṭabrīsī (d. 548/1154) in its bibliography. This commentary retains its position in the third edition, with additional support from al- Ṭabāṭabāʿī's (1904–81) *al-Mizān fī tafsīr al-qurʾān*. The presence of both commentaries may be due to the involvement of Quraish Shihab in the translation committee, as he is a figure who is willing to consider Shīʿī sources, and *al-Mizān fī tafsīr al-qurʾān* is one of the sources he uses in his *Tafsir al-Misbah*. Neither of these commentaries is present in the bibliography of the fourth edition.

38 Departemen Agama Republik Indonesia, i, pp. 40–41.

39 Walid A. Saleh, 'Preliminary Remarks on the Historiography of Tafsir in Arabic: A History of the Book Approach', *Journal of Qur'anic Studies*, 12 (2010), 6–40 (p. 11), https://doi.org/10.3366/E146535911000094X; Walid A. Saleh, 'The Qur'an Commentary of al-Bayḍāwī: A History of *Anwār al-tanzīl*', *Journal of Qur'anic Studies*, 23.1 (2021), 71–102 (p. 72), https://doi.org/10.3366/jqs.2021.0451; Claude Gilliot, 'Exegesis of the Qur'ān: Classical and Medieval', ed. by Jane Dammen McAuliffe, *Encyclopaedia of the Qur'ān* (Leiden; Boston; Köln: Brill, 2002), 99–124 (p. 115).

40 Ahmad Najib Burhani, 'Sectarian Translation of the Quran in Indonesia: The Case of the Ahmadiyya', *Al-Jāmiʿah: Journal of Islamic Studies*, 53.2 (2015), 251–82, https://doi.org/10.14421/ajis.2015.532.251-282; Moch. Nur Ichwan, 'Differing Responses to an Ahmadi Translation and Exegesis: "The Holy Qur'ân" in Egypt and Indonesia', *Archipel*, 2001, 143–61, https://doi.org/10.3406/arch.2001.3668.

This survey has also found that Indonesian sources do not have a substantial role in QT. The introduction acknowledges several Indonesian Qur'an commentaries and translations, both in the national and regional languages. Two commentaries and eleven translations are mentioned explicitly by title and author, and some others—mentioned vaguely—are attributed to various religious communities, such as the Muhammadiyah, Persis, and al-Ittihad Islamijah.[41] However, despite the fact that these works predated QT and ought to have been available to the committee should they have wished to use them, the only Indonesian commentaries included in the bibliography to the first edition were those of Mahmud Yunus, Ahmad Hassan (1887–1958), Hasbi Ash-Shiddieqy (his *An-Nūr*), and Zainuddin Hamidy (1907–57) and Fakhrudin Hs. (b. 1906). Hasbi's second commentary, *al-Bayān,* is the only addition to the bibliography of the second edition, and Quraish Shihab's *al-Misbah* is the only further addition to that of the third edition. It is also worth mentioning that the commentaries by A. Hassan and Zainuddin Hamidy and Fakhruddin Hs. are dropped from the bibliographies of the third and fourth edition. Hamka's (1908–81) lack of involvement in the committee of the first edition made much sense politically (see Chapter Three), and his *al-Azhar* was still in the formation phase during the writing of the first edition, yet the absence of his commentary from the bibliographies of all the following editions is intriguing. In contrast, Hasbi Ash-Shiddieqy's *An-Nur* is included in the bibliography of all editions, and his *al-Bayan* is there from the second edition to the fourth. Quraish Shihab's *Tafsir al-Misbāh* was included in the third edition only a year after its publication in 2001. (The inclusion of Hasbi and Shihab's works in the bibliography gives a clear signal that the works written by individual committee members can have an impact on the text of QT.) Finally, the *Tafsīr al-Munīr,* or otherwise *Maraḥ labīd,* by Muḥammad Nawāwī al-Bantānī (1813–97), a nineteenth-century Indonesian exegete, makes an appearance in the third edition, but is no longer present in the fourth edition—and his work is not even acknowledged in the introduction. This is perhaps surprising, because Nawāwī is a figure with a distinguished reputation in Indonesian Islamic intellectual history, and his works, including *Tafsīr al-Munīr,* are

41 Departemen Agama Republik Indonesia, i, pp. 42; 45.

widely studied in *pesantren* across Java. Despite this, however, it appears that his work failed to make a substantial contribution to QT.

The bibliographies of the various editions of QT point to a particular perception of the hierarchy of Qur'an commentaries held in the Indonesian *tafsīr* tradition. Despite the fact that the Arabic commentaries are typically considered to be of differing merit, they are presented as a single group of prominent authorities in QT—as long as they are approved Sunnī works.[42] In practice, these Arabic commentaries are referred to in a random manner that most of the time seems to depend on the personal choice of the commentator/translator, and there does not seem to be any differentiation between them, in terms of scope and approach. There seems to be no difference whether one refers to al-Ṭabarī's *Jāmiᶜ al-bayān* or *al-Jalālayn,* despite the fact that the two works are very different. In other words, as is typical of the Sunnī *tafsīr* tradition, the multitude of interpretations provided in these different commentaries are viewed as part of a wide range of possible interpretations of the meaning of the Qur'an, from which one can select a view considered suitable to a particular situation. It is this particular hermeneutical perspective that lies behind a common expression found in *tafsīr* in Indonesia, written or oral: *menurut para mufassir...* ('according to the exegetes...').[43]

These Arabic commentaries have clearly been allocated a place at the top of the hierarchy of *tafsīr* sources in the Indonesian *tafsīr* tradition, and were consulted in the initial phrases of the translation process, when the translation teams were seeking to determine meaning. Below them commentaries by Indonesian authors are listed, all of which, in all editions, are written in the Indonesian national language. Not one single commentary written in a regional language makes its way onto the list of sources in any of the editions of QT, despite the fact that some of

42 What is classified as an approved Sunnī work here is not necessarily derived from al-Dhahabī as he writes in his *al-Tafsīr wa al-mufassirūn,* but rather from the gradual development of the *tafsīr* tradition in Indonesia. The works widely read in Indonesia and those classified by al-Dhahabī might be similar, but the emergence, transmission, and preservation of Sunnī *tafsīr* in Indonesia predates his *al-Tafsīr wa al-mufassirūn.*

43 Pink's analysis of the sources used by Quraish Shihab illustrates this phenomenon. Shihab seems to prioritize modern commentaries, but when providing views from classical and pre-modern *tafsīrs*, he refrains from explicitly identifying the commentators and instead leaves them generally unnamed.

them are mentioned in the introduction. This indicates that the primary importance of Indonesian commentaries, in terms of the QT project, lies in the fact that they express the meaning of the Qur'an in Indonesian. These works play a role insofar as they provide a point of comparison. In this context, when it comes to the fourth edition, even though Quraish Shihab's *Al-Qur'an dan Maknanya* is not listed in the bibliography, it may well have been the most influential Indonesian work at the stage when the committee, having agreed on a given verse's meaning, turned its attention to formulating the best Indonesian expression. This hierarchical perception also explains the minor role attributed to *al-Munīr* of Nawāwī al-Bantānī, even though it was written in Arabic. The committee's apparent disregard for his work reflects just how much they value Arabic works from the Middle East above any commentaries produced by Indonesian scholars.[44]

The Indonesian *tafsīr* tradition's reliance on Sunnī sources stretches back to the seventeenth century. Daneshgar correctly suggests that the majority of Qur'an commentaries written in the Malay-Indonesian world before the nineteenth century and early twentieth century relied heavily on classical Arabic works, such as the *tafsīrs* of al-Jalālayn, al-Bayḍāwī (d. 791/1388), and al-Khāzin (d. 725/1324).[45] Thus, when it comes to Indonesian-authored *tafsīrs*, the anonymous manuscript of *al-Kahf* drew from al-Baghawī (d. 516/1122), al-Khāzin, and al-Bayḍāwī,[46] while ᶜAbd al-Raᵓūf al-Singkīlī's (1615–93) *Tarjumān al-mustafīd* relied much on *Tafsīr al-Jalālayn* as well as al-Bayḍāwī and al-Khāzin.[47] In the nineteenth century, Nawāwī al-Bantanī's *al-Tafsīr al-munīr* referred to Fakhr al-Dīn

44 Bruinessen suggests that the modernization of the *pesantren* and *surau* in Java and Sumatra effectively displaced locally authored works, in favor of Arabic sources. Martin van Bruinessen, 'Kitab Kuning: Books in Arabic Script Used in the Pesantren Milieu: Comments on a New Collection in the KITLV Library,' *Bijdragen Tot de Taal-, Land- En Volkenkunde* 146, no. 2/3 (1990), p. 239.

45 Majid Daneshgar, 'The Study of Qurᵓān Interpretation in the Malay-Indonesian World: A Select Bibliography', in *The Qurᵓān in Malay-Indonesian World: Context and Interpretation*, ed. by Majid Daneshgar, Peter G. Riddell, and Andrew Rippin (London, New York: Routledge, 2016), pp. 7–21.

46 Peter G. Riddell, 'Classical Tafsīr in the Malay World: Emerging Trends in Seventeenth-Century Malay Exegetical Writing', in *The Qurᵓān in Malay-Indonesian World: Context and Interpretation*, ed. by Majid Daneshgar, Andrew Rippin, and Peter G. Riddell (London, New York: Routledge, 2016), p. 26.

47 Riddell, 'Classical Tafsīr in the Malay World: Emerging Trends in Seventeenth-Century Malay Exegetical Writing', p. 30.

al-Rāzī's *al-Futūḥāt al-ilāhiyya* and *al-Tafsīr al-Kabīr*, as well as *Sirāj al-munīr, Tanwīr al-miqbās,* and the *tafsīr* of Abū al-Suᶜūd (d. 982/1574). Anthony Johns suggests that *al-Tafsīr al-Kabīr* was the major source for *Maraḥ labīd,*[48] and, in the same period, Ṣaliḥ Darāt mentions that both *al-Jalālayn* and *al-Tafsīr al-Kabīr* were among his sources.[49] The recurring presence of al-Bayḍāwī and al-Rāzī is important, because it indicates that the commentaries that became central to Sunnī *tafsīr* scholarship in the Middle Eastern heartlands also found their way into Southeast Asia and, in particular, Indonesia. Given this legacy, the choice of the particular selection of commentaries mentioned in QT makes perfect sense.

It is also interesting to note that, although it was one of the most prominent Qur'an commentaries in the twentieth century, Ibn Kathīr's *tafsīr* is not mentioned in the bibliography of the first edition of QT; it is only included from the second edition onwards. Nevertheless, the significance of its omission should not be overstated, and does not in fact suggest that this commentary did not play a role in the first edition as well. Not only is the bibliography to the first edition not necessarily exhaustive, but Ibn Kathīr's *tafsīr* is ubiquitous throughout the Islamic world, and has been one of the most common sources used by those writing commentaries and translations in Indonesia since the twentieth century,[50] not long after it first came to prominence.[51] Although Indonesian commentaries written before the twentieth century, such as the anonymous *al-Kahf,* and *Tarjumān al-mustafīd,* and *Tafsīr al-Munīr* do not seem to rely on Ibn Kathīr, Indonesian *mufassir*s writing in the mid-twentieth century, such as Hasbi Ash-Shiddieqy and Zainuddin Hamidy-Fakhruddin Hs. did. Given this, it is highly likely that Ibn

48 Anthony H. Johns, 'Qurʾān Exegesis in the Malay-Indonesian World: An Introductory Survey', in *Approaches to The Qur'an in Contemporary Indonesia.*, ed. by Abdullah Saeed (Oxford: Oxford University Press, 2005), pp. 17–41 (p. 28).

49 Cf. Abdul Mustaqim, 'The Epistemology of Javanese Qurʾanic Exegesis: A Study of Ṣāliḥ Darat's Fayḍ al-Raḥmān', *Al-Jāmi'ah: Journal of Islamic Studies,* 55.2 (2017), 357–90 (pp. 368; 380), https://doi.org/10.14421/ajis.2017.552.357-390.

50 van Bruinessen, 'Kitab Kuning: Books in Arabic Script Used in the Pesantren Milieu: Comments on a New Collection in the KITLV Library', p. 253.

51 Johanna Pink, 'The Fig, the Olive, and the Cycles of Prophethood: Q 95:1–3 and the Image of History in Early 20th-Century Quraʾnic Exegesis', in *Islamic Studies Today: Essays in Honor of Andrew Rippin,* ed. by Majid Daneshgar and Walid A. Saleh (Leiden; Boston: Brill), pp. 317–38 (p. 337).

Kathīr's writings have had some impact on the content of the first edition, despite not being mentioned in the bibliography (especially given that Hasbi Ash-Shiddieqy was a member of the translation team).

The rise to pre-eminence of Ibn Kathīr's *tafsīr* during the twentieth century, which may be connected to Rashīd Riḍā (1865–1935),[52] opens up another interesting facet of the hermeneutical background of QT, given that the connection of this Egyptian scholar with Indonesian Islamic scholarship is widely recognized.[53] Saleh has suggested that Ibn Kathīr came to prominence late in the twentieth century, following the rising influence of Salafi and Azhari hermeneutics on the Qur'an at the expense of the classical Sunnī-Ashᶜarite hermeneutics represented by scholars such as al-Bayḍāwī, al-Rāzī, and al-Zamakhsharī.[54] The arrival of Ibn Kathīr's *tafsīr* in Indonesia at this point demonstrates the growing importance of the Cairo-Indonesia connection in nineteenth-century Indonesian Islamic intellectual history.

The Cairo connection also introduced Indonesian *tafsīr* scholarship to modern developments in *tafsīr* in Egypt as well as the wider Arabo-Islamic intellectual sphere. Daneshgar suggests that commentaries written in Indonesia during the twentieth century bear witness to an influx of modern views, methodologies, and approaches from throughout the Arab world, especially Egypt, through the works of figures such as Muḥammad ᶜAbduh (1849–1905), Rashīd Riḍā, Ṭanṭawī Jawharī (1870–1940), and Sayyid Quṭb (1906–66).[55] Indonesian translators and exegetes such as Zainuddin Hamidy and Fakhruddin Hs., Hasbi Ash-Shiddieqy, and Hamka read the new works with great enthusiasm. It is no wonder, then, if traces of the intellectual legacy of these scholars can be found in QT. The continuing influence of al-Azhar can also be seen in the fact that a number of the additional commentaries and *ᶜulūm al-Qurʾān* literature introduced in the second and particularly the third editions of QT were

52 Rashīd Riḍā is the editor for the publication of Ibn Kathīr's commentary that was sponsored by the royal house of the Ḥijāz, al-Imām ᶜAbd Allāh ibn Saᶜūd. See Saleh, 'Preliminary Remarks on the Historiography of Tafsir in Arabic: A History of the Book Approach', p. 15.

53 Michael Francis Laffan, *Islamic Nationhood and Colonial Indonesia: The Umma Below the Winds* (London, New York: RoutledgeCurzon, 2003), p. 114.

54 Saleh, 'Preliminary Remarks on the Historiography of Tafsir in Arabic: A History of the Book Approach', p. 10; Saleh, 'The Qur'an Commentary of al-Bayḍāwī', p. 73.

55 Daneshgar, p. 21.

published in Cairo. This makes sense, given that graduates of al-Azhar consistently held important positions on the committee.

Saleh has posited that, in the context of Arabic Qur'an commentaries, the Salafi-Azharī[56] school of hermeneutics is involved in a clear struggle for ideological supremacy with the classical-Ashᶜarī school, but in Indonesia, Ibn Kathīr and al-Ṭabarī, representing the first school, and al-Bayḍāwī, al-Rāzī, and al-Zamakhsharī, representing the second, form a single group of prominent *tafsīr* authorities, as mentioned earlier. Indonesian *tafsīr* scholarship to this day does not approach the two schools as having an antagonistic relationship. This means that modern Egyptian *tafsīr* works might not have the same reception among Indonesian readers as they do elsewhere, for they require a willingness to adopt a reformist/modern stance—a position not every Indonesian scholar agrees with, especially those who are traditionalists. Nevertheless, the presence of a number of Azhar graduates on the various QT committees has meant that these more modern trends have naturally seeped into the pool of sources referenced during the production of QT. In short, as far as QT is concerned, the inclusion of such a wide variety of commentaries in the bibliography shows that the translation is a composite of several trends in the *tafsīr* tradition, and does not follow one single interpretive thread.

Conclusion

In an interview I held with Muchlis M. Hanafi, the director of the LPMQ, he stated that the interpretive authority of QT belongs to the *ulama*, whereas the state is merely the facilitator. This statement, I suggest, tells us a lot about the hermeneutical processes at work in QT. The collective nature of the translation generates an idea of consensus, which is why QT has been considered as having greater authority than individual translations. Indeed, QT has paradoxically marginalized the individual contributions of committee members by

56 One should not assume that Salafi and Azharī ideas are identical. In this issue, the Qur'anic hermeneutics developed by Azharī scholars follows the Taymiyyan school. Saleh argues that classical Sunnī *tafsīr* scholarship was primarily built upon philology, whereas Ibn Taymiyya directed his energy towards the Qur'an and *hadīth*. For more on this, see Saleh, 'Preliminary Remarks on the Historiography of Tafsir in Arabic: A History of the Book Approach', p. 10.

implementing a three-step procedure, moving from individual research and translation, to committee consensus, to final authorization. QT's status as a collaborative, collective work also means that the translation in many ways reflects ideas held by the Indonesian *ulama* about how to conceptualize translation and how to conduct it. It is clear that the consensus of those involved is that the translation of the Qur'an should be closely tied to the source text, as evidenced by the theoretical exposition of the genre of Qur'an translation put forward in paratextual elements such as the introduction, and the particular role assumed by the *gandul* method, despite its gradually waning influence. Though the translation team seem to define Qur'an translation as a specific genre that is different from *tafsīr*, they certainly situate it within the *tafsīr* tradition. *Tafsīr* has a strong presence in QT both at the textual and subtextual level, effectively making this Qur'an translation a translation of a composite text that comprises the Qur'an and *tafsīr*. We can also say that QT is a product of the *ulama*, insofar as they rely on tradition and its sources perfectly situate it within the prolonged history of the *tafsīr* tradition. Furthermore, as a collective work, QT embodies a shared hermeneutical ideology that values the classical Sunnī tradition and modern Arabic commentaries above any Indonesian commentaries (including commentaries by an Indonesian written in Arabic).

Zadeh suggests that 'translation is not an either/or proposition, but rather represents a continuum in the push and pull of meaning and its form.'[57] The hermeneutical processes at work in the production of QT demonstrate exactly this. QT is a work that reflects the push and pull between attempts to distance translation from *tafsīr* and to present both translation and interpretation simultaneously, and between the ideal of translation as being tied as closely as possible to the source text and the competing ideal that it should communicate with its readers more freely through the idiomatic use of the target language.

57 Zadeh, p. 13.

5. Between Official Translation and the Official Reform

This chapter and the following one deal with the translation output of the *Al-Qur'an dan Terjemahnya* project. In this chapter, I analyze the translation choices made by the committee at the level of phrases and diction by analyzing their translation of several selected verses and exploring how these take into account the development of Islamic thought in Indonesia. The translations provided in the various different editions of QT are compared to developments that have taken place over time in discussions on Islamic thought in Indonesia. However, this is undertaken with the caveat that this study aims to understand QT as an official state project and, accordingly, the developments in Islamic thought that are taken into consideration in the analysis are those that have been influenced or fashioned by the state. This qualification leads us to consider the concept of official reform of Islamic affairs as understood within the Indonesian context. To what extent do the translations provided in the various editions of QT resonate with the ideas developed as part of official Islamic discourse in Indonesia? This is the question that will be discussed in this chapter.

Official attempts to implement reforms to Islamic affairs in Indonesia cover a broad spectrum, including the bureaucratization of *ḥajj* and Islamic charity (*zakāh*), reform of the Islamic legal and court system, and reforms in Islamic education. This volume is restricted to the study of reforms in intellectual dynamics, that is to developments in Islamic thought, on the basis that the content of QT is interpretive in nature and thus might reflect such changes. The discussion here is limited to two fields of reform, namely reforms in Islamic education and law. Education reforms are manifested through state control over the Islamic higher education system and changes to the curriculum, and are reflected in

 https://doi.org/10.11647/OBP.0289.05

the history of state Islamic higher education institutes in Indonesia (STAIN, IAIN, and UIN).[1] The most notable effects of education reforms have been the introduction of a historical approach to religious study and the reinterpretation of several key Islamic concepts.[2] In the field of *tafsīr* especially, education reforms have led to the emergence of new insights into the interpretation of the Qur'an, while legal reforms have resulted in the introduction of laws that entail substantial modifications to the classical law transmitted through traditional *fiqh*. In both cases, it is of clear interest to explore how QT might render the verses relevant to this field.

This chapter focuses primarily on a selection of verses that address two themes, namely gender and religious pluralism. They include verses on marriage and polygamy (Q 4:3), the political rights of women (Q 4:34), creation (Q 4:1) and religious tolerance or pluralism (Q 1:7 and Q 3:19). However, it is necessary to clarify that these are by no means the only verses pertaining to reforms in education and Islamic law, but simply a small sample. These verses have been chosen for analysis here because they illustrate how the religious discourse of the state has influenced the ways particular Qur'anic key words are translated. For example, this chapter discusses the issue of political rights of women raised by rendering a particular word, *qawwāmūn*, as either '*pemimpin*' ('leader') or '*pelindung*' ('protector/guardian'), because one of these translations has been used to support the idea that women should not become political leaders. On the other hand, this chapter will not address, for example, the issues surrounding inheritance raised by Q 4:11 as these do not pertain to translational problems per se. This chapter will also discuss whether the Qur'an acknowledges other religions in the case of Q 3:19, as the debates on this are based in the question of whether to translate the term *al-islām* in this verse as either referring to the institutionalized religion of Islam or as an act of submission to God regardless of religion.

---

1 Moch. Nur Ichwan, 'Official Reform of Islam: State Islam and the Ministry of Religious Affairs in Contemporary Indonesia, 1966–2004' (unpublished doctoral dissertation, Tilburg University, 2006), pp. 160–62, https://pure.uvt.nl/portal/en/publications/official-reform-of-islam(f07a60f1-bf55-4979-8ea1-bab6e45a42ac).html; Ronald A. Lukens-Bull, *Islamic Higher Education in Indonesia: Continuity and Conflict* (New York: Palgrave Macmillan, 2013), p. 44.

2 Abdullah Saeed, 'Towards Religious Tolerance Through Reform in Islamic Education: The Case of The State Institute of Islamic Studies of Indonesia', *Indonesia and the Malay World*, 27.79 (1999), 177–91 (p. 185); Lukens-Bull, pp. 47–61.

However, it will not consider the occurrence of an essentially identical issue in Q 2:62, i.e., the question of whether Hinduism and Buddhism belong to the category of *ahl al-kitāb* ('the people of the book'), because the issue is not affected by the way we translate this verse, and the discussion depends on the way the verse is understood or contextualized in a more general sense. Additionally, gender issues are given particular attention in this study, following the statement of the current director of Lajnah Pentashihan Mushaf Al-Qur'an, (LPMQ, The Qur'anic Text Review Board) of feminist critiques of QT.[3]

The following analysis identifies the hermeneutical problems presented by each verse and juxtaposes the renderings of the various editions of QT with other materials produced as part of the state's wider reform project. When it comes to legal reform, the relevant materials are the 1974 Marriage Law and the 1991 Kompilasi Hukum Islam (KHI, The Compilation of Islamic Law). When it comes to Islamic educational reform, this study takes into consideration a number of relevant intellectual contributions that are directly or indirectly related to attempts by the state to shape religious discourse. The materials that can be directly related to this include *Wanita Islam Indonesia dalam Kajian Tekstual dan Kontekstual* (Indonesian Muslim Women in Textual and Contextual Studies, henceforth: *Wanita Islam Indonesia*) edited by Marcoes-Natsir and Meuleman (1993), an edited volume comprising papers presented at a conference on gender issues organized by MORA,[4] and *Rekonstruksi Metodologis Wacana Kesetaraan Gender dalam Islam* (Methodological Reconstruction of the Gender Equality Discourse in Islam, henceforth: *Rekonstruksi Metodologis*), a volume that came out of a joint project between the State Islamic Institute (currently: State Islamic University) Sunan Kalijaga Yogyakarta and McGill-ICIHEP.[5] 'Indirectly related materials,' refers here to the intellectual output of individuals who at some point were involved in state-run or state-controlled Islamic education projects.

3 Personal interview with Muchlis M. Hanafi.

4 *Wanita Islam Indonesia dalam Kajian Tekstual dan Kontekstual: Kumpulan Makalah Seminar*, ed. by Lies M Marcoes-Natsir and Johan Hendrik Meuleman, INIS, 1 (Jakarta: INIS, 1993).

5 Siti Ruhaini Dzuhayatin and others, *Rekonstruksi Metodologis Wacana Kesetaraan Gender dalam Islam*, PSW IAIN Sunan Kalijaga Yogyakarta (Yogyakarta: Pustaka Pelajar, 2002).

Q 4:1, The Creation Verse

The interpretation of Qur'anic verses relating to the creation of humankind is one of the focal points of contention for Muslim feminists, and this is especially the case for Q 4:1, as this particular verse has been used to legitimize gender inequality. The issue is rooted in the verse's suggestion that creation started with a man, Adam, and that his female companion, Ḥawa (Eve), was created after and from him. This led to a view that situates men as superior to women, whereas women are servants of men.

يـٰأيها ٱلناس ٱتقوا ربكم ٱلذى خلقكم من نفس وٰحدة وخلق منها زوجها...

> People, be mindful of your Lord, who created you from a single soul, and from it created its mate...

The hermeneutical problem in this verse revolves around complexities in understanding what the verse associates *nafs wāḥida* ('a single soul') with, what the pronoun *hā* in *minhā* ('from it') refers to, and what *zawjahā* ('its mate') means. Most Qur'an commentaries identify *nafs wāḥida* as referring to Adam, thus making him God's first human creation. The pronoun *hā* in *minhā* is considered to refer back to *nafs*, while *zawjahā* is considered to refer to Ḥawa. When it comes to the phrase *minhā*, Qur'an commentaries almost always provide further identification about which part of Adam Ḥawa was created from. Referring to a *ḥadīth* transmitted by al-Bukhārī (810–70), Ibn Kathīr (d. 1372), for example, asserts that she was created from Adam's rib.[6] Thus, according to this reading of the verse, God created Adam first, and from Adam's rib He created his female pair, namely Ḥawa.

However, there is another way to understand the verse. Fakhr al-Dīn al-Rāzī (d. 1210) presents two lines of interpretations in his *Mafātīḥ al-ghayb*;[7] the first is the one mentioned above, and the second is the view of Abū Muslim al-Aṣfahānī (1277–1365), who suggests that *minhā* does not refer to a part of Adam's body, but rather to a material from which Adam was created. Accordingly, Ḥawa was a creature formed of the same material as Adam, rather than from his rib. However, al-Rāzī provides this view only to criticize it. He argues that viewing

6 ʿImād al-Dīn Abū al-Fidāʾ Ismāʿīl Ibn Kathīr, *Al-Tafsīr al-qurʾān al-ʿaẓīm*, 15 vols (Giza: Muʾassasa Qurṭuba, 2000), iii, p. 333.

7 Fakhr al-Dīn al-Rāzī, *Mafātīḥ al-ghayb*, 32 vols (Beirut: Dār al-Fikr, 1981), ix, p. 167.

Ḥawa as being created from the same material as Adam would mean that human beings were created not from *nafs wāḥida* ('a single self or soul') but *nafsāyn* ('two selves'). Despite this criticism, some Qur'an commentators of the later generations, such as ᶜAbduh (1849–1905), Rashīd Riḍā (1865–1935), al-Qāsimī (d. 1332), and al-Ṭabāṭabāᶜī (1903–81), prefer this second view. Rashīd Riḍā, for example, suggests that the rib story cannot be justified on the basis of the Qur'anic text, and that commentators took it from the Old Testament.[8]

The first interpretation, however, remains the prevalent one, and has been transmitted and reproduced within *tafsīr* across generations. It is therefore no surprise that QT, in principle, follows this interpretive view, albeit with some shifts between the different editions that deserve a closer look.

First edition	*Hai sekalian manusia, bertakwalah kepada Tuhan-mu jang telah mentjiptakan kamu dari* **seorang diri (Adam)**, *dan dari padanja Allah mentjiptakan* **isterinja (Hawa)**...
	[O mankind, be mindful of your Lord, who created you from **a single self (Adam)**, and from it Allah created **his wife (Hawa)**...]
Second/Saudi edition	*Hai sekalian manusia, bertakwalah kepada Tuhan-mu yang telah menciptakan kamu dari* **diri yang satu**, *dan dari padanya Allah menciptakan* **isterinya**...
	[O mankind, be mindful of your Lord, who created you from **a self that is one**, and from it Allah created **its wife...**]
Third edition	*Wahai manusia! Bertakwalah kepada Tuhanmu yang telah menciptakan kamu dari* **diri yang satu (Adam)**, *dan (Allah) menciptakan* **pasangannya (Hawa) dari (diri)nya**...
	[O mankind! Be mindful of your Lord, who created you from **a self that is one (Adam)**, and (Allah) created **his wife (Hawa) from it/him(self)...**]
Fourth edition	*Wahai manusia, bertakwalah kepada Tuhanmu yang telah menciptakanmu dari* **diri yang satu (Adam)** *dan Dia menciptakan darinya* **pasangannya (Hawa)**...
	[O mankind, be mindful of your Lord, who created you from **a self that is one (Adam)**, and He created from it/him **its/ his wife (Hawa)...**]

8 Rashīd Riḍā, *Tafsīr Al-Manār*, 11 vols (Cairo: Dār al-Manār, 1947), iv, p. 330.

The shifts between these editions in this particular verse are abundant. The first edition renders *nafs wāḥida* as *'seorang diri'* (lit. 'a single self') and identifies the self with Adam by placing his name in parenthesis immediately afterwards. The word *zawjahā* is translated as *'istrinya'* ('his wife') and likewise identified as Ḥawa in parenthesis. Accordingly, the pronoun *hā* in *minhā,* in this context, is unambiguously read as referring to *nafs,* which stands for Adam. The second/Saudi edition changes the translation of *nafs wāḥida* from *'seorang diri'* (lit. 'a single self') into *'diri yang satu'* (lit. 'self that is one'). This edition does not explicitly identify *nafs wāḥida* as Adam and *zawjaha* as Hawa. The third edition follows the Saudi edition's rendering of *nafs wāḥida* as *'diri yang satu',* but reinserts the parenthesis identifying the *nafs* as Adam. The translation of *zawjahā* also shifts from *'istrinya'* ('his wife') to a more generic word *'pasangannya'* ('his pair') and again qualifies this with an additional parenthesis identifying this 'pair' as Hawa. There is also a shift in the translation of *minhā* from *'dari padanya'* (lit. 'from her') to *'dari (diri)nya'* (lit. 'from itself'), most probably to emphasize the idea that the pronoun *hā* refers back to the feminine word *nafs* instead of Adam. The fourth edition only makes one change to the translation provided in the third, a shift in the presentation of *minhā* from *'dari (dirinya)nya'* (lit. 'from itself') to *'darinya'* (lit. 'from her').

The shifts in the translation of this particular verse are commented on in the footnotes that accompany this verse. The first, the second, and the Saudi editions have an identical note for the phrase *khalaqa minhā zawjaha,* which seems to resemble the commentary on this verse provided by al-Rāzi in *Mafātīḥ al-ghayb*:

> *Maksud dari padanya menurut jumhur mufassirin ialah dari bagian tubuh (tulang rusuk) Adam a.s. berdasarkan hadis riwayat Bukhari dan Muslim. Disamping itu ada pula yang menafsirkan dari padanja ialah dari unsur yang serupa, yakni tanah, yang daripadanya Adam a.s. diciptakan.*

> [The meaning of it [the phrase] according to the majority of commentators is a body part (the rib) of Adam as. based on a hadith transmitted by Bukhari and Muslim. In addition to that, others interpret the phrase as coming from the same origin, which was soil, from which Adam as. was created.]

The fourth edition introduces a new note that is placed after the phrase *rijālan kathīran wa nisā*ᵓ ('countless men and women') that occurs later in Q 4:1, which reads:

> *Ayat ini menegaskan bahwa Nabi Adam a.s. dan Hawa tidak diciptakan melalui proses evolusi hayati seperti makhluk hidup lainnya, tetapi diciptakan secara khusus seorang diri, lalu diciptakan pasangannya dari dirinya. Mekanismenya tidak dapat dijelaskan secara sains. Barulah anak-anaknya lahir dari proses biologis secara berpasang-pasangan sesuai kehendak-Nya*
>
> [This verse emphasizes that the Prophet Adam and Eve were not created through a natural evolution like other creatures, but [Adam] was created by a specific means as one self, and [God] then created from him his spouse. The mechanism cannot be scientifically explained. Only afterwards were their descendants born through the biological process in pairs following His wish.]

This issue has been the subject of disputes between scholars in Indonesia. Yunahar Ilyas (1956–2020), for example, subscribes to the traditional view on the verse. In his MA thesis, defended at the Institut Agama Islam Negeri (currently: Universitas Islam Negeri) Sunan Kalijaga Yogyakarta, he supported the association of *nafs wāḥida* with Adam and *zawjahā* with Ḥawa. He admits that Q 4:1 does not give clear information about the creation of Adam and Ḥawa. However, he derives that association from an intratextual comparison of Q 4:1 with other verses. Q 35:11,[9] Q 37:11,[10] and Q 15:26[11] all reveal that the first human being was created from dust or clay, while Q 3:59[12] says that Adam was created from dust; hence, he argues, Adam, the first human being, was created from dust. Adam, in fact, is the only creature the Qur'an tells us was made of dust. When it comes to the phrase *minhā zawjahā*, Ilyas follows al-Rāzī's view, and considers that if Ḥawa was created from dust in the same way that Adam was, it would contradict the notion of *nafs wāḥida*.[13]

Nasaruddin Umar, in contrast, contends that associating the *nafs wāḥida* with Adam is problematic. That is because the Qur'an, in all of its 295 uses of the word *nafs*, is never definitively using it to refer to Adam. According to him, Q 42:11 relates the term to the origin of animals. He employs a philological analysis and concludes that the

---

9 It is God who created you from dust and later from a drop of fluid [...]

10 So [Prophet], ask the disbelievers: is it harder to create them than other beings We have created? We created them from sticky clay.

11 We created man out of dried clay formed from dark mud.

12 In God's eyes Jesus is just like Adam: He created him from dust, said to him, 'Be', and he was.

13 Yunahar Ilyas, *Feminisme dalam Kajian Tafsir Al-Qur'an Klasik dan Kontemporer* (Yogyakarta: Pustaka Pelajar, 1997), pp. 108; 113.

phrase *nafs wāḥida* is mentioned in its indefinite form (*nakira*) in Q 4:1, and this suggests that it refers to the first resource from which Adam was created, not to Adam himself. For that reason, he translates the phrase as *'diri yang satu'*, 'a single self', or on another occasion as 'a single person', without explicitly linking this to Adam. Additionally, he says, the word *zawj* could grammatically be either masculine or feminine, on the basis of which he argues that in Q 4:1 it means *'pasangan genetis jenis manusia'* ('genetic-pair of human species').[14] To support his argument, Umar refers to the views of Muḥammad ᶜAbduh who, in his *al-Manār*, also refuses to associate *nafs wāḥida* with Adam, and agrees with al-Aṣfahānī's view that *minhā* refers to the same source as Adam. Umar also refers to al-Zamakhsharī's (d. 538/1144) view that the conjunction *wa* ('and') in *wa khalaqa minhā* refers to some hidden clause, and should thus be interpreted as reading *min nafs wāḥida ansha*ᵓ*ahā* ('from the same resource, He created her').[15]

Quraish Shihab, in *Wanita Islam Indonesia*, presents both interpretations, citing key figures in support of each. However, he seems to agree with Rashīd Riḍā, suggesting that the Qur'an does not provide clear information indicating that Ḥawa was created from Adam's rib or that she was created differently from him. Hence, he suggests it is best to understand the rib narrative as a figurative expression.[16] Zaitunah Subhan and Nasaruddin Umar are in the same camp as Shihab in this regard.[17] In his discussion of this aspect of Q 4:1, Umar refers to al-Rāzi's citation of Abū Muslim al-Aṣfahānī's opinion that the phrase *minhā* does not refer to Adam's rib, but instead means that Hawa was created from the same original material as Adam, i.e., *turāb* ('soil'). He criticizes al-Rāzi for not thoroughly elaborating on this view but instead presenting al-Aṣfahānī's argument only to criticize it, while in fact, in

---

14 Nasaruddin Umar, *Argumen Kesetaraan Gender Perspektif Al-Qur'ān* (Jakarta: Paramadina, 1999), p. 174.

15 Umar, *Argumen Kesetaraan Gender Perspektif Al-Qur'ān*, pp. 236–45; Nasaruddin Umar, *Ketika Fikih Membela Perempuan* (Jakarta: Gramedia, 2014), pp. 135–36.

16 M. Quraish Shihab, 'Konsep Wanita Menurut Quran, Hadis, dan Sumber-Sumber Ajaran Islam', in *Wanita Islam Indonesia dalam Kajian Tekstual dan Kontekstual: Kumpulan Makalah Seminar*, ed. by Lies M Marcoes-Natsir and Johan Hendrik Meuleman, INIS, 1 (Jakarta: INIS, 1993), pp. 3–18 (p. 6).

17 Zaitunah Subhan, *Tafsir Kebencian: Studi Bias Gender dalam Tafsir Qur'an* (Yogyakarta: LKiS, 1999), p. 173.

Umar's opinion, al-Aṣfahānī's view could serve as a valid comparative argument for a majority interpretation.[18]

At this point, it is tempting to suggest that there is a push and pull going on between the interpretation provided in QT and developments in Indonesian Islamic intellectual discourse on the creation issue which is reflected in the shifts in translation in the various editions. The first edition is clear; it associates *nafs wāḥida* with Adam and *zawjahā* with Ḥawa, thereby subscribing to the view of the majority of Qur'an commentaries. The second and Saudi editions then remove both associations, leaving the words unidentified. An individual familiar with the dispute about *nafs wāḥida*—whether it refers to Adam or the material from which Adam was created—might entertain the idea that translating the phrase literally, without any further elaboration, indicates a preference for the latter option. Additionally, the shift from *'seorang diri'*, which has a strong personal nuance, to *'diri yang satu'*, which could be considered impersonal, could be interpreted as a shift from associating *nafs wāḥida* with Adam, the view of the majority, to the material from which Adam was created, i.e., the view proposed by ᶜAbduh, Riḍā, al-Qāsimī, and Umar.[19] (And it is worth noting at this point that the commentaries of ᶜAbduh, Riḍā and al-Qāsimī are all listed in the bibliography of this edition of QT.) However, the third and the fourth editions seemingly backtrack and explicitly reassert the association of Adam and Hawa with *nafs wāḥida* and *zawjahā,* in a move that seems to confirm QT's conformity with the traditional majority consensus.

Despite this apparent change, I contend that in this case QT is actually consistent in its aim to subscribe to the theological views of the majority. Although the shifts in the translation of this verse might seem to be of significant import, in fact they are not. The removal of the explicit association of Adam and Ḥawa with the phrases *nafs wāḥida* and *zawjahā,* and the shift from *'seorang diri'* to *'diri yang satu'* in the second/Saudi edition does not, in fact, reflect a substantial theological or interpretive shift, because both editions retain the identical footnote

18 Umar, *Argumen Kesetaraan Gender Perspektif Al-Qur'ān*, p. 240.

19 Zaitunah Subhan observed that the shift from *'seorang diri'* to *'diri yang satu'* also occurred in *Al-Qur'an dan Tafsirnya*. She argues that, with this shift, this commentary accords with an interpretation that sees *nafs wāḥida* as the material from which Adam was created. See Subhan, p. 55.

found in the first edition. Even though the footnote does mention al-Aṣfahānī's alternative reading, we can deduce that this interpretation was considered marginal from the fact it was relegated to the footnote, rather than inserted into the main text, as the interventions relating to Adam and Ḥawa were. Likewise, the shift from *'seorang diri'* to *'diri yang satu'* does not indicate a move towards the impersonal nuance of the word, but rather demonstrates the tendency to adopt a more literal approach in translation, according to which the noun-adjective construction (*nafs wāḥida*) is rendered into a phrase in the Indonesian language that uses the same structure (*'diri yang satu'*).

On the other hand, the shift from the use of *'istri'* ('wife') to *'pasangan'* ('spouse'/'pair') to translate *zawj* in the third edition might appear to have rather more significant interpretive implications. The word *Istri* refers to the marital relationship, and it is a feminine form. *Pasangan,* on the other hand, is genderless and suggests a more primordial relationship between men and women, a concept which Nasaruddin Umar calls 'a genetic-pair of the human species' (*'pasangan genetis spesies manusia'*).[20] Furthermore, the absence of any footnotes on this point in this edition could be read as implying that the QT committee at this point may no longer have found the classical commentary on this verse relevant, and therefore abandoned it. This does, indeed, seems to be the case, until one recognizes that *'diri yang satu'* as the translation of *nafs wāḥida* in the third edition of QT is associated with Adam, and *zawjahā,* although translated as a genderless *'pasangan',* is connected to Hawa. Therefore, this different wording cannot be seen as an avoidance of making explicit associations, in order to reflect the ambiguity of the original text of the Qur'an. The removal of the footnote also does not reflect an interpretive shift, but is instead the result of attempts to produce a shorter, more compact translation.[21] Overall, the changes made to the translation of this verse in the third edition do not reflect an interpretive reorientation. Finally, the fourth edition essentially follows the third edition, but

---

20 Nasaruddin Umar, *Argumen Kesetaraan Gender Perspektif Al-Qur'ān,* p. 174.

21 Hamam Faizin suggests that the removal of the footnote is more than technical. Instead, it shows that the committee wants to shut down disputes and rejects the idea that Hawa was created from a part of Adam's body. I found his argument uncompelling because he does not propose any evidence as to why the removal of the footnote should mean that the committee supports one view and rejects the other. He does not analyze the actual translation closely either. Hamam Faizin, *Sejarah Penerjemahan Al-Quran di Indonesia* (Ciputat: Gaung Persada, 2022), p. 320.

adds one more change: it includes a footnote that not only restates the traditional view on the creation of Adam and Ḥawa, but also poses a response to scientific ideas on evolution which, in principle, ignore or reject the idea of divine creation.

In general, the rendering of key words, the addition of material in parentheses, and the use of footnotes all indicate the reliance of QT on the majority positions put forward in pre-modern Qur'an commentaries, and demonstrate an indifference to the alternative, progressive interpretation of Q 4:1 put forward by modern commentators and Muslim feminist scholars. Here, I agree with Shihab, who suggests that QT follows this line of interpretation because it reflects the view of the majority.[22] Despite all the shifts between the editions of QT, they consistently subscribe to the traditional view, suggesting that the first human being created was Adam, and Hawa was generated from part of his body. Al-Ṭabarī (d. 311/923), Ibn Kathīr, al-Qurṭubī (d. 671/1272), al-Zamakhsharī, al-Baghawī (d. 516/1122), and al-Ṣuyūṭī (d. 911/1505), unanimously associate the word *nafs* with Adam and *zawj* with Ḥawa, and some mention the *riwāya* which explains that Ḥawa was created from the rib of Adam when he was sleeping. Although Riḍā and al-Qāsimī are named in the bibliography of all editions of QT, it is evident that the alternative reading promoted by these authors has not affected the translation of this verse. Accordingly, the official reforms made in Islamic education and thought in this case have not been accommodated by QT, insofar as the alternative, modernist reading of this verse is essentially rejected.

Q 4:3, Marriage and Polygamy

The Islamic view on polygamy revolves around the interpretation of Q 4:3:

وإن خفتم ألا تقسطوا فى ٱليتٰمىٰ فٱنكحوا ما طاب لكم من ٱلنساء مثنىٰ وثلٰث وربٰع فإن خفتم ألا تعدلوا
فوٰحدة أو ما ملكت أيمٰنكم ذٰلك أدنىٰ ألا تعولوا

> If you fear that you will not deal fairly with orphan girls, you may marry whichever [other] women seem to you, two, three, or four. If you fear that you cannot be equitable [to them], then marry only one, or your slave(s): that is more likely to make you avoid bias.

22 Shihab, p. 5.

A first glance at this verse reveals that it deals with two subjects, orphaned girls (*al-yatāmā*) and women (*al-nisā*ᵓ). The word *al-yatāmā* generally includes both boys and girls, but the historical context of the verse, as will be discussed later, and the textual context of this part of the verse—which deals with marriage—indicate that this verse refers specifically to orphaned girls. When it comes to the treatment of this verse by the classical *mufassirūn*, most commentators explain the marriage-related issues it touches on in terms of their historical and textual context.

Al-Ṭabarī writes about four different events that are considered to provide historical context for the revelation of Q 4:3; one of which might have relatively different interpretive consequences to the others. All the events, however, share one basic principle in that they deal with the wealth and marriage of orphans. Later Qur'an commentaries mostly report only one of these events. They recount that ᶜUrwa ibn Zubayr asked ᶜĀᵓisha, one of Muhammad's wives, about the verse. In her response, ᶜĀᵓisha mentioned an individual who was interested in marrying an orphan girl who he had custody of for her beauty and wealth and who, because he was her custodian, felt a temptation to not provide her with the proper dowry. The verse was then revealed to make it clear that this attitude was undesirable, and to prevent such acts, explaining that a man who is interested in marrying an orphaned girl should carry out his obligations to fulfill her rights; otherwise, he should refrain from marrying her and marry another (non-orphaned) woman instead.[23]

Rashīd Riḍā is one of the few commentators to emphasize that the main concern of Q 4:3 is the protection of the rights of orphans and their dignity. He cites Muḥammad ᶜAbduh who, as Riḍā writes, suggests that the edict on marriage and polygamy is mentioned within the framework of the verse's prohibition against taking orphans' wealth, even through marriage. He also says that the verse is a guideline intended to put an end to abuses practiced against orphans and women, such as marrying an orphan without the proper dowry, or for their money, or preventing others from marrying them with the intention of exploiting their wealth, and also marrying one or more women without fulfilling their rights.[24]

---

23 Abū Jaᶜfar Muḥammad ibn Jarīr al-Ṭabarī, *Jāmiᶜ al-bayān ᶜan taᵓwīlī āyi al-qurᵓān*, ed. by ᶜAbullāh ibn ᶜAbd al-Muḥsin al-Turkī, 24 vols (Cairo: Dār Hijr, 2001), vi, p. 358.

24 Riḍā, iv, p. 348.

The primary issue in this verse for many, however, lies in the question of the permissibility of polygamy. Most Qur'an commentaries share the view that polygamy is allowed with up to four wives, as the wording of the verse suggests. Ibn Kathīr, for example, suggests that polygamy is a matter of *ibāḥā* ('permissibility'): in case an individual fears he is incapable of being just to orphan girls, he is entitled to marry up to four non-orphaned women of his choice.[25] In fact, the issue of whether polygamy is permitted or not was not even a question for many pre-modern Qur'an commentaries; instead, they focused on issues of dealing fairly with orphans, whether one should marry them, and ensuring fair treatment of multiple wives. The overall picture was that polygamy was viewed as the norm, while monogamy was an option for those who feared they would be unable to manage multiple marriages fairly. Some more modern Qur'an commentaries, however, raise the issue of the ideal marriage. Rashīd Riḍā, for example, is of the opinion that the ideal marriage in Islam is monogamous, whereas polygamy is a conditional option. In this, he follows the view of his teacher, Muḥammad ᶜAbduh, who sees polygamy as an arduous option that should only be undertaken in specific situations.[26]

Let us see how QT renders the verse:

First edition *Dan djika kamu takut tidak akan dapat berlaku adil terhadap* **(hak2)**[27] **perempuan jang jatim (bilamana kamu mengawininja)**, *maka kawinilah* **wanita2 (lain) jang kamu senangi**: *dua, tiga atau empat. Kemudian djika kamu takut tidak akan dapat berlaku adil, maka (kawinilah) seorang sadja, atau budak2 jang kamu miliki. Jang demikian itu adalah lebih dekat kepada tidak berbuat aniaja.*

[And if you fear that [you] will not deal fairly with **(the rights) of girls who are orphan (if you marry them)**, then marry **(other) women of your choice**, two, three, or four. Then if you fear that [you] cannot be equitable, then (marry) only one, or the slaves that you have. That is closer to preventing [you] from doing injustice]

25 Ibn Kathīr, iii, p. 339.

26 Riḍā, iv, p. 349. To emphasize his point, he elaborates on the possibility that polygamy could be a source of bigger social problems, and is therefore allowed only in very limited situations.

27 The addition of the numeric figure '2' was the common way to indicate plural word forms in Indonesian writings. Currently, it is occasionally used in non-official

Second/Saudi edition	*Dan jika kamu takut tidak dapat berlaku adil terhadap* **(hak-hak) perempuan yatim (bilamana kamu mengawininya)**, *maka kawinilah* **wanita-wanita (lain) yang kamu senangi**: *dua, tiga atau empat. Kemudian jika kamu takut tidak dapat berlaku adil, maka (kawinilah) seorang saja, atau budak-budak yang kamu miliki. Yang demikian itu adalah lebih dekat kepada tidak berbuat aniaya.* [And if you fear that [you] will not deal fairly with **(the rights) of orphan girls (if you marry them),** then marry **(other) women of your choice,** two, three, or four. Then if you fear that [you] cannot be equitable, then (marry) only one, or the slaves that you have. That is closer to preventing [you] from doing injustice]
Third edition	*Dan jika kamu khawatir tidak akan mampu berlaku adil terhadap* **(hak-hak) perempuan yatim (bilamana kamu menikahinya)**, *maka nikahilah* **perempuan (lain) yang kamu senangi**: *dua, tiga atau empat. Tetapi jika kamu khawatir tidak akan mampu berlaku adil, maka (nikahilah) seorang saja, atau hamba sahaya perempuan yang kamu miliki. Yang demikian itu lebih dekat agar kamu tidak berbuat zalim.* [And if you fear that [you] will not be able to deal fairly with **(the rights) of orphan girls (if you marry them),** the marry **(other) women of your choice,** two, three, or four. But if you fear that [you] cannot be equitable, then (marry) only one, or the female slaves that you have. That is closer for you from avoiding injustice]
Fourth Edition	*Jika kamu khawatir tidak akan mampu berlaku adil terhadap* **(hak-hak) perempuan yatim (bilamana kamu menikahinya)**, *nikahilah* **perempuan (lain) yang kamu senangi**: *dua, tiga, atau empat. Akan tetapi, jika kamu khawatir tidak akan mampu berlaku adil, (nikahilah) seorang saja atau hamba sahaya perempuan yang kamu miliki. Yang demikian itu lebih dekat untuk tidak berbuat zalim.* [If you fear that [you] will not be able to deal fairly with **(the rights) of orphan girls (if you marry them),** thus marry **(other) women of your choice,** two, three, or four. However, if you fear that [you] will not be able to be equitable, (marry) only one, or the female slaves that you have. That is closer to not doing injustice]

---

writings.

The translations of Q 4:3 provided in all four editions are quite straightforward. Each word in the Arabic source text finds its corresponding Indonesian word in a relatively synonymous grammatical structure and composition, with only slight differences that work to accommodate Indonesian language structures and the incorporation of *tafsīr* material, and there is barely any variation between the target text in the different editions. There are some small shifts, but these are insignificant from the perspective of this study: *'takut'* ('fear', 'afraid') changes to *'khawatir'* ('worry'); *'wanita'* ('woman', 'female') to *'perempuan'* ('woman', 'female');[28] *'mengawini'* ('to marry') to *'menikahi'* ('to marry'); *'aniaya'* ('oppress') to *'zalim'* ('oppress'); *'budak-budak'* ('slave') to *'hamba sahaya'* ('slave'); *'kemudian'* ('then', 'furthermore') to *'tapi'* ('but', 'however'), and then *'akan tetapi'* ('however'); *'kepada'* ('to') to *'agar'* ('so that'), and then to *'untuk'* ('for'); and the omission of *'maka'* ('so that') in the fourth edition which is related to the development of this grammatical feature of the Indonesian language rather than issues of interpretation.

The translations of this verse provided in QT are consistent with the interpretation and commentary provide in many Qur'an commentaries. This is particularly true when it comes to most of the commentaries that are listed in the QT bibliographies. The word *al-yatāmā* in the key part of the verse—*wa in khiftum an lā tuqsiṭū fī al-yatāmā* ('And if you fear that you will not deal fairly with orphan girls')—is translated with additional materials in parentheses that clarify that this is referring to *'hak-hak'* ('their rights'), and that it applies to *'bilamana kamu menikahinya'* ('if you marry them'). It is quite certain that the parentheses are intended to accommodate the historical information transmitted in the aforementioned report from ᶜĀʾisha in the target text. *'Hak-hak'* ('the rights') refers to the part of the story that deals with the provision of

28 It has been suggested that the shift from *wanita* to *perempuan* reflects a certain development in gender ideology in Indonesia. The term *wanita* suggests the meaning of 'refined and reserved female behavior', while *perempuan* reflects 'a more dynamic and strong notion of womanhood.' The term *wanita* was widely used to subordinate women as dependent on men during the New Order period when the husband's government position also determined his wife's position. See Siti Ruhaini Dzuhayatin, 'Gender and Pluralism in Indonesia', in *The Politics of Multiculturalism: Pluralism and Citizenship in Malaysia, Singapore, and Indonesia*, ed. by Robert W. Hefner (Honolulu: University of Hawaii Press, 2001), pp. 260–62, http://www.redi-bw.de/db/ebsco.php/search.ebscohost.com/login.aspx%3fdirect%3dtrue%26db%3dnlebk%26AN%3d104410%26site%3dehost-live; Faizin, p. 295.

an orphan's dowry as a right that should be provided on marriage. It is also worth noting that, as a consequence of the ᶜĀʾisha report, many Qur'an commentaries qualify this part of the verse with the phrase *idhā nakaḥtumūhunna* or *tazawwajtumūhunna* ('if you marry them'); the addition of the phrase *'bilamana kamu menikahi'* in QT mirrors this. Additionally, the insertion of the word *lain* ('other') in *'perempuan (lain) yang kamu senangi'* to translate *mā ṭāba lakum min al-nisāʾ* ('whichever women seem to you') certainly seems to come from the same report. There is no additional explanation provided for the phrase *mathnā wa thulāthā wa rubāᶜ* ('two, three, or four') that qualifies the instructional verb *fa-nkiḥū* ('marry') in the source text. The absence of any textual gloss or explanation here indicates that the translation team might have taken its meaning for granted or found it self-explanatory. That at this point the committee saw no need for additional explanation does, however, indicate that they understood polygamy to be the norm.

While the body of the translation for this verse is quite straightforward, the shifting use of footnotes across the editions of QT is interesting. The first two editions both have two footnotes, the third edition adds one more, and the fourth edition removes the footnotes altogether. The note added in the third edition concerns a shift of wording from *'budak'* to *'hamba sahaya'* (both refer to 'slave') in the translation of *mā malakat aymānukum* (lit. 'what your right hands possess'). The note explains that the slavery system depicted in this verse no longer exists. As slavery is a topic that lies beyond the scope of our discussion, this leaves us with two notes to discuss.

The first note provides an explanation for the verb *taᶜdilū* ('be equitable'), and reads as follows:

First edition	*Berlaku adil ialah perlakuan jang adil dalam meladeni isteri seperti pakaian, tempat, giliran dll, jang* **bersifat lahirijah**. [Being equitable means being just in fulfilling **the physical needs** of wives, such as clothing, places, and sexual intercourse]
Third edition	*Third edition: Berlaku adil ialah perlakuan yang adil dalam memenuhi kebutuhan istri seperti pakaian, tempat, giliran dan lain-lain* **yang bersifat lahiriah dan batiniah.** [Being equitable means being just in fulfilling **the physical and non-physical** needs of wives, such as clothing, places, and sexual intercourse.]

The third edition introduces a change to the note. The first, second, and Saudi editions define *adil* ('just') as being limited to tangible physical matters (*lahiriah*), such as clothing, housing and sexual intercourse. This note accords with explanations given in most Qur'an commentaries, which limit the notion of *ᶜadl* to material aspects, equating it with *qism* ('distribution') and *nafaqa* ('living costs').[29] The third edition does not seem to be satisfied with how *adil* was defined in the previous editions. Accordingly, it expands the note to indicate that *ᶜadl* in this verse does not relate solely to physical matters (*lahiriah*), but also non-physical matters (*batiniah*). In short, this amendment to the interpretation of this verse means that the husband is asked to also be just in terms of providing affection and psychological support for his wife or wives. At this point, QT departs from the majority of Qur'an commentaries. Even Rashīd Riḍa and ᶜAbduh, who in *al-Manār* idealize monogamy and suggest that polygamy is an arduous option, exclude affection from their definition of what *ᶜadl* is required of husbands with multiple wives.

Let us now move on to the second note, which provides additional explanation for the Arabic *fa-wāḥidatan* ('[marry] only one'), and which reads as follows:

> *Islam memperbolehkan poligami dengan syarat-syarat tertentu. Sebelum turun ayat ini poligami sudah ada, dan pernah pula dijalankan oleh para Nabi sebelum Nabi Muhammad s.a.w. Ayat ini membatas poligami sampai empat orang saja.*
>
> [Islam allows polygamy with specific requirements. Before this verse was revealed, polygamy already existed and was also practiced by prophets before the Prophet Muhammad pbuh. This verse limits polygamy to four wives only.]

The note is short but eloquently sets out QT's views on polygamy. Despite its minimal length, the note proposes four fundamental arguments on the issue. First, it says that Islam unquestionably allows polygamy. This argument relies on the textual features of the verse that expressly permit polygamy by providing instructions about the number of wives a man may have. Second, it clarifies that there are requirements (*syarat-syarat tertentu*) that those who desire polygamous marriage are obliged to fulfill. (QT, however, does not explicitly mention these requirements,

29 For example, Jalāl-u-dīn Muḥammad ibn Aḥmad ibn Muḥammad al-Maḥallī and Jalāl-u-dīn ᶜAbd-l-raḥmān ibn Abī Bakr al-Ṣuyūṭī, *Tafsīr Al-Imāmayn al-jalīlayn* (Dār Ibn Kathīr), p. 77.

which means that the readers are expected to find out what they are on their own.) Third, it states that polygamy is an ancient practice that was recognized and performed by the prophets that preceded Muhammad. It does not explicitly mention that Muhammad himself had a polygamous marriage. Nevertheless, the inclusion of the word *'pula'* ('also') in the note implies that the translators considered it common knowledge that does not require an explicit reminder. Fourth, we are told that Islam only allows polygamy with up to four wives, which is, again, a reference to information given in the text of the verse.

The positioning of this note is quite curious. The note is a justification of polygamy, yet it is appended to the word *fa-wāḥidatan* ('marry only one') instead of *mathnā wa thulāthā wa rubā*^{c} ('two, three, or four'). The reader of QT might overlook this positioning issue, or consider it as a marginal or irrelevant detail. Nevertheless, the fact that this note remains in this position in all four editions of QT, even after two comprehensive revisions by a coordinated committee, indicates that there might be an intention behind it. To put it into perspective, a look at Qur'an commentaries reveals that the discussion about the issue of the number of spouses allowed for marriage is also usually incorporated into discussion of the phrase *mathnā wa thulāthā wa rubā*^{c} rather than *fa-wāḥidatan*. I would argue that there is an implied emphasis here. One may wonder as to why the part of the verse that addresses polygamy (*mathnā wa thulātha wa rubā*$^{\supset}$) is translated literally, while the part that addresses monogamy (*fa-wāḥidatan*) is thought to need additional explanation, even if only in a footnote.

Let us now examine what stance the official state policy takes with regards to polygamy. The 1974 Marriage Law legislates for monogamy and stipulates that 'a man shall be allowed to have one wife only; a woman shall be allowed to have one husband only,' but allows polygamy with restrictions. The main requirement resonates with the provision of the Qur'an, that the husband should be able to treat all his wives and children fairly but, in a departure from the Qur'anic provision, requires court approval for polygamous marriages. In order to obtain approval, the petitioner must convince the court of his capability to maintain multiple marriages and prove that he has the permission of his present wife (or wives). This permission has to be submitted in writing and should be based on direct testimony provided by the wife in court. The court, however, can only grant the proposed polygamous marriage after examining whether the wife can perform her marital duties, whether she has become disabled or contracted an incurable disease, or whether she cannot give birth. The KHI does not propose anything that differs substantially from the 1974 Marriage Law. In principle, it allows polygamy, albeit subject to strict requirements.

The publication of the first edition of QT in 1965 preceded the Marriage Law by almost a decade. The translation and the law disagree over the issue of monogamy as the ideal form of marriage, but share the same opinion that polygamy is allowed with specific requirements. Consequently, it is tempting in this context to assume that the 1974 Marriage Law partly follows in the footsteps of QT on this issue, on the basis that they are both state projects, and it would be unsurprising if they were synchronized. However, it would be somewhat far-fetched to come to this conclusion. The Marriage Law presents a set of actual requirements and procedures for polygamous marriage, whereas the translation does not. After the 1974 Marriage Law had been introduced, QT could have included the state's legal restrictions for polygamy in a footnote, had they been synchronized. That is however not the path QT follows, even after the first comprehensive revision took place in 1989–90. That is also the case for the KHI, introduced in 1991, and for the third edition of QT (2002). Of course, it would realistically be impossible to include all the requirements and procedures of polygamy proposed by the Marriage Law and the KHI in QT in the limited space available in the Qur'an translation. Nevertheless, the translation does not give even the slightest hint that, for example, polygamy is only possible with the permission of any pre-existing wife or wives and special dispensation by a court, or make any reference to the 1974 Marriage Law or the KHI.

When it comes to the general intellectual discourse among Muslim scholars and academics in Indonesia, views on polygamy are unsurprisingly split: one camp allows it, while the other forbids it. The first camp suggests that polygamy is a part of sharia law, and hence considers the rejection of it as effectively a rejection of Islam. In current popular culture, polygamy is framed as one of the most important elements of piety, for both men and women. Freedom of expression in post-Suharto Indonesia saw an increase in the promotion of polygamy in the popular media and events such as the controversial 'polygamy awards'.[30] In the political context, polygamy is occasionally used to attract the political sympathy of voters during elections. On the flip side, polygamy is denounced by the opposite camp as an outdated practice that discriminates against women and should be abolished on the basis that it has been the root of social problems such as economic hardship, intra-familial disharmony, and neglected wives and children. There is, however, a middle ground. This third group does wish to ban polygamy absolutely, but would like to introduce somewhat tighter regulations for those who wish to arrange a polygamous marriage.

Those who promote or approve of polygamy tend to base their views in a literal reading of the Qur'anic text and the view on this given by the majority of Qur'an commentaries. Some Indonesian scholars of Islam, however, have reservations about this stance, suggesting that it demonstrates gender bias. Siti Ruhaini Dzuhayatin, for example, in a 2002 article included in *Rekonstruksi Metodologis*, argues that this verse is actually concerned with social protection for orphans and widows, but was misinterpreted by the classical *mufassir*s as being intended to accommodate men's sexual drives.[31] Another contribution in the same volume by Nasaruddin Umar points to a widely used method of *tafsīr*, namely *taḥlīlī* ('analytical') *tafsīr*,[32] as at the root of what he views as

---

30 In the early 2000s, a successful entrepreneur and practitioner of polygamy, Puspo Wardoyo, actively publicized his support for polygamy through television and radio talk shows, speeches and seminars, and books and newspaper advertisements. He worked with an Islamic scholar, Syahrin Harahap, and a well-known preacher, Aa Gym, to campaign for the idea that 'polygamy is better than *zina* (adultery).' In 2003, he sponsored a "Polygamy Award" to promote polygamy. See Nina Nurmila, *Women, Islam and Everyday Life: Renegotiating Polygamy in Indonesia*, Women in Asia (New York: Routledge, 2009), pp. 64–77.

31 Siti Ruhaini Dzuhayatin, 'Pergulatan Pemikiran Feminis dalam Wacana Islam di Indonesia', in *Rekonstruksi Metodologis Wacana Kesetaraan Gender dalam Islam*, PSW IAIN Sunan Kalijaga Yogyakarta (Yogyakarta: Pustaka Pelajar, 2002), pp. 3–26 (p. 18).

32 *Tafsīr taḥlīlī* is the most commonly used *tafsīr* methodology, according to which one interprets the text at the level of the verse, commenting on the verses one after another, following the canonical order. This method allows an exegete to give his/her full attention to each specific verse, but there is a risk that reading the verses in isolation might obscure an appreciation of the holistic Qur'anic worldview on a particular matter. By reading the verse in isolation from others, and attending only to the literal features of the text, the verse can become detached from its historical context, in this case obscuring the fact that its central message is about protecting the rights of vulnerable orphan girls from potential oppression, and instead reading the verse in an entirely different way.

the gender-biased interpretation of Q 4:3, due to the fact that it requires one to look at each verse in isolation from both the Qur'an as a whole and the historical context. Unsurprisingly, he then boldly suggests that there is no prominent *tafsīr* that is not gender-biased.[33] The answer to this problem, Umar suggests, is the thematic method (*tafsīr mawḍūʿī*). Unlike *tafsīr taḥlīlī, tafsīr mawḍūʿī* requires the exegete to gather together verses that relate to the same topic. Only by looking closely at all of the verses together can one achieve a holistic view of the Qur'an's teachings on a particular topic. In the context of polygamy, Umar suggests that while the *taḥlīlī* approach would result in a view that allows polygamy, interpreting the verse using the *mawḍūʿī* approach would restrict polygamy, or even prohibit it altogether. He bases his argument on the content of another, significant verse that relates to polygamy, Q 4:129:

> ولن تستطيعوا أن تعدلوا بين ٱلنساء ولو حرصتم فلا تميلوا كل ٱلميل فتذروها كٱلمعلقة وإن تصلحوا وتتقوا فإن ٱلله كان غفورا رحيما
>
> You will never be able to treat your wives with equal fairness, however much you desire to do so, but do not ignore one wife altogether, leaving her suspended [between marriage and divorced]. If you make amends and remain conscious of God, He is most forgiving and merciful

This verse is considered to disqualify the possibility of being just to multiple wives, and Umar argues that it could be understood as an argument for the prohibition of polygamy precisely because it asserts the impossibility of complying with the requirement to be just. Some other scholars take a slightly different view of this verse and argue that while it may appear to forbid polygamy totally, it actually allows it with strict requirements.[34] ʿAbduh and al-Marāghī (d. 1952), for example, suggest that despite the Qur'an's directive that a husband must treat multiple wives with equal fairness, he is actually exempt from this when it comes to an aspect that he could never be expected to control, namely his affectionate preferences.[35]

---

33 Nasaruddin Umar, 'Metode Penelitian Berperspektif Gender tentang Literatur Islam', in *Rekonstruksi Metodologis Wacana Kesetaraan Gender dalam Islam*, PSW IAIN Sunan Kalijaga Yogyakarta (Yogyakarta: Pustaka Pelajar, 2002), pp. 85–106 (p. 86).

34 Umar, 'Metode Penelitian Berperspektif Gender tentang Literatur Islam', pp. 97–98; Umar, *Argumen Kesetaraan Gender Perspektif Al-Qur'ān*, pp. 281–86.

35 Riḍā, iv, p. 348; Aḥmad Muṣṭafā al-Marāghī, *Tafsīr Al-Marāghī*, 30 vols (Cairo: Muṣṭafā al-Bāb al-Ḥalab wa Awlāduh, 1946), v, pp. 72–73.

Umar himself does not provide an explicit final opinion on the legal status of polygamy, though, and in his *Rekonstruksi Metodologis* article he is quite equivocal on the subject. On the one hand, he provides contextual rationalization to help make sense of the verse. He emphasizes that the verse was revealed in the context of warfare, and that the Muslim population in the early period of Islam consisted of more women than men, and hence it was only sensible that a verse revealed during that time would allow polygamy. Additionally, he stresses the need to analyze the verse using other methodologies, for example those applied by scholars such as Fatima Mernissi, Amina Wadud, Fazlur Rahman, and Toshihiko Izutsu, all of whom implicitly object to the practice of polygamy.[36] However, in another book, he states that although many *ulama* justify polygamy, it can only be applied with requirements, and supports this position by referring to contemporary scholars such as ᶜAbduh, al-Marāghi, and Wahbah al-Zuhayli who allow polygamy with strict requirements.[37]

Umar's criticism of the dangers inherent in *tafsīr taḥlīlī* methodology is also relevant to QT. As with almost all Qur'an translations, QT follows the sequence of the ᶜUthmānic *muṣḥaf* and, because it reads the text in linear fashion, it risks rendering Q 4:3 in isolation from other relevant verses. Following Umar's line of argument, the unquestioning position taken by the earlier editions of QT on the issue of polygamy comes from reading Q 4:3 individually, rather than in juxtaposition with other verses such as Q 4:129. However, one of the notes appended to this verse in the third edition shows an interesting development. As discussed earlier, there is a shift in the footnote in this edition that relates to the subject of ᶜ*adl*. The first, second, and Saudi editions define ᶜ*adl*/*adil* ('justice') as being limited to tangible physical matters (*lahiriah*), such as clothing, housing, and sexual intercourse, whereas the third edition adds that ᶜ*adl* in this verse does not relate solely to physical matters (*lahiriah*), but also to the non-physical (*batiniah*).

We can be sure of one thing about the change to this footnote, which is that this shift was the result of discussion amongst the committee with regards to the scope of ᶜ*adl* in the verse. The new note seems to combine the notion of ᶜ*adl* in this verse with the stipulations about the

36 Umar, *Argumen Kesetaraan Gender Perspektif Al-Qur'ān*, pp. 282–85.
37 Umar, *Ketika Fikih Membela Perempuan*, pp. 126–34.

treatment of multiple wives provided in Q 4:129. Despite the fact that QT follows the 'old-school' *taḥlīlī* approach, the view provided in this note indicates that a comprehensive reading of verses that address the same concern has had its influence on the QT target text. We can also posit that developments in Islamic thought resulting from official reforms have made their mark on the translation in this case.

Finally, the fourth edition removes all the notes that had previously been provided for this particular verse. I would like to argue that this shows another shift, and that now the QT team has decided that they do not want to engage with the ongoing debates around the issue of polygamy. Controversial events, such as the aforementioned polygamy awards, have successfully raised the confidence of practitioners of polygamy, who are now more open about the subject in public.[38] The increased levels of freedom of expression and belief in Indonesia in the aftermath of the fall of the New Order have opened up opportunities for people to promote a plethora of ideas, including polygamy, and polygamy has consequently become increasingly acceptable to the extent that it has even become a means for Muslim politicians to attract support. Polygamy has become the subject of endless discussions and, given the status of QT as the official Qur'an translation of the state, the translation committee appear to be wary of getting embroiled in this controversial, ongoing debate.

Q 4:34, The Political Rights of Women

ٱلرجال قوٰمون على ٱلنساء بما فضل ٱلله بعضهم علىٰ بعض وبما أنفقوا من أمولهم

> Husbands are the *qawwāmūn* of their wives, with [the bounties] God has given to some more than others and with what they spend out of their own money...

Q 4:34 is frequently referred to as the 'de-justification' for female leadership. The verse essentially deals with domestic issues between husbands and wives, but commentators have historically extended the meaning of the verse to denote the superiority of men over women in all walks of life. This interpretation comes from a particular understanding

38 Nurmila, p. 70.

of the word *qawwāmūn*. Most classical Qur'an commentaries explain the word as indicative of the natural superiority of men over women. The fiercest supporter of this view might be Ibn Kathīr, who sets out in detail the many attributes that make men superior to women. For him, the phrase *al-rijāl qawwāmūn* ᶜ*alā al-nisā*ᵓ means that man is the leader (*'ra*ᵓ*īs'*), the superior (*'kabīr'*), the judge (*'hākim'*), and the educator (*'mu*ᵓ*addib'*) of women. He emphasizes this concept with unequivocally repeated notions, going on to say 'because men (*al-rijāl*) are better (*afḍal*) than women (*al-nisā*ᵓ), and a man (*al-rajul*) is better/finer (*khayr*) than a woman,' in his explanation for the subsequent phrase, *bimā faḍḍala llāhu ba*ᶜ*ḍahum* ᶜ*alā ba*ᶜ*ḍ*. He suggests that this is why all of the prophets are men, as are the greatest kings, and then justifies his interpretation with a prophetic tradition that says that a community led by a woman would not be successful (*lan yaflaḥ qawm wallaw amrahum imra*ᵓ*a*).[39] This kind of view seems to transcend time. Even the progressive Abū al-Aᶜlā al-Mawdūdī (1903–79) believes that women, due to their physical disadvantages, can only manage simple household affairs,[40] and Rashīd Riḍā, in a segment of his interpretation of the polygamy verse, suggests that men's superiority over women is a natural phenomenon.[41]

Let us move to QT. The editions of QT display several changes in the rendering of Q 4:34.

First edition	**Kaum laki2** *adalah* **pemimpin** *bagi* **kaum wanita**, *oleh karena Allah telah melebihkan sebahagian mereka (laki2) atas sebahagian jang lain (wanita), dan karena mereka (laki2) telah menafkahkan harta mereka...* [**Mankind** is the **leader** of **womankind**, because Allah has given more to some of them (mankind) over the others (womankind), and because they (mankind) spent out of their wealth...]

39 ᶜImād al-Dīn Abū al-Fidāᵓ Ismāᶜīl Ibn Kathīr, *Al-Tafsīr al-Qur*ᵓ*ān al-*ᶜ*aẓīm*, 15 vols (Giza: Muᵓassasa Qurṭuba, 2000), iv, p. 20.

40 Dzuhayatin, 'Pergulatan Pemikiran Feminis dalam Wacana Islam di Indonesia', p. 16.

41 Riḍā, iv, p. 354.

Second/Saudi Edition	**Kaum laki-laki** *itu adalah* **pemimpin** *bagi* **kaum wanita,** *oleh karena Allah telah melebihkan sebahagian mereka (laki-laki) atas sebahagian yang lain (wanita), dan karena mereka (laki-laki) telah menafkahkan sebagian dari harta mereka...* [**Mankind** is the **leader** of **womankind**, because Allah has given more to some of them (mankind) over the others (womankind), and because they (mankind) spent out of their wealth...]
Third Edition	**Laki-laki (suami)** *itu* **pelindung** *bagi* **perempuan (istri)**, *karena Allah telah melebihkan sebagian mereka (laki-laki) atas sebagian yang lain (perempuan), dan karena mereka (laki-laki) telah memberikan nafkah dari hartanya...* [**Men (husbands)** are the **protectors of women (wives)**, because Allah has given more to some of them (men) over the others (women), and because they (men) spent out of their wealth...]
Fourth Edition	**Laki-laki (suami)** *adalah* **penanggung jawab** *atas para* **perempuan (istri)** *karena Allah telah melebihkan sebagian mereka (laki-laki) atas sebagian yang lain (perempuan) dan karena mereka (laki-laki) telah menafkahkan sebagian dari hartanya...* [**Men (husbands)** are **the bearers of responsibility/ custodians for women (wives)**, because Allah has given more to some of them (men) over the others (women), and because they (men) spend out of their wealth...]

We can identify several changes in the way the editions of QT render this verse into Indonesian. At a general level, there are a number of changes that relate to language style, such as the change from *'ialah'* to *'adalah'* (both are the different forms of the verb 'to be'); *'di balik pembelakangan suaminja'* ('behind the back of her husband') to *'ketika suami tidak ada'* ('when her husband is not around'); and *'nasehatilah mereka'* ('advise them') to *'beri nasihat kepada mereka'* ('give them a piece of advice'). The other changes are related to interpretive problems, such as the removal of *'kaum'* ('the people') before *'laki-laki'* ('man') and *'wanita'* ('woman'); the addition of *'suami'* ('husband') and *'istri'* ('wife') in brackets; and the shift from *'pemimpin'* ('leader') to first *'pelindung'* ('protector'/'guardian') and finally *'penanggung jawab'* ('bearer of responsibility'/ 'custodian').

The use of the word *'pemimpin'* ('leader') to translate *qawwāmūn* vividly reflects the interpretive tendency that QT follows. It is likely that the committee was influenced in this by Ibn Kathīr's reading of *ra'īs* ('leader') as the meaning of *qawām*. Additionally, because the word *'kaum'* ('people') has connotations of normalization and generalization, the phrase *'kaum laki-laki itu adalah pemimpin bagi kaum wanita'* ('mankind is the leader of womankind') suggests a normative, primordial and general hierarchy that positions mankind as leaders of womankind. This is, again, perhaps derived from Ibn Kathir's statement 'men are better than women, and a man is better/finer than a woman.'

Against this backdrop, the third and fourth editions of QT display a substantive change in the way the committee interprets this verse. First, the committee decided to render *qawāmūn* as *'pelindung'* ('protector'/'guardian') rather than *'pemimpin'* ('leader') for the third edition, and further revised this for a third time to *'penanggung jawab'* ('bearer of responsibility'/'custodian') for the fourth edition. *Pemimpin* in the Indonesian language is a word that suggests an unequal hierarchical relationship between the parties at stake, which means that *'laki-laki pemimpin bagi wanita/perempuan'* ('men are leaders of women') carries an additional connotation that men occupy a higher social standing than women. *Pelindung,* on the other hand, does not designate a hierarchical social position. It is rooted in *lindung,* which means 'taking cover,' as in *tentara berlindung di belakang pohon,*[42] which means 'a soldier seeks cover behind a tree.' In this expression, the tree is *pelindung* for the person who is hiding behind it. Therefore, the shift from *'pemimpin'* to *'pelindung'* can be seen as indicative of an increased gender awareness among the QT translation team.

However, the committee that worked on the fourth edition of QT evidently did not consider *'pelindung'* an ideal translation for *qawāmūn.* Although it does not carry an explicitly hierarchical connotation, *'pelindung'* could still be understood to convey such an idea. This can be seen from one of the semantic connotations of *'melindungi'*—the verb form of *pelindung*—that means *'mengayomi'*. *'Mengayomi'* is a word

42 Tim Penyusun Kamus Pusat Bahasa, 'Lindung', *Kamus Bahasa Indonesia* (Jakarta: Pusat Bahasa, 2008), p. 864.

which is used with the meaning of affectionate care shown by parents to their children, or educators to their pupils, and so on. For example, *'aku berlindung kepada Allah'* ('I seek protection from/in Allah') is a widely used translation for the *taᶜāwudh* formula with which one should start reciting the Qur'an.[43] This expression situates Allah as *pelindung* and humankind as its object, and it is obvious that in this sense the word is used with a hierarchical nuance. Accordingly, a person with a patriarchal mindset could interpret the word *pelindung* in Q 4:34 as implying an unequal social relationship between men and women. In this context, the transition from *'pemimpin'* to *'pelindung'*, despite the semantic shift, fails to excise the interpretation that women are not the equals of men. This led the committee to change the translation of *qawwāmūn* again, to *'penanggung jawab'* ('bearer of responsibility/custodian'). *Penanggung jawab* is an idiom that means 'someone who is in charge or responsible for a matter,' and has no nuance of unequal social relationships between the parties at stake. The question of whether *'tanggung jawab'* is a proper equivalence for *qawamūn* is a matter of debate. Nevertheless, the ongoing discussions that have now resulted in the choice of *'tanggung jawab'* reflect a continuous willingness to rehabilitate the interpretation of this verse from a patriarchal way of thinking.

Other substantial changes introduced in the third edition and maintained in the fourth edition are the removal of *'kaum'* before *'laki-laki'* (*al-rijāl*) and *'perempuan'* (*al-nisāᵓ*) and the addition of two parentheses, *'suami'* ('husband') and *'istri'* ('wife') after the same words. As mentioned above, the use of the word *'kaum'* before both words suggests a normative, primordial and general hierarchy of mankind and womankind. By using this word, the verse can only be read as meaning that men intrinsically and primordially occupy a higher position than women. Its removal and its substitution with *'suami'* and *'istri'* create a shift in meaning, so that the verse is now interpreted as making more specific reference to domestic and familial affairs. While the original reading found in the first edition is commonly used as a justification for the ineligibility of women for any political leadership position, the changes introduced in the last two editions dissociate this verse from the issue of the political rights of women. In sum, the change

43 The formula goes: *aᶜūdhu bi 'llāh min al-shaiṭān al-rajīm* ('I seek protection from/in Allah from the accursed Devil').

from *'kaum'* to the insertion of *'suami'* and *'istri'* in parenthesis and the shift from *'pemimpin'* ('leader') to *'pelindung'* ('one who safeguards') to *'penanggung jawab'* '(bearer of responsibility'/'custodian') are a clear sign that the verse is no longer interpreted by the QT translation team as referring to a natural gender-based hierarchy, nor is it a justification for the rights of men or women to lead, or be excluded from leadership positions.

In Indonesia, the verse has been frequently cited by those opposed to women's rights. Budhy Munawwar-Rachman, in his contribution to *Rekonstruksi Metodologis*, suggests that this idea comes from a perspective that interprets the verse from a hierarchical point of view, according to which men are ontologically superior to women.[44] Siti Ruhaini Dzuhayatin, in the same volume, suggests that the verse adjures Muslim men to treat their wives well, but then goes on to interpret it as saying that a woman must be submissive and obedient to her husband.[45] As a result of such readings of Q 4:34, the idea of women in leadership positions managing groups that include men is unfathomable for some Indonesians.

It is against this background that Quraish Shihab, in a contribution to *Wanita Islam Indonesia*, asserts that Q 4:34 has been the source of justification for the relegation of women to an inferior political role, and assertions that they should never be leaders. Furthermore, Shihab also points out that many contemporary exegetes have argued against this idea, stating that the verse deals with the issue of domestic affairs rather than political rights. The oft-cited prophetic *ḥadīth* that contends that women's leadership would not be successful has a specific context, and another *ḥadīth* that asserts that women are less intelligent is problematic and should be rejected. On the other hand, he continues, there are several prophetic *ḥadīth*s that in fact support the idea of women's rights. He also refers to Q 9:71,[46] another Qur'anic verse that can be read as supportive

44 Budhy Munawar-Rachman, 'Penafsiran Islam Liberal atas Isu-Isu Gender dan Feminisme', in *Rekonstruksi Metodologis Wacana Kesetaraan Gender dalam Islam*, PSW IAIN Sunan Kalijaga Yogyakarta (Yogyakarta: Pustaka Pelajar, 2002), pp. 27–84 (p. 39).

45 Dzuhayatin, 'Pergulatan Pemikiran Feminis dalam Wacana Islam di Indonesia', p. 15.

46 'The believers, both men and women, *awliyā*ᶜ (support) each other; they order what is right and forbid what is wrong; they keep up the prayer and pay the prescribed

of women's rights and which is, he suggests, intended to encourage men and women to cooperate in managing their everyday affairs. This verse assigns the word *awliyāʾ* to both men and women. He points out that the word *awliyāʾ* in this verse contains the meaning of *'kerja sama'* ('teamwork'), *'bantuan'* ('help'/'assistance'), and *'penguasaan'* ('governance'). Shihab also references a number of other verses which were revealed in the light of events involving women during the early years of Islam, and also uses them to argue that women have an equal right to leadership as men.[47]

Nasaruddin Umar agrees with Quraish Shihab's argument against the classical interpretation of Q 4:34. He argues that *'pemimpin'* is not equivalent to *qawāma*,[48] and thus referring to this verse as the justification for objections to women's rights is incorrect. Like Shihab, he refers to ʿAbduh, who refuses to say that leadership is the privilege of men. While Shihab essentially provides a comparative analysis of the interpretation of classical and contemporary exegetes, Umar instead provides a philological analysis, saying that the word *al-rijāl* has connotations of gender rather than sex, and that gender, unlike sex, is a culturally constructed concept. Accordingly, any verse mentioning *al-rijāl* and *al-nisāʾ* should be understood contextually, with consideration of the correlation between the text and the particular socio-cultural circumstance in which it was revealed.[49] This argument implies that women during the early age of Islam, as recorded in the Qur'an, were deprived of the political right to leadership, but that this should not necessarily be the case in the current context of Indonesia.

At this point, it is evident that the shift in the translation of Q 4:34 in the various editions of QT resonates with the dynamics of intellectual discourse on Islam and gender in Indonesia. The first and second editions that render *al-rijāl* as *'kaum laki-laki'*, *al-nisāʾ* as *'kaum perempuan'*, and *qawwāmūn* as *'pemimpin'* conform to the prevalent trend in Qur'an

---

alms; they obey God and His Messenger. God will give His mercy to such people: God is almighty and wise.'

47 Shihab, pp. 13–16.

48 Umar, *Ketika Fikih Membela Perempuan*, p. 279.

49 Umar, *Argumen Kesetaraan Gender Perspektif Al-Qur'ān*, pp. 150; 172; Nasaruddin Umar, 'Kajian Kritis terhadap Ayat-ayat Gender (Pendekatan Hermeneutik)', in *Rekonstruksi Metodologis Wacana Kesetaraan Gender dalam Islam*, PSW IAIN Sunan Kalijaga Yogyakarta (Yogyakarta: Pustaka Pelajar, 2002), pp. 107–49 (p. 118).

commentaries to consider man as naturally superior to woman. Then, the third edition introduces substantive changes. The removal of *'kaum'* and the addition of *'suami-istri'* resonates with the reservations of modern-day Indonesian intellectuals such as Siti Ruhaini Dzuhayatin, Budhy Munawwar-Rachman and Quraish Shihab, all of whom associate the verse with domestic, familial affairs rather than the public sphere. The philological analysis of Umar regarding *al-rijāl* and *al-nisā*ᵓ might not be explicitly identified in this shift, however in the third and fourth editions the QT committee obviously share his objection to the view that *qawāmun* corresponds to *'pemimpin'*. In this light it is worth noting that Quraish Shihab was one of the committee members during the second revision of QT between 1998 and 2002 when the third edition of the translation was being produced, and was one of the honorary figures invited to participate in the third revision of 2016–19.

In addition to the changing intellectual trends among Indonesian exegetes, one other political event might also have played a role in this interpretive shift. In 1999, Indonesia held its first democratic election, after three decades of authoritarian government under the New Order. During the election, the rise of Megawati Sukarnoputri, the leader of the Partai Demokrasi Indonesia Perjuangan (PDI-P, The Indonesian Democratic Party of Struggle), generated concerns among many Muslim leaders, not only because the leadership of PDI-P was dominated by Christians, but also due to her gender and the fact that she was not considered 'Islamic' enough. Megawati's main opposition were the PPP and a number of hardline Muslim organizations, and they invoked Q 4:34 to promote the idea that women's leadership was unacceptable. Despite their efforts, the PDI-P won the general election, but Megawati lost the race for the presidency, which was awarded to Abdurrahman Wahid in October 1999. President Abdurrahman Wahid, however, failed to hold on to power and was impeached on 23 July 2001, after which Megawati was appointed as president.[50]

50 Azyumardi Azra, 'The Use and Abuse of Qur'anic Verses in Contemporary Indonesian Politics', in *Approaches to The Qur'an in Contemporary Indonesia*, ed. by Abdullah Saeed, The Institute of Ismaili Studies (Oxford: Oxford University Press, 2005), pp. 193–208 (p. 14); Clarissa Adamson, 'Gendered Anxieties: Islam, Women's Right, and Moral Hierarchy in Java', *Anthropological Quarterly*, 80.1 (2007), 5–37 (p. 14).

The process of the election, Megawati's defeat, and her eventual presidency took place during the second revision of QT, between 1998 and 2002. It seems inevitable that such a prominent political event and the controversy it had generated would become a subject of discussion for the revision committee. Thus, in addition to the presence of Quraish Shihab on the committee, Megawati's political journey to the presidency also probably influenced the changing opinions about how to translate the word *qawāmūn* in the third edition of QT.

Q 1:7 and Q 3:19: Religious Tolerance and Pluralism

The history of discussions of religious pluralism and the Qur'an in Indonesia is pretty diverse and rich, both in terms of theme and approaches. The debates revolve around a number of Qur'anic verses, along with prophetic traditions and segments of the life of the prophet Muhammad, that were read with a fresh, new perspective. These notions deal with issues such as the depiction of other religious communities in the Qur'an, eschatology, the theological status of the *ahl al-kitāb* and various other figures, as well as stories shared by the Qur'an and the Bible. This section only discusses how QT treats two relevant cases, Q 1:7 and Q 3:19, because both involve issues that relate to the complexities of translating various Qur'anic terms rather than issues of interpretation in a more general sense. Q. 1:7 reads as follows:

صرٰط ٱلذين أنعمت عليهم غير ٱلمغضوب عليهم ولا ٱلضالين

> The path of those You have blessed, those who incur no anger and who have not gone astray.

Here is how the QT renders the verse in its various editions:

First edition	*(Jaitu) djalan orang2 jang telah Engkau anugerahkan ni'mat kepada mereka; bukan (djalan) mereka* **jang dimurkai** *dan bukan (pula djalan)* **mereka jang sesat**. [(namely) the path of those You have blessed with bounties for them, not (the path of) those **who are angered** and (also) not (the path of) those **who have gone astray**.]

Second edition	*(Yaitu) jalan orang-orang yang telah Engkau anugerahkan ni'mat kepada mereka; bukan (jalan)* **mereka yang dimurkai** *dan bukan (pula jalan)* **mereka yang sesat**. [(namely) the path of those You have blessed with bounties for them, not (the path of) those **who are angered** and (also) not (the path of) those **who have gone astray**.]
The 1997 copy of the Saudi edition[51]	*(yaitu) jalan orang-orang yang telah Engkau anugerahkan ni'mat kepada mereka; bukan (jalan) mereka* **yang dimurkai (Yahudi)**, *dan bukan (pula jalan)* **mereka yang sesat (Nasrani)**. [(namely) the path of those You have blessed with bounties for them, not (the path of) those who **are angered (the Jews)** and (also) not (the path of) those **who have gone astray (the Christians)**.]
The 2016 copy of the Saudi edition	*(yaitu) jalan orang-orang yang telah Engkau anugerahkan ni'mat kepada mereka; bukan (jalan) mereka yang dimurkai (orang-orang yang mengetahui kebenaran dan meninggalkannya), dan bukan (pula jalan) mereka yang sesat (orang-orang yang meninggalkan kebenaran karena ketidaktahuan dan kejahilan).* [(namely) the path of those You have blessed with bounties for them, not (the path of) those who **are angered (those who know the truth but refrain from it)** and (also) not (the path of) those **who have gone astray (those who renounce the truth due to their stupidity and ignorance)**.]
Third edition	*(yaitu) jalan orang-orang yang telah Engkau beri nikmat kepadanya; bukan (jalan)* **mereka yang dimurkai,** *dan bukan (pula jalan)* **mereka yang sesat.** [(namely) the path of those You have blessed with bounties for them, not (the path of) those **who are angered** and (also) not (the path of) those **who have gone astray**.]
Fourth edition	*(yaitu) jalan orang-orang yang telah Engkau beri nikmat, bukan (jalan)* **mereka yang dimurkai** *dan bukan (pula jalan)* **orang-orang yang sesat**. [(namely) the path of those You have blessed with bounties, not (the path of) those **who are angered** and (also) not (the path of) those **who have gone astray**.]

51 The Saudi edition does not indicate the year of the publication of their copies. The date assigned for these copies is based on the year each copy was distributed to Indonesian pilgrims.

The translations of Q 1:7 in the first, second, third, and fourth editions of QT do not entail any substantial changes. They all render the verse almost literally, and the slight difference in the fourth edition is due to its adaptation of the translation to a more contemporary linguistic structure. The Saudi edition, however, is distinctive, particularly in its translation of *al-maghḍūb ᶜalayhim* and *al-ḍāllīn*, and includes an additional note that does not exist in any of the editions printed in Indonesia. Furthermore, this edition has two different renderings. The earlier Saudi edition explicitly mentions the Jews and the Christians in its translation of *al-maghḍūb ᶜalayhim* and *al-ḍāllīn*, respectively, whereas the latter revises it with a longer description.

The differences between the two Saudi editions present two interesting issues. First, the King Fahd Complex has been publishing the text of the second edition of QT since 1990, and as far as the current LPMQ officials are concerned, they have no information about any changes made in the Saudi edition since then. In the case of this particular verse, a change has been implemented in the latter copy (the ones I obtained are the 1997 and 2016 copies), but there is no information about when the change might have taken place. However, an incident involving an English translation printed by King Fahd Complex, *The Noble Qur'an: English Translation of the Meaning and Commentary* by Taqī al-Dīn al-Hilālī (1894–1987) and Muḥammad Muḥsin Khān (b. 1927), can give us a clue as to what might have taken place. Like the earlier edition of the Saudi edition of QT, the earlier edition of the Hilālī-Khan translation associated *al-maghdūb* with 'the Jews' and *al-Ḍāllīn* with 'the Christians.' This translation drew harsh criticism for its polemical tone and was thus rephrased using a longer description, perhaps, as suggested by Stefan Wild, some time after 9/11.[52]

The second issue is interpretive. The earlier Saudi edition makes explicit mention of Jews and Christians in its translation of this verse, thereby taking a bold stance against both religious communities. This translation choice finds its justification in the pre-modern Arabic *tafsīr* tradition: many of these commentaries do indeed interpret the phrase as referring to Jews and Christians, such as, for example, al-Ṭabari, Ibn Kathīr, al-Qurṭubī, and al-Ṣuyūṭī, to name only a few. The latter Saudi

52 Stefan Wild, 'Muslim Translators and Translations of the Qur'an into English', *Journal of Qur'anic Studies*, 17.3 (2015), 158–82 (pp. 173–74), https://doi.org/10.3366/jqs.2015.0215.

edition substitutes the explicit reference to Jews and Christians with an explanation in parenthesis. Thus, *al-maghḍūb* is explained as meaning *'orang-orang yang mengetahui kebenaran dan meninggalkannya'* ('those who know the truth but refrain from it'), while *al-ḍāllīn* is clarified as referring to *'orang-orang yang meninggalkan kebenaran karena ketidaktahuan dan kejahilan'* ('those who renounce the truth due to their stupidity and ignorance'). This reading is similar to that provided in *Tafsīr al-Muyassar*[53] (which is also published by the King Fahd Complex as a kind of guide to Qur'an translation).[54] Given the glaring resemblance between the two, and the importance of Ibn Kathīr for Salafī hermeneutics,[55] it is likely that the explanations provided in the parenthesis are taken from Ibn Kathīr's characterization of Jews and Christians in his commentary for this verse.[56] In short, the Saudi edition has changed from explicitly mentioning the name of these two religious communities to instead referring to their characteristics as informed by Ibn Kathīr's Qur'an commentary.

However, unlike the edition published by King Fahd Complex, all of the editions published in Indonesia were reluctant to explicitly associate the phrases *al-maghḍūb ʿalayhim* and *al-ḍāllīn* with Jews and Christians, despite the prevalence of this interpretation in the classical *tafsīr* tradition. Instead of mentioning both religious communities explicitly, they opt to comment on the phrasing in notes. The note in the first and the second edition reads: *'yang dimaksud dengan mereka yang dimurkai dan mereka yang sesat ialah semua golongan yang menyimpang dari ajaran Islam'* ('the meaning of 'those with whom [God] is wrathful and those who go astray' is all communities who stray from the teachings of Islam'). The third edition changes this to *'Mereka yang dimurkai adalah mereka yang sengaja menentang ajaran Islam. Mereka yang sesat adalah mereka yang sengaja mengambil jalan lain selain ajaran Islam'* ('Those with whom

53 Nukhbat al-ʿUlamāʾ al-Tafsīr, *Tafsīr Al-Muyassar* (Medina: Mujammaʿ al-Malik Fahd li Ṭibāʿāt al-Muṣḥaf al-Sharīf, 2008), p. 1.

54 Mykhaylo Yakubovych, 'Qur'an Translations into Central Asian Languages: Exegetical Standards and Translation Processes', *Journal of Qur'anic Studies*, 21.1 (2022), 89–115 (p. 91), https://doi.org/10.3366/jqs.2022.0491.

55 Walid A. Saleh, 'Preliminary Remarks on the Historiography of Tafsir in Arabic: A History of the Book Approach', *Journal of Qur'anic Studies*, 12 (2010), 6–40 (p. 34), https://doi.org/10.3366/E146535911000094X.

56 ʿImād al-Dīn Abū al-Fidāʾ Ismāʿīl Ibn Kathīr, *Al-Tafsīr al-Qurʾān al-ʿaẓīm*, 15 vols (Giza: Muʾassasa Qurṭuba, 2000), i, p. 223.

[God] is wrathful are those who deliberately confront the teachings of Islam. Those who go astray are those who deliberately take a path other than the teachings of Islam'). There is thus no clear mention of either religious community in the notes to any of the first three editions, a firm indication of the fact that the committee indeed deliberately refrained from mentioning such an established, mainstream reading. The reason, for Muchlis M. Hanafi, the director of the LPMQ, is that the Jews and the Christians mentioned in those commentaries were originally only referenced as examples by the *tafsīr* tradition.[57] Eventually, the fourth edition does not include any footnote on this issue, probably in an attempt to avoid engaging in the debate on it entirely.

The reluctance of QT to engage in inter-religious polemics is sensible given that Indonesia is home to several different religious communities, including Christians. Accordingly, explicitly singling out a particular religion in such a widely read, state-produced translation would potentially undermine interreligious harmony, which is always an issue that is fraught with peril in the Indonesian context. Nevertheless, the initial adjustment of the Saudi edition reflects that the committee members, specifically from the King Fahd Complex, were unsatisfied with the original wording of the first edition, although it was most probably driven by theological concerns. Thus, the difference of interest between the Indonesian and Saudi authorities, in this case, brought about a difference in translation decisions. Furthermore, if Wild's observation about the Hilālī-Khān translation is correct, the change of the translation of this verse in the latter Saudi edition of QT might also have something to do with 9/11, and was thus related to the King Fahd Complex's response to the global context instead of MORA's initiative.

Let us now turn our attention to Q 3:19, which begins with the phrase:

إن ٱلدين عند ٱلله ٱلإسلٰم

True religion, In God's eyes, is Islam

Here is how the editions of QT render the relevant text:

57 Mohammad, p. 79.

First edition	*Sesungguhnja agama (jang diridhai) di sisi Allah hanjalah Islam*	[Verily, the religion (that is accepted) by Allah's side is only Islam]
Second/Saudi edition	*Sesungguhnya agama (yang diridhai) di sisi Allah hanyalah Islam*	[Verily, the religion (that is accepted) by Allah's side is only Islam]
Third edition	*Sesungguhnya agama di sisi Allah ialah Islam*	[Verily, the religion in Allah's side is only Islam]
Fourth edition	*Sesungguhnya agama (yang diridhai) di sisi Allah ialah Islam*	[Verily, the religion (that is accepted) by Allah's side is only Islam]

It is very clear that the editions of QT share a common rendition of this verse, and that the addition of '*yang diridhai*' ('which is blessed') in brackets in the first and fourth editions serves only as emphasis. The removal of this phrase from the third edition does not seem to have a specific reason; it is likely that it is simply a result of the editorial decision to shorten the target text in this edition. None of the editions provide any annotation for this verse.

An alternative translation of this verse was suggested by Nurcholish Madjid (1939–2005) in 1992. In his *Islam, Doktrin, dan Peradaban,* he translates the verse as '*Sesungguhnya agama bagi Allah ialah sikap pasrah kepadanya* (*al-islām*)' ('Verily, religion before Allah is submission to Him [*al-islām*]') and argues that this reading is the core teaching of the Qur'an. This is to say, according to his reading, the term *al-islām* in this verse refers to its generic meaning of 'submission' instead of the historical meaning according to which it signifies Islam as an institutionalized religion. While the latter interpretation of the verse implies an exclusivist reading of the word *islām*, according to which salvation can only be obtained by following the tenets of the Islamic faith, the former suggests a pluralist approach to other religions; that all religions teach compassion and submission to God.[58] Madjid is pretty much consistent in the way he treats *islām* in his translation. Almost

58 Nurcholish Madjid, *Islam: Doktrin dan Peradaban* (Jakarta: Paramadina, 1992), p. 3.

all of the words derived from the verbal root *s-l-m* are translated as meaning *'pasrah'* ('to submit'). His argument is that, because the term is repeatedly used in relation to the predecessors of Muhammad, *islām* is not the religion of Muhammad alone, but also of Nūh (Noah), Ibrāhīm (Abraham), Iṣḥāq (Isaac), and Yaᶜqūb (Jacob). Madjid points out that the Qur'an tells us that Ibrāhīm delivered a message to his successor, Yaᶜqūb, through Iṣḥāq, to submit (*aslim*) to God in Q 2:131–132. He also mentions that the verb *s-l-m* is, in fact, also used in relation to Jesus (ᶜĪsā) in Q 3:52. Judaism and Christianity, he continues, are rooted in this message, and therefore, both religions are *al-islām*.[59]

The various QT translation teams do not go so far as to accommodate Madjid's vision in their translations. Even though, in some cases, they do render words derived from *s-l-m* with its generic meaning of 'submit,' as in Q 2:131 and Q 3:52, they cannot be more explicit in mentioning Islam as an institutionalized religion revealed through Muhammad in those cases where it matters the most. Thus, when it comes to Q 2:132, the first, second, and Saudi editions of QT render the phrase *illā wa antūm muslimūn* ('unless you [pl.] are Muslim') as *'kecuali dalam memeluk agama Islam'* ('unless you embrace Islam'), while the third edition renders it as *'kecuali dalam keadaan muslim'* ('unless you are in the state of being a *Muslim*'). This is also the case for Q 3:19.

The discrepancy in the approach to the translation of Q 1:7 and Q 3:19 is significant. Social and interreligious harmony has always been a major concern for the Indonesian government, as it is for MORA. Nevertheless, this does not mean that those working on the various QT teams subscribe to the more liberal view when it comes to religious pluralism. The state wishes to reduce the potential for interreligious tensions and maintain harmony among its citizens. But the rejection of a pluralistic reading in these two verses indicates that, despite wishing to avoid explicit condemnation of other religions, those producing the translation are not willing to go so far as accepting that all religions are the same before God. As a consequence, QT continues to conform to the widely accepted theological position taken by Sunnī Islam.

59 Madjid, pp. 456–59.

Conclusion

This chapter has revealed that there is no formal connection between QT and the 1974 Marriage Law and KHI. The translations of the polygamy verse provided in QT seem to be somewhat accommodating of the voices of progressive scholars who object to polygamy, emphasizing that the required criteria of *ᶜadl* also refers to affection in marriage. However, there is no direct reference to the legal requirements for polygamous marriage as mentioned in the Marriage Law of 1974 and the KHI, which the committee clearly could have chosen to include in the translation if they wished: from a political point of view, QT is the project of the state, like the Marriage Law and the KHI.[60] This was, however, a path that the committee never took.

When it comes to the issue of official reform to Islamic education, state reforms have contributed to the emergence of distinctive religious discourses in Indonesia. However, it should be noted that these reforms are not monolithic, as it is clear that different scholars and *ulama* hold a multiplicity of views on various subjects. The individual works of scholarship by academics such as Nasaruddin Umar, Zaitunah Subhan, and Yunahar Ilyas that this study takes into account were all originally written and defended as either Master's or doctorate theses in state-funded Islamic higher education institutions. However, the approaches and opinions that emerge from these works demonstrate very different types of scholarship: while Ilyas sticks to the widely recognized views provided in the majority of Qur'an commentaries, the others show a willingness for re-interpretation and innovation. At this point, however, we can identify which overall position the state wishes to affirm. Out of all the individual academic works (which I classed as 'indirectly

60 Politically, MORA is more than capable of synchronizing all these texts. Additionally, from the exegetical point of view, the KHI was initiated as the national *madhhab* according to the conception of *ijmāᶜ* ('consensus'). This means that, in addition to the explanations given in Qur'an commentaries, the requirements for polygamy mentioned in the law and KHI could be considered as a legal opinion, and hence, could also be placed in the prolonged history of the development of Islamic law. Therefore, the committee could easily have referenced the law as a source in their translation. On the national *madhhab*, see R. Michael Feener, 'Indonesian Movements for the Creation of a "National Madhhab"', *Islamic Law & Society*, 9.1 (2002), 83–115; Howard M. Federspiel, *Indonesian Muslim Intellectuals of the 20th Century*, Southeast Asia Background Series, no. 8 (Singapore: Institute of Southeast Asian Studies, 2006), pp. 53–54.

related' materials in the introduction to this chapter), those that were eventually incorporated into the two volumes that were published as MORA projects—*Wanita Islam Indonesia* and *Rekonstruksi Metodologis*—were those in which figures such as Nasaruddin Umar and Zaitunah Subhan were involved. In contrast, Yunahar Ilyas, for example, has not received the same affirmation. This implies that MORA was inclined to favor the reformist ideas of Nasaruddin Umar and Zaitunah Subhan, while leaving out work written by Yunahar Ilyas.

Against this backdrop, I argue that a heavy reliance on classical Sunnī Qur'an commentaries provides the basic backbone of QT, and it generally only selectively accommodates modernist or reformist ideas. The translation shifts between the editions of QT in each sample case indicate the existence of substantial discussions between the committee members, the results of which show different degrees of adherence to the ideas developed from the attempts of the state to reform and guide religious discourse. On the issue of the first creation of human beings, the translation teams do not seem to be interested in the reformist view. When it comes to issues relating to marriage and polygamy, the influence of new ideas was present in the third edition, albeit in a somewhat ambiguous way, but the team working on the fourth edition clearly made a decision to avoid controversy. Of all these issues, women's rights is the only area that sees a shift between the editions of QT that resonates with the dynamics of the wider intellectual discourse on Islam and gender in Indonesia. Finally, QT seems to implicitly support the idea of religious tolerance, but does not go so far as to subscribe to the liberal view of religious pluralism. Discussion of the sample verse that relates to women's rights also demonstrates that sometimes significant changes to QT are led by political events, and that state reform of religious discourse is not the sole impetus for the interpretive shifts in the target text.

Finally, the interpretive issues QT tackles, and the ones that it leaves out, indicate an essential trait of this translation: it refrains from controversy. For example, the alternative translation of Q 3:19 proposed by Nurcholish Madjid has proven to be provocative and has led to accusations and condemnation from many in the Muslim community.[61]

61 Greg Barton, 'Indonesia's Nurcholish Madjid and Abdurrahman Wahid as Intellectual 'Ulama': The Meeting of Islamic Traditionalism and Modernism

This both reflects and re-affirms something I have mentioned in the previous chapter, the fact that those overseeing the project have consciously avoided inviting the participation of figures known for controversial ideas. Having such individuals involved would actually be counterproductive for QT, as it is intended for the general reader. Producing a radical, modernist translation of the Qur'an would be contentious and would only diminish its credibility and, by association, the credibility of the Ministry of Religious Affairs, among Indonesia's Muslim community.

in Neo-Modernist Thought', *Studia Islamika*, 4.1 (1997), 30–81, http://dx.doi.org/10.15408/sdi.v4i1.786.

6. The Official Translation and Ideological Vocabulary of the State

This chapter will undertake a textual analysis of the rendition of five terms in *Al-Qur'an dan Terjemahnya* in order to investigate the translation decisions that the various QT committees have made when it comes to verses that present ideological problems. The first two are the translations of the word(s) *aḥad/wāḥid* ('one') when used of God, and the translation of *khalīfa* ('successor'). These terms are problematic in the Indonesian context, because *esa* ('one') is a term that is used in the ideological vocabulary of the state whereas *khalīfa* has recently been used by the Hizbut Tahrir Indonesia (HTI, the Indonesian Branch of Hizb ut-Tahrir) to undermine the state's authority. The third and fourth cases involve two terms that some scholars consider to have political and ideological significance in the history of Indonesia: *awliyāʾ* in Q 5:51, and *akābir mujrimīha* ('chief evildoers') in Q 6:123. Nadirsyah Hosen, an Indonesian Professor of Law at Melbourne University, has suggested that the pre-1998 edition of QT rendered the word *awliyāʾ* ('friends, allies, managers') in Q 5:51 as *'pemimpin-pemimpin'* ('leaders') to reflect attitudes towards the New Order 'Interreligious Harmony' government project (*Kerukunan Umat Beragama*). It would have been, he says, counterproductive at the time to translate *awliyāʾ* as *'teman setia'* ('loyal friend'), as the third edition, which was produced in the aftermath of the fall of Suharto in 1998, does. When it comes to Q 6:123, Moch. Nur Ichwan, a Professor of Islamic Studies in Sunan Kalijaga State Islamic University Yogyakarta, has argued that the shift in translation of this verse was, likewise, driven by political circumstances. The initial translation was revised during the New Order period in 1974, Ichwan

 https://doi.org/10.11647/OBP.0289.06

suggests, into a formulation that was sympathetic to the government. The discussion of these verses in this chapter will scrutinize the assessments provided by both scholars. In the last subsection, the analysis focuses on the translation of *ūlu al-amr* ('those in command') in Q 4:59 and 83, which was translated in some editions of QT as *'pemegang kekuasaan'*, ('power holder'), a familiar political concept during the New Order period. This chapter uses these terms to explore the extent to which ideological constraints influence the work of the committee.

Esa and *Khalifah:* Pancasila or Islamic Caliphate

When dealing with the presence of ideological vocabulary of the state within QT, *esa* has precedence over all other words. It is one of the very important keywords in the foundation of the state, Pancasila, the first verse of which affirms *Ketuhanan Yang Maha Esa* ('belief in one Almighty God'). Likewise, QT, the official Qur'an translation of the state, almost always renders the particular, crucially significant word, *aḥad-wāhid,* as *'Maha Esa'* ('Almighty') across all its editions. Does this have anything to do with the politicization of the Qur'an translation?

As mentioned above, *Ketuhanan Yang Maha Esa* is the officially recognized formulation of the first verse of Pancasila as set out in the constitution, and defines the state of Indonesia as being submissive to God. Yet, as mentioned in Chapter One, this principle has a history. It is the result of the negotiations that took place between the founding fathers shortly before the declaration of independence, and replaces a previous formulation that placed Muslims in a privileged position compared to other religions: *Ketuhanan dengan kewajiban menjalankan syari'at Islam bagi pemeluk-pemeluknya* ('Belief in God with the obligation to carry out the Islamic sharia for its believers'). This formula contradicts an idea of the future Indonesia as a unified state that encompasses people of various ethnic and religious identities. Eventually, it became clear that a shift was needed to alleviate discontent among non-Muslim Indonesian communities, who mainly resided in the Eastern part of Indonesia. Thus, *Ketuhanan Yang Maha Esa* is a concept that represents the ideal of a unified, independent Indonesia, that is founded in belief in God and guarantees the same rights to its citizens regardless of their religion. It is a statement that declares the importance of belief in God, but not exclusively the Islamic God.[1]

However, because of the fact that the concept of *Ketuhanan Yang Maha Esa* emerged from a political compromise, there is a certain degree of vagueness in the term that leaves it open to interpretation; while some place emphasis on a specifically Islamic interpretation, others have a more inclusive view of it.[2] For Indonesian Muslims, *esa* stands at the heart of their theology. This word represents the uppermost principle of Islamic faith, namely *tawḥīd* ('oneness, unity'). The amendment of the first verse of Pancasila may have thwarted the aspiration of some Muslim leaders to make the Islamic faith the foundation of the state, but the current formula, to some extent, resonates with its core teaching as *Maha Esa* is an Indonesian phrase that is mainly used in relation to God in the monotheistic worldview.

Maha is an adverb used to signify 'mighty,' and is typically used of God; for example, '*Maha Pengasih*' and '*Maha Penyayang*' are both possible renditions for the Arabic *al-raḥmān al-raḥīm* (two of God's ninety-nine Names, both of which are variations on the word 'merciful'). As for *esa*, it is rooted in the Austronesian language, and basically means '*satu*' ('one'). Some languages in this region, such as Malay and Sundanese, use the word exclusively to refer to God but others, such as Talaud and Simalur, do not.[3] *Kamus Besar Bahasa Indonesia* (KBBI, The Main Dictionary of Indonesian Language) defines it usage in modern Indonesian as meaning '*tunggal*' ('sole') or '*satu*' ('one'), without any emphasis on its exclusiveness to God. In fact, although the example sentences it provides to explain *esa* are closely related to God, the KBBI also cites a couple of local proverbs that use the word *esa* and are not

1 B. J. Boland, *The Struggle of Islam in Modern Indonesia* (Dordrecht: Springer Netherlands, 1971), pp. 27–38, https://doi.org/10.1007/978-94-017-4710-3; Moch. Nur Ichwan, 'Official Reform of Islam: State Islam and the Ministry of Religious Affairs in Contemporary Indonesia, 1966–2004' (unpublished doctoral dissertation, Tilburg University, 2006), pp. 48–49, https://pure.uvt.nl/portal/en/publications/official-reform-of-islam(f07a60f1-bf55-4979-8ea1-bab6e45a42ac).html; Ismatu Ropi, *Religion and Regulation in Indonesia* (Singapore: Springer Singapore, 2017), pp. 70–71, https://doi.org/10.1007/978-981-10-2827-4; Martin van Bruinessen, 'Genealogies of Islamic Radicalism in Post-Suharto Indonesia', *South East Asia Research*, 10.2 (2002), 117–54 (p. 120).

2 Ropi, pp. 89; 219.

3 'ACD—Austronesian Comparative Dictionary—Cognate Sets—e', http://www.trussel2.com/acd/acd-s_e1.htm?zoom_highlight=esa.

related to God. The current colloquial use of the word seems to connote the same sense as Malay does, using it specifically in relation to God. For example, one cannot say *saya memiliki esa computer* ('I have *esa* [one] computer'), instead one says *saya memiliki satu computer* ('I have *satu* [one] computer'). Given all of this, the phrase *Maha Esa* is one that is highly significant for Muslims in Indonesia.

In all editions of QT, *esa* is used to translate the vast majority of Qur'anic occurrences of *aḥad* and *wāḥid* that refer to God, while they are commonly translated as '*satu*' when referring to anything other than God. There are only two exceptions to this: when it comes to Q 29:46, all editions of QT translate *wāḥid* as '*satu*' instead of '*esa*', most probably because the word *wāḥid* in this verse conveys the meaning 'the same God': 'our God and your God are *wāḥid* (the same God)'. (For the sake of comparison, Abdel Haleem translates the verse as 'our God and your God are one [and the same].'[4]) The second exception is Q 38:5 ('How can he claim that all the gods are but one God (*illāhan wāḥidan*)?...'), in which all but the first edition translates the word as '*satu*'. The committee seems to prefer this rendition because the verse conveys the statement of the *mushrikūn* ('polytheists'), whose religious ideas prevent them from accepting the concept of God's oneness.

The words *aḥad* or *wāḥid*, used with reference to God, occur in twenty-three verses of the Qur'an. The instance for which most Qur'an commentaries provide the most nuanced explanation is that found in Q 2:163, 'Your God is the one God (*illāhun wāḥidun*): there is no god but He, Most Gracious, Most Merciful.' They vary in the extent of their explanations for the word *wāḥid*, the range of issues they discuss, their points of view, and the supporting material they bring into their discussions, yet they seem to be in agreement that the word *wāḥid* in this verse has the connotation of uniqueness. This word identifies God as an absolute unique being, to whom nothing is similar (*mithl*) or analogous (*naẓīr*). The commentaries often also discuss the practical ramifications of this idea for Muslims; it requires Muslims to worship no one other than God, consider nothing equal to Him, and not name anything other than Him God. In short, when used in relation to God, the words *wāḥīd* and *aḥad* represent the main tenet of Islamic theology: *tawḥīd*. In more

4 M. A. S. Abdel Haleem, *The Qur'an* (Oxford: Oxford University Press, 2004), p. 255.

practical terms, the word *aḥad* occurs in the second shortest *sūra* of the Qur'an, *al-Ikhlāṣ*, which is taught to children at a very early age and may even be the *sūra* that is most often recited in Muslims' daily prayers.

Thus, there are two different concepts of *esa*. The first is an Islamic *esa* that is the local equivalent for *aḥad*/*wāḥid*, the Qur'anic conceptualization of monotheism, and which has a theologically exclusive connotation. The second is the Pancasila *esa* that defines Indonesia as a religiously observant yet neutral state. At this point, it is tempting to identify the existence of one of the most important words in the ideological apparatus of the state, *esa*, in the official Qur'an translation as the state's imposition of its ideology in QT. It is a feasible assumption indeed, given that MORA is tasked with 'mak[ing] *Ketuhanan Yang Maha Esa* an operative principle in public life'[5] and, as discussed in Chapter Three, successive Indonesian governments have had specific interests in the production of QT.

This assumption, however, seems unwarranted. For starters, the rendering of *aḥad*/*wāḥid* as *esa* in QT is consistently exclusive; it always relates to Islamic monotheism, and is intended for a Muslim readership. Accordingly, one cannot compare QT's interpretation of *esa* to that of Indonesian legal texts in the 1950s and 1960s, such as the blasphemy law; while the former addresses a theologically exclusive conception intended for a Muslim readership, the latter have binding legal force and have had far-reaching consequence for citizens of other faiths.[6] Secondly, the rendition of *aḥad*/*wāḥid* as *esa* was not introduced by QT. Ropi suggests that the phrase *Ketuhanan Yang Maha Esa* was not one that was often used in the political debates between Muslims and secular nationalists prior to Indonesian independence, and was actually an accidental invention during the formulation of the 1945 constitution.[7] Nevertheless, the translation of *aḥad*/*wāḥid* as '*esa*' had been quite prevalent in the Indonesian *tafsīr* tradition long before 1965 when QT first made its

5 Boland, p. 108.

6 Zainal Abidin Bagir, 'Defamation of Religion Law in Post-Reformasi Indonesia: Is Revision Possible?', *Australian Journal of Asian Law*, 13.2 (2013), 1–16; Kikue Hamayotsu, 'The Limits of Civil Society in Democratic Indonesia: Media Freedom and Religious Intolerance.', *Journal of Contemporary Asia*, 43.4 (2013), 658–77; Ropi, p. 112; Alfitri, 'Religious Liberty in Indonesia and the Rights of Deviant Sects', *Asian Journal of Comparative Law*, 3.1 (2008), 1–27, https://doi.org/10.2202/1932-0205.1062.

7 Ropi, pp. 74; 90.

appearance, and even before Pancasila was officially inaugurated as the foundation of the state in 1945. For example, this translation can be found in the works of Mahmud Yunus (1899–1982) and Ahmad Hassan (1887–1958), both of which were published two decades before Pancasila was issued. Going back further, Hamzah Fansuri (d. *c.* 1590) used *'esa'* in his rendition of Q 2:255, and an anonymous manuscript of *al-Kahf* and *Tarjumān al-mustafīd* by ᶜAbd al-Raᵓūf al-Singkīlī (1615–93) composed in the seventeenth century also translated *wāḥid* as *'esa'* in Q 18:10,[8] and (in the case of *Tarjumān al-mustafīd*) in Q 12:39.[9] In short, the tradition of using *esa* with reference to God's 'oneness' predates Pancasila.

As well as being used in the actual translation, *esa* is also used occasionally in the forewords to QT. Its use here could have a different signification because, unlike the actual text of the translation, the foreword is a blank space, in which the author is free to elaborate on its use if they wish. That said, the use of *esa* in the forewords of QT is at best as vague as the use of *Ketuhanan Yang Maha Esa* in Pancasila. Nevertheless, because QT was first produced during the Guided Democracy of Sukarno, it may be intended to convey the idea of the religiously observant yet neutral state, following the reenactment of the 1945 constitution in 1959. Likewise, when the word was used by Suharto, it may have also chimed well with his desukarnoization project. Thus, *esa* in the forewords is mentioned along with, and framed under the concept of, Pancasila of the state or the ruling government.

At this point, it appears that QT conveys two concepts of *esa:* the Qur'anic *esa* and *esa* of Pancasila. The first is *esa* that is based in Islamic theology, and which is inherited through the Islamic intellectual legacy. The second has a more recent significance that should be understood in the context of the ideological battle taking place, first and foremost, during the formation of the Indonesian constitution, and harks back to the replacement of the seven words removed from the Jakarta Charter. In this context, it denotes a universal deity, as part of the inclusive agenda intended to accommodate the equal status of non-Muslim citizens in the country. The former makes its presence in the actual translation of

8 Riddell, *Malay Court Religion, Culture and Language: Interpreting the Qur'ān in 17th Century Aceh*, pp. 29; 130.

9 ᶜAbd al-Raᶜūf ibn ᶜAlī al-Fanṣūrī al-Sinkīlī, *Tarjumān al-mustafīd* (Singapore: Sulaymān Marᶜī, 1951), p. 241.

the Qur'anic text, whereas the latter is used in the forewords written by government officials. The use of *esa* to translate *aḥad/wāḥid* in the Qur'anic text does not denote the ideological presence of the state in QT, but its use in the foreword does.

There are two other, inter-related dimensions to the translation of *aḥad/wāḥid* as *'esa'*, that relate to the consistent and incrementally increasing distribution of QT over the decades, and the privilege it holds as the official translation of the state. First, the translation of *aḥād-wāḥīd* as *'esa'* seems to have become the norm. Previously, it was not always the case, and some other translations, such as those by Zainuddin Hamidy (1907–57) and Fakhruddin Hs. (b. 1906), A. Hasan, and Mahmud Yunus, did not always use *esa* on every occasion in which *aḥād* or *wāḥīd* is used in relation to God (although they all do use *esa* in some verses). Likewise, in his *Tafsīr Juz ʿAmmā Bahasa Melayu,* written in 1938, Jama'in Abdul Murad (b.1900) translates the word *aḥad* in Q 112:1 as *'satu',* not *esa.*[10] In contrast, nowadays it has become natural to translate *aḥad/wāḥid* as *'esa'* when it is related to God. Almost all of the Qur'an translations published after QT consistently make this choice, even including a translation which was written with the explicit intention of challenging QT and the authority of the state, the *Tarjamah Tafsiriah* of Muhammad Thalib. QT, therefore, has probably contributed to normalizing this particular usage. Secondly, the normalization of this translation emphasizes the 'Islamic' dimension of Pancasila; in other words, it influences how people perceive the Pancasila notion of *Ketuhanan Yang Maha Esa,* fostering a tendency to consider the notion as exclusively Islamic.

It is certainly clear that, as indicated earlier, a rather Islamic interpretation of *Ketuhanan Yang Maha Esa* has prevailed since the early days of Indonesian independence. As early as 1953, Agus Salim, one of the leaders of Masyumi, wrote of his concerns about state unity because of the perceived association of *Ketuhanan Yang Maha Esa* with Q 5:44, 45 and 47, verses that condemn those who do not rule according to God's law.[11] Two years earlier, Hamka wrote *Urat Tunggang Pantjasila,* in which he interprets *Ketuhanan Yang Maha Esa* as referring to submission before

10 Jama'in Abdul Murad, *Tafsīr Juzʾ ʿAmmā Bahasa Melayu* (Patani: Maṭbaʿa ibn Halābī), p. 175.

11 Agus Salim, *Ketuhanan Yang Maha Esa* (Jakarta: Bulan Bintang, 1977), p. 10.

God. He also suggests that Indonesian Muslims have throughout history been driven in their struggle for Indonesian independence by this kind of belief.[12] Ropi suggests that this Islamic interpretation was intended to 'rebuild the psychological confidence' of Muslims following their failures in the struggle to establish an Islamic state and in Islamizing the state's stance on religion.[13]

Let us look at a recent example of this in action. In 2017, through the Government Regulation in Lieu of Law (PERPPU) No. 2/2017, the government officially dissolved the HTI, one of several Indonesian Islamist movements that continue to challenge the authority of the state. The grounds for the government action were the conviction that the HTI posed a threat to the unity of Indonesia because of their intensive campaign for the establishment of an Islamic caliphate. The HTI challenged the regulation in the administrative court. In his plea, Eggi Sudjana, the HTI advocate, citing the main premise of the regulation that any mass organization which contradicts Pancasila should be dissolved, claimed that the regulation was irrelevant because it effectively disbanded any religion other than Islam. According to Sudjana, the Pancasila concept *Ketuhanan Yang Maha Esa* is only relevant to monotheistic religions, and the only monotheistic religion practiced in Indonesia is Islam: Christianity has a trinity, Hinduism has Trimurti, and Buddhism does not have any concept of God.[14]

The plea from Sudjana shows that there are cases in which an 'Islamic' interpretation of *Ketuhanan Yang Maha Esa* is directed against the state. Muhammad Rizieq Syihab, for example, argues, in a similar vein to Eggi Sudjana, that *Ketuhanan Yang Maha Esa* is a concept that is recognized only within Islamic theology.[15] Syihab thus restricts the relevance of *Ketuhanan Yang Maha Esa* in Pancasila to Islam only, rather than reading it as a neutral statement that supports religious diversity. This interpretation paves the way for Syihab to argue that the implementation of Islamic laws in Indonesia is only possible through a

12 Hamka, *Urat Tunggang Pantjasila* (Jakarta: Pustaka Keluarga, 1951).

13 Ropi, pp. 90–91.

14 Eggi Sudjana, 'Perbaikan Permohonan Perkara Nomor : 58/PUU-XV/2017', 15 September 2017.

15 Al-Habib Muhammad Rizieq Bin Husein Syihab, 'Pengaruh Pancasila terhadap Penerapan Syariah Islam di Indonesia' (unpublished Dissertation, Universiti Malaya, 2012), p. 58.

true understanding of Pancasila. True Pancasila, according to Syihab, is the Jakarta Charter version that states *Ketuhanan dengan kewajiban menjalankan syariat Islam bagi pemeluk-pemeluknya* rather than the revised, more inclusive, wording. Syihab's interpretation of Pancasila is Islamic and exclusive, and through it he aims to justify the implementation of Islamic law in the country.

This brings us to the next word that will be discussed in this chapter: *khalīfa*, often translated into English as 'vicegerent', 'ruler,' or 'leader'. Let us start by discussing the significance of this Qur'anic term to the HTI. The HTI is the Indonesian wing of Hizb ut-Taḥrīr (The Liberation Party), which was founded in Jerusalem by Taqī al-Dīn al-Nabhānī (1909–77). It is a political party that fights for an Islamic caliphate that goes beyond national borders and aims to implement Islamic law and establish a global caliphate. The HTI has wide support in Indonesia, and a conference held by the party in Jakarta in 2007 was attended by something like 80,000 people, even though it had been operating underground between its initial emergence in the 1980s and 1998.[16] The freedom of expression guaranteed by the state after the *Reformasi* has enabled exponential growth and support for Islamic movements such as the HTI. Its Qur'an and *ḥādith* based rhetoric appeals to many Indonesians, especially the urban youth. Their idea of a caliphate dismisses the concept of Indonesia as a nation-state and aims at implementing a single governing system for all the Muslims, and thus the HTI are categorically opposed to Pancasila.

The word *khalīfa* features frequently in the rhetoric used by the HTI to advocate for their goal of an Islamic caliphate, and herein lies the importance of our second key word. The word *khalīfa* is mentioned only twice in the Qur'an: in Q 2: 30[17] and Q 38:26.[18] In the plural form, there

16 van Bruinessen, 'Overview of Muslim Organizations, Associations and Movements in Indonesia', p. 38; Meerim Aitkulova, 'Hizb Ut-Tahrir: Dreaming of Caliphate', in *Handbook of Islamic Sects and Movements*, ed. by Muhammad Afzal Upal and Carole M. Cusack, Brill Handbook on Contemporary Religion, 21 (Leiden - Boston: Brill, 2021), pp. 402–20 (pp. 42–46).

17 '[Prophet], when your Lord told the angels, "I am putting a successor (*khalīfa*) on earth," they said, "How can You put someone there who will cause damage and bloodshed, when we celebrate Your praise and proclaim Your holiness?" but He said, "I know things you do not."'

18 'Dāwud, We have given you mastery (*khalīfa*) over the land. Judge fairly between people. Do not follow your desires, lest they divert you from God's path: those who

are references to *khalāʾif* in Q 6:165,[19] Q 35:39[20] and *khulafāʾ* in Q 27:62.[21] None of the verses deals specifically with a governmental system, hence, they say nothing about the necessity of re-establishing an Islamic caliphate modeled on the early history of Islam as proposed by the HTI. Q 2:30, '[Prophet], when your Lord told the angels, "I am putting a *khalīfa* (successor) on earth,"' deals with the issue of human existence in the world as the *khalīfa* of God, and Q 38:26, 'Dāwud, We have given you *khalīfa* (mastery) over the land' relates to Dāwud, who became a *khalīfa* (ruler), meaning he should rule justly. However, since the *Reformasi*, the HTI has overwhelmingly used the term *khilāfa* (Islamic caliphate) in its public propaganda, a word that they conflate with the Qur'anic term *khalīfa*, which they have co-opted into the framework of their ideas of a caliphate. For this reason, opponents of the HTI, both at individual and state level, have sought to clarify what the Qur'anic *khalīfa* means as a way to undermine the HTI's discourse. During the hearing on the dissolution of the HTI held in 2018, Yudian Wahyudi, the then Rector of UIN Sunan Kalijaga (and current Chairman of Badan Pembinaan Ideologi Pancasila, BPIP, The Agency for Pancasila Ideology Education), emphasized that the Qur'an did not justify HTI's concept of an Islamic caliphate and that the Qur'anic word *khalīfa* has nothing to do with this idea. Instead, this word, according to Wahyudi, refers to human beings in terms of all their positive and negative potential to manage the world.[22]

There is initially nothing interesting about the way QT translates *khalīfa*. All editions are consistent in not translating the word but instead

wander from His path will have a painful torment because they ignore the Day of Reckoning.'

19 'It is He who made you successors (*khalāʾif*) on the earth and raises some of you above others in rank, to test you through what He gives you. [Prophet], your Lord is swift in punishment, yet He is most forgiving and merciful.'

20 'It is He who made you [people] successors (*khalāʾif*) to the land. Those who deny the truth will bear the consequences: their denial will only make them more odious to their Lord, and add only to their loss.'

21 'Who is it that answers the distressed when they call upon Him? Who removes their suffering? Who makes you successors (*khulafāʾ*) in the earth? Is it another god beside God? Little notice you take!'

22 M. Djidin and Sahiron Syamsuddin, 'Indonesian Interpretation of the Qur'an on Khilāfah: The Case of Quraish Shihab and Yudian Wahyudi on Qur'an, 2: 30–38', *Al-Jami'ah: Journal of Islamic Studies*, 57.1 (2019), 143–66, https://doi.org/10.14421/ajis.2019.571.143-166; Saidurrahman and Azhari Akmal Tarigan, *Rekonstruksi Peradaban Islam Perspektif Prof. K.H. Yudian Wahyudi, Ph.D.* (Jakarta: Prenadamedia Grup, 2019), pp. 135–37.

using the original Arabic word, either with or without the additional gloss *'penguasa'* ('ruler', 'authority') in parenthesis. However, things become more interesting when the third edition introduces a footnote for Q 2:30, which the fourth edition refines. The footnote in the third edition reads: *'khalifah bermakna pengganti, pemimpin, atau penguasa'* (*'khalifah* means successors, leaders, or rulers'), while that of the fourth edition goes: *'Di dalam Al-Qur'an kata khalīfah memiliki makna pengganti, pemimpin, penguasa, atau pengelola alam semesta'* ('in the Qur'an, the word *khalīfa* has the meaning of successors, leaders, rulers, or managers of the universe'). There is thus a slight change, but both footnotes essentially reflect the view provided by the *tafsīr* tradition.

The lack of footnoting in the first two editions shows that the committee was initially not concerned with giving any additional explanation for *khalīfa.* Most likely, this reflects the fact that they considered it self-explanatory. Yet, in the third edition the committee finds it necessary to give an extra explanation, and it is safe to assume that this is due to the growing public discourse on the word caused by the rhetoric used by the HTI as the movement continued to grow in popularity. Events during the Jakarta gubernatorial election in 2017 and 'Aksi Bela Islam' (ABI, Defending Islam Action) (on which there will be more in the next chapter) then provided the momentum for the HTI to attract even more support, and the word *khalīfa* in the Qur'an became increasingly identified with the concept of the Islamic caliphate. The addition of a note in the third edition limits the meaning of *khalīfa* to the concept of leadership and allows HTI sympathizers to connect the word with the political significance of their interests. The fourth edition eventually adds one more meaning in the footnote, 'managers of the universe,' which is similar to that proposed by Wahyudi during the aforementioned hearing, in that the word is stripped of any political nuance.

The case of *aḥad/wāḥid* and *khalīfa* gives us an indication of the way the QT committee deals with words with ideological significance in Indonesia. In both cases, the translation provided in QT reflects that fact that even though external affairs might have influenced the decision of the committee, they keep their interpretation in line with the view provided by the *tafsīr* tradition. The connotative range of the word *esa* develops to follow two different trajectories and, with the rise of Islamism after the *Reformasi*, the exclusively Islamic interpretation of Pancasila challenges the religiously neutral and the inclusive Islamic interpretations. The state has taken measures to counter such challenges, including the dissolution of the HTI and later Front Pembela Islam (FPI, The Islamic Defender Front). Yet, in the context of the official Qur'an translation, its intervention is minimal. In fact, it appears that those working on the translation of QT tend to be disinterested in the growing discourse surrounding the symbolic meaning of *esa* and instead stick to the Qur'anic sense of *esa* that has been transmitted since the early Islamization of the Malay-Indonesian world. While this line of interpretation could be considered exclusivist, the committee does not seem to be concerned. When it comes to *khalīfa*, QT shows its support of the state's interests, but—as is the case with *esa*—they do not want to go beyond the interpretive range expressed in the *tafsīr* tradition.

Q 5:51, *Awliyāʾ*: '*Pemimpin-pemimpin*' ('Leaders') or '*Teman Setia*' ('Loyal Friend')

Q 5:51 is another Qur'anic verse that has ideological complications in the Indonesian context. It prohibits Muslims from making Jews and Christians *awliyāʾ*, making this a word that could have possible ideological consequences in terms of the constitution of the state, the political rights of its citizens, and Muslims' attitudes towards non-Muslim minorities in the country.[23] The word *awliyāʾ* itself presents a relatively sophisticated hermeneutical problem. The ambiguous nature of the word has ramifications when it comes to deciding how to interpret and translate it, and how to convey the significance of the word in each particular Qur'anic usage, especially given the polyvalent views provided in Qur'an commentaries. It represents a profound challenge for any translator seeking equivalence and raises concerns about whether to opt for a linguistically faithful rendition or not, and

23 In the global context, Pink suggests that the verse is 'loaded with possible ideological implications concerning the attitude towards the West, the state of Israel, and non-Muslim minorities in Muslim majority societies.' Johanna Pink, 'Tradition and Ideology in Contemporary Sunnite Qur'ānic Exegesis: Qur'ānic Commentaries from the Arab World, Turkey, and Indonesia and Their Interpretation of Q 5:51', *Die Welt Des Islams*, 50 (2010), 3–59 (p. 7), https://doi.org/10.1163/157006010X489801.

how much liberty to take in conveying what could be considered as the intended meaning in each particular instance. These interpretive issues often lead to ideological disputes that include taking this verse as a justification for refusing to associate with Jews and Christians. The verse reads as follows:

> يٰأيها ٱلذين ءامنوا لا تتخذوا ٱليهود وٱلنصـٰرىٰ أولياء بعضـهم أولياء بعض ومن يتولهم منكم فإنهٔ منهم إن ٱلله لا يهدى ٱلقوم ٱلظـٰلمين
>
> You who believe, do not take the Jews and Christians as allies (*awliyāʾ*): they are allies (*awliyāʾ*) only to each other. Anyone who takes them as an ally (*yatawallahum*) becomes one of them—God does not guide such wrongdoers...

A survey of the interpretations given in Qur'an commentaries on this verse reveals a number of semantic possibilities in the reading of *awliyāʾ*. For example, it is interpreted as meaning helpers (*anṣār*) and allies (*ḥulāfāʾ*), as in al-Ṭabari (d. 311/923);[24] having good social relationships, as in al-Shawkāni (d. 1250/1834);[25] being dependent on their support, making them brothers, and showing affection towards them, as in Fakhr al-Dīn al-Rāzi (d. 1210), al-Alūsī (d. 1270/1854), the two Jalāls, and al-Qāsimī (d. 1332).[26] Some commentators, such as Ibn Kathīr (d. 1372) and al-Zamakhsharī (d. 538/1144), report a story about ᶜUmar ibn al-Khaṭṭāb's disapproval of Abū Mūsā al-Ashᶜarī's approval of a report that was written by a Christian. In the context of this story, Ibn Kathīr adds one more meaning to his discussion of *awliyāʾ*: that the verse warns against making them entrusted persons by whom Muslims'

24 Abū Jaᶜfar Muḥammad ibn Jarīr al-Ṭabarī, *Jāmiᶜ al-bayān ᶜan taʾwīl āy al-qurʾān*, ed. by ᶜAbullāh ibn ᶜAbd al-Muḥsin al-Turkī, 24 vols (Cairo: Dār Hijr, 2001), viii, p. 507.

25 Royal Aal al-Bayt Institute for Islamic Thought, 'Tafsīr Maḥāsin al-taʾwīl / Muḥammad Jamāl al-Dīn al-Qāsimī (d. 1332 AH) sūrat al-Māʾida 51', *Altafsir.Com*, https://www.altafsir.com/Tafasir.asp?tMadhNo=0&tTafsirNo=102&tSoraNo=5&tAyahNo=51&tDisplay=yes&UserProfile=0&LanguageId=1.

26 Fakhr al-Dīn al-Rāzī, *Mafātīḥ al-ghayb*, 32 vols (Beirut: Dār al-Fikr, 1981), xii, pp. 17–18; Abū al-Faḍl Shihāb al-Dīn al-Sayyid Maḥmūd al-Alūsī, *Rūḥ al-maᶜānī fī tafsīr al-qurʾān wa al-sabᶜ al-mathānī*, 30 vols (Beirut: Iḥyāʾ al-Turāth al-ᶜArabī), vi, p. 156; Jalāl-u-dīn Muḥammad ibn Aḥmad ibn Muḥammad al-Maḥallī and Jalāl-u-dīn ᶜAbd-l-raḥmān ibn Abī Bakr al-Ṣuyūṭī, *Tafsīr Al-Imāmayn al-Jalīlayn* (Dār Ibn Kathīr), p. 117; Royal Aal al-Bayt Institute for Islamic Thought, 'Tafsīr Maḥāsin al-taʾwīl / Muḥammad Jamāl al-Dīn al-Qāsimī (d. 1332 AH) sūrat al-Māʾida 51'.

affairs are handled.[27] However, reading Q 5:51 in conjunction with the next verse elicits another semantic dimension of *awliyāʾ*, as verse 52 contains a segment that explains the motive behind the prohibition of taking Jews and Christians as *awliyāʾ*, namely 'we are afraid fortune may turn against us' (*nakhshā an tuṣības dāʾira*), thereby implying that the verse is concerned with Muslims seeking protection from the Jews and the Christians for their fear of misfortune.

The word *awliyāʾ* is mentioned in forty-two places across the Qur'an. In general, it is translated using a wide range of options in Qur'an translations and commentaries produced and distributed in Indonesia. The most popular of those options is to render it as *'pemimpin-pemimpin'* ('leaders'), and this is the case in many translations of Q 5:51. This translation implies that the verse is understood to negate the possibility of non-Muslim leadership in Indonesia, a position that directly contradicts the constitution.[28] Accordingly, this verse has been constantly employed in the political arena in Indonesia in order to prevent non-Muslims from occupying significant political positions. In 1974, a periodical affiliated with Persis called *Al-Muslimun* used this interpretation of *awliyāʾ* as the basis for its proposal that Muslims retract their support for political

27 ʿImād al-Dīn Abū al-Fidāʾ Ismāʿīl Ibn Kathīr, *Al-Tafsīr al-qurʾān al-ʿaẓīm*, 15 vols (Giza: Muʾassasa Qurṭuba, 2000), v, p. 253; Ibn ʿUmar al-Zamakhsharī, *Al-Kashshāf ʿan ḥaqāʾiq ghawāmiḍ al-tanzīl wa ʿuyūn al-aqāwīl fī wujūh al-taʾwīl*, 6 vols (Riyad: Maktaba al-'Abīkān, 1998), ii, p. 249.

28 The issue of the criteria for eligibility for the office of President of the Republic of Indonesia formed part of the disputes during the preparations for Independence. Again, the issue pertains to the extent to which religion plays a role in the state. During a meeting of the PPKI, the founding fathers had a heated debate on Article 6 of the then-proposed constitution which stated: 'The President is an indigenous person whose religion is Islam.' Wahid Hasyim suggested that 'if the president is Muslim, his orders would be justified in Islam, and this would make a great impact.' Agus Salim objected to Wahid Hasyim's proposal, but somehow, Sukarno initially endorsed it. However, the requirement that the president must be a Muslim was eventually eliminated and Article 6 was modified to read: 'The President shall be a native Indonesian.' According to the reformatted version of the article, there are four pre-conditions: candidates must be Indonesian citizens by birth; they must never have held, of their own accord, another citizenship; they must never have committed treason; and they must be spiritually and physically able to carry out the duty and obligation of the President and/or Vice-President. Nadirsyah Hosen, 'Race and Religion in the 2012 Jakarta Gubernatorial Election: The Case of Jokowi Ahok', in *Religion, Law and Intolerance in Indonesia*, ed. by T. Lindsey and H. Pausacker, Routledge Law in Asia (London, New York: Taylor & Francis, 2016), pp. 180–94 (p. 181); Ichwan, 'Official Reform of Islam: State Islam and the Ministry of Religious Affairs in Contemporary Indonesia, 1966–2004', pp. 49–54.

parties that include Christian candidates. More recently, during the 1999 elections, Majelis Ulama Indonesia (MUI, Indonesian Ulama Council) and the Muhammadiyah urged Muslims to participate in the elections and to refrain from voting for any political party that had non-Muslim candidates, in response to the fact that about 40 percent of PDI-P candidates were allegedly non-Muslims.[29] Finally, since the *Reformasi* Q 5:51 has been politicized and is frequently used to hinder non-Muslim political leadership in Indonesia.

For QT, the problem presented by Q 5:51 is, again, reflected in a shift in translation in the third edition. The editions of the translation render the verse as follows:

First edition	*Hai orang*^{2} *jang beriman, djanganlah kamu mengambil orang*^{2} *Jahudi dan Nasrani* **mendjadi pemimpin**^{2}**(mu)**: *sebahagian mereka adalah* **pemimpin** *bagi sebahagian jang lain. Barangsiapa diantara kamu mengambil mereka* **mendjadi pemimpin,** *maka sesungguhnja orang itu termasuk golongan mereka. Sesungguhnja Allah tidak memberi pimpinan kepada orang*^{2} *jang zalim.* [People who believe, do not take the Jews and Christians as your leaders (*awliyāʾ*): some of them are leaders to some others. Anyone of you who takes them as leaders, they indeed become one of them. Verily, Allah does not give leadership to wrongdoers]
The 1977 copy of the first edition	*Wahai orang-orang yang beriman, janganlah kamu menjadikan orang Yahudi dan Nasrani sebagai* **wali(mu)**; *sebahagian mereka adalah* **wali** *bagi sebahagian yang lain. Barangsiapa diantara kamu mengambil mereka* **menjadi wali,** *maka sesungguhnya orang itu termasuk golongan mereka. Sesungguhnya Allah tidak memberi petunjuk kepada orang-orang yang zalim.* [People who believe, do not you take the Jews and Christians as your ***wali***: some of them are ***wali*** to some others. Anyone of you who takes them as ***wali***, they indeed become one of them. Verily, Allah does not give guidance to wrongdoers]

29 Hosen, 'Race and Religion in the 2012 Jakarta Gubernatorial Election: The Case of Jokowi Ahok', p. 182.

Second/Saudi edition	*Hai orang*^{2} *yang beriman, janganlah kamu mengambil orang-orang Yahudi dan Nasrani* **menjadi pemimpin-pemimpin(mu)***: sebahagian mereka adalah* **pemimpin** *bagi sebahagian yang lain. Barangsiapa diantara kamu mengambil mereka* **menjadi pemimpin,** *maka sesungguhnya orang itu termasuk golongan mereka. Sesungguhnya Allah tidak memberi petunjuk kepada orang-orang yang zalim.* [People who believe, do not you take the Jews and Christians as **your leaders**: some of them are **leaders** to some others. Anyone of you who takes them as **leaders**, they indeed become one of them. Verily, Allah does not give guidance to wrongdoers]
Third Edition	*Wahai orang-orang yang beriman! Janganlah kamu menjadikan orang Yahudi dan Nasrani sebagai* **teman setia(mu)**; *mereka satu sama lain* **saling melindungi**. *Barangsiapa di antara kamu yang* **menjadikan mereka teman setia**, *maka sesungguhnya dia termasuk golongan mereka. Sungguh, Allah tidak memberi petunjuk kepada orang-orang yang zalim.* [People who believe! Do not you take the Jews and Christians as your **loyal friends**: they are **protecting each other**. Anyone of you who takes them as **loyal friends**, they indeed belong to them. Verily, Allah does not give guidance to wrongdoers]

The first edition renders *awliyāʾ* as *'pemimpin-pemimpinmu'* ('your leaders'). The 1977 copy of this edition shifts the translation of *awliyāʾ* to *'wali'*, using the singular form of the original Arabic word, which is in ubiquitous use in Indonesian. The second and Saudi editions, interestingly, recall the initial translation from the first edition (the 1965 copy). A substantive change occurs in the third edition, shifting the translation of *awliyā* to *'teman setia'* ('loyal friends'), whilst the fourth edition sticks to this latter translation. The rendering of *awliyāʾ* as *'wali'* as in the 1977 copy of the first edition is most probably due the ambiguity of the word, which led the committee working on this edition to refrain from giving any interpretive preference. When it comes to *Pemimpin-pemimpin* ('leaders'), several scholars, as will become clear, suggest that this meaning arguably does not find direct justification in the Qur'an commentaries. *Teman setia* ('loyal friends'), on the other hand, does; it is semantically close to the concepts of allies (*ḥulāfāʾ*),

brotherhood, and showing affection. Taking into account the strict reliance of the committee upon Qur'an commentaries, the shift to *'teman setia'* in the third and fourth editions makes sense. At this point, it is worth investigating why the translation teams that worked on the first, second, and Saudi editions decided on this particular meaning over the other available options, and what the cause of the shift to *'teman setia'* was.

Without a direct justification for the use of *pemimpin-pemimpin* for *awliyāʾ* that is grounded in *tafsīr*, it is reasonable that some scholars consider this translation as narrow and inaccurate, and as distorting the meaning of the original verse and deviating from established readings. In the case of the periodical *Al-Muslimun* mentioned above, the American political scientist Jeremy Menchik has noted that *Al-Muslimun* quotes two verses in which the term *awliyāʾ* was translated as *'ketua-ketua'* ('the leaders'/'the chiefs'). He compares the Arabic-Indonesian translation given in *Al-Muslimun* with an (unidentified) Arabic-English translation, and the Arabic-Indonesian translation strikes him as unusual: the Arabic-English translation renders the term *awliyāʾ* as 'allies,' 'patrons,' 'protectors', helpers,' 'sponsor,' 'guardian,' 'supporters,' or 'friends,' while the Arabic-Indonesian opts for *ketua* ('chief').[30]

Ahmad Sahal, an Indonesian scholar, voices the same concern as Menchik, based on his analysis of a number of English translations: *The Meaning of the Holy Qur'an* by Yusuf Ali, *The Message of the Qur'an* by Muhammad Asad, Abdel Haleem's *The Qur'an*, Marmaduke Pickthal's *The Glorious Qur'an*, N.J. Dawood's *The Koran*, M.H. Shakir's *The Quran*, and T.B. Irving's *The Qur'an*, all of which translate the word as 'friends', 'protector', 'allies', and 'sponsors'. By looking into these English translations, Sahal wants to demonstrate that the popular translation of *awliyāʾ* into Bahasa Indonesia as *'pemimpin-pemimpin'* is misleading and, to use his terminology, distorted. *Awliyāʾ*, he suggests, is the plural form of *walī*, which relates to the concept of *walāʾ* or *muwāla*; both have the meaning of friendship and alliance on the one hand, and protection and patronage on the other; he excludes leadership. This misleading translation, Sahal suggests, might result from the incorrect assumption

30 Jeremy Menchik, '"Do Not Take Unbelievers as Your Leaders" The Politics of Translation in Indonesia', *Mizan*, 2016, http://www.mizanproject.org/do-not-take-unbelievers-as-your-leaders/.

that the word *awliyāʾ* comes from the root *wilāya*, which means *'kepemimpinan'* ('leadership') and *'kepemerintahan'* ('governance'). The flaw in this assumption, Sahal suggests, is obvious, because the word *awliyāʾ* is not accompanied by the preposition *ʿalā* in the verse in question, and *awliyāʾ* only refers to leadership when it is used in conjunction with *ʿalā*.[31]

Johanna Pink agrees with Menchik and Sahal that the translation of *awliyāʾ* as *'pemimpin-pemimpin'* is inaccurate, for, according to her, 'friendship' is cited as the preferred meaning of *awliyāʾ* in classical Arabic Qur'an commentaries. For QT, she argues, the decision to opt for *'pemimpin-pemimpin'* reflects an uncritical reliance on Indonesian Qur'an commentaries, such as those by Mahmud Yunus, A. Hassan, and Hamka. Considering the hermeneutical hierarchy of QT's sources, this assessment seems unwarranted, not to mention that Hamka is not mentioned in any of QT's bibliographies.[32] Pink also echoes the criticism of this translation made by Quraish Shihab, who suggests that *awliyāʾ* in fact denotes some form of closeness that blurs the boundaries between Muslims and non-Muslims.[33] Pink's stance is supported by two Indonesian scholars, Nadirsyah Hosen and Ahmad Ishomuddin, who argue that if one refers to the explanations provided in the *tafsīr* tradition on this verse, none of the authoritative classical commentaries connect the word *awliyāʾ* in Q 5:51 to 'leadership.'[34]

---

31 The article was published for the first time in *Majalah Tempo* in the context of the 2012 Jakarta gubernatorial election when Joko 'Jokowi' Widodo and Basuki, a.k.a. Ahok, took office. The idea was reproduced and republished in *Koran Tempo* with a slight difference in 2016, again in the context of the Jakarta gubernatorial elections. Akhmad Sahal, 'Haramkah Pemimpin Non Muslim?', *Majalah Tempo*, 16 August 2012; Akhmad Sahal, 'Haramkah Pemimpin Non Muslim?', *Koran Tempo*, 25 April 2016.

32 See Chapter Four.

33 Pink, 'Tradition and Ideology in Contemporary Sunnite Qur'ānic Exegesis: Qur'ānic Commentaries from the Arab World, Turkey, and Indonesia and Their Interpretation of Q 5:51', pp. 43–44.

34 Ishomuddin delivered his argument as part of his testimony during the court case of religious blasphemy brought against Basuki Tjahaja Purnama. Mahkamah Agung Republik Indonesia, *Putusan Nomor 1537/Pid.B/2016/PN.Jkt Utr. Tahun 2017 Ir. BASUKI TJAHAJA PURNAMA Alias AHOK* (Jakarta: Direktori Putusan Mahkamah Agung Republik Indonesia, 2017), p. 407, https://putusan.mahkamahagung.go.id/putusan/e8b1049e890f1bf53511d70ffa120602; Nadirsyah Hosen, 'Tafsir Awliya': Bagaimana Kita Harus Bersikap?', *Mengkaji ISLAM Kontekstual Bersama Gus Nadir*, 2017, http://linkis.com/nadirhosen.net/multi/oHlq2; Nadirsyah Hosen, 'Meluruskan Sejumlah Tafsir Surat Al-Maidah 51',

In his analysis of the interpretation of *awliyāᵓ* in *Al-Muslimun*, Menchik suggests that the preference of the periodical for *'ketua-ketua'* ('the leaders'/'the chiefs') as the corresponding word for *awliyāᵓ* cannot be explained by semantic and philological arguments,[35] because it reflects pragmatic political motives. In 1954, *Persatuan Islam* was preparing for a national democratic election, and its main opponents were the nationalist and communist parties. The fact that both the nationalists and communists opposed the implementation of Islamic law by the state on the one hand, and that the Christians were potential allies for both nationalists and communists on the other, inspired them to encourage Muslim voters to vote only for a Muslim party. Menchik argues that the shift away from translating the Qur'anic term *awliyāᵓ* with words such as 'friends' or 'allies' to 'leaders' was due to the politicization of translation in *Al-Muslimun* with the intention of influencing the election.

I would here argue that the fact that Menchik makes recourse to only a few English Qur'an translations means that his analysis of translators' semantic considerations is premature. Arabic dictionaries offer a large range of semantic options for *w-l-y*, the verbal root of *awliyāᵓ*. While it is true that the word has the connotation of 'alliance' and 'friendship,' the semantic range of the verb *w-l-y* and its various derivations is flexible, and the meanings of its various forms range from 'helper,' 'friend,' 'ally,' 'authority,' 'power,' 'having legal power over someone' (in a family relationship, inheritance line, marriage, and captivity), to the verbs 'to help/support,' 'to manage,' 'to administer,' 'to love,' and 'to arbitrate a quarrel.'[36]

NU Online Suara Nahdlatul Ulama, 2016, http://www.nu.or.id/post/read/71937/meluruskan-sejumlah-tafsir-surat-al-maidah-51.

35 Menchik also disassociates this problem from the point of view of the ideological vision of Al-Muslimun. Although Al-Muslimun is affiliated with Persis which was identified as a radical fundamentalist, extreme modernist, or Islamist organization, comparable to the Egyptian Muslim Brotherhood or Jamaat al-Islāmi in Pakistan. However, there was also material promoting religious tolerance and the protection of religious freedom and Christian churches in some places within the same edition. Menchik, '"Do Not Take Unbelievers as Your Leaders" The Politics of Translation in Indonesia'.

36 *Muᶜjam al-Waṣīṭ* explains various meanings of the word, including those with the dimension of 'leadership,' 'management,' 'authority,' and the like. *Waliya al-syaiᵓ wawaliya ᶜalayhi wilāya* translates to *malaka amrahu wa qāma bihi* ('to master/control its affairs and administer it'); *waliya fulān wa waliya ᶜalayhi* means 'to help' or 'to love'; *waliya al-bilād* means 'to control' (*taṣallaṭa ᶜalayhi*); and *tawalla al-syaiᵓ* means 'to manage' (*adbara*). Aḥmad ibn Fāris suggests the root w-l-y denotes something

This semantic range is apparently evident to Mahmud Yunus, an Indonesian translator who has written an Arabic-Indonesian dictionary as well as a Qur'an translation. The entry for *w-l-y* provided in his dictionary points to his understanding of the semantic range of the word in the Qur'an and is, it seems, heavily in debt to *Mu*ᶜ*jam al-Waṣīṭ*. He gives the term various meanings, including 'to protect', 'to help,' 'to love,' and of course, 'to rule or to be the ruler of a land.'[37] Similarly, those are the options he had when he was translating *awliyā*ᵓ in the Qur'an. Perhaps unsurprisingly given this, in his *Tafsir Qur'an Karim Bahasa Indonesia*, Yunus translates the word with twelve different meanings across its various uses in the Qur'an; as *'pemimpin'* ('the leader'), *'kawan-kawan'* ('friends'), *'teman setia'* ('the loyal friends'), *'wali'*, *'penolong* '('the helper'), *'pengikut'*, ('followers') *'Tuhan'* ('the God'), *'yang berhak menguasai'* ('sovereign'), *'pelindung'* ('protector'), *'saudara seagama'* ('brothers in religion'), *'sekutu'* ('allies'), and *'kekasih'* ('lovers'). This use of different meanings depending on the context of the verse is also practiced by the anonymous contributor to *Al-Muslimun*, A. Hassan, and

close; *al-walyu* means *al-qarbu*. The expression *al-mawlā* refers to someone who liberates a captive (*al-mu*ᶜ*tiq*), a liberated captive (*al-mu*ᶜ*taq*), a friend (*al-ṣāḥib*), ally (*al-ḥalīf*), cousin (*ibn al-*ᶜ*amm*), helper (*al-nāṣir*), and neighbor (*al-jār*). Somebody who manages somebody elses affairs is a *wālī*. With reference to the latter, Ibn Fāris conveys an expression that demonstrates the verb (*waliya*) used to mean managing someone's affairs (*wa kullu man waliya amra ākhara fahuwa waliyyuhu*). The alternative form of the plural is *al-walā*ᵓ which means *al-muwālūn*, as illustrated in the expression *al-walā*ᵓ *fulān*. Ibn Mandhūr associates the word with the name of God, *al-Waliyy*, which means the Helper (*al-Nāṣir*), while *al-Wāli* means the Owner/ Authority over everything (*mālik al-ashyā*ᵓ *jamī*ᶜ*iha al-mutaṣarrif fīhā*). The latter indicates *al-wilāya*, which, he quotes from Ibn al-Athīr, is marked by management (*al-tadbīr*), capacity (*al-qudra*), and action/performance (*al-fi*ᶜ*l*). While *al-wilāya* means power and authority (*al-sulṭān, al-imāra*), it also has the dimension of 'supporting and helping' (*al-nuṣra*). *Al-nuṣra* has the same meaning as *al-walāya*. Quoting from Sibawayh, Ibn Mandhūr states that *al-wilāya* refers to the name of something you manage and administer (*ism limā tawallaytahu wa qumta bihi*). Like Ibn Fāris, Ibn Mandhūr discloses various meanings of *mawlā*, one of which is *al-walī alladhī waliya* ᶜ*alayka amraka*. On *tawalla*, Ibn Mandhūr provides a number of examples that explain the meaning of the word as 'to help and/or to manage people's affairs.' *Al-Muwālā* (*wālā-yuwālī*) means 'one who arbitrate the quarrel' and 'one who love.' See Ibn Mandhūr, 'Waliya', *Lisān al-'arab* (Cairo: Dār al-Ma'ārif, 1981), pp. 4920–26; *Majma' al-lugha al-'arabiyya, Mu'jam al-Waṣīṭ*, 4th edn (Cairo: Maktaba al-Syurūq al-Duwaliyya, 2004), pp. 1057–58; Abū Ḥasan Aḥmad Ibn Fāris, *Mu*ᶜ*jam Maqāyis al-luga*, ed. by ᶜAbd al-Salām Muhammad Hārun, 6 vols (Beirut: Dār al-Fikr, 1979), vi, pp. 141–42.

37 Mahmud Yunus, *Kamus Arab-Indonesia* (Jakarta: Hidakarya Agung, 1989), pp. 506–07.

the committee of QT, although they do not agree on the same translation in each specific instance of the word.

Turning now to QT and the renditions of Q 5:51 given in its text, Nadirsyah Hosen makes a similar point to Menchik, claiming that the translation of *awliyāʾ* as *'pemimpin-pemimpin'* in QT reflects an ideological bias towards the New Order governmental project. The translation of *awliyāʾ* into 'leaders', he explains, is found in the pre-1998 edition of QT, while the current version has been revised to include a shift from *'pemimpin'* to *'teman setia'*. According to him, *'pemimpin-pemimpin'* was deliberately chosen in the earlier editions to support the government's promotion of religious harmony during a period in which the government's focus was on maintaining the unity of Indonesia. To translate *awliyāʾ* as *'teman setia'* ('loyal friend') would contradict the program of multicultural inclusivity by effectively telling Muslims not to associate with Christians, and would lead to social tensions. However, after the fall of Suharto the committee revised the translation to *'teman setia'*. The reasoning behind the shift was absent from Hosen's explanation, but clearly he thinks the current translation is better because it subscribes to the views presented in classical Qur'an commentaries, as he says 'they put back [in] what the classical Muslim scholars said in their commentaries.'[38]

Hosen's argument is, however, anachronistic. The project of interreligious harmony was formally introduced during the New Order era,[39] and it is obvious that Hosen is trying to identify QT as the product

38 Hosen delivered his observation while responding to the polemical context of Q.5:51 in the Jakarta 2017 gubernatorial election in a podcast called 'Talking Indonesia' uploaded on the 'Indonesia at Melbourne' blog. He also wrote a significantly summarized version in a serialized tweet commonly known in Indonesia as *kultwit* (an abbreviation from *kuliah twitter*, which means 'tweet-lecture') from his Twitter account in order to gain more attention from his Indonesian followers (his serial tweets were compiled and re-shared by a random account) and re-open the discussion on the topic during what seems to be a routine speech in front of an Indonesian community in Australia (where he currently resides); the video is available on his personal website. Dave McRae, 'Talking Indonesia: Ahok, Race, Religion, and Democracy', Talking Indonesia, http://indonesiaatmelbourne.unimelb.edu.au/talking-indonesia-ahok-race-religion-and-democracy/; Murtadha, 'Penjelasan Kenapa "Awliya" Pernah Diterjemahkan "Pemimpin" di Masa ORBA by @Nadir_Monash', *Chirpstory*, 2016, https://chirpstory.com/li/333681.

39 Tarmizi Taher, the Minister of Religious Affairs of Indonesia between 1993 and 1998, revealed that the term Kerukunan Umat Beragama was officially introduced into the Broad Guidelines of State Policy (Garis Besar Haluan Negara, GBHN), following a

of the New Order regime, just as Federspiel and Feener have done.[40] This assumption is inaccurate as QT was, in fact, produced during the power transition from the Old Order to the New Order, and the first volume of the first edition of QT, which includes Q 5:51, was published under Sukarno in 1965, while the second and third volumes were published under Suharto, in 1967 and 1969 respectively. Additionally, Hosen fails to recognize that the rendition of *awliyā᾽* as *'pemimpin-pemimpin'* in QT is not an exclusive and unprecedented case. In my opinion, connecting the translation of *awliyā᾽* as *'pemimpin-pemimpin'* to the New Order project is historically inaccurate, and associating the revision from *'pemimpin-pemimpin'* to *'teman setia'* in the 2002 edition with the fall of Suharto is equally invalid.

Another historical dimension which might go some way to explaining the Indonesian tradition of translating *awliyā᾽* as *'pemimpin-pemimpin'* can be found in the country's colonial history, specifically, as Johanna Pink argues, in terms of the perceptions Indonesians have of the Dutch.[41] For Indonesians, the Dutch are connected with two identities: the colonizer and the Christian missionary.[42] In the context of colonization, during the early twentieth century the Dutch were considered 'illegitimate leaders' by the Indonesian populace.[43] The colonizers administered

---

presidential and ministerial Decision, based on the speech of K.H.M. Dachlan, the Ministry of Religious Affairs during the opening of the Interreligious Conference (Musyawarah Antara Agama) on November 30, 1967. The politics of interreligious harmony was later heavily indebted to the concepts introduced by A. Mukti Ali, the Minister of Religious Affairs between 1971 and 1978. Ali created more feasible principles for policies of religious harmony, which included acceptance (*prinsip mengakui*), respect (*menghargai eksistensi agama lain*), and cooperatation (*bekerja sama*) between religons. See Sila, p. 123.

40 Moch. Nur Ichwan, 'Negara, Kitab Suci Dan Politik: Terjemahan Resmi Al-Qur'an Di Indonesia', in *Sadur Sejarah Terjemahan Di Indonesia Dan Malaysia*, ed. by Henri Chambert-Loir (Jakarta: Kepustakaan Populer Gramedia, 2009), pp. 417–33 (p. 419).

41 Pink, 'Tradition and Ideology in Contemporary Sunnite Qur'ānic Exegesis: Qur'ānic Commentaries from the Arab World, Turkey, and Indonesia and Their Interpretation of Q 5:51', p. 53.

42 Deliar Noer, 'The Rise and Development of the Modernist Muslim Movement in Indonesia During the Dutch Colonial Period (1900–1942)' (unpublished doctoral dissertation, Cornell University, 1963), pp. 7; 30.

43 Taufik Abdullah, an Indonesian historian, explains the evolution of political images of the Dutch during their occupation of the Indonesian peninsula as a cultural nuisance, occupants of the mythological world and representations of the modern or the West. The last perception mainly spans the period from the early twentieth century until the Independence Day of the Republic of Indonesia, when the

the social, political, and economic affairs of Indonesia, while Christian missionaries successfully attracted religious converts. In fact, the Dutch Vereenigde Oostindische Campagnie (VOC) made the Protestant Church an independent department in their administration because they needed to oversee and control the missionaries so as to avoid conflict with the indigenous Muslim population and maintain their political position in Indonesia.[44] The centuries of Dutch rule created a specific form of historical trauma, which makes its appearance in the exegetical treatment of Q 5:51 in Indonesia.

The existence of the translation of *awliyāʾ* as *'pemimpin-pemimpin'* prior to the publication of QT, as Pink suggests, tells us a story about the connection of colonial history and the interpretation and translation of the Qur'an in Indonesia. During this colonial period, A. Hassan and Mahmud Yunus both chose to translate *awliyāʾ* as *'pemimpin'*, however neither of them explain their preference. Hamka, however, was very aware of the influence colonialism had had on Indonesian culture, and a detailed elaboration in his *Tafsir al-Azhar* (1967) supports the idea that the preference of Indonesian commentators/translators for rendering *awliyāʾ* as *'pemimpin'* was influenced by colonial history. His views on the Dutch, which can be assumed to reflect widely held views, convey a perception of them as Christian colonizers. In his commentary, he highlights the impact of the imposition of Dutch as the state's official language on the social and cultural lives of Indonesians, as well as commenting on the influence of modern rationality on the role of religion in Indonesia. He also addresses the disappearance of the widely-used *Jawi* script, another result of Dutch colonialism.[45] Such experiences can be considered as the driving force for not only Hamka but also his predecessors, all of whom had somewhat similar experiences. In this particular instance, the collective memory of colonialism has contributed to shaping the exegetical preferences of Indonesian Qur'an translators, including those

sentiment of *kemajuan* ('modernizing') and national dignity were articulated. See Taufik Abdullah, 'History, Political Images and Cultural Encounter: The Dutch in the Indonesian Archipelago', *Studia Islamika; Vol 1, No 3 (1994): Studia Islamika*, 2014, http://journal.uinjkt.ac.id/index.php/studia-islamika/article/view/848/726.

44 Husni Mubarok, 'Babak Baru Ketegangan Islam dan Kristen di Indonesia (Book Review)', *Studia Islamika*, 21.3 (2014), 579–601 (pp. 579–601).

45 Kevin W. Fogg, 'The Standardisation of the Indonesian Language and Its Consequence for Islamic Communities', *Journal of Southeast Asian Studies*, 46.1 (2015), 86–110 (p. 91), https://doi.org/doi:10.1017/S0022463414000629.

working on QT. Although colonialism had ended in 1945, during both the Old Order and the New Order, competition between Muslims and Christians was apparent. During the New Order period Indonesian Christians enjoyed political privileges which their Muslim neighbors did not, and many well-educated Christian scholars held strategic positions in government. In the face of this, Muslim leaders and *ulama* saw a need for action to prevent further Christianization of Indonesia by urging people to only vote for Muslim leaders.[46]

The idea that the rendering of *awliyā᾿* as *'pemimpin-pemimpin'* is a reflection of colonial history makes sense, but is only a part of the story. The translations produced during the colonial period had indeed rendered the word *awliyā᾿* as 'leaders.' It is also true that the memory of colonialism remained a determining factor in the preferences of later translators. However, the association of *awliyā᾿* with the concept of leadership and management was already present in Southeast Asian Qur'anic literature a very long time ago, and is, for example, found in *Tarjumān al-mustafīd* in the seventeenth century (although not in Q 5:51). The manuscript of *Tarjumān al-mustafīd*, held in Perpustakaan Nasional Republik Indonesia (PNRI, The National Library of the Republic of Indonesia) under the code ML. 291, indeed renders *awliyā᾿* in Q 5:51 not as 'leadership,' but rather as *'orang yang damping yang berkasih-kasihan'* ('people who are close and loving to each other'). The contemporary Indonesian meaning of *damping* is 'next to', and in ancient Malay it was probably associated with 'being close', while *'berkasih-kasihan'* means 'being in reciprocal love'. Accordingly, the word *awliyā᾿* is here associated with two meanings: being close and feeling reciprocal love towards each other. It is not about leadership. However, in other verses the manuscript renders *awliyā᾿* using words related to management and authority. For example, in Q 4:144 it is translated as *'mengampukan pekerjaan kamu'* ('to give [somebody] charge over your affairs'), and in Q 4:89, it is translated as *'segalayang memerintah yang kamu damping'* ('all who order [who are] close to you'). This leads to the argument that, while it is true that *awliyā᾿* in Q 5:51 is not translated into words related to leadership and the *tafsīr* tradition also does not interpret it as such, other verses that incorporate the word *awliyā᾿* probably do contain that meaning. *Tarjumān al-mustafīd*

46 Hosen, 'Race and Religion in the 2012 Jakarta Gubernatorial Election: The Case of Jokowi Ahok', p. 183.

has shown us that this is the case for Q 4:144 and Q 4:89,[47] and the same is true for many other instances of translations of *awliyāʾ* in QT. Even though QT has revised the translation of the word in Q 5:51 to *teman setia*, this does not mean that the 'leadership' meaning is erased from the translation. In fact, the instances where *awliyāʾ* is translated into '*pemimpin*' in the 2002 edition is higher in number than the 1965–99 editions; seven instances compared to six.

This analysis of *Tarjumān al-mustafīd* informs us about something that is missing from the previous analysis. Perhaps due to the fact that Q 5:51 receives more attention that the other verses that mention *awliyāʾ*, observers have limited their discussion of this word to what the *tafsīr* tradition has to say about this particular verse. However, as already mentioned, although one might not find any Qur'an commentaries associating the word *awliyāʾ* in Q 5:51 with leadership, there are indeed a number of commentaries that interpret instances of this word in other verses with the nuance of 'management.' For example, many Qur'an commentaries associate the word *awliyāʾ* in Q 2:257, 'As for the disbelievers, their allies (*awliyāʾuhum*) are false gods who take them from the light into the depths of darkness', with *mutawallī umūrahum* (those who oversee people's matters). This interpretation is mentioned in, for example, al-Thaᶜlabi's (467) *al-Kashf wa al-bayān*, followed by al-Wāḥidī's (d. 468 H) *al-Wajīz*, Ibn Jawzī's (1116–1201) *Zād al-masīr*, and the *tafsīr*s of al-Bayḍāwī (d. 791/1388) and al-Nasafī (d. 710/1310). Additionally, the views on the issue of leadership expressed in non-*tafsīr* works by a number of classical Muslim scholars, such as al-Māwardī (d. 1058), al-Ghazālī (d. 1111), Qāḍī ᶜIyāḍ (d. 1149), and al-Nawāwī (d. 1277), as well as contemporary scholars such as al-Mawdūdī (1903–79) conveys the belief that a ruler/Imam/Caliph/leader should be a Muslim.[48] Given this, the translators' decision to render *awliyāʾ* as '*pemimpin*' in Q 5:51 does not seem to be completely divorced from the *tafsīr* tradition. While colonial history might play a role in this choice, the justification for this interpretation was already established within the *tafsīr* tradition, just not in terms of the interpretation of Q 5:51.

47 Cited from the manuscript in the National Library of the Republic of Indonesia, code ML 291.

48 Hosen, 'Race and Religion in the 2012 Jakarta Gubernatorial Election: The Case of Jokowi Ahok', p. 183.

As mentioned earlier, the fourth edition retains the third edition's translation of the word *awliyāʾ*. However, this edition does actually introduce a change, albeit to the footnote. In this edition, the phrase 'loyal friends' is appended with a footnote, which directs the reader to a footnote on *awliyāʾ* presented earlier, in Q 3:28,[49] which reads:

> *Kata 'auliyā'' adalah bentuk jamak dari kata 'waliy'. Secara harfiah kata ini berarti dekat sehingga menunjukkan makna teman dekat, teman akrab, teman setia, kekasih, penolong, sekutu, pelindung, pembela, dan pemimpin. Kata 'waliy' dan 'auliya'' dalam AlQur'an diulang 41 kali.*[50] *Maknanya berbedabeda sesuai dengan konteks ayat.*
>
> [The word '*awliyāʾ*' is the plural form of the word '*walī*'. It literally means 'near' and thus denotes 'close friend', 'intimate companion', 'loyal friend', 'lover', 'helper', 'ally', 'protector', 'defender', and 'leader'. The word '*walī*' and '*awliyāʾ*' are repeated 41 times in the Qur'an. Their meanings vary according to the context of the verse.]

This footnote clearly indicates that the committee wishes to inform readers about the ambiguity and multiple possible meanings of *awliyāʾ*, providing detail that was absent in previous editions. This is a new intervention in the text, which almost certainly stems from the controversy that arose around the interpretation of this word, which will be discussed in the next chapter. As we will see, many Indonesian Muslims believe that the correct translation for *awliyāʾ* is '*pemimpin-pemimpin*' rather than '*teman setia*', and many (if not most) of them must have anticipated that the wording would be changed in the new edition of QT. However, because the committee decided to keep '*teman setia*', a disclaimer footnote was deemed necessary.

In conclusion, the preference of the translation committees was for using '*pemimpin-pemimpin*' as the translation of *awliyāʾ* in Q 5:51 in some earlier editions of QT, but this changed and the committees opted for '*teman setia*' in the third and fourth editions. This section has so far shown that in the context of the ambiguity of *awliyāʾ*, external constraints, in this

49 It is unclear, however, why this footnote is assigned to Q 3:28, as this is not the first time the word *awliyāʾ* appears in the Qur'an.

50 There seems to be some mistake here. Muchlis M. Hanafi stated in an interview for a press release from the Ministry of Religious Affairs that this word appears forty-two times in the Qur'an. Further investigation reveals that this word appears forty-two times in forty different verses.

case the collective memory of colonialism, may have been at work in the translators' decision to opt to translate *awliyā᾿* as *'pemimpin-pemimpin'*. However, one of the other possible meanings of *awliyā᾿* involves the concept of leadership and the use of this word in other verses is also interpreted by the *tafsīr* tradition with this semantic signification. Thus, even though the *tafsīr* tradition does not associate *awliyā᾿* in Q 5:51 with leaders, the translators of QT were quite certainly influenced by their knowledge of *tafsīr* in their rendering of this word in other verses. As for the shift to *teman setia* in the third and fourth editions, this must have been the result of a decision by the committee to stick closely to the views presented in the *tafsīr* tradition for this particular verse rather than being influenced by other, external constraints. However, it is necessary to underline the fact that this particular shift in the translation of Q 5:51 does not erase the use of *'pemimpin-pemimpin'* for *awliyā᾿* in QT. The committee seems to continue to take the view that, in some cases, the word *awliyā᾿* means *'pemimpin-pemimpin'*, but in others, it does not.

Q 6:123, *Akābir Mujrimīha*: *'Penjahat Terbesar'* or *'Pembesar yang Jahat'*

The shifts in the translation of Q 6:123, particularly between the first, second, and third editions of QT, provide perhaps the most intriguing instance of an interpretive decision in which external constraints resulting from the government's ideology seem to have made their presence felt. First of all, let us see how the *tafsīr* tradition explains the verse, which reads as follows:

وكذلك جعلنا فى كل قرية أكٰبر مجرميها ليمكروا فيها

> And so We have put chief evildoers in every city to perpetrate their schemes there...

The hermeneutical problem presented by this verse is the identification of who exactly it is that the Qur'an identifies here as *akābir mujrimīhā*, the 'chief evildoers'. There seems to be a consensus in the classical Arabic *tafsīr*s that the first word, *akābir* (literally 'big' or 'great'), refers to *ᶜuzhamā᾿* ('great people'), *ru᾿asā᾿* ('chiefs/leaders'), and *mutraf* ('lavish people'). Al-Ṭabarī suggests that *akābir* means *ᶜuẓamā᾿*. Ibn

Kathīr also mentions the same view, adds *ruᵓasāᵓ* as another meaning, and then, referring to a number of other relevant verses, also interprets the word as *mutraf*. The second word, *mujrimīhā*, is composed of a plural masculine *mujrimūn* and the pronoun *hā* which refers back to the word *qarya* ('village/city') earlier in the verse. The meaning of this word is apparently straightforward; al-Ṭabarī translates it *ahl al-shirk* ('polytheists') and *(ahl) al-maᶜṣiyya* ('wrongdoers') and al-Qurṭubī (d. 671/1272) renders it *fussāq* ('those who are disobedient'). These interpretations are essentially representative of the range of views provided and reproduced in other classical Qur'an commentaries. Some *tafsīrs* explain that the verse was revealed to console the Prophet Muhammad over the resistance he was facing from the elites of his community, reassuring him that every other messenger of God before him had encountered a comparable reception from their people, and that this same situation would occur in every society. Al-Baghāwī (d. 516/1122) provides a nice summary: 'the oppressor in every country will emerge from those with power and authority, while the followers of the prophet are the *ḍuᶜafāᵓ* ('the weak').'[51]

At this point it seems that the verse is not that problematic and its meaning is quite straightforward. However, there was an interesting controversy around this verse in the early 1990s that involved QT. It began with a letter in the daily newspaper *Pelita* in which a reader voiced concerns over the substantial difference in the translations of this verse given in QT and *Al-Qur'an dan Tafsirnya,* despite the fact that both were published by the same institution; QT translates *akābir mujrimīha* as *'penjahat-penjahat yang terbesar'* ('the greatest criminals'), while *Al-Qur'an dan Tafsirnya* renders it as *'pembesar-pembesar yang jahat'* ('the infamous leaders'). The reader called this shift *taḥrīf* ('corruption'),

51 Abū Jaᶜfar Muḥammad ibn Jarīr al-Ṭabarī, *Jāmiᶜ al-bayān ᶜan taᵓwīlī āyi al-qurᵓān*, ed. by ᶜAbullāh ibn ᶜAbd al-Muḥsin al-Turkī, 24 vols (Cairo: Dār Hijr, 2001), ix, p. 537; ᶜImād al-Dīn Abū al-Fidāᵓ Ismāᶜīl Ibn Kathīr, *Al-Tafsīr al-qurᵓān al-ᶜaẓīm*, 15 vols (Giza: Muᵓassasa Qurṭuba, 2000), vi, p. 161; Royal Aal al-Bayt Institute for Islamic Thought, 'Tafsīr al-Jāmiᶜ li Aḥkām al-Qurᵓān / al-Qurṭubī (d. 671 AH) Sūrat al-Anᶜām 123', *Altafsir.Com*, https://www.altafsir.com/Tafasir.asp?tMadhNo=0&tTafsirNo=5&tSoraNo=6&tAyahNo=123&tDisplay=yes&UserProfile=0&LanguageId=1; Royal Aal al-Bayt Institute for Islamic Thought, 'Tafsīr Maᶜālim al-tanzīl / al-Baghawī (d. 516 AH) Sūrat al-Anᶜām 123', *Altafsir.Com*, https://www.altafsir.com/Tafasir.asp?tMadhNo=0&tTafsirNo=13&tSoraNo=6&tAyahNo=123&tDisplay=yes&UserProfile=0&LanguageId=1.

which is always a sensitive allegation to make with regards to the Qur'an. The controversy escalated and the QT translation committee, the MUI, and a number of experts were called in to clarify the situation. Ibrahim Hosen (1917–2001), the head of the committee responsible for *Al-Qur'an dan Tafsirnya,* suggested that readers should give preference to *Al-Qur'an dan Tafsirnya* on the basis that the committee reviewed QT while they were writing *Al-Qur'an dan Tafsirnya.* Muchtar Natsir (1924–2004), the Head Imam of the Istiqlal Mosque, suggested that the difference arose from the different references used for each work: QT's reading depends on the commentary of Abū Suᶜūd, *Gharāʾib al-qurʾān* (author unidentified) and the commentary of 'Al-Fariid' (unidentified) (the latter two commentaries are not mentioned in the bibliography), whereas *Al-Qur'an dan Tafsirnya* refers to *Tafsīr al-Qurṭubī.* He and Hasan Basri (1920–98), the head of the MUI, proposed forming a committee to solve this problem. Finally, the Ministry of Religious Affairs, through the head of the Centre for Research and Development of Religious Literature (Pusat Penelitian dan Pengembangan Lektur Agama), Hafiz Dasuki, discounted the accusation of *taḥrīf.* Dasuki asserted that the difference between the two translations reflected a variation of interpretation instead of corruption.[52]

Considering the timing of the controversy, it was very likely that the reader in question might have read the second edition of QT, which does indeed render the phrase *akābir mujrimīhā* as *'penjahat-penjahat yang terbesar'* ('the greatest criminals'). This issue becomes more interesting when one takes into account the fact that the first edition translates the phrase as *'pembesar-pembesar yang jahat'* ('the infamous leaders'), just like *Al-Qur'an dan Tafsirnya.* Thus, not only do QT and *Al-Qur'an dan Tafsirnya* differ in their treatment of this phrase, but the different editions of QT also treat it differently. It is worth noting that this shift was not the result of the comprehensive revision that took place in 1989–90, but occurred in 1974 as one of the sporadic changes that were implemented

52 I did not obtain the daily *Pelita* that published the actual reader's opinion. Nevertheless, I had direct access to *Majalah Tempo* which on 25 April 1992 reported the responses from relevant authorities on this issue. Julizar Kasiri, Siti Nurbaiti, and Wahyu Muryadi, '"Penjahat Besar" atau Pembesar yang Jahat', *Majalah Tempo,* 25 April 1992, pp. 77–78.

during an ad hoc revision of the translation.[53] Eventually, the third edition changed the translation once again, reverting to the reading given in the first edition, after which, finally, the fourth edition changed it to *'orang-orang jahatnya sebagai pembesar'* ('its criminals as leaders'). Unlike the first two editions, the third and fourth editions include an identical footnote that says: *'menurut sebagian mufassir, akābir mujrimīha ialah para penjahat-penjahat terbesar'* ('according to some exegetes, *akābir mujrimīha* means "the greatest criminals"'). With this footnote, the later translations seem to credit the previous edition, acknowledging that *'penjahat-penjahat terbesar'* is one valid meaning for *akābir mujrimīha.* Alternatively, the inclusion of this footnote might simply reflect the fact that there was a debate within the translation team about how to interpret the verse which failed to reach a consensus, and so a decision was made to accommodate both meanings.

Here is the summary of the shifts of the translation in this verse:

First edition	*Dan demikianlah Kami adakan pada tiap*^{2} *negeri* **pembesar**^{2} **jang djahat** *agar mereka mengadakan tipu dadja dalam negeri itu...*
	[And so We have put in every city infamous leaders to perpetrate their schemes there...]
The 1974 copy	*Dan demikianlah, Kami adakan pada tiap-tiap negeri* **penjahat-penjahat yang terbesar** *agar mereka melakukan tipu daya di negeri itu...*
	[And so We have put in every city the greatest criminals to perpetrate their schemes there...]
Third edition	*Dan demikianlah pada setiap negeri Kami jadikan* **pembesar yang jahat** *agar melakukan tipu daya di negeri itu...*
	[And so in every city We have put infamous leaders to perpetrate their schemes there...]
Fourth edition	*Demikian pula pada setiap negeri Kami jadikan orang-orang jahatnya sebagai pembesar agar melakukan tipu daya di sana...*
	[And so in every city We have put its criminals as the leaders to perpetrate their schemes there...]

53 Ichwan addresses the 1974 edition as one distinct edition, the second edition. This study, however, suggests that the second edition was not produced until 1990 (see Chapter Two). Ichwan, 'Negara, Kitab Suci dan Politik: Terjemahan Resmi Al-Qur'an di Indonesia', p. 424.

The shift of the translation in 1974, which was produced during the early period of the New Order, and the decision of the committee to retake the old translation in the second revision that took place in 1998–2002, when the New Order had collapsed, have led observers to view it as an example of the politicization of Qur'an translation. Ichwan suggests that the initial shifts in the translation were driven by the political climate of the state. He believes that the New Order regime thought that the first translation had potential to harm their authority and therefore decided a change was needed.[54] Islah Gusmian is on board with Ichwan; he suggests that this is one example of the *'otosensor'* ('self-censorship') that occurred in the production of *tafsīr* and which was conditioned by the authoritarian ideology of the state during the years of the New Order.[55]

Both observations make sense. By translating the phrase as *'pembesar-pembesar yang jahat'* ('the infamous leaders'), the first edition of QT effectively puts the Indonesian leadership in the spotlight and describes them as potentially infamous. This was unacceptable during the New Order period, when the government could not be questioned or criticized. A normative reading of the verse could potentially lead to distrust of the government, and any anti-government activists motivated by religious sentiment could easily recite the verse in their protests against the government, a situation that the New Order government always aimed to constrain. Thus, the 1974 edition of QT saw a change in the wording of this verse to *'penjahat-penjahat yang terbesar'* ('the greatest criminals'), so as to soften its nuance. The leaders were not under the spotlight anymore; instead, the reader was directed towards criminals. Then, after the collapse of the New Order, the translation shifted back to its original rendition.

Despite this hypothesis, it is impossible to be more definitive about whether this case is actually an instance of politicization as we have no concrete information about the actual motives for the change to the wording of Q 6:123. It was either, first, a direct instruction from the president, or someone on his behalf, or individuals in the governmental

54 Ichwan, 'Negara, Kitab Suci dan Politik: Terjemahan Resmi Al-Qur'an di Indonesia', p. 424.

55 Gusmian, *Tafsir Al-Qur'an dan Kekuasaan di Indonesia: Peneguhan, Kontestasi, dan Pertarungan Wacana*, p. 301.

structures, or secondly, there was a sense of discomfort amongst the committee members at the prospect of translating the verse in a way that could be read as directly pointing to the government, especially at a time during which MORA was under the tight control of the New Order regime.[56] Ichwan seems to prefer the first possibility, while Gusmian goes with the latter. Unfortunately, there is no information about the internal debates within the committee, nor any record that any instruction was given by the president or any another government official. However, on the basis that the edition of *Al-Qur'an dan Tafsirnya* read by the reader who complained to *Pelita* translated *akābir mujrimīhā* as *'pembesar-pembesar yang jahat'*, and the fact that there was no record of discomfort from the government on this issue, it seems likely that although the authoritarian New Order government (which actively suppressed political Islam in its early period) might have influenced the interpretive decision made by the QT translation team, it did not actively demand that the committee change the translation; if this were the case, the first edition of *Al-Qur'an dan Tafsirnya* would not have translated the phrase *akābir mujrimīhā* as *'pembesar-pembesar yang jahat'*, the interpretation avoided in the 1974 copy of QT. It is, however, safe to say that the political climate during the production of QT may well have induced anxiety and discomfort amongst the translation team, who wished to avoid producing a translation that could potentially be considered as making a political critique of the government.

So far, I have argued that the initiative to change the translation of *akābir mujrimīhā* from *'pembesar-pembesar yang jahat'* to *'penjahat-penjahat yang terbesar'* might very well have come from the committee. This then raises an important question: if this change was motivated by political concerns, is this revision exegetically illegitimate? This question is significant because it can cast light on how the committee managed to find a solution to potentially problematic passages of the Qur'an when facing external constraints such as political circumstances. In other words, did the committee abandon their reliance on the *tafsīr* tradition when faced with conflicting external constraints?

To answer this question, I will turn to the wording of the two translations in question. The first thing to note is that there is no

56 Ropi, p. 221.

significant shift of lexicon between *pembesar-pembesar yang jahat* and *penjahat-penjahat yang terbesar*; both essentially consist of the words *'besar'* and *'jahat'*. *Besar* is an adjective that literally means 'big' or 'large,' but also has the connotations of nobility, greatness, or power. *Jahat* is also an adjective, and literally means 'bad,' 'evil,' 'malevolent.' The prefix *pe(m)* appended to *besar* (*pembesar*) changes the word to a noun and associates it with a person, creating the meaning of someone noble, great, or in power. The word *pembesar* is synonymous with *'pemimpin', 'penguasa', 'pemegang tampuk pimpinan', 'pejabat'*; all are words with the semantic connotation of leadership, authority and power, nobility, and domination.[57] Likewise, the prefix *pe(n)* appended to *jahat* (*penjahat*) also makes it a noun and personalizes the word, suggesting the meaning of a criminal, evildoer, or sinner, whereas the prefix *ter* appended to *jahat* (*terjahat*) keeps the word as an adjective but formulates it in superlative form. Accordingly, *jahat* in the construction *pembesar-pembesar yang jahat* qualifies the noun *pembesar. Pembesar-pembesar yang jahat,* accordingly, would literally mean 'the noble, great, or in power men who are bad, evil or malevolent,' or in short, 'the infamous leaders.' On the other hand, the construction of *penjahat-penjahat yang terbesar* has *penjahat* standing as the main word and *terbesar* is its adjective in the superlative form. It would mean 'the criminals who are the greatest' or, in idiomatic English, 'the greatest criminals.'

Our question at this point is whether *'pembesar-pembesar yang jahat'* and *'penjahat-penjahat yang terbesar'* are both actually valid renderings for *akābir mujrimīhā,* and hence whether the shift between both renderings is exegetically legitimate. A review of grammatical views on the verse is needed at this point. While the grammatical aspects of the text do not seem to be of the utmost interest to the classical exegetes in the context of this verse, the commentaries provide two possible options in this regard. Al-Rāzī and al-Qurṭubī both suggest that the verb *jaᶜala* ('to make') requires two objects. The first object they specify is *mujrimīhā,* while the second is *akābir.* In this grammatical reading of the verse, the second object is placed before the first. Additionally, al-Rāzī suggests that the construction of *akābir mujrimīhā* cannot be a genitive (*iḍāfa*), for

57 Tim Penyusun Kamus Pusat Bahasa, 'Pembesar', *Kamus Bahasa Indonesia* (Jakarta: Pusat Bahasa, 2008), p. 189; 'Lema "Pembesar"—Tesaurus Tematis Bahasa Indonesia', http://tesaurus.kemdikbud.go.id/tematis/lema/pembesar.

it would make it an incomplete sentence.[58] Thus, the English translation for this grammatical reading is: 'We have **made** [verb] in every city its **leaders** [2nd object] (its) **criminals** [1st object]', or if we transposition the objects, 'We have **made** [verb] in every city its **criminals** [1st object] [from] its **leaders** [2nd object].'

Following this grammatical analysis, the closest translation would be the one provided by the fourth edition, i.e., *'orang-orang jahatnya sebagai pembesar'* ('its criminals as the leaders'), a construction that explicitly follows the verb plus two objects structure. This creates a more straightforward meaning in the target text because it transposes the two objects from their original places in the source text. Neither *'pembesar-pembesar yang jahat'* nor *'penjahat-penjahat yang terbesar'* are consistent with this 'verb plus two objects' structure. In both expressions, *'pembesar-pembesar'* ('leaders') and *'penjahat-penjahat'* ('criminals') are respectively the only objects, whereas *jahat* and *terbesar* are adjectives, emphasized by *yang*.

I would argue that, despite the slight grammatical inaccuracy, *'pembesar-pembesar yang jahat'* ('infamous leaders') is the closest rendering to the way commentators such as al-Ṭabarī and Ibn Kathīr explain the verse, and this is especially true when one comes to the grammatical analysis provided by al-Qurṭubī and al-Rāzī. Despite failing to follow the original grammatical structure of the Arabic, *'pembesar-pembesar yang jahat'* maintains the semantic connotation that is intended by the original *akābir mujrimīhā*, i.e., leaders that are infamous, or infamous people who have become leaders. In the construction *'penjahat-penjahat yang terbesar'* ('the greatest criminals'), on the other hand, the element of leadership is missing; the criminals, (or the greatest criminals), may or may not also be leaders. Al-Rāzī excludes the possibility of *akābir mujrimīhā* being a genitive construction, and if one agrees with this, the translation of *akābir mujrimīhā* as *'penjahat-penjahat yang terbesar'* could be justified. Following this line of analysis, the shift from *'pembesar-pembesar yang jahat'* to *'penjahat-penjahat terbesar'* is, on the other hand, much more questionable.

There is also a second opinion on the grammatical features of this verse. Al-Bayḍāwī agrees that *jaᶜala* requires two objects. The first object,

58 Fakhr al-Dīn al-Rāzī, *Mafātīḥ al-ghayb*, 32 vols (Beirut: Dār al-Fikr, 1981), xiii, p. 183.

for him, is *fī kulli qarya*, whereas the second is *akābir*. He views *mujrimīhā* as *badl* ('substitution') or, in contrast to al-Rāzī, the second particle of the genitive construction. Al-Bayḍāwī also adds that it is possible to consider *akābir* as a superlative adjective standing as the first participle of a genitive construction.[59] Thus, the English translation for this grammatical reading is: 'We have **made** [verb] **in every city** [1st object] **its leaders** [2nd object] **the criminals** (*badl*/substitution)—or, **the greatest criminals** [2nd object composed with genitive construction). According to this view, *'penjahat-penjahat yang terbesar'* is one of the meanings intended by *akābir mujrimīhā*, and accordingly, the shift in question is legitimate.

At this point, I have shown that both readings, *'pembesar-pembesar yang jahat'* and *'penjahat-penjahat terbesar'*, can find legitimation in the classical *tafsīr*s, and this may well explain the inclusion of the alternative reading in the footnote in the third and fourth editions. Although it is feasible that a political constraint was behind the translation committee's decision to change the translation in the second edition, it could also be convincingly argued that the committee may have made this change on the basis of the *tafsīr* tradition. One other important observation to make is that the fourth edition decides to avoid a certain degree of ambiguity inherent in the various renderings from previous editions of QT. Instead of making a choice between *'pembesar-pembesar yang jahat'* and *'penjahat-penjahat yang terbesar'*, the latest edition instead chooses to be more literal in its translation of this phrase.

Q 4:59 and 83, *Ūlu al-Amr*: *'Pemegang Kekuasaan'*

The analysis above has demonstrated that leadership is an important ideological issue in Indonesian politics, and the rendering of *awliyāʾ* into *'pemimpin-pemimpin'* has a strong connection to the state's relationship with Islam. Here, I turn my attention to another phrase that is interpreted within the context of leadership, namely the phrase *ūlu al-amr* (lit. 'those in command') in Q 4:59 and Q 4:83. As a matter of fact, *w-l-y*, the root

59 Royal Aal al-Bayt Institute for Islamic Thought, 'Tafsīr Anwār al-tanzīl wa asrār al-taʾwīl / al-Bayḍāwī (d. 685 AH) Sūrat al-Anʿām 123', *Altafsir.Com*, https://www.altafsir.com/Tafasir.asp?tMadhNo=0&tTafsirNo=6&tSoraNo=6&tAyahNo=123&tDisplay=yes&UserProfile=0&LanguageId=1.

from which *awliyā*ᵓ is derived, is commonly used in the compound construction of *walī al-amr,* which is considered synonymous with *ūlu al-amr.* Sukarno was awarded the title *walī al-amr ḍarūr bi shawkah* ('de facto interim holder of power') in 1954,[60] and on more than a few occasions the government has been associated with the phrase *ūlu al-amr.*[61]

Ūlu al-amr is mentioned in two places in the Qur'an, i.e., Q 4:59 and Q 4:83, and a subtle politicization of translation can be identified in the way this phrase has been translated in both instances. Q 4:59 reads as follows:

يـٰأيها ٱلذين ءامنوا أطيعوا ٱلله وأطيعوا ٱلرسول وأولى ٱلأمر منكم

> You who believe, obey God and the Messenger, and *ūlu al-amr* among you

The classical Sunnī *tafsīr* tradition offers various interpretations of this verse. Al-Ṭabarī provides a number of *riwāyah*s that associate the word with leaders, the *ulama,* or the companions of the prophet.[62] Ibn Kathīr provides a similar range of interpretive suggestions. However, unlike al-Ṭabari, Ibn Kathīr relates the interpretation of *ūlu al-amr* (as referring to the *ulama*) to such early influential exegetical authorities as Ibn ᶜAbbās, Mujāhid, ᶜAṭāᵓ, Ḥasan al-Baṣrī, and Abū ᶜĀliya, expressing it as synonymous with *ahl al-ᶜilm wa al-fiqh wa al-ᶜulamā*ᵓ ('the people of knowledge and jurisprudence and the scholars').[63] These three interpretations are supported widely by early *tafsīr* authorities, and essentially inform the interpretive views of later Qur'an commentaries.

---

60 Steven Drakeley, 'Indonesia's Muslim Organisations and the Overthrow of Sukarno', *Studia Islamika*, 21.2 (2014), 197–232 (p. 203), https://doi.org/10.15408/sdi.v21i2.1039.

61 For example, during court testimony for a polygamy case in 2007, Huzaiman T. Yanggo, a Professor of Sharī'a at State Islamic University Syarif Hidayatullah Jakarta, and also a member of the MUI's Fatwa Commission, as well as the current QT revision committee, supported the state's limitation on polygamous marriages. In her testimony, she described the state as *ūlu al-amr*. See Alfitri, 'Whose Authority? Contesting and Negotiating the Idea of a Legitimate Interpretation of Islamic Law in Indonesia', *Asian Journal of Comparative Law*, 10 (2016), 191–212 (p. 199), https://doi.org/10.1017/ASJCL.2016.1.

62 Abū Jaᶜfar Muḥammad ibn Jarīr al-Ṭabarī, *Jāmiᶜ al-bayān ᶜan taᵓwīlī āyi al-qurᵓān*, ed. by ᶜAbullāh ibn ᶜAbd al-Muḥsin al-Turkī, 24 vols (Cairo: Dār Hijr, 2001), vii, p. 173.

63 ᶜImād al-Dīn Abū al-Fidāᵓ Ismāᶜīl Ibn Kathīr, *Al-Tafsīr al-qurᵓān al-ᶜaẓīm*, 15 vols (Giza: Muᵓassasa Qurṭuba, 2000), iv, p. 130.

One different interpretation, however, is given by Fakhr al-Dīn al-Rāzi. He connects the verse to the hierarchy of the sources of Islamic teaching recognized in *uṣūl al-fiqh*—the holy scripture, the *sunna* ('the practice and precedent of Muhammad'), *ijmāᶜ, and qiyās* ('analogy'). *Ūlu al-amr,* al-Rāzi suggests, refers to *ijmāᶜ*, and the source of *ijmāᶜ* is the collective *ahl al-ḥall wa al-ᶜaqd* (lit. 'people who loosen and bind').[64] He rejects the interpretation of *ūlu al-amr* as referring to *umarāᵓ* ('leaders') as he thinks that the order to obey the *umarāᵓ* is already included in the order to be obedient to God and the Prophet.[65] By associating the *ulama* with *ahl al-ḥalli wa al-ᶜaqd*, al-Rāzi gives us insight into the institutionalization of the *ulama* during his time. However, he is the only one to provide this interpretation, which means that his commentary is somewhat marginal.

The exegetes' discussions are generally concerned with determining which of the three interpretive possibilities provides the best meaning for *ūlu al-amr.* Their discussions usually take into account two meanings, 'leaders' and '*ᶜulamāᵓ*,' and somehow exclude the interpretive possibility that the phrase refers to the companions of the Prophet. Al-Ṭabari prefers *umarāᵓ*, given the supporting evidence for this reading provided by dozens of *riwāyas*. While indecisive on the issue in his *al-Durr al-manthūr,* al-Suyūṭī seems to be in line with al-Ṭabari in his co-written *al-Jalālayn* and provides only one meaning, *aṣḥāb al-wilāyah* ('the master of a region').[66] Unlike al-Ṭabari and *al-Jalālayn,* some other commentators such as al-Qurṭubī, Ibn Kathīr, al-Biqāᶜī (1406–80), al-Zamakhsharī, etc., believe that both 'leaders' and '*ulama*' are equally acceptable interpretations of *ūlu al-amr;* the former reading is supported by dozens of *riwāyahs* (in line with al-Ṭabarī's opinion), while the latter is supported by the following phrase in the verse, *wa in tanazaᶜtum fi syaiᵓ fa-ruddūhu ila 'llāh wa rasūlihi* ('If you are in dispute over any matter, refer it to God and the Messenger'). This phrase, they suggest, indicates that there could be no one who can comprehend the word of God and

64 This terminology, in medieval political theory, refers to legal scholars who elect and depose a caliph on behalf of the wider Muslim community. In the modern context, it has been adapted in the context of parliament. See Muhammad Qasim Zaman, 'Ahl Al-Ḥall Wa-l-ᶜaqd', ed. by Kate Fleet and others, *Encyclopaedia of Islam* (Koninklijke Brill NV), https://doi.org/10.1163/1573-3912_ei3_COM_0027.

65 Fakhr al-Dīn al-Rāzī, *Mafātīḥ al-ghayb*, 32 vols (Beirut: Dār al-Fikr, 1981), x, p. 148.

66 al-Maḥallī and al-Ṣuyūṭī, p. 87.

the *sunna* of the prophet other than the *ᶜulamāᵓ*. In other words, there is no hierarchy between the word choices; both meanings have equal representation through *ūlu al-amr.*

Let us move now to the classical *mufassir*'s interpretations of Q 4:83:

وإذا جاءهم أمر من ٱلأمن أو ٱلخوف أذاعوا بهۦ ولو ردوه إلى ٱلرسول وإلىٰ أولى ٱلأمر منهم لعلمه ٱلذين يستنبطونهۥ منهم

> Whenever news of any matter comes to them, whether concerning peace or war, they spread it about; if they referred it to the Messenger and *ūli al-amr* among them, those seeking its meaning would have found it out from them...

The *tafsīr* tradition essentially provides the same meanings for *ūlu al-amr* here; as referring to either the companions of the prophet, the *ulama,* or leaders. Again, just as in the previous verse, the issue of whether *ūlu al-amr* equally means all of those things or whether one meaning is more appropriate than the others also preoccupies the exegetes. However, most of the commentaries interpret the phrase as referring to either the historical Companions of the Prophet (probably because Q 4:83 talks about a specific event during his life), or to 'those with knowledge', i.e., the *ulama.* Al-Ṭabarī provides a number of *riwāyas* that gloss the phrase *ūlu al-amr* as meaning *ᶜulamāᵓihim* or *al-fiqh fī al-dīn wa al-ᶜaql* ('the *ulama* among them [i.e., the Companions], or the experts in religious [knowledge] or intelligence'). Al-Baghawī interprets it as referring to the intellectuals among the Companions, such as the four rightly guided caliphs, while *al-Muntakhab* interprets it as *kibār al-ṣaḥāba* ('the great man of the Companions [of the prophet]'). Al-Qurṭubī also interprets the word as *umarāᵓ al-sarāyā* ('a person with authority') and *ahl al-ᶜilm wa al-fiqh* ('those with intelligence and knowledge').[67]

67 al-Ṭabarī, vii, p. 253; Royal Aal al-Bayt Institute for Islamic Thought, 'Tafsīr Maᶜālim al-tanzīl / al-Baghawī (d. 516 AH) Sūrat al-Anisāᵓ 85', *Altafsir.Com*, https://www.altafsir.com/Tafasir.asp?tMadhNo=0&tTafsirNo=13&tSoraNo=4&tAyahNo=83&tDisplay=yes&UserProfile=0&LanguageId=1; Royal Aal al-Bayt Institute for Islamic Thought, 'Tafsīr Al-Muntakhab fī tafsīr al-qurᵓān al-karīm / Lajna al-qurᵓān wa al-sunna Sūrat al-Nisāᵓ 83', *Altafsir.Com*, https://www.altafsir.com/Tafasir.asp?tMadhNo=9&tTafsirNo=65&tSoraNo=4&tAyahNo=83&tDisplay=yes&UserProfile=0&LanguageId=1; Royal Aal al-Bayt Institute for Islamic Thought, 'Tafsīr al-Jāmiᶜ li aḥkām al-qurᵓān / al-Qurṭubī (d. 671 AH) Sūrat al-Nisāᵓ 85', *Altafsir.Com*, https://www.altafsir.com/Tafasir.asp?tMadhNo=0&tTafsirNo=5&tSoraNo=4&tAyahNo=83&tDisplay=yes&UserProfile=0&LanguageId=1.

Let us examine how QT renders both verses. Here is how Q 4:59 was translated across different editions of QT:

First edition	*Hai orang-orang yang beriman, ta'atilah Allah dan ta'atilah Rasul-(Nya), dan* **orang-orang yang memegang kekuasaan** *diantara kamu...* [You who believe, obey Allah and obey (His) Prophet, and **the people who hold power** among you]
The 1974 copy	*Hai orang-orang yang beriman, ta'atilah Allah dan ta'atilah Rasul (Nya), dan* **ulil amri** *di antara kamu...* [You who believe, obey Allah and obey (His) Prophet, and ***ulil amri*** among you]
Third Edition	Hai orang-orang yang beriman! Taatilah Allah dan taatilah Rasul (Muhammad), dan **Ulil Amri (pemegang kekuasaan)** di antara kamu... [You who believe, obey Allah and obey (His) Prophet, and ***Ulil Amri*** (**power holders**) among you]

There is thus a slight change in the translation of Q 4:59 across the editions of QT. The first edition renders *ūlu al-amr* as *'orang-orang yang memegang kekuasaan'* (lit. 'the people who hold power'). The 1974 copy prefers to refrain from translating the word, leaving it as an Arabic word written in transliteration, *'ulil amri'*. The second and Saudi editions retain this rendering. The third and fourth editions basically also opt for transliteration, only they also echo the initial translation, albeit using a shorter expression, *'pemegang kekuasaan'* ('the bearers of power'), which is placed in parenthesis.

In Q 4:83, the word *ūlu al-amr* is left untranslated in all of the editions of QT. The fourth edition seeks internal consistency and therefore, as for Q 4:59, leaves the phrase untranslated and adds *'pemegang kekuasaan'* ('the bearers of power') in parenthesis. Some of the editions give an additional explanation in their footnotes. Thus, the first, the second, and the Saudi editions contain the footnote: *'ialah tokoh-tokoh sahabat dan para cendikiawan diantara mereka'* ('[They are] the companions [of the Prophet] and the intellectuals among them'). The third edition conveys the same message in a shorter expression; *'tokoh-tokoh sahabat rasul'* ('the figures from the Companions of the Prophet'). Both notes clearly indicate QT's reliance on the classical *tafsīr* tradition in terms of the attention they give to the historical context of the verse, by following their lead in reading the phrase as referring to the Companions of the Prophet.

From the interpretive point of view, the translation of both verses provided in QT is clear and the level of changes across its editions is hardly substantial. There is a high probability that the QT readership would not care greatly whether *ūlu al-amr* in the verse is translated as 'bearers of power' or left untranslated; both options are clear and comprehensible and can be considered to have similar signification and, most importantly, both are justified by the *tafsīr* tradition.

However, despite being arguably insignificant, the shifts from '*orang-orang yang memegang kekuasaan*' to '*ulil amri*' and eventually to '*ulil amri (pemegang kekuasaan)*' in Q 4:59 point to a series of internal debates within the various translation committees that resulted in subtly different translation decisions. No doubt, these debates were driven by the existing interpretive options provided by the *tafsīr* tradition and the committees' views on the best way to accommodate these in their translations. The team working on the first edition decided to include one meaning, that of 'leaders', and completely omitted mention of any other interpretive possibility. The translation shift made in the 1974 copy might indicate two considerations. *First,* the committee working on the 1974 edition may have been unsatisfied with the existing translation because it omitted the other, equally valid, interpretive options. Going with transliteration instead of preferring one of the possible options would solve this problem. In other words, because they refused to actually translate the phrase, the reader was expected to extrapolate the meaning from the words by themselves. Second, the phrase *ūlu al-amr* is a familiar one in the Indonesian context, which means there is a high chance that if it was left untranslated, it would be fully understood without explanation. Finally, leaving *ūlu al-amr* untranslated might also lead the reader to seek an explanation for this word by themselves in *tafsīr* works. The final shift, introduced in the third edition, to include the phrase '*pemegang kekuasaan*', 'the bearers of power', in parentheses following the untranslated original phrase shows that the translation committee that worked on this edition decided to, again, privilege one interpretation over the others.

Regardless of all the interpretive changes in the rendition of Q 4:59 in QT, in the translation it is placed as the initial verse of a thematic block that gives more insight into how QT (or rather its translation committees) actually views the meaning of *ūlu al-amr* in this verse. As mentioned earlier, QT divides the Qur'anic *sūras* into thematic sections, or blocks, which are often given subtitles. Q 4:58 is the beginning of one such thematic block on the theme of *Dasar-dasar Pemerintahan* ('the foundation of government') that continues for the next thirteen verses. As indicated earlier, the thematic blocks in QT follow the scheme used in Muḥammad Maḥmūd Ḥijāzī's *Tafsīr al-Wāḍiḥ*. However, there is a possibility that on this occasion the thematization is also inspired by al-Rāzī and al-Zamakhsharī, who relate Q 4:59 to the preceding verse. As the previous verse instructs people to be just and 'render the trusts,' (*tuʾaddū al-amānāt*) they read Q 4:59 as instructing people to obey those who are in charge of implementing justice. The note introduced in the third edition only emphasizes this preference, suggesting that obedience towards *ūlu al-amr* is only required as long as 'those in command' adhere to the Qur'an and the Sunna.

From a methodological point of view, the translation committees clearly approached this verse through the *tafsīr* tradition, relying on the Qur'an commentaries to lead their interpretations. Viewed in this light, it would not have been incorrect for them to give preference to either interpretation, *ʿulamāʾ* or 'leaders', in their translation of *ūlu al-amr* in either verse. Nevertheless, it is worthy of mention that, despite all the options, the interpretive decision of the committee ultimately justifies the authority of 'leaders' over that of religious scholars, a position that clearly benefits the state. Taking into account the interpretive options provided by the *tafsīr* tradition and the decisions made by the various QT committees, in my opinion this rendering points to a subtle politicization of this Qur'an translation.

Conclusion

This section shows that QT essentially relies on information derived from the *tafsīr* tradition to inform its reading of the Qur'anic text. This attitude to some extent limits the part that politics plays in the translation. This is not to say that the content of this translation is completely free from the influences of any sort of ideological interest. However, even in cases where the politicization of translation has been identified, it is clear that the committee persistently seeks a solution to ideological problems through recourse to the views provided in Qur'an commentaries.

The use of *esa* in the foreword positions QT within the framework of the general state project, yet its use as a translation for *aḥad/wāḥid* is consistent with the Qur'anic concept as transmitted by *tafsīr*. The same is true of the translation of *awliyāʾ*. Although the constitution in Indonesia does not limit the rights of non-Muslims to run for the presidency, this vision is not imposed on QT; in a number of verses containing the word *awliyāʾ* it is translated as *'pemimpin-pemipin'* ('leaders').

The other two cases explored in this chapter, however, seem to indicate the influence of the government on the content of QT. The translation of *akābīra mujrimīha* as *'pembesar-pembesar yang jahat'* may have led to an uncomfortable situation for the translation committee that worked on the second edition during the New Order era, as they modified the translation to *'penjahat-penjahat terbesar'*, amending the reading so that this verse related to 'criminals' rather than 'leaders', thereby shifting the focus away from the government. A milder influence has been identified in the treatment of the phrase *ūlu al-amr*. Although the Qur'an commentaries seem to be in considerable agreement on its meaning—as referring both to leaders and religious scholars—QT binds the word to the concepts of governance and leadership, and ignores the other meaning. This shows how a method recognized in *tafsīr*, namely selection of a preferred meaning out of a number of cited opinions, has made way for a more subtle politicization of translation. Above all, what these case studies show is that QT, as the official state Qur'an translation, is able to maintain its form as a *tafsīr*/translation even though it faces ideological problems, and that allegations that QT distorts and manipulates the Qur'anic source text, as some have argued (with specific reference to the translation of *awliyāʾ*), are unjustified.

7. One Translation, Two Faces: The Ambivalent Authority of the Official Qur'an Translation

In 2016 and 2017 Indonesia witnessed one of the most significant political moments in its history since the *Reformasi*, as a highly divisive event that seemed set to shape the future of Indonesian society and politics unfolded, namely the gubernatorial election of Jakarta. The candidacy of Basuki Tjahaja Purnama—a Christian of Chinese ethnicity who had ascended to the prized governorship of the capital city after Jokowi left office to pursue the presidency—was monopolized by the issue of his religious credentials and ethnic origins, which overshadowed any substantive debate on the quality of his governance, or questions of the personal integrity and accountability of any of the candidates. Given its status as the capital of Indonesia, Jakarta is considered representative of Indonesia as a whole, and this means that local politics have a greater significance in terms of the broader landscape of national politics, and the conservative Muslim elements of the Indonesian population considered the prospect of a Christian governor in this capital to be particularly undesirable. The race grew dramatic, involving three massive rallies held under the banner of 'Aksi Bela Islam' (ABI, Defending Islam Action), an indictment against Basuki Tjahaja Purnama, otherwise known as Ahok, for religious blasphemy, and his eventual imprisonment.

Given that the election was effectively a stage for identity politics based on the religious credentials of the candidates, it was only to be expected that the politicized use of the Qur'an would be in evidence. Indeed, Indonesian politics has a precedent for such practices. In 1971,

 https://doi.org/10.11647/OBP.0289.07

the Golongan Karya party used Q 48:18[1] to justify their political interests and sway people toward voting for them, while the PPP did just the same with Q 5:95 and 97.[2] In the 1999 election, the political use of Q 4:34 was ubiquitous because of the participation of a female candidate, Megawati Sukarnoputri. That year saw various Qur'anic terms enter the common vernacular, such as *balda ṭayyiba* ('a good land'), *jihād fī sabīlillāh* ('struggling/striving in Allah's cause') and *al-baghy* ('injustice, tyranny').[3] During the 2017 Jakarta gubernatorial election, the debates revolved around Q 5:51, a literal reading of which, as discussed in the previous chapter, prohibits Muslims from making *awliyāʾ* of Jews and Christians. As I propose in this chapter, Indonesian Qur'an translations, particularly QT, played a significant role in events on the political stage as they unfolded.

Discussions have abounded on this particular political moment, covering various approaches and issues, especially with regards to the role of the ABI and the issue of the blasphemy case against Ahok. To my surprise, the question of the part played by Indonesian Qur'an translations has been overlooked, despite the omnipresence of the Qur'an during the election and the pivotal role Qur'an translations arguably played in determining its outcome. This chapter therefore discusses how Qur'an translations, particularly the official QT translation, contributed to the political battleground of the 2017 Jakarta gubernatorial election. The case brings us to consider Q 5:51 anew for several reasons: the hermeneutical problems presented in the verse, the political problems it may raise for Indonesia in the future and, most importantly for the current context, the different ways the editions of QT rendered the key word *awliyāʾ* in this verse. This case provides us with a good entry point through which to understand how Indonesian

1 The verse has been translated as: 'God was pleased with the believers when they swore allegiance to you [Prophet] under the tree: He knew what was in their hearts and so He sent tranquillity down to them and rewarded them with a speedy triumph.' Golongan Karya is a political party whose emblem is a big banyan tree, which makes the reason for their choice of this verse obvious because it unites the concepts of allegiance, the tree, and triumph.

2 Both verses contain the word *kaʿba* which is the emblem of the respective party.

3 Azyumardi Azra, 'The Use and Abuse of Qur'anic Verses in Contemporary Indonesian Politics', in *Approaches to The Qur'an in Contemporary Indonesia*, ed. by Abdullah Saeed, The Institute of Ismaili Studies (Oxford: Oxford University Press, 2005), pp. 193–208.

Muslims perceive the 'officiality' of QT. This chapter therefore seeks to answer two main questions: To what extent did the Qur'an translation play a role in this particular debacle? And what can we learn from these events about the way Indonesians perceive QT given its status as the official Qur'an translation of the state?

Ahok and Q 5:51: A Politicized Verse

Having embarked on the capital city's ambitious transformation project as the governor from 2014 until 2017, a venture which gained traction among the city's residents and had already shown results, Ahok was confident that he would win the opportunity to extend his administration for another five years. In the 2017 Jakarta gubernatorial election, he competed against Agus Harimurti Yudhoyono, the son of the former president Susilo Bambang Yudhoyono, who ran with Sylviana Murni, and also against Anies Rasyid Baswedan, who ran with Sandiaga Uno, all of whom were Muslims. As the only Christian in the race, Ahok teamed up with a Muslim, Djarot Saiful Hidayat. Given that they had the advantage of being incumbents, the Ahok-Djarot pairing was preferred by the respondents in a number of surveys and the odds seemed to slightly favor their re-election. However, amid indications that the race would be tight, Muslim hardliners intensified their campaign to discourage Muslims from voting for Ahok-Djarot with the rhetoric 'choose anyone but Ahok-Djarot.' As Ahok and Djarot were officially assigned the second slot in the ballot paper out of the three candidate pairs, a *hadith* that asserts that 'Allah loves odd numbers' was also appropriated by the hardliners in their campaign. Muslims in Jakarta were encouraged to vote for either number one (Agus-Silvy) or three (Anies-Sandi) on the ballot paper, but not number two (Ahok-Djarot).

The defeat of Agus-Silvy in the first round left Ahok-Djarot and Anies-Sandi competing against each other in the runoff. This inevitably divided voters into two camps, each with their own discourse and biases. Those who supported Ahok campaigned on the issue of *kebhinekaan* ('diversity') and accused the opposing camp of trying to undermine Indonesia's diversity, calling on the specter of 'shariatization' and radicalism, which they associated with the hardliner groups that gathered in Anies' camp. On the other side, the Anies-Sandi supporters framed themselves as defenders of Islam and the Qur'an, who aimed to protect Muslims and Islam from a hostile religious blasphemer (*penista agama*) who endangered religious harmony. Muslims who supported Ahok-Djarot were denounced as *munāfiq* ('hypocrites') or *zindiq* ('disbelievers or heathens'). Ahok's Chinese origins were also pitted against those of Anies, who is a descendent of the Haḍramawt community in Indonesia.[4]

Although Ahok was predicted to win, objections to his leadership in Jakarta had actually emerged prior to the election. Ahok, who ran as vice governor to the Muslim candidate Jokowi in 2012, ascended effectively unelected to the governorship of the capital city following Jokowi's successful presidential run in 2014. This created an unacceptable situation for some Muslims, as it conflicted with an idea current in political Islam that a non-Muslim cannot govern a Muslim community. This notion, as discussed in the previous chapter, is partly founded on the text of Q 5:51, which is believed by many of Ahok's opponents to forbid Muslims from appointing a non-Muslim as their leader. The verse states:

> You who believe, do not take the Jews and Christians as *awlīyāʾ*; they are *awlīyāʾ* only to each other. Anyone who takes them as *awlīyāʾ* becomes one of them—God does not guide such wrongdoers.[5]

If read literally, this verse prohibits Muslims from a specific relationship with Jews and Christians which is described using the term *awliyāʾ*. Though the word encompasses many semantic possibilities, but a number of Qur'an translations in Indonesia, including the first, second, and the Saudi editions of QT, translate it as *'pemimpin-pemimpin'* ('the leaders'), thus implying that Muslims are prohibited from choosing non-Muslims as their leaders. It was this verse, and this particular translation of it, that were used against Ahok and his nomination as a candidate, and which fueled the opposition protests that were led by the hardliner Front Pembela Islam (FPI, The Islamic Defender Front). To delegitimize Ahok's leadership, the FPI even appointed a governor

4 Ahmad Najib Burhani, 'Ethnic Minority Politics in Jakarta's Gubernatorial Election', *ISEAS Perspective*, 39, 2017.

5 The translation belongs to that of Abdel Haleem, but the rendering of the word *awliyā'* is deliberately left out because the very interpretation of the word is the centre of the controversy. Haleem himself translates the word as ally.

of their own, Fakhrur Rozi, although he never officially took up an administrative position.

Ahok is no Islamic scholar, and it is thus reasonable to assume that, at the time, he was not fully aware of the far-reaching and nuanced hermeneutical complications that emerge from Q 5:51. That, however, did not prevent him from having a particular opinion on the verse. In 2008, Ahok published a 'political autobiography', *Merubah Indonesia: The History of Basuki Tjahaja Purnama* (Changing Indonesia: The History of Basuki Tjahaja Purnama), in which he speaks of his political career. In a subchapter titled "Berlindung di Balik Ayat Suci" (Hiding Behind the Holy Verses) he writes as follows:

> *Selama karir politik saya dari mendaftarkan diri menjadi anggota partai baru, menjadi ketua cabang, melakukan verifikasi, sampai mengikuti pemilu, kampanye pemilihan bupati, bahkan sampai gubernur, ada ayat yang sama yang saya begitu kenal digunakan untuk memecah belah rakyat dengan tujuan memuluskan jalan meraih puncak oleh oknum yang kerasukan 'roh kolonialisme'.*
>
> ...
>
> *Dari oknum elite yang berlindung di balik ayat suci agama Islam, mereka menggunakan surat al-Maidah 51. Isinya melarang rakyat menjadikan kaum Nasrani dan Yahudi menjadi pemimpin mereka, dengan tambahan jangan pernah memilih kafir menjadi pimpinan. Intinya, mereka mengajak agar memilih pemimpin dari kaum yang seiman.*
>
> *Padahal, setelah saya tanyakan ke teman-teman, ternyata ayat ini diturunkan pada saat adanya orang-orang Muslim yang ingin membunuh Nabi Besar Muhammad SAW dengan cara membuat koalisi dengan kelompok Nasrani dan kelompok Yahudi di tempat itu. Jadi, jelas bukan dalam rangka memilih kepala pemerintahan, karena di NKRI kepala pemerintahan bukanlah kepala agama/ imam kepala.*[6]
>
> [Throughout my political career, ever since I registered as a new member of a party, to becoming the chairman of the chapter, to [undergoing the political] verification process [when applying for candidature], and while I took part in election campaigns for positions in local government, and even for the governorship, there is this particular verse, which I have got to know so well, that has been used to divide people and to smooth the path to the top by elements who are dazed by 'the phantom of colonialism'.
>
> ...

6 Basuki Tjahaja Purnama, *Merubah Indonesia: The History of Basuki Tjahaja Purnama* (Jakarta: Center for Democracy and Transparency, 2008), p. 40.

> The elites who hide behind the Islamic holy verses used *al-Māʾida* 51. It forbids people from making Christians and Jews their leaders, [and they] add 'do not ever vote a kafir to be [your] leader.' In short, they call on people to choose leaders from their own faith.
>
> But when I asked friends, apparently the verse was revealed during the time when some Muslims wanted to kill the Prophet Muhammad—peace be upon him—by allying with Christians and Jews. So, clearly it has nothing to do with electing the head of government, because in the NKRI (Negara Kesatuan Republik Indonesia, the Unitary State of the Republic of Indonesia), the head of government is not a religious leader/the head imam.]

As indicated by these three paragraphs, Ahok learned about Q 5:51 from his political experiences, when his political opponents used the verse in a discriminatory manner against him on the basis that he is a Christian. This discrimination started when he stood for election as Regent of Bangka Belitung in 2007, when he faced political opponents who quoted Q 5:51 against him. Pamphlets and brochures citing Q 5:51, along with rhetoric intended to prevent Muslims from voting for non-Muslim candidates, were brought into play, and the verse was also referenced during religious sermons.[7] The fact that Ahok entitled the relevant chapter of his biography "Memilih BTP, Bukan SARA" ('To vote for BTP is not SARA') gives us a clear insight into his views on the way the verse has been used against him: BTP stands for his name, Basuki Tjahaja Purnama, and SARA is an abbreviation of *Suku, Agama, dan Ras* (tribe, religion, and race), three categories of discrimination in Indonesia.

Clearly, Ahok believes Q 5:51 has a different interpretation to that which has been used against him. For Ahok, the verse has nothing to do with modern political elections, rather it refers to a specific issue related to religious leadership. His understanding, as he himself says, is formed on the basis of information provided by a friend to the effect that the verse was revealed during a particular historical situation in the seventh century. According to this interpretation, the suggestion that this verse has anything to do with political elections is unjustifiable. While Ahok has never identified the person he consulted, it is quite easy to infer their

7 'Putusan Nomor 1537/Pid.B/2016/PN.Jkt Utr. Tahun 2017 Ir. BASUKI TJAHAJA PURNAMA Alias AHOK' (Jakarta: Direktori Putusan Mahkamah Agung Republik Indonesia, 2017), p. 343, https://putusan.mahkamahagung.go.id/putusan/e8b1049e890f1bf53511d70ffa120602.

identity. During the 2007 gubernatorial election of Bangka Belitung, Ahok gained support from, among others, an Islamic party called the PKB (Partai Kebangkitan Bangsa, National Awakening Party). A senior member of the PKB, the late former president of Indonesia and leader of Nahdlatul Ulama, Abdurrahman Wahid (1940–2009), better known as Gus Dur, played a vital part in that election and openly supported Ahok. Gus Dur attended Ahok's campaign rallies and delivered a speech in which he underlined his understanding that Q 5:51 does not talk about governance and that those who quoted the verse to undermine Ahok's candidacy and political legitimacy, therefore, misunderstood the verse. Gus Dur's support, however, did not bring Ahok to triumph in that election, as he eventually lost by a small margin.

In 2012, Ahok stood for election in Jakarta and paired with Joko Widodo. Again, in this political arena, religious sentiments took over. The PKS (Partai Keadilan Sejahtera, Prosperous Justice Party) backed Hidayat Nurwahid, who cultivated a political image as a pious candidate. On the other hand, Jokowi was accused of being an '*Islam abangan*' ('nominal Muslim'), or even an outright communist, while Ahok's religious credentials were again called into question. Brochures and pamphlets gave way to social media memes and the use of politically charged religious sermons continued. Rhoma Irama, a famous *dangdut* musician, gave a speech explicitly calling on people not to vote for a non-Muslim candidate in which he quoted Q 4:144 to support his argument. (Q. 4:144, *You who believe, do not take the disbelievers as allies and protectors instead of the believers: do you want to offer God clear proof against you*, is understood similarly to Q 5:51.) Despite the heightened religious sentiments, Jokowi and Ahok won the election.[8]

The Accusation of Religious Blasphemy

During all the elections he has competed in, including the 2017 Jakarta gubernatorial elections, Ahok has remained consistent in his stance

8 Jokowi-Ahok's experience in the 2012 Jakarta gubernatorial election is described by Nadirsyah Hosen as the only other political event in Indonesia in which a religious issue did not successfully influence the outcome. See Hosen, 'Race and Religion in the 2012 Jakarta Gubernatorial Election: The Case of Jokowi Ahok', in *Religion, Law and Intolerance in Indonesia*, ed. by T. Lindsey and H. Pausacker, Routledge Law in Asia (London, New York: Taylor & Francis, 2016), pp. 180–94 (p. 181).

on the interpretation of Q 5:5. On the basis of his understanding of its meaning, he made a number of public statements in which he insisted that his political opponents should refrain from using the verse against him. Apparently, one particular event during which he delivered his opinion on the Q 5:51 verse brought the issue to another level, and led to allegations against him of religious blasphemy.

Ahok's administration in Jakarta was never totally free from protests by Islamists. Their opposition heightened after Ahok made reference to Q 5:51 in a speech he delivered during an official visit to *Kepulauan Seribu* on 17 September 2016, where he encouraged local fishermen to support and join a fishing project proposed by the government. His visit took place shortly before the election, and he tried to convince the fishermen, who were mostly Muslims, not to worry about the election results as they would not have any effect on the project as a whole. His main concern was that he himself was a Christian, while the people he was speaking to were Muslims, and that there was a campaign to prohibit people from voting for him based on his religious credentials. He urged the fishermen to join him and support the project regardless of their religious views on the political role of non-Muslims or their political preferences in the forthcoming election. In doing so, he insisted that they did not have to be hesitant about the project even if they would not be voting for him.

Ahok is typically blunt, and in the speech he delivered that day his allusion to Q 5:51 was accompanied by the words *dibohongi* ('deceived') and *dibodohi* ('fooled'), and it was his usage of this terminology that inflamed the controversy. Here is the complete transcript of his speech, which was used as the centerpiece of the blasphemy accusation against him:

> *... ini pemilihan kan dimajuin. Jadi kalo saya tidak terpilih pun saya berhentinya Oktober 2017. Jadi kalo program ini kita jalankan dengan baik pun bapak ibu masih sempet panen sama saya sekalipun saya tidak terpilih jadi gubernur. Jadi cerita ini supaya bapak ibu semangat; jadi ga usah pikiran, 'ah.. nanti kalau ga kepilih, pasti Ahok programnya bubar.' Engga... saya sampai Oktober 2017. Jadi jangan percaya sama orang—kan bisa aja dalam hati kecil bapak ibu ga bisa pilih saya, ya kan, dibohongi pakai surat Al-Māʾida 51, macem-macem itu, itu hak bapak ibu. Yah jadi kalo bapak ibu, perasaan gak bisa kepilih nih, karena saya takut masuk neraka, karna dibodohin gitu, ya enga papa. Karena ini kan panggilan pribadi bapak ibu. Program ini jalan saja. Jadi bapak ibu gak usah merasa gak enak; dalam nuraninya ga bisa milih Ahok, gak suka sama Ahok nih,*

tapi programnya gua kalo terima, ga enak dong jadi utang budi, jangan bapak ibu punya perasaan ga enak nanti mati pelan-pelan loh kena stroke.

[...the election would be held earlier [than planned]. So even if I am not elected again, I will step down [from the governorship] in October 2017. So, if we manage to run this program well, you will still be able to harvest with me, even though I may not be elected governor again. So, [I tell you] this to encourage you, so you do not have to be worried, 'If [he] is not re-elected, Ahok's program would be disbanded.' That is not the case, I [will still be in office] until October 2017. So, do not believe what people say—it is possible that deep in your heart [you know] you could not vote for me, isn't it, [because you have been] *deceived* using *al-Māʾida* 51 and so on; that is your right. So, if you feel you cannot vote for me, because you are afraid of going to hell—because [you have been] *fooled*—it is okay. That is your personal call. [No matter what happens], this program will continue to run. So, you do not have to be apprehensive; [just because you feel] in your heart that you cannot vote for Ahok, you do not like Ahok, but you accept his program, so you feel indebted to me; do not, you must not! Or otherwise, you will slowly die from a stroke.]

Ahok uploads the videos of his meetings and other government programs to the official government website, and this particular speech was no exception. He had already been criticized several times for his blunt rhetoric and harsh diction, but this specific speech generated controversy of another dimension: blasphemy. The main issue revolved around whether or not Ahok explicitly denounced the Qur'an as an untruthful scripture. One particular social media user, Buni Yani, was alleged to have edited the video, transcribed the speech, and shared it via his social media account on 6 October 2016. (He was eventually charged for manipulating the transcript.[9]) He began his transcript with a rhetorical question in capitalized script: *'PENISTAAN TERHADAP AGAMA?'* ('A BLASPHEMY ON RELIGION?'), which he followed with a selectively edited segment of Ahok's speech:

'Bapak-Ibu (pemilih Muslim)... dibohongi Surat Al Maidah 51'... (dan) 'masuk neraka (juga Bapak-Ibu) dibodohi'

['Ladies and gentlemen, [you] (Muslim voters)... are deceived by *Sūrat al-Māʾida* 51'... (and) 'are going to hell, (also you are) fooled.']

9 On Buni Yani's role in the controversy, see Lizzy van Leeuwen, 'Onderzoek De Zaak-Buni Yani "Hij Ging Met Niemand Om"', *De Groene Amsterdammer*, 2017, https://www.groene.nl/artikel/hij-ging-met-niemand-om.

Yani closed his post with the statement *'Kelihatannya akan terjadi sesuatu yang kurang baik dengan video ini'* ('It seems something bad will come from this video').

The most striking feature of the transcript is the fact that Yani omitted a word which is semantically significant in Indonesian grammar. What Ahok expressed as *'dibohongi pakai surat Al-Māʾida 51'* ('[being] deceived *using al-Māʾida* 51') apparently became *'dibohongi surat Al-Māʾida 51'* ('[being] deceived [*by*] *al-Māʾida* 51') at Yani's hands. The omission of the word *pakai* has a significant impact on the whole discourse as it substitutes the grammatical position of Q 5:51. Yani's edits changed its grammatical status so that it became the subject of the sentence, thereby conveying the meaning that *al-Māʾida* 51 is an active subject deceiving people, i.e., that they are deceived by the text itself rather than by the manipulation of the text by other people, which laid Ahok open to accusations that he was impugning the truthfulness and holiness of the Qur'an. The original wording of his speech, however, references Q 5:51 as a tool through which his opponents deceive people: it does not talk about the verse itself but instead refers to the way that it is used.

This part of Ahok's speech would always be a grammatically complicated sentence when transcribed into written Indonesian, because it consisted of a main clause and several overlapping sub-clauses. In his edits to the text, Yani also cut out some words, which meant that not only did he mislead people about the nuance of Ahok's message, but he also made it look as if Ahok made a straightforward denunciation of the Qur'an by presenting Ahok's statement as a simple grammatical structure. In short, with his edited transcript, Yani distorted Ahok's original wording into a single, simple sentence that could only inspire a hostile reaction from readers.

Ahok's supporters criticized Yani's transcript for being deceptive and argued that the notion of blasphemy occurred only in Yani's interpretation of Ahok's speech. They believed that Ahok would never have been accused of blasphemy had Yani not distorted his words. However, the effect of the transcript was instant and inflammatory as it went viral on social media with millions of shares the day after it was posted. The discourse it created is clearly reflected in the following excerpt from an article published in Dewan Da'wah News:

> *Dengan memakai seragam PNS—artinya ia sedang dinas menjalankan tugasnya, Ahok mengatakan kepada audiens yang dihadapinya (muslim di Kepualauan Seribu-Red) bahwa mereka dibohongi oleh surat Al Maidah 51. Kata-kata itu mengandung makna yang jelas bahwa Al-Qur'an (Surat Al-Maidah: 51) adalah bohong, dan orang yang menyampaikan Al-Qur'an (Surat Al-Maidah: 51) adalah pembohong. Menuduh Al-Qur'an (Surat Al- Maidah: 51) bohong adalah penistaan agama, dan menuduh orang yang menyampaikan Al-Qur'an (Surat Al-Maidah: 51) pembohong adalah penghinaan terhadap Nabi SAW, ulama, ustadz, kyai, mubalig.*[10]
>
> [Wearing a civil servant uniform—which meant that he was on official duties, Ahok said to the audience ([a group of] Muslims in Kepulauan Seribu), that they were fooled by *al-Māʾida* 51. Those words had a clear meaning: that the Qur'an (*al-Māʾida* 51) is a lie, and that the people who preach it (*al-Māʾida* 51) are liars. Denouncing the Qur'an (*al-Māʾida* 51) as a lie is blasphemy, and denouncing its preachers (*al-Māʾida* 51) as liars is an insult towards the prophet Muhammad, peace be upon him, [and to the] *ulama, ustadz, kyai,* and *muballig.*]

Ahok's wording as reported in this excerpt has a similar tone to that found in Yani's transcript. It explicitly mentions the idea of '*dibohongi oleh surat al-Ma'idah*' ('[being] deceived *by al-Māʾida* 51'). The use of the word *oleh* ('by') in this article is actually an even more explicit indication that Q 5:51 was used as an active subject. Interestingly, while Yani admitted that he mistakenly missed out the word *pakai* ('to use'), he denied the consequence of that omission. He argued that whether Ahok stated it with or without using the word *pakai,* his speech was blasphemous nonetheless. In other words, whether Ahok expressed his conviction that the Qur'an was being deceitfully manipulated as a tool, or claimed that Qur'an itself was deceptive, for Yani his speech was blasphemous.

The controversy escalated into three massive rallies, the ABI, which were held on 14 October, 4 November, and 2 December 2016. These rallies are said to be the biggest ever in Indonesian history and are claimed to have been attended by seven million people, although other estimates put the number somewhere between two and three million. Moh. Nur Ichwan marks this as the most significant mobilization undertaken by the FPI, which had typically only been able to mobilize relatively small

10 Humas Dewan Da'wah Islamiyah Indonesia, 'Menista Islam Ahok Menghitung Hari', *Dewan Da'wah News*, October 2016.

groups of people in the past. He suggests that the FPI may have been so successful in organizing the rallies because they persuaded Majelis Ulama Indonesia (MUI, Indonesian Ulama Council) to get involved.[11] Prior to the rallies, on 9 October 2016, the Jakarta branch of the MUI released a warning and demanded an apology from Ahok for his blasphemous speech. Two days later, the central MUI released a statement, namely '*Pendapat dan Sikap Keagamaan*' (Opinion and Religious Motion),[12] that stated:

1. The Qur'an *sūra al-Māʾida* 51 contains an explicit prohibition against appointing Jews or Christians as leaders. This verse is one of the legal prohibitions against the appointment of non-Muslims as leaders.
2. The *ulama* is obliged to preach the content of *al-Māʾida* 51 to the Muslim community and to tell them that appointing a Muslim leader is compulsory.
3. Every Muslim should believe in the truthfulness of *al-Māʾida* 51 as legal guidance for appointing a leader.
4. Declaring that *al-Māʾida* 51—which prohibits appointing Jews or Christians as leaders—is untruthful is *haram* and is classified as blasphemy against the Qur'an.
5. The deceitful claim concerning the *ulama* who deliver *al-Māʾida* 51 as a means of prohibition against appointing a non-Muslim as a leader demonstrates contempt for the *ulama* and the Muslim community.[13]

---

11 Moch. Nur Ichwan, 'MUI, Gerakan Islamis, dan Umat Mengambang', *Jurnal Maarif*, Setelah 'Bela Islam': Gerakan Sosial Islam, Demokratisasi, dan Keadilan Sosial, 11.2 (2016), 87–104 (pp. 94–95).

12 Ichwan suggests that the nature of *Pendapat dan Sikap Keagamaan* is political, and that it is effectively a type of statement that used to be called *tausiyah* and does not have legal consequences. However, activists considered these statements to be equivalent to *fatwas*, as has been proven by the establishment of the GNPF MUI (Gerakan Nasional Pengawal Fatwa MUI/The National Movement of the Escort of the Fatwa of MUI). Din Syamsuddin and Ma'ruf Amin are of the opinion that Sikap Keagamaan is more powerful than a *fatwa*. See Ichwan, 'MUI, Gerakan Islamis, dan Umat Mengambang', p. 98.

13 Editor Mui, 'Pendapat dan Sikap Keagamaan MUI terkait Pernyataan Basuki Tjahaja Purnama', *Majelis Ulama Indonesia*, 2017, http://mui.or.id/id/berita/pendapat-dan-sikap-keagamaan-mui-terkait-pernyataan-basuki-tjahaja-purnama/.

The *Pendapat Keagamaan* statement called for the government to take immediate action against Ahok's controversial speech. The government, however, was hesitant to take legal action. Amien Rais, the late chief of Majelis Permusyawaratan Rakyat (MPR, People's Consultative Assembly) complained about the president's silence over the incident,[14] and the FPI accused the government of protecting Ahok.[15] In the aftermath of the MUI's motion, the GNPF MUI (Gerakan Nasional Pengawal Fatwa MUI/The National Movement of the Escort of the Fatwa of MUI)[16] was established, from members affiliated with several Islamist organizations; the FPI, the FUI (Front Umat Islam, Front of the Muslim Community), and the HTI (Hizbut Tahrir Indonesia, the Indonesian Branch of Hizb ut-Tahrir). Even though this movement explicitly associated itself with the MUI, the MUI did not formally acknowledge the association, despite the fact that the primary figures of GNPF MUI included MUI officials, namely Bachtiar Nasir and Zaitun Rusmin.[17] The GNPF MUI, under the leadership of Bachtiar Nasir and Rizieq Syihab, alongside some notable names—politicians such as Amien Rais, and musicians such as Ahmad Dhani—successfully led the three rallies, attracting protesters not only from Jakarta but from across the whole of Indonesia. Although most of the people who visited Jakarta to attend the rallies took regular means of transportation, some covered distances of 250–300 km on foot.[18] They considered it a religious call; as was clearly symbolized by the name of the rallies, *Aksi Bela Islam* (Defending Islam Action).[19]

---

14 Amien Rais, 'Amien Rais: Bung Jokowi, Selesaikan Skandal Ahok', *Republika Online,* 29 October 2016, section Khazanah, http://www.republika.co.id/berita/dunia-islam/islam-nusantara/16/10/28/ofqben385-amien-rais-bung-jokowi-selesaikan-skandal-ahok.

15 Hafizd Mukti, 'FPI: Pemeriksaan Terbuka, Langkah Jowoki Lindungi Ahok', *CNN Indonesia,* 5 October 2016, https://cnnindonesia.com/nasional/20161105213504-12-170576/fpi-pemeriksaan-terbuka-langkah-jokowi-lindungi-ahok/.

16 Soon enough, the MUI took steps to put themselves apart from the GNPF MUI. It then introduced its new name, GNPFU (*Gerakan Nasional Pengawal Fatwa Ulama* / The National Movement of the Escort of the Fatwa of Ulama).

17 Ichwan, 'MUI, Gerakan Islamis, dan Umat Mengambang', p. 97.

18 Randy Wirayudha, 'FOKUS: Keteguhan Ribuan Santri Ciamis Long March 300 Km Ke Jakarta', *Okezone News*, 29 November 2016, section National, https://news.okezone.com/read/2016/11/29/337/1554370/fokus-keteguhan-ribuan-santri-ciamis-long-march-300-km-ke-jakarta.

19 Ichwan suggests that there are two kinds of masses who join the rallies: floating *umma* and floated *umma*. The first refers to unaffiliated people who follow a certain organization when it comes to one specific issue, and another organization when

After three months, the controversy brought Ahok to trial for religious blasphemy. The main concern of the prosecutors, as they frequently emphasized, was ethical. Their argument was based on Ahok's statement *'dibohongin pakai surat Al-Māʾida 51'* ('[being] deceived using *sūra al-Māʾida'*) and *dibodohin* ('[being] fooled [with it]'). To emphasize this, many witnesses and expert witnesses on the prosecutors' side insisted that Ahok's blasphemy had nothing to do with whatever the correct interpretation of Q 5:51 might be; it was exclusively about his abusive attitude to the Qur'anic scripture. K.H. Ma'ruf Amin, then the head of the MUI and the current Vice President of Indonesia, stated that he and his MUI colleagues did not even discuss the interpretation of the verse in their preparatory meetings about the case. His statement, however, can be understood as rhetorical, and intended to emphasize his concern with the improper way in which Ahok had spoken of the scripture.[20] He interpreted Ahok's phrasing as offensive to the Islamic faith and considered his words to be blasphemous based on several Qur'anic verses: Q 2:231, Q 6:70, Q 5:51, Q 3:28, and Q 4:144. For Amin, to suggest that the Qur'an can be used a tool of deceit is itself blasphemous because it offends the underlying belief of Muslims in the holiness and inimitability of the Qur'an.[21] Yunahar Ilyas (1956–2020), a Muhammadiyah-affiliated theologian, supported Amin, stating that the phrase *'dibohongi pakai surat Al-Māʾida'* indicated that Ahok had alleged that that verse was utilized as a tool of deceit. In his opinion, this was inappropriate because the Qur'an is truthful and cannot be a source of any falsehood.[22] Muhammad Rizieq Syihab, the head of the FPI, cited a *hadīth* that says *man shakka fī al-Qurʾān fa-qad kafara* ('whoever has doubts about the Qur'an is an infidel'), clearly suggesting that it is forbidden

it comes to another issue, while the latter category refers to members of a certain organization, such as the Muhammadiyah or Nahdlatul Ulama, who in this case follow the GNPF MUI instead of the official stance taken by the organization of which they are a member. Ichwan proposes some possible reasons for their preferences, but does not discuss the potential role of Qur'an translations. Ichwan, 'MUI, Gerakan Islamis, dan Umat Mengambang', p. 99.

20 'Putusan Nomor 1537/Pid.B/2016/PN.Jkt Utr. Tahun 2017 Ir. BASUKI TJAHAJA PURNAMA Alias AHOK', p. 120.

21 'Putusan Nomor 1537/Pid.B/2016/PN.Jkt Utr. Tahun 2017 Ir. BASUKI TJAHAJA PURNAMA Alias AHOK', p. 122.

22 'Putusan Nomor 1537/Pid.B/2016/PN.Jkt Utr. Tahun 2017 Ir. BASUKI TJAHAJA PURNAMA Alias AHOK', p. 234.

to have any doubts about the Qur'an, let alone to associate it with dishonesty.[23]

Not only did a number of the witnesses during the trial deem it insensitive to describe the Qur'an as a tool that could be used to deceive, some went even further and asserted that Ahok had attacked the actual truth of Q 5:51. Even though they did not explicitly say so, the proponents of this view were probably supporting Yani's argument about the insignificance of the word *'pakai'*. By saying *'dibohongi pakai surat al-Māʾida 51,'* they argue, not only did Ahok suggest that the Qur'an was being used as a tool for deceit, but also as a source of untruth. While describing it as a tool may be neutral, to suggest that it is a source of deceit would be more profound. Their narrative was that Ahok accused the *ulama* of telling people about something from an untruthful source. In other words, the *ulama* lied, used false information, and the information they gave came from the Qur'an. According to this narrative, the claim that the Qur'an is used as a tool for deceit is also coupled with its description as a source of untruthfulness, thereby implying that the content of the Qur'an itself is untruthful.

Ahok's perceived hostility against the Qur'an was not the only point of concern for the prosecutors. They also interpreted his speech as being disrespectful toward the *ulama*. Accordingly, Ma'ruf Amin asserted that the *ulama* have an obligation to preach the Qur'an to the Muslim community, and that Q 5:51 is no exception. Ahok's claim that people were deceived using Q 5:51, he claimed, amounted to accusing the *ulama* of lying.[24] Yunahar Ilyas agreed with Amin's argument and suggested that even though Ahok did not explicitly state who exactly deceives people using Q 5:51, it is the *ulama* who have the authority to explain the verse. Thus, Ahok must have been accusing the *ulama* of deceiving people with the Qur'an. Rizieq Syihab and Irena Handono went even further: they said that Ahok was hostile to anybody preaching Q 5:51, namely all Muslims, the *ulama*, the prophet's companions, the prophet himself, and even Allah.[25]

---

23 'Putusan Nomor 1537/Pid.B/2016/PN.Jkt Utr. Tahun 2017 Ir. BASUKI TJAHAJA PURNAMA Alias AHOK', p. 307.

24 'Putusan Nomor 1537/Pid.B/2016/PN.Jkt Utr. Tahun 2017 Ir. BASUKI TJAHAJA PURNAMA Alias AHOK', p. 126.

25 'Putusan Nomor 1537/Pid.B/2016/PN.Jkt Utr. Tahun 2017 Ir. BASUKI TJAHAJA PURNAMA Alias AHOK', pp. 49; 303–06.

Responding to this, the main argument of the defense attorney and witnesses in their testimony was based on allegations about the politicization of religion. To support their argument, they testified to Ahok's good relationship with his Muslim colleagues, and gave the example of his governmental program, which benefited Muslims. Unsurprisingly, they also cited the attitude of his political opponents in every election in which he had participated. They argued that Ahok's minority status as a Christian of Chinese origin had been exploited continuously by his opponents, and that Q 5:51 was the recurring tool they used to try to undermine his constitutionally guaranteed political rights. Ahmad Ishomuddin, an Islamic scholar with NU affiliation, suggested that the tactics used by Ahok's opposition were the same as those used by the PPP when they tried to dissuade people from supporting the Golongan Karya party by using the Qur'anic story of the expulsion of Adam and Eve from Paradise and making connections between the forbidden tree in the Garden of Eden and the party's emblem, a banyan tree. To use the Qur'anic text in such a way, Ishomuddin contended, was a form of prevarication, as the verse in question had nothing to do with elections. For him, that was also true in the context of Q 5:51.[26] Using these arguments, the defense contended that Ahok's statement had to be understood as his response to the politicization of religion, which had effectively inserted the Qur'an into the political discourse of the election.

The defense furthermore argued that the prosecutors' failure to understand the relevant section of Ahok's speech correctly was because they detached it from its overall context. Rahayu Surtiati, a linguist, suggested that the phrase *jangan percaya sama orang* (lit. 'do not believe in people') in Ahok's statement should not have been understood literally, as it functioned as an idiom with specific significance. She argued that Ahok meant 'do not believe in hearsay,' referring to his personal experience as set out in his book, *Merubah Indonesia,* as his political opponents cited the verse against him, which spread hearsay. It would, she said, be incorrect to interpret Ahok's words as suggesting that everyone who cites Q 5:51 are liars who should not be believed.[27]

26 'Putusan Nomor 1537/Pid.B/2016/PN.Jkt Utr. Tahun 2017 Ir. BASUKI TJAHAJA PURNAMA Alias AHOK', p. 416.

27 'Putusan Nomor 1537/Pid.B/2016/PN.Jkt Utr. Tahun 2017 Ir. BASUKI TJAHAJA PURNAMA Alias AHOK', p. 399.

Another linguist, Herminigildus Bambang Kaswanti Purwo, suggested that Ahok's speech had been interpreted incorrectly by the prosecutors, and that his words had been taken out of context. He suggested that the proper way to assess Ahok's speech is through pragmatic, not semantic methods, and through its significance, not its lexical meaning. The fact that the people of *Kepulauan Seribu* whom Ahok spoke to did not initially take issue with the speech showed that the statement was harmless. It was only after the edited video was circulated that people began to be concerned.[28] Two further witnesses for the defense, Risa Permana Deli and Sahiron Syamsuddin, were also concerned about decontextualization. The former suggested that judging this problem based solely on the decontextualized words used by Ahok would potentially lead to a bias in understanding the case, as if the issue were merely a linguistic problem. The latter suggested that a holistic context would quickly reveal that Ahok's concerns were focused on his political opponents, who employed the verse against him in a polemical sense during the gubernatorial election.[29]

Al-Qur'an dan Terjemahnya and the Interpretive Dimension of the Blasphemy Allegations

As mentioned above, the prosecutors' strategy was to insist on pursing the ethical aspects of the issue, focusing on Ahok's alleged disrespect for the Islamic holy text. According to their arguments, both the connection between Ahok's speech and the forthcoming elections, and the issues surrounding the actual interpretation of the verse should be put aside. Nevertheless, the political and interpretive dimensions of the controversy were used as the basis of Ahok's defense, and this meant that disputes over the meaning of the Q 5:51 continued to spark heated controversy.

As discussed in the previous chapter, the word *awliyāʾ* encompasses a wide range of semantic options. With regard to this particular controversy, two meanings came to the fore: 'leadership' and 'friendship.'

28 'Putusan Nomor 1537/Pid.B/2016/PN.Jkt Utr. Tahun 2017 Ir. BASUKI TJAHAJA PURNAMA Alias AHOK', pp. 466–71.
29 'Putusan Nomor 1537/Pid.B/2016/PN.Jkt Utr. Tahun 2017 Ir. BASUKI TJAHAJA PURNAMA Alias AHOK', pp. 474; 521.

On this particular occasion, the concepts of leadership and friendship are not just different; they are contradictory. The first meaning was used to justify the accusation of blasphemy brought against Ahok, while the latter was used to deny it.

Outside the courtroom, public figures who supported both sides delivered their arguments by making speeches at rallies, engaging in media interviews and academic seminars, preaching sermons, and publishing articles in mainstream and social media. Video excerpts circulated of speeches and interviews featuring such figures as Rizieq Syihab, Bachtiar Nasir, and Amien Rais, who presented a clearly defined interpretation of Q 5:51. Leading figures in the opposing camp, such as Ahmad Sahal, Nadirsyah Hosen, Hamka Haq, and Ahmad Ishomuddin, used the same media to criticize their opponents. Those in favor of the prosecution of Ahok insisted on '*pemimpin-pemimpin*' ('leaders') as the correct interpretation of *awliyāʾ*, while the opposing camp disputed this view. For them, *awliyāʾ* corresponded to friendship, not leadership, and they argued that the verse was not about politics or leadership. Ahok's speech was, they claimed, a valid response to the abuse and politicization of the verse.

There were also two, massively popular, conflicting booklets that were published online at the end of 2016 and early 2017 which received a lot of attention.[30] The first book, *7 Dalil Umat Islam DKI dalam Memilih Gubernur* ('7 Postulates for Muslims of DKI in Electing the Governor'—henceforth: *7 Dalil*) provides seven arguments in favor of Ahok and his political ambitions. One of the arguments refuted the legitimacy of

30 Neither booklet was published according to the regular mechanism of book publishing in Indonesia, which stipulates that books should be published through a legal publishing house with the official sanction of the National Library of the Republic of Indonesia, which provides all publications with an ISBN. The first booklet is *7 Dalil Umat Islam DKI dalam Memilih Gubernur*, written by Muhammad Taufiq Damas and published through an organization called RelaNu (Relawan Nusantara). The partiality of this organisation for Ahok is apparent as they invited him to their commemoration of the *Santri* Day on 21 October 2016 and of the Birth of the Prophet Muhammad in January 2017. *7 Dalil Umat Islam* includes excerpts of religious advice (*tawṣiyya*) in its preface written by Ahmad Ishomuddin, the NU leader who later became an expert witness for Ahok during his trial. The second booklet, *Haram Memilih Pemimpin Non-Muslim* (HMPN), is a direct refutation of the first, written by Sayyid Muhammad Hanif Alattas, and published through an organization named Front Santri Indonesia. This booklet includes a preface by Muhammad Rizieq Syihab, one of the leaders of the FPI, who later testified against Ahok at trial.

rendering *awliyāʾ* as *'pemimpin-pemimpin'*, a reading which would hinder Ahok's political career. According to *7 Dalil*, Q 5:51 does not concern political leadership in a democratic country such as Indonesia. It suggests that as long as the individual in question is capable of providing good governance, a Christian can be elected to a leadership position. In doing so, *7 Dalil* includes an analogy provided by the Indonesian exegete Quraish Shihab which poses the question 'If one has to choose between an experienced pilot (or doctor) who is a non-Muslim, and an inexperienced one who is a Muslim, which one is preferable?'[31]

The second booklet, *Haram Memilih Pemimpin Non-Muslim* ('It is Forbidden to Appoint a Non-Muslim Leader'—henceforth: HMPN) challenges *7 Dalil*, arguing that appointing a non-Muslim as a leader in a Muslim community would harm the nobility of Islam and would make it possible for the said leader to commission policies through which non-Muslims might dominate and have control over Muslims. It emphasizes the fact that Q 5:51 is not the only verse in the Qur'an to prohibit the appointment of non-Muslims as leaders, and argues that in order to understand Q 5:51 one needs to also take all of these related verses into account.[32] The *tafsīr* tradition, HMPN suggests, is unanimous in its view on the meaning of these verses, and there is therefore a consensus about the legal precepts that can be deduced from them. In Q 5:51 alone, the use of the verb *tattakhidhū* ('do not take') indicates a strong prohibition, and because the word *awliyāʾ* is mentioned in an indefinite form (*nakira*) it has a general meaning. Any attempt to specify its meaning, according to the argument put forward in HMPN, is invalid unless it is supported by textual references that elaborate the meaning in greater detail. HMPN also references notable figures in the Islamic intellectual tradition who interpreted the verse as a prohibition against appointing a non-Muslim leader, such as ᶜUmar ibn al-Khaṭṭāb, the second rightly guided caliph, who rejected a report written by one Abū Mūsā on the basis that it had been written by a Christian secretary. ᶜUmar is said to have cited Q 5:51 in his rejection, mentioning it as his source of inspiration to do so. HMPN also relates a similar story that

31 The analogy is not a part of Shihab's interpretation in Tafsir Al-Mishbāh, but it forms a part of his Ramadan preaching. See '[Tafsir Al Misbah] Surah Al Maidah Ayat 051–054 Part 02', *Youtube*, https://www.youtube.com/watch?v=QT23mUC8Aes.

32 For instance, Q 3:28 and 118, Q 58:22, Q 60:1, Q 9:71 and several others.

involved ᶜUmar ibn ᶜAbd al-ᶜAzīz, the eighth Umayyad caliph, and refers to scholars and/or *mufassirs* such as al-Jūwaynī (1028–85), al-Māwardī (d. 1058) and al-Qurṭubī (d. 671/1272), even including an Indonesian commentator, Hamka (1908–81). With regard to Ahok's argument that the verse was restricted in its applicability because it referred only to a specific historical moment as set out in the *sabab al-nuzūl* ('occasion of revelation') for this verse, HMPN rebuts *7 Dalil* on the basis of the principle of *al-ᶜibra bi-ᶜumūm al-lafẓ lā bi-khuṣūṣ al-sabab* ('weight is given to the universality of the linguistic expression, not the particular circumstances when it was uttered'),[33] suggesting that the verse has universal significance and cannot be limited to a specific context.

As far as the blasphemy case is concerned, the far-reaching dispute taking place in the wider world was brought into the courtroom, and turned it into a stage on which each side presented their conflicting interpretations of Q 5:51. K.H. Ma'ruf Amin suggested that Q 5:51 denotes a prohibition against Muslims electing a non-Muslim leader, on the basis that a semantic preference for interpreting as *'pemimpin'* ('leader') or *'penguasa'* ('sovereign'/'ruler') is indicated by its association with the verb *ittakhadha* ('to make/to appoint'). He highlighted that the verse also states that God threatens Muslims who disobey this injunction, and that they will be held accountable for every choice they have made.[34] Supporting Ma'ruf Amin, Hamdan Rasyid, an Islamic scholar, recognized the various meanings that the word *awliyāʾ* can encompass, but argued that, in Q 5:51, the proper reading is *'pemimpin-pemimpin'* ('leaders'). He suggested that the same meaning was used in the Indonesian context when the NU named Sukarno *'Waliyyul Amri.'*[35]

Other witnesses for the prosecution, Irena Handono, Habib Muchsin, Wilyuddin Abdul Rasyid Dani—all Islamic preachers—interpreted the word *awliyāʾ* as referring to a general form of leadership, both religious and secular. They argued that not only does the word refer to presidency and governorship, it is also relevant to the smallest unit of governance,

33 I would like to thank Walid Saleh and Mohammed Fadel for their help with the nuances of the English wording for this translation, as well as Helen Blatherwick for acting as an intermediary.

34 'Putusan Nomor 1537/Pid.B/2016/PN.Jkt Utr. Tahun 2017 Ir. BASUKI TJAHAJA PURNAMA Alias AHOK', p. 123.

35 'Putusan Nomor 1537/Pid.B/2016/PN.Jkt Utr. Tahun 2017 Ir. BASUKI TJAHAJA PURNAMA Alias AHOK', pp. 193–95.

such as a village leader, and to cultural leadership such as a classroom chairman (*ketua kelas*), the head of an economic union (*kepala koperasi*), or the leader of a specific Muslim community.[36]

Ma'ruf Amin, Miftahul Akhyar (the deputy leader of Nahdlatul Ulama) and M. Amin Suma (a professor of *tafsīr*), among others, elaborated on the reasoning behind this claim of universality. They suggested that an understanding of the Qur'an is derived from the textual features of the verse. The initial phrase, *yā ayyuhā alladhīna āmanū* ('O believers') indicates that what follows in the verse is an exclusive theological call to Muslims. *Lā* ('do not') in *lā tattakhidhū* ('do not take') is a *lā* of prohibition (*lā nahy*) which implies that what it prohibits is completely forbidden (*taḥrīm*). They acknowledged that the Islamic traditional commentaries on this verse do indeed include an occasion of revelation (*sabab al-nuzūl*). However, they argued, this only has interpretive weight as long as it does not contradict the lexical meaning of the text, referring to a principium *al-ᶜibra bi-ᶜumūm al-lafẓ lā bi-khuṣūṣ al-sabab.* Yunahar Ilyas provided a more extensive analysis of the use of *asbāb al-nuzūl* with regard to Q 5:51. He argued that the *riwāyahs* on the context of the revelation of Q 5:51 in this case do not determine the interpretation of the verse because the terminology used in the *tafsīrs* to introduce the *riwāya* in this case indicates that the authenticity of the story is uncertain. The Qur'an commentaries do not say *'sabab nuzul ayat ini adalah'* ('the *sabab nuzūl* of this verse is'); instead, they emphasize the questionability of the story by using the unconvincing phrasing *nuzilat fī*... ([the verse was] revealed in...).[37]

Expert witnesses on the defense side argued against the translation of *awliyāʾ* as *'pemimpin-pemimpin'.* Sahiron Syamsuddin, an Islamic scholar, suggested that to properly understand the word *awliyāʾ* in Q 5:51, one needs to understand its meaning during the period of the Qur'an's revelation. According to a *ḥadīth*, the Prophet Muhammad once said, *'man ᶜāda waliyya* [...]' ('Whoever fights against my *walī* [...]'). Based on this, Sahiron argued that associating the word *walī* with *'pemimpin'* ('leader') was historically impossible, because Muhammad was already the leader

36 'Putusan Nomor 1537/Pid.B/2016/PN.Jkt Utr. Tahun 2017 Ir. BASUKI TJAHAJA PURNAMA Alias AHOK', pp. 23; 55; 81–82.

37 'Putusan Nomor 1537/Pid.B/2016/PN.Jkt Utr. Tahun 2017 Ir. BASUKI TJAHAJA PURNAMA Alias AHOK', pp. 132; 197; 200; 244; 311–14.

of the *walī* mentioned in the *hadīth*. The logical meaning then becomes 'friend', on the basis that the Prophet was saying 'whoever fights against my friends [...]'. Sahiron Syamsuddin suggested that this reading of *walī* was also valid for Q 5:51 and that, historically speaking, the word would mean *'teman setia'* ('loyal friend'), rather than *'pemimpin'* ('leader').[38] Ahmad Ishomuddin, an Islamic scholar, provided testimony affirming that the word *walī/awliyāʾ* could carry two or more meanings, and that none of the thirty Qur'an commentaries he had examined interpreted the word with a semantic field relating to leadership. Masdar Farid Mas'udi, also an Islamic scholar, although he did not testify to the correct meaning of *awliyāʾ*, agreed with Ishomuddin that the verse is exclusively relevant to the milieu of war. He criticized his counterparts who had considered the notion of prohibition in Q 5:51 as a general and absolute prohibition. Whether the word *awliyāʾ* is translated as *'teman setia'* or *'pemimpin'*, he suggested that the verse should be understood in the light of other verses on the basis of the methodological principle of *tafsīr al-Qurʾān bi-l-Qurʾān* ('interpretation of the Qur'an with the Qur'an'), and that interpreting Q 5:51 in isolation from other relevant verses would result in a flawed conclusion. According to him, as Indonesia is not in a state of war, a Muslim should maintain good relationships with Christians and Jews, on the basis of intratextual reference to Q 60:8–9, which states that God does not forbid Muslims from being just to those who do not fight against them. Based on this verse, he suggested, discrimination against non-Muslims is prohibited.[39]

The prosecution criticized this line of argument. They argued that the interpretation of *awliyāʾ* as *'teman setia'* ('loyal friend') would not save Ahok from the allegation of religious blasphemy. That was because, first of all, his blasphemy lay in his insensitive attitude towards the Qur'an and Muslims' faithfulness to it rather than his interpretation of the verse in question. Secondly, they asserted that the argument presented by the defense attorney and expert witnesses for the defense was self-defeating. Even if the correct translation for *awliyāʾ* in Q 5:51 is *'teman setia'* ('loyal friend'), rather than *'pemimpin'* ('leader'), if the Qur'an prohibits one from befriending a non-Muslim in other verses, appointing one as a

38 'Putusan Nomor 1537/Pid.B/2016/PN.Jkt Utr. Tahun 2017 Ir. BASUKI TJAHAJA PURNAMA Alias AHOK', p. 517.

39 'Putusan Nomor 1537/Pid.B/2016/PN.Jkt Utr. Tahun 2017 Ir. BASUKI TJAHAJA PURNAMA Alias AHOK', pp. 510–11.

leader is, clearly, even more strongly prohibited. Rizieq Syihab argued that even though the *ᶜulamāᵓ* provide various different views about the meaning of *awliyāᵓ* in this verse, they share a specific vision that this verse is a legal basis for the prohibition of appointing non-Muslims as leaders. Although they might have different opinions on the exact meaning of *awliyāᵓ*, they do not disagree on its legal implications.[40]

Ahmad Ishomuddin responded to this criticism by pointing out that the reasoning provided by the prosecutors was flawed because they carelessly ignored the *ᶜilla* ('the legal reason for the revelation of a verse'). Based on the *sabab al-nuzūl* for Q 5:51, he explains, the *ᶜilla* for the prohibition in the verse related to an act of hostility and betrayal carried out during a state of war. In his conclusion, he went on to assert that the verse only talks about religious leadership, i.e., *imām al-ṣala* ('the imam of prayers'), not political leadership, as Gus Dur once explained.[41]

Finally, after months of controversy and debates played out in the mass and social media, and many discussions, conferences, and rallies, the court eventually found Ahok guilty of blasphemy. He was sentenced to two years in prison, and also lost the election. The final decision of the court was in favor of reading *awliyāᵓ* as referring to '*pemimpin*'. The following paragraph cites from the verdict document:

> *Bahwa Surat Al-Maidah ayat 51 yang merupakan bagian dari Al Qur'an sebagai Kitab Suci agama Islam berdasarkan terjemahan Departemen/ Kementerian Agama adalah "Wahai orang-orang yang beriman, janganlah kamu mengambil orang-orang Yahudi dan Nasrani menjadi pemimpin—pemimpin(mu); sebahagian mereka adalah pemimpin bagi sebahagian yang lain. Barangsiapa di antara kamu mengambil mereka menjadi pemimpin, maka sesungguhnya orang itu termasuk golongan mereka. Sesungguhnya Allah tidak memberi petunjuk kepada orang-orang yang zalim.", di mana terjemahan dan interpretasinya menjadi domain bagi pemeluk dan penganut agama Islam, baik dalam pemahamannya maupun dalam penerapannya.*[42]
>
> [Surah al-Māᵓida verse 51, which is a part of the Qur'an, the holy book of Islam, based on the translation of the Ministry of Religious Affairs, states "You who believe, do not take the Jews and Christians as your leaders:

40 'Putusan Nomor 1537/Pid.B/2016/PN.Jkt Utr. Tahun 2017 Ir. BASUKI TJAHAJA PURNAMA Alias AHOK', pp. 311–14.

41 'Putusan Nomor 1537/Pid.B/2016/PN.Jkt Utr. Tahun 2017 Ir. BASUKI TJAHAJA PURNAMA Alias AHOK', pp. 407–08; 427; 433.

42 'Putusan Nomor 1537/Pid.B/2016/PN.Jkt Utr. Tahun 2017 Ir. BASUKI TJAHAJA PURNAMA Alias AHOK', p. 5.

> they are the leaders to each other. Anyone who takes them as their leader becomes one of them–God does not guide such wrongdoers", the translation and interpretation [of the Qur'an] is the domain of Muslims, either in interpretation or in practice.]

The preceding account has shown how the case against Ahok was driven by political motives, religious sentiment, and also the interpretive aspect of the Qur'an.[43] The politicization of the Qur'an, the response to it, and the considerable pressure exerted by the masses who had been effectively mobilized by Ahok's opponents eventually resulted in yet another successful prosecution for blasphemy in Indonesia. However, while the role of the propaganda put out by the GNPF MUI was undeniably a significant factor in attracting and maintaining people's attention, I contend that the role of Qur'an translations cannot be underestimated in the way this controversy played out.

The interpretive dispute that played out in the courtroom was clearly, I would argue, informed by the different renditions of this verse provided in the various Qur'an translations in circulation in the country. The part played by QT in the Ahok debate was probably the most significant as, in fact, it might be the most influential translation due to its wide readership and its status as the official translation of the state—as will be discussed in the next section. More importantly, as discussed in the previous chapter, QT renders the instance of *awliyāʾ* in Q 5:51 in two different ways across its editions: the first, second, and the Saudi edition translate it as *'pemimpin-pemimpin'* ('leaders'), whereas the third edition renders it *'teman setia'* ('friends') (the fourth edition still did not exist at this time). This difference in wording helped to form and amplify partisanship in the context of the blasphemy allegations and the election.

The idea that 'leaders' is the correct translation for *awliyāʾ* may come from a number of sources, especially for individuals with training in Islamic scholarship who are capable of diving deep into the Islamic intellectual legacy. However, it is evident that for some people this

43 Assyaukanie suggests that a number of businessmen whose enterprises were put into jeopardy during Ahok's administration were also responsible for the mobilization of the rally. See Luthfie Assyaukanie, 'Unholy Alliance: Ultra-Conservatism and Political Pragmatism in Indonesia | THC ASEAN', *Thinking Asean*, 2017, http://thcasean.org/read/articles/327/Unholy-Alliance-Ultra-Conservatism-and-Political-Pragmatism-in-Indonesia.html.

reading came from the earlier editions of QT (the Saudi edition is still widely distributed to those undertaking the *hajj*), as a number of witnesses explicitly cited the translation in their testimony. Ten of the prosecution witnesses referred to the editions of QT that render *awliyāʾ* as *'pemimpin-pemimpin'*. It is worth noting that some of them did not seem to be aware of the fact that this translation had been revised over time and that the third edition had changed its wording to *'teman setia'* more than a decade earlier. Similarly, some of them did not seem to understand the complexities of the semantic range of the word *awliyāʾ*, let alone the interpretive issues it raises. Unsurprisingly, the court presents it with the meaning of 'leaders' in its verdict document, as demonstrated above.

The reading of *awliyāʾ* as referring to the concept of friendship presented in the court was, in a similar vein, taken from the third edition of QT. There are a number of words for friendship in the Indonesian lexicon, such as *kawan* or *teman*, and the fact that the phrase *'teman setia'* ('loyal friend') was consistently chosen in this case is almost definitely influenced by the fact that the third edition of QT chose this particular wording to translate *awliyaʾ*. The defense attorney referred to this rendition in their response to the reference made by prosecutors to the earlier editions of QT, arguing that the earlier editions did not translate it correctly, as evidenced by the revision that was implemented in the newest edition. The understanding of the verse provided in the third edition, they argued, makes it clear that it has no relevance to elections or to the political rights of non-Muslims, and, consequently, should exempt Ahok from any allegation of blasphemy. The different editions of QT were frequently cited during the trial both to justify and to disprove the discourse on both sides.

It is clear that throughout the whole affair there was a consistent binary opposition between one group and the other, and that the different translations of *awliyāʾ* provided by the various editions of QT were a focal point in the disputes. Furthermore, the conflict had become so heated that it led to a situation in which there was no such thing as an unbiased opinion. The discourse was all about whether *awliyāʾ* means *'pemimpin'* or *'teman setia'*, and hence whether Ahok was blasphemous or not. The scholarly elites on both sides voiced their opinions so as to justify a monovalent interpretation of their choice to others. The intensive mobilization of the masses orchestrated by Islamist groups and the MUI's motion, as well as the counterargument of their opponents, spurred people into participating in the debate. While the Islamic academic elite may have had reasonable grounds for their respective views, based in years of study and a nuanced understanding of the issues at hand, most ordinary people knew nothing more than what they were told by their religious leaders and the translations of the Qur'an to which they had access. The narratives and arguments put forward by the scholars were then reproduced on various media platforms, and eventually widely distributed via social media. As a result, anybody could get involved in the debate, sharing their own views and perspectives and becoming active participants in the process. In short, the specific political climate in which the allegations and the subsequent court case emerged morphed into a bitter partisanship, to which Indonesians translations of the Qur'an, and QT in particular, had contributed.

Imagining the State Authority in the Translation

Analyzing the public reception towards QT against this particular political background can give us important clues about what the notion of the 'officiality' of this translation means to its Indonesian readership. The dispute over the correct translation of Q 5:51 and the historical sequence of events reflect, at least to some extent, how Indonesian Muslims perceive QT. This is particularly apparent in the distrust of the government that was demonstrated when they were considered to be slow to act in prosecuting Ahok for blasphemy, and the belief of some that the government was biased in Ahok's favor. Given its status as the official translation of the state, public perceptions of and attitudes to the government somehow also affected popular perceptions of QT.

The most dramatic moment of the entire controversy, in terms of the involvement of QT, occurred in the context of accusations concerning the authenticity of the third edition of the QT translation. These accusations claimed that this edition of QT, or any other translation that uses '*teman setia*' ('loyal friend') instead of '*pemimpin-pemimpin*' ('leaders'), is 'a fraudulent Qur'an' (*Al-Qur'an palsu*). The accusation was initially made by Mustafa Nahra through his Twitter account on

20 October 2016. He began with *'Innalillahi wa innaillaihi roojiuun,'*[44] a Qur'anic phrase which is often read on the occasions of misfortune, particularly death, before stating *'Telah dibagikan Al-Qur'an PALSU ke sekolah2'*[45] ('The FRAUDULENT Qur'an has been distributed to schools'). Nahra's concern, however, seemed to be about more than a difference in translation. His tweet was written in a passive voice which did not mention the subject, i.e., those who were responsible for distributing the supposed fraudulent Qur'an. This indicates that, as well as being troubled by the actual wording of the verse, he was concerned by the apparent attempt to furtively change the translation of the Qur'an and distribute it through schools in the current political atmosphere. He was suspicious that the Qur'an had been deliberately edited in order to save Ahok from the blasphemy accusation. Nahra urged people to check their *mushaf*, and even to inspect bookstores, and to come forward if anyone found a Qur'an with a *fabricated* translation, suggesting that he might do something about it.[46]

Nahra's narrative of the fraudulent Qur'an generated anxiety and led to suspicion. He was supported by one of the MUI leaders, Tengku Zulkarnain (1963–2021),[47] who posted the following on his Twitter account:

> *Al Qur'an Terjemahan Baru Muncul. 'Waliy' Diartikan 'Kawan Setia'. DUIT Bergerak Mau Tipu Umat. Jadi KAWAN SETIA Saja HARAM Apalagi Penguasa?*
>
> [A new Qur'an translation has appeared. 'Waliy' is translated as 'a loyal friend'. MONEY moves to deceive people. Even becoming a LOYAL FRIEND is PROHIBITED, let alone a ruler?]

44 The phrase, properly transcribed as *Innā li-'lāh wa innā ilayhi rāji^{c}ūn* ('we belong to God and to Him we shall return'), is a Qur'anic phrase mentioned in Q 2:156.

45 The addition of the numeric figure '2' is the common way to indicate plural word forms in non-official writings in Indonesia.

46 Bayu Hermawan, 'Netizen Dihebohkan dengan "Berubahnya" Tafsir Al Maidah Ayat 51', *Republika Online*, 22 October 2016, section Nasional, http://www.republika.co.id/berita/nasional/umum/16/10/22/offxlk354-netizen-dihebohkan-dengan-berubahnya-tafsir-al-maidah-ayat-51.

47 Dr. H. Tengku Zulkarnain passed away on 10 Mei 2021 from Covid-19. May he rest in peace along with all who died as a result of the pandemic.

Zulkarnain seemed to be relatively careful in his statement regarding the accusation of the fraudulent Qur'an, and this may reflect an awareness on his part that a change in translation did not equate to fabrication. However, given his failure to clarify Nahra's accusation, Zulkarnain's statement, in fact, amplified the indictment and fanned more suspicion. Even though neither Nahra or Zulkarnain explicitly said so, their allegations were undoubtedly directed at people who supported Ahok.

The controversy and suspicion became fiercer when the government, through the Ministry of Religious Affairs, was accused of being an actor behind the so-called underground movement to save Ahok from the accusations of blasphemy. Indeed, in an attempt to bolster the blasphemy discourse, the GNPF MUI quite frequently suggested that the government was supportive of Ahok. They made insinuations about the close relationship between Jokowi and Ahok, pointing out that they were partners during Jokowi's Jakarta governorship before he became president.

The identification of MORA with the 'fraudulent Qur'an' first arose on the Internet. Following up his first series of tweets, which opened up the issue, Nahra then encouraged his Twitter followers to check their *mushafs,* take a screenshot of the translation of the relevant verse, and post it to their accounts, tagging Nahra's account so that he could trace which publishing house had published the so-called fabricated Qur'an. He also encouraged people to check their mobile Qur'an apps and said that anyone finding *awliyāʾ* rendered as *'teman setia'* should delete the app. Many people followed him. Due to Nahra's intervention, the perception of two kinds of Qur'an appeared, a *'safe'* Qur'an and a *'fabricated'* one, and this likewise divided the publishers of Qur'ans into 'trustworthy' and 'untrustworthy' categories. During Nahra's exchange with his followers, a member of the Local Representative Council, Fahira Idris (@fahiraidris) was as reactive as Nahra. She confirmed the change in translation, and to provide evidence, shared a screenshot of Q 5:51 from the translation of the Saudi edition, which translates *awliyāʾ* as *'pemimpin'*. She claimed to have called the publishing house that produced her translation, which informed her that all of the Qur'an copies which were edited were ordered by the Ministry of Religious Affairs (*semua Al Qur'an yg 'diedit' tsb, atas instruksi Departemen Agama*).

Nahra's accusation and Zulkarnain's supporting tweet were vague in their nature and did not explicitly indicate who the actor behind this change in translation was. Against this backdrop, Idris' statement brought the controversy to a new level, given her suggestion that it was the government that was behind the supposed fabrication of the Qur'an. The publisher that Idris contacted was correct that the revision was executed by order of the Ministry of Religious Affairs, but the full story was that the Qur'an publishing industry had been publishing the third edition of QT since 2004, some thirteen years prior to Ahok's speech and the subsequent controversy. Notwithstanding this, Idris' statement was, ironically, unquestioningly taken as concrete proof that the government indeed sided with Ahok.

The online exchanges that took place between Mustafa Nahra, Tengku Zulkarnain, and Fahira Idris reveal their lack of awareness about the workings of the Qur'an publishing industry and the production of Qur'an translations in Indonesia. As stated above, they did not seem to understand that the shift from '*pemimpin-pemimpin*' to '*teman setia*' occurred during the second revision which took place in 1998–2002. Nor did they understand that, unless it was a personal translation authored by a particular figure, all *mushaf*s that include a translation printed in Indonesia have incorporated the official translation of the Ministry of Religious Affairs. This was made evident when Nahra compared the newly published third edition of QT to the older editions, and when Idris contrasted the recently published Qur'an translation in Indonesia with the Saudi edition, without acknowledging that all of them use QT as a template. However, over time, when more and more people shared their *mushaf* and identified the publishers, they eventually realized that identifying the Qur'an translation in Indonesia by publisher was irrelevant, because nearly all *mushafs* published in Indonesia were based on the QT template. They also eventually realized that the change to '*teman setia*' had taken place at some time in the 2000s, even though they were not sure of the exact year the revision took place. Both Nahra and Idris then deleted their misleading tweets (although both can still easily be found, as Nahra's tweet was quoted directly on a news portal, and the screenshot of Idris' tweet is still available on the Internet). In fact, Idris now explicitly denies associating this revision with the conflict between Ahok and the GNPF MUI.[48]

48 Kabul Astuti, 'Soal Perubahan Tafsir Al Maidah 51, Fahira akan Tanyakan Kemenag', *Republika Online*, 23 October 2016, section Nasional, http://www.republika.co.id/

Recognizing how the accusations of a fraudulent Qur'an could get seriously out of hand, the Minister of Religious Affairs, Lukman Hakim Saifuddin, reacted through his twitter account, @lukmansaifuddin, tweeting that 'The news stating that there was a fabrication of the Qur'an and that the ministry instructed its fabrication is incorrect.' A clarification was then published on MORA's official website in the form of an interview with Muchlis M. Hanafi, the director of the Lajnah Pentashihan Mushaf Al-Qur'an (LPMQ, The Qur'anic Text Review Board). In this interview, Hanafi rebutted the idea that the ministry had ordered any publishing houses to fabricate the Qur'an. He explained that the term *awliyā͗* was used forty-two times in the Qur'an and was translated in various ways depending on the context, and addressed the role of the Ministry of Religious Affairs in the publication of the Qur'an and its translation. He pointed out that the ministry merely acted as the facilitator for the *ulama* in this context, and that the translation and interpretation of the Qur'an was the responsibility of the *ulama.* Hanafi also responded to the allegations of a 'fake' Qur'an by explaining that a Qur'an translation was different to the Qur'an itself. According to him, the translation represented only the understanding of the translator of the Qur'an, and a change in the translation does not mean a change in the Qur'an.[49]

Mustafa Nahra, Tengku Zulkarnain and Fahira Idris might be oblivious to the finer subtleties of the nature of translation, the history of the translation of the Qur'an in Indonesia, and the intricacies of the Qur'an publication process in Indonesia. Nevertheless, their responses to what they thought to be a change in the translation of the Qur'an and the explicit *Al-Qur'an palsu* accusation exacerbated mistrust of the government. This mistrust towards the government and QT led to the re-emergence of an old critique of the official translation that initially appeared in 2010 as part of the attempt of Majelis Mujahidin Indonesia

---

berita/nasional/umum/16/10/23/ofgnj0361-soal-perubahan-tafsir-al-maidah-51-fahira-akan-tanyakan-kemenag; Ahmad Muhajir, 'Fahira Idris Benarkan Ada Perubahan Terjemah Al-Qur'an', *Gontornews,* 2016, http://gontornews.com/2016/10/24/fahira-idris-benarkan-ada-perubahan-terjemah-al-quran/.

49 Khoiron, 'Soal Terjemahan Awliyā sebagai "Teman Setia", Ini Penjelasan Kemenag', *Kementrian Agama Republik Indonesia,* 2016, https://kemenag.go.id/berita/read/417806/soal-terjemahan-awliy---sebagai----teman-setia-----ini-penjelasan-kemenag.

(MMI, The Council of Indonesian Warriors) to delegitimize the state's religious discourse (see Chapter Four). Arifin Ilham (1969–2019), one of the proponents of the GNPF MUI, was reported to have discouraged people from using QT and encouraged them to substitute it with the *Tarjamah Tafsiriyah* of Muhammad Thalib, coincidentally the late chief of MMI.

The story of the objections Thalib voiced towards QT in this critique became relevant in the context of the blasphemy case because it demonstrates the connection between public perceptions of the government on the one hand, and QT on the other hand. Following the ABI, the government attempted to limit the growing influence of their sympathizers, in part by issuing the Government Regulation in Lieu of Law (PERPPU) No. 2/2017 that allows the state to dissolve organizations that were deemed to be at odds with state ideology. Using this regulation, the government dissolved the HTI. To protest against this, they attempted to delegitimize the government by, among other things, denouncing QT. Thus, the old story of the disagreement between Muhammad Thalib and MORA was reproduced and redistributed with the aim of maintaining, and exacerbating, the public's distrust of the government. In response, as reported on the official website of the Ministry of Religious Affairs, Muchlis M. Hanafi defended QT. He explained that Muhammad Thalib's criticisms do not reflect on the integrity of QT, and that Muslims are allowed to choose whichever translation they prefer. As the ministry did in response to Thalib when he originally made his criticism of QT public, Hanafi invited Arifin Ilham to participate in a discussion.[50]

The clumsy accusations made about the 'fraudulent Qur'an' created a new awareness in people that they should look beyond the hermeneutical aspects of a particular Qur'an translation to determine whether or not it is authoritative. That is evident in the emergence of the idea that there is a 'safe' and a 'fraudulent Qur'an' and the categorization of publishers as trustworthy or untrustworthy.[51] Fahira

50 Khoiron, 'Penjelasan tentang Dugaan Kesalahan Terjemah Al Quran Kementrian Agama', *Kementrian Agama Republik Indonesia*, 2017, https://kemenag.go.id/berita/read/504945/penjelasan-tentang-dugaan-kesalahan-terjemah-al-quran-kementerian-agama.

51 This categorization had immediate consequences. One publication house filed a police complaint when their *mushaf* was posted online along with a comment

Idris thought that the Qur'an translation from Saudi Arabia had greater validity than any translations available in Indonesia, although ironically she did not acknowledge that the Saudi edition also uses the second edition (1990) of QT. However, soon enough, people recognized that nearly all *mushafs* in Indonesia incorporate the QT translation of the text. When it comes to the contested translation of *awliyā*ʾ in Q 5:51, those in favor of translating the word as 'leader' started deliberately mentioning that the reason they referred to QT was because it was the official state translation. In the courtroom, Novel Chaidir Hasan, an FPI activist and witness for the prosecution, for example, stated that he deliberately quoted QT in his testimony precisely because it was the translation recognized by the government (he appeared to confuse 'commissioned by the government' with 'recognized by the government'). Likewise, the indictment document quoted the pre-2002 edition of QT, because it was so frequently referenced during the trial itself.

While the reference made by the prosecutors to the pre-2002 edition of QT has a hermeneutical basis, the indications that their reference to QT is conscious and deliberate is intriguing. Generally speaking, as is often the case with the reception of translations in general throughout the world, Indonesian Muslims take Qur'an translations for granted, that is to say that they are not really aware of the authorship of a certain translation of the Qur'an and the interpretive issues this can entail. It was only after a series of events—the ABI rallies, the fraudulent Qur'an accusations, and the re-emergence of Thalib's objection to QT—that they started to be aware that the authorship of a text can have implications for how that text is read. Thus, there is the idea that political power influences the degree of legitimacy of a specific Qur'an translation.

The accusations about a fraudulent Qur'an and the re-emergence of Muhammad Thalib's exchange with MORA, and the way Novel Chaidir Hasan explicitly indicated the motive behind his reference to QT during the trial are illustrative of two conflicting attitudes towards QT as the official government translation. On the one hand, the government is accused of manipulating the translation for their own political interests, implying a distrust of it. On the other hand, Ahok's opponents deliberately referred to QT to support their arguments in court, implying

---

discouraging people from buying it on the basis that it was untrustworthy because it rendered *awliyā*ʾ as *teman setia* instead of *pemimpin-pemimpin*.

a level of recognition of its authority. Although these two approaches may seem contradictory on the surface, they share one thing: they both speak to conceptions about the imagined authority of the state. The readers of QT imagine that there is a certain quality that is associated with a state-authorized translation of the Qur'an. Typically, a translation of the Qur'an contains a hermeneutical aspect, as it is a new space in which the message of a holy book in the source language, Arabic, is transferred into the target language. However, its status as the official translation has led people to think that the authority of the state also resides in the translation. QT, therefore, has more than hermeneutical significance: people do not only refer to QT because of perceptions of its hermeneutical value or the intellectual authority of the authors, but also because of their understanding that it is authoritative precisely because it has official status. The official Qur'an translation, therefore, carries a burden of officiality.

Conclusion

The 2017 Jakarta gubernatorial election was an historic event that continues to shape current political developments in Indonesia. The blasphemy issue, the rallies, and the sentiments that grew from it have had tangible effects. As far as QT is concerned, the election and subsequent trial leads us to several interesting observations. In the context of the constant politicization of the Qur'an, particularly Q 5:51, and its use to undercut the rise of a Christian candidate to a position of political leadership, the dynamics of the discourse lead us to some conclusions about the officiality of QT.

The underlying problem presented by Q 5:51 lies in the contradiction between the constitution—which guarantees the political rights of all citizens regardless of their religious credentials—and a Qur'anic verse that is commonly cited as prohibiting the appointment of a non-Muslim leader. Consequently, although the constitution guaranteed the political rights of Basuki Tjahaja Purnama, his opponents could always employ the verse to further their political interests. This juxtaposition is exactly what the 2017 Jakarta gubernatorial election has shown us.

The politicization of the Qur'an and the public response to this led to a series of events, from blasphemy allegations and rallies to the allegations of a fraudulent Qur'an, and eventually to the guilty verdict against Ahok. Although Islamist groups and the MUI were the primary drivers of the rallies, the role played by Qur'an translations in this controversy cannot be underestimated. I contend that QT made a significant contribution to the discourse used by both sides, and that this is connected to the two different interpretations of the verse provided in the different editions of QT. While one reading provided a sense of justification for the allegations of blasphemy, the other translation stands as the primary premise for the counter-arguments about the abuse and politicization of the Qur'an. The two different renditions of the key word *awliyāʾ*, which are rooted in deep and far-reaching hermeneutical complications, result in an irreconcilable ideological contradiction. This contradiction, in turn, has contributed to shaping the partisan attitudes of the masses.

The Indonesian citizens' perceptions of the state are also reflected in their attitude to the official translation of the Qur'an. Where there is distrust towards the state, the official translation is regarded with suspicion. Conversely, in another context where the authority of the state is deemed necessary, the translation is considered authoritative. This clearly illustrates the fact that QT is a text that is judged on more than its hermeneutical merits: it also has the burden of officiality, and ideas of state authority are intertwined with perceptions about the authority of the translation.

Concluding Remarks: What Is an Official Qur'an Translation?

This study has investigated the official Qur'an translation produced by the Ministry of Religious Affairs of the Republic of Indonesia, *Al-Qur'an dan Terjemahnya*. It has discussed how the state acts as the producer of Qur'an translations and what the consequences of this are for the work itself. In general, this study has revealed that QT contributes to maintaining the religious authority of the state through the adoption of mainstream Sunnī theology rather than through any close governmental control of the translation process with the aim of explicitly voicing government ideology or promoting the religious policy of the state. Hence, any assumption that QT is intended to create a standardized national Islamic discourse is an overstatement. Despite the fact that the translation is nominally produced by the Ministry of Religious Affairs, the *ulama* who make up the translation committee enjoy interpretive authority and are able to draw freely on traditional Sunnī sources in making their translation decisions. The appointment of a translation committee, rather than a single translator, is, however, a way for the state to exercise its authority as the protector of the interests of its Muslims citizens, because it means that QT does not have a single author, and the text is thus not connected to any particular figure or ideology but is rendered impersonal. Furthermore, the fact that QT is translated by a committee, as well as the choice of committee members, means that the translation follows a conventional, traditional reading of the Arabic source text and eschews controversy. QT thus perpetuates the authority and image of the state or the ruling government as meeting the interests of its Muslim population.

In Chapter One, it was pointed out that Sunnism has contributed to the formation of the democratic Indonesian state as an orthodox

 https://doi.org/10.11647/OBP.0289.08

theism that shapes the state's affairs on religion, which is termed as Godly nationalism and explained as a co-evolutionary process between the state and religion. This implies that Sunnism is an inherent part of the state's Islamic identity and informs its policies. For this reason, on the basis of a strong connection between QT and the Sunnī *tafsīr* tradition, one might be tempted to associate QT as belonging to this co-evolutionary process, which goes some way to proving the idea that the production of QT is intended to create a standard, state-approved Islamic discourse. However, I argue here that the history of QT is not reflective of the co-evolution of state and religion. QT's reliance on Sunnī sources is driven by the genealogical nature of the Arabic *tafsīr* tradition, whereas the state in this context only adopts that tradition. In other words, the Sunnī tradition has profoundly affected the nature of the state's official Qur'an translation, and its production processes, yet the state's involvement in the production of QT does not affect the living Sunnī *tafsīr* tradition. This can be seen from the fact that the number of interpretive 'adjustments' to the source text made in QT with the intention of aligning the target text with state ideology and policies is extremely limited. In fact, we can even find interpretive instances that go against government policy. The reason for this is that, for one thing, while QT falls under the wider structure of the state's projects on religion, it does not constitute a strategic project intended to influence or define the political orientation of the state. Secondly, the interpretive authority of QT has been handed over to the *ulama,* the bearers of the Sunnī Islamic tradition. It is true that the production processes of QT entail authorization of the final text by the Ministry of Religious Affairs, but this authorization is not equivalent to a legislative process. Even though QT is an official Qur'an translation, it is still just a translation, not a law or a government regulation that occasions a degree of binding force on Indonesian citizens.

Over the course of its history, there have been four main editions and two other secondary editions of QT. The initial edition was the product of the transition of power from Sukarno's Guided Democracy to Suharto's New Order Indonesia. It was printed in three volumes: the first volume was published under the governance of the first president, whereas the other two were produced under his successor. The joint committee set up by MORA and the Saudi King Fahd Complex in 1989–90 when the Saudi institution decided to extend their Qur'an translation project to cover the Indonesian language has generally been considered to have resulted in the publication of just one revised edition, but I have argued that the version(s) of QT printed by the King Fahd Complex has/have followed a distinctive trajectory to those printed in Indonesia, either by MORA, the Qur'an publishing industry, or other players. The work of this joint committee thus actually resulted in two distinct editions: the second and the Saudi editions. Another review and revision process was undertaken in 1998–2002, due to both a growing demand and readership and criticisms of the existing edition. This revision resulted in the third edition of QT. Since that time, a growing concern with the preservation of regional languages within MORA has led the ministry to extend the Qur'an translation project to encompass a number of regional languages: dozens of translations into regional languages have already been published, and there are more to come. Finally, between 2016 and 2019, a further revision took place, which resulted in the fourth edition of QT. Even though it was officially launched at the end of 2019, this edition was yet to reach the market when this study was finalized.

As has been discussed in Chapter Two, the different editions of QT do not only entail changes in the target text, but also encompass technical elements and metatextual aspects of the work. This includes factors such as the development of the spelling and transliteration system, layout and typesetting, the visual presentation of the book, and the move to a digital format, as well as the original print format. The transformation of the text at this level has been affected by both the readers of QT and the Qur'an publishing industry, which has played a major part in driving such changes. In general, Qur'an translations used to be a distinctive subgenre, but recently the translation has been integrated into the Arabic *mushaf*. Qur'an publishers in Indonesia print different editions of the Qur'an using different formats to meet different needs, for example some target a specific readership (e.g., children or women), some include a specific additional feature (memorization or *tajwid* guidance), or are produced in a luxurious format intended to be part of a dowry or gift. QT has been fully integrated into the *mushaf* industry and is manifested in a wide variety of forms. The government is open to such innovations in the use of QT in Qur'an production as it means that QT consistently maintains its readership.

The presence of the state and the ideology of the current government make themselves felt in the forewords of QT. These constitute a blank space, unrestricted by the boundaries of the Qur'anic text, that have allowed successive governments to deploy their political and ideological vocabularies. These forewords show that QT was initially a part of Sukarno's aim to ground and elaborate his synthetic ideology, *Nasakom,* as well as to establish his image as a religious leader. When Sukarno stepped down from the presidency and was replaced by Suharto in 1965, the new president made QT a part of his developmentalist project, in which religion was contextualized in a purely religious framework. He cleansed the translation of all traces of Sukarno's footprints to such an extent that contemporary readers might be confused by its initial history, and an 'unideological' QT has been the rule since that time. In the post-Suharto period, when Indonesia experienced the rise of Islamism, QT encountered criticism from the MMI as part of its overall agenda of questioning the authority of the state. An explosion caused by a suicide bomber in 2011 led to an escalation in such criticism and there were allegations that QT was the cause of the terrorist attack. The MMI demanded that the state withdraw QT from distribution and openly apologize to the public, and urged even more strongly that the King Fahd Complex cease printing their edition of QT. The government was left with no choice but to respond to these criticisms and to undermine MMI's discourse, as defending QT was defending its own authority.

The forewords to the various editions of QT also inform us that it was not produced merely to facilitate access to the meaning of the Qur'an for those Indonesian Muslims with no competency in Arabic, but also to enable those who were unfamiliar with modern Indonesian to experience the language through the Qur'an translation. Along with other projects, most notably the establishment of Islamic higher education, QT is one means through which the government seeks to fulfill its aim of making Indonesian the language of Islamic scholarship in the country. More recently, the government has expanded this aim to encompass the idea of preserving Indonesian regional languages through translations of the Qur'an, in the belief that because of the high regard and respect in which the Qur'an is held by believers this would benefit their attempts to preserve regional languages in danger of extinction.

As for the actual hermeneutic basis of the translation, the government has always given interpretive authority to the *ulama.* For each edition, a translation committee is formed, and their translation starts with individual inquiries, and then moves to regular plenary sessions. The first edition of the resulting text was authorized by the Ministry of Religious Affairs, while the national congress of *ulama* of the Qur'an have approved further editions. The Saudi edition is the exception, as the King Fahd Complex has its own authorization processes in place. The translation procedures mean that QT is truly a collaborative, collective project, a feature that creates a sense of its being an impersonal text, and gives it a higher level of authority than any individual translation. The names of the translators are mentioned in the text, but this is intended to credit their service more than their intellectual contributions; indeed, the individual contributions of the translators are completely invisible in the translation. It is interesting, though, that despite the fact that QT is produced by members of the *ulama*, it is widely referred to as the MORA translation.

When it comes to the theological dimension of QT, the interpretive decisions made within its text consistently follow the mainstream Sunnī outlook, as the interpretive freedom of the *ulama* manifests in a heavy reliance on the Sunnī *tafsīr* tradition. As a result, there is no formal connection between QT and other MORA projects such as the modernization of family law and Islamic thought. The committee is not interested in synchronizing QT with developments in the Marriage Law or the Compilation of Islamic Law, and the government does not attempt to push them in that direction. The interpretive developments that are implemented between one edition and the next point to the existence of substantial discussions within the various translation committees, but only selectively accord with the progressive discourse on Islamic thought that is supported by the state in the other projects. Even when the committee encounters an intersection between the state's ideological vocabulary and Qur'anic terms and concepts, they can produce a disinterested translation, as they have done with their translation of *aḥad* as *esa*. The scholars working on QT are also free to maintain an interpretation that categorically contradicts the constitution, such as their rendition of *awliāʾ* as *'pemimpin'*. When the translation seems to support the government discourse, as in the more subtle case of *ūlu al-amr* and the more controversial *akābira mujrimīha*, this is because the translation committee has sought their solution within the *tafsīr* tradition. As far as the committee is concerned, going beyond the accepted interpretive boundaries as set out in *tafsīr* does not seem to be an easy option. When it comes to the state's interests, the various QT translation committees have supported them as long as the interpretive range of the *tafsīr* allows it, as is evident from their selection and reproduction of views from the *tafsīr* tradition.

I have said earlier that the hermeneutical procedures followed by QT give it a level of authority over other, individually authored translations. The case study of the Jakarta gubernatorial election clearly demonstrates how QT has assumed an authority that goes beyond the hermeneutical to encompass a sense of institutionalized authority. QT has a wide readership because it is the official Qur'an translation of the state, and is imbued with the authority accorded to it by this status. Those members of the public who trust the government tend not to question the translation of the Qur'an provided by QT, while those who are critical of the government are also critical of QT.

So, what actually characterizes QT as an official Qur'an translation? It originated from a national development plan initiated by the highest political institution in the state, the Majelis Permusyawaratan Rakyat Sementara (MPRS, Provisional People's Consultative Assembly) and was executed under the supervision of the Ministry of Religious Affairs. The translation committee was formed by MORA, while the translation itself was a collective, collaborative hermeneutical process that included authorization from either the ministry or the congress of *ulama*. This process has made it impossible to ascribe the translation to any particular translator or group of translators, and it has therefore been ascribed to the institution that oversees the project, MORA. Furthermore, its official status is accepted, and arguably approved, by its readership. The forewords included in the various editions indicate that it is not free from the influence of government policy, however the content of the translation may or may not support the state's stance on a particular religious issue. This is because, from the perspective of the translation committees, the primary objective of the target text is to reproduce the generally accepted Sunnī reading of the Qur'an. This undoubtedly precludes any explicit state-supported politicization of the translation, but the translators demonstrate a strong tendency for avoiding controversy, which we can assume is in no small part motivated by their desire to maintain public trust in the translation.

This leads to another question: what are the fundamental elements that constitute the genre of the institutional Qur'an commentary produced in this Muslim majority region? First of all, the commissioning institution (the state in this case), the readership, and the translation committee are three important variables that interact in the production of the translation. In producing the translation, the state undoubtedly gives consideration to the prevailing theological views of the community, and this has led to a particular approach to selecting the members of the translation committees. Thus, the hermeneutical principles which the committees bring to their translations are predictable. This leads to a situation where the translation reproduces the prevailing theology, the readers will accept this reading of the text readily, and the state enjoys public confidence in their state Qur'an.

When it comes to translation methodology, the theoretical exposition provided by the translators gives few clues as to how they approached the actual work of translation. The theorization they do provide casts more light on their theological beliefs, and their view of the Qur'an as inimitable, divine revelation with extraordinary linguistic impact. It does seem clear that the work of the translation teams was largely shaped by their views on the Qur'an and their knowledge of *tafsīr*, and their approach may well have been influenced more by prevailing policy on language, for example, than a well-defined theory of Qur'an translation.

This brings me to my final point. Another aspect of QT that is key to an understanding of the nature of the text lies in the fact that any Qur'an translation is the translation of a composite text: it is not simply the translation of the Qur'an in isolation from its secondary literatures. However, QT is not a translation in which the translators make overt and sustained recourse to the secondary literatures, whether *fiqh* or *tafsīr* for example. Nevertheless, the *tafsīr* tradition is much more present in the translation than it might appear to be on the surface. The interpretive possibilities and boundaries provided by the *tafsīr* tradition are always at work in the background, and it frequently makes its presence felt, often even substituting for the original Qur'anic text. While traditional translation theories take into account the push and pull between the text and translators and reflect on the (in)visibility of the latter, in Qur'an translation, one must not forget to investigate the (in)visibility of *tafsīr*.

Bibliography

Abdullah, Taufik, 'History, Political Images and Cultural Encounter: The Dutch in the Indonesian Archipelago', *Studia Islamika; Vol 1, No 3 (1994): Studia Islamika*, 2014, http://journal.uinjkt.ac.id/index.php/studia-islamika/article/view/848/726

—, 'Islam, State and Society in Democratizing Indonesia: An Historical Reflection', *Studia Islamika; Vol 18, No 2 (2011): Studia Islamika*, 2014, http://journal.uinjkt.ac.id/index.php/studia-islamika/article/view/432/285

Abdullah, Taufik, and Endjat Djaenuderadjat, eds., *Sejarah Kebudayaan Islam Indonesia: Tradisi, Intelektual, dan Sosial*, 2nd edn (Jakarta: Direktorat Sejarah, Direktorat Jenderal Kebudayaan, Kementerian Pendidikan dan Kebudayaan, 2017)

Abuza, Zachary, *Political Islam and Violence in Indonesia* (London, New York: Routledge, 2007)

'ACD—Austronesian Comparative Dictionary—Cognate Sets—e', http://www.trussel2.com/acd/acd-s_e1.htm?zoom_highlight=esa

Adamson, Clarissa, 'Gendered Anxieties: Islam, Women's Right, and Moral Hierarchy in Java', *Anthropological Quarterly*, 80.1 (2007), 5–37

Afif, Zarkasi, Harits Fadly, Ali Akbar, Syatri Jonni, Mustopa Mustopa, Ahmad Jaeni, and others, 'Preferensi Masyarakat dalam Penggunaan Al-Qur'an Digital', *SUHUF Jurnal Pengkajian Al-Qur'an dan Budaya*, 11.2 (2018), 185–214

Ahmad, Mirza Bashir-ud-din Mahmud, *Introduction to The Study of The Holy Qur'ān* (Surrey: Islam International Publications Limited, 2016)

Ahmad, Nur, 'Sejarah Makna Kitab Gandul dalam Tradisi Pesantren', *alif.id*, 2018, https://alif.id/read/nur-ahmad/sejarah-makna-kitab-gandul-dalam-tradisi-pesantren-b212819p/

Aitkulova, Meerim, 'Hizb Ut-Tahrir: Dreaming of Caliphate', in *Handbook of Islamic Sects and Movements*, ed. by Muhammad Afzal Upal and Carole M. Cusack, Brill Handbook on Contemporary Religion, 21 (Boston: Brill: Leiden, 2021), pp. 402–20

Akbar, Ali, 'Pencetakan Mushaf Al-Qur'an di Indonesia', *SUHUF*, 4.2 (2015), 271–87, https://doi.org/10.22548/shf.v4i2.57

Alfian, 'Islamic Modernism in Indonesian Politics: The Muhammadijah Movement during the Dutch Colonial Period (1912–1942)' (unpublished doctoral dissertation, The University of Wisconsin, 1969)

Alfitri, 'Religious Liberty in Indonesia and the Rights of Deviant Sects', *Asian Journal of Comparative Law*, 3.1 (2008), 1–27, https://doi.org/10.2202/1932-0205.1062

—, 'Whose Authority? Contesting and Negotiating the Idea of a Legitimate Interpretation of Islamic Law in Indonesia', *Asian Journal of Comparative Law*, 10 (2016), 191–212, https://doi.org/10.1017/ASJCL.2016.1

Ali, Lukman, *Ikhtisar Sejarah Ejaan Bahasa Indonesia* (Jakarta: Pusat Pembinaan dan Pengembangan Bahasa, 1998)

Ali, Muhamad, 'The Muhammadiyah's 47th Congress and "Islam Berkemajuan"', *Studia Islamika; Vol 22, No 2* (2015)*: Studia Islamika*, 2015, http://journal.uinjkt.ac.id/index.php/studia-islamika/article/view/1978/1557

Aljunied, Khairudin, *Muslim Cosmopolitanism: Southeast Asian Islam in Comparative Perspective* (Edinburgh: Edinburgh University Press, 2017)

'Alquran Digital Kemenag Sudah Bisa Diunduh di Google Play Store', *Republika Online*, 2016, https://republika.co.id/berita/dunia-islam/islam-nusantara/16/08/31/ocriqt313-alquran-digital-kemenag-sudah-bisa-diunduh-di-google-play-store

al-Alūsī, Abū al-Faḍl Shihāb al-Dīn al-Sayyid Maḥmūd, *Rūḥ al-maᶜānī fī tafsīr al-qurʾān wa al-sabᶜ al-mathānī*, 30 vols (Beirut: Iḥyāʾ al-Turāth al-ᶜArabī), VI

Amin, Ma'ruf, 'Khittah Islam Nusantara', *Kompas* (Jakarta, Agustus 2015)

Andrianto, M. Fahri, M.R. Nababan, and Eva Farhah, 'The Impact of Translation Techniques on Translation Methods of Qur'an Translation of Indonesian Ministry of Religion on Fawatih Al-Suwar', *International Journal of Linguistics, Literature and Translation*, 4.6 (2021), 291–98, https://doi.org/10.32996/ijllt.2021.4.6.34

antaranews.com, 'Kemenag Luncurkan Terjemahan Al Quran dalam Bahasa Daerah', *Antara News*, https://www.antaranews.com/berita/602379/kemenag-luncurkan-terjemahan-al-quran-dalam-bahasa-daerah

Aspinall, Edward, *Opposing Suharto: Compromise, Resistance, and Regime Change in Indonesia*, Contemporary Issues in Asia and the Pacific (California: Stanford University Press, 2005)

Assegaf, Umar Faruk, 'The Rise of Shi'ism in Contemporary Indonesia: Orientation and Affiliation' (unpublished master's thesis, The Australian National University, 2012)

Assyaukanie, Luthfie, 'Unholy Alliance: Ultra-Conservatism and Political Pragmatism in Indonesia | THC ASEAN', *Thinking Asean*, 2017, http://thcasean.org/read/articles/327/Unholy-Alliance-Ultra-Conservatism-and-Political-Pragmatism-in-Indonesia.html

Astuti, Kabul, 'Soal Perubahan Tafsir Al Maidah 51, Fahira akan Tanyakan Kemenag', *Republika Online*, 23 October 2016, section Nasional, http://www.republika.co.id/berita/nasional/umum/16/10/23/ofgnj0361-soal-perubahan-tafsir-al-maidah-51-fahira-akan-tanyakan-kemenag

Awwas, Irfan S, 'Ideologi Teroris dalam Terjemah Qur'an Depag', *Majalah Gatra*, 27 April 2011, pp. 26–27

—, 'Kontroversi Tarjamah Harfiyah', in *Koreksi Tarjamah Harfiyah Al-Qur'an Kemenag RI: Tinjauan Aqidah, Syariah, Mu'amalah, Iqtishadiyah*, by Muhammad Thalib (Yogyakarta: Maᶜhad An-Nabawy, 2011), pp. 11–22

Azra, Azyumardi, *Islam Nusantara: Jaringan Global dan Lokal* [*Historical Islam: Indonesian Islam in Global and Local Perspective*], trans. by Iding Rosyidin Hasan (Bandung: Mizan, 2002)

—, 'Islamic Reform in Southeast Asia: Assimilations, Continuity and Change', in *Muslim Reform in Southeast Asia: Perspectives from Malaysia, Indonesia, and Singapore*, ed. by Syed Farid Alatas (Singapore: Majlis Ugama Islam Singapura, 2009)

—, *Jaringan Ulama Timur Tengah dan Kepulauan Nusantara Abad XVII & XVIII: Akar Pembaruan Islam Indonesia* (Jakarta: Kencana, 2013)

—, 'Naskah Terjemahan Antarbaris: Kontribusi Kreatif Dunia Islam Melayu-Indonesia', in *Sadur Sejarah Terjemahan di Indonesia dan Malaysia*, ed. by Henri Chambert-Loir (Jakarta: Kepustakaan Populer Gramedia, 2009), pp. 435–43

—, *The Origins of Islamic Reformism in Southeast Asia: Networks of Malay-Indonesian and Middle Eastern ᶜUlamāʾ in the Seventeeth and Eighteenth Centuries*, Southeast Asia Publication Series (Allen & Unwin and University of Hawai'i Press, 2004)

—, 'The Use and Abuse of Qur'anic Verses in Contemporary Indonesian Politics', in *Approaches to The Qur'an in Contemporary Indonesia*, ed. by Abdullah Saeed, The Institute of Ismaili Studies (Oxford: Oxford University Press, 2005), pp. 193–208

Azra, Azyumardi, Dina Afrianty, and Robert W. Hefner, 'Pesantren and Madrasah: Muslim Schools and National Ideals in Indonesia', in *Schooling Islam: The Culture and Politics of Modern Muslim Education*, ed. by Robert W. Hefner and Muhammad Qasim Zaman (Princeton and Oxford: Princeton University Press, 2007), pp. 172–98

Badan Pengembangan dan Pembinaan Bahasa, 'Zat', *KBBI Daring*, 2016, https://kbbi.kemdikbud.go.id/entri/zat

Bagir, Zainal Abidin, 'Defamation of Religion Law in Post-Reformasi Indonesia: Is Revision Possible?', *Australian Journal of Asian Law*, 13.2 (2013), 1–16

Baidan, Nashruddin, *Terjemahan Al-Qur'an: Studi Kritis terhadap Terjemahan Al-Qur'an yang Beredar di Indonesia* (Yogyakarta: Pustaka Pelajar, 2017)

Barton, Greg, 'Indonesia's Nurcholish Madjid and Abdurrahman Wahid as Intellectual 'Ulama': The Meeting of Islamic Traditionalism and Modernism in Neo-Modernist Thought', *Studia Islamika*, 4.1 (1997), 30–81, http://dx.doi.org/10.15408/sdi.v4i1.786

Bobzin, Hartmut, 'Translation of the Qur'an', ed. by Jane Dammen McAuliffe, *Encyclopaedia of the Qur'ān* (Leiden; Boston; Köln: Brill, 2006), 340–54

Boland, B. J., *The Struggle of Islam in Modern Indonesia* (Dordrecht: Springer Netherlands, 1971), https://doi.org/10.1007/978-94-017-4710-3

Bräuchler, Birgit, 'Islamic Radicalism Online: The Moluccan Mission of the Laskar Jihad in Cyberspace.', *Australian Journal of Anthropology*, 15.3 (2004), 267–85

van Bruinessen, Martin, 'Genealogies of Islamic Radicalism in Post-Suharto Indonesia', *South East Asia Research*, 10.2 (2002), 117–54

—, 'Ghazwul Fikr or Arabization? Indonesian Muslim Responses to Globalization', in *Southeast Asian Muslims in the Era of Globalization*, ed. by Ken Miichi and Omar Farouk (New York: Palgrave Macmillan, 2014), pp. 61–85, the citation is from the online copy on author's site: https://www.academia.edu/2839951/Ghazwul_fikri_or_Arabisation_Indonesian_Muslim_responses_to_globalisation

—, 'Global and Local in Indonesian Islam', *Southeast Asia Studies*, 37.2 (1999), 158–75

—, 'Introduction: Contemporary Development in Indonesian Islam and the "Conservative Turn" of the Early Twenty First Century', in *Contemporary Development in Indonesian Islam: Explaining the 'Conservative Turn'*, ed. by Martin van Bruinessen (Singapore: ISEAS Publishing, 2013), pp. 1–20

—, 'Kitab Kuning: Books in Arabic Script Used in the Pesantren Milieu: Comments on a New Collection in the KITLV Library', *Bijdragen Tot de Taal-, Land- En Volkenkunde*, 146.2/3 (1990), 226–69

—, *Kitab Kuning, Pesantren dan Tarekat*, trans. by Farid Wajidi and Rika Iffati (Yogyakarta: Gading Publishing, 2012)

—, 'Overview of Muslim Organizations, Associations and Movements in Indonesia', in *Contemporary Development in Indonesian Islam: Explaining the 'Conservative Turn'*, ed. by Martin van Bruinessen (Singapore: ISEAS Publishing, 2013), pp. 21–59

—, 'Pesantren and Kitab Kuning: Continuity and Change in a Tradition of Religious Learning', in *Texts from the Islands: Oral and Written Traditions of Indonesia and the Malay World*, ed. by Wolfgang Marschall (Berne: The University of Berne Institute of Ethnology, 1994), pp. 121–46, the citation is from the online copy on author's site: https://www.academia.edu/2524271/Pesantren_and_kitab_kuning_Continuity_and_change_in_a_tradition_of_religious_learning

—, 'Secularism, Islamism, and Muslim Intellectualism in Turkey and Indonesia: Some Comparative Observations', in *Ketika Makkah Menjadi Las Vegas: Agama, Politik dan Ideologi*, ed. by Mirza Tirta Kusuma (Jakarta: Gramedia, 2014), pp. 130–57

—, 'What Happened to the Smiling Face of Indonesian Islam?: Muslim Intellectualism and the Conservative Turin in Post-Suharto Indonesia', in *RSIS Working Paper* (Nanyang Technological University, 2011)

Burdah, Ibnu, 'Ṭarīqat al-tarjama al-waẓīfiyya al-muᶜjama al-muᶜallaqa: taṣawwur ᶜām wa al-baḥth al-tārikhiy ᶜanhā', *Journal of Indonesian Islam*, 5.2 (2011), 353–76, http://dx.doi.org/10.15642/JIIS.2011.5.2.353-377

Burhani, Ahmad Najib, 'Defining Indonesian Islam: An Examination of the Construction of the National Islamic Identity of Traditionalist and Modernist Musilms', in *Islam in Indonesia: Contrasting Images and Interpretations*, ed. by Jajat Burhanudin and Kees van Dijk, ICAS Publication Series (Amsterdam: Amsterdam University Press, 2013), XVI, 25–48

—, 'Ethnic Minority Politics in Jakarta's Gubernatorial Election', *ISEAS Perspective*, 39, 2017

—, 'Muhammadiyah', ed. by Kate Fleet, Gudrun Krämer, and Everett Rowson, *Encyclopaedia of Islam*, https://referenceworks.brillonline.com/entries/encyclopaedia-of-islam-3/*-COM_36688

—, 'Pluralism, Liberalism, and Islamism: Religious Outlook of Muhammadiyah', *Studia Islamika*, 25.3 (2018), 433–70, https://doi.org/10.15408/sdi.v25i3.7765

—, 'Sectarian Translation of the Quran in Indonesia: The Case of the Ahmadiyya', *Al-Jāmi'ah: Journal of Islamic Studies*, 53.2 (2015), 251–82, https://doi.org/10.14421/ajis.2015.532.251-282

—, 'When Muslims Are Not Muslims: The Ahmadiyya Community and the Discourse on Heresy in Indonesia' (unpublished doctoral dissertation, University of California, 2013)

Burhanudin, Jajat, 'The Triumph of Ruler: Islam and Statecraft in Pre-Colonial Malay-Archipelago', *Al-Jāmi'ah: Journal of Islamic Studies*, 55.1 (2017), 211–40, https://doi.org/10.14421/ajis.2017.551.211-240

Bush, Robin, *Nahdlatul Ulama and the Struggle for Power within Islam and Politics in Indonesia* (Singapore: ISEAS Publishing, 2009)

Damami, Muhammad, Syaefan Nur, Sekar Ayu Aryani, and Syafa'atun Almirzanah, 'Prof. Dr. H. A. Mukti Ali, M.A.', in *Lima Tokoh IAIN Sunan Kalijaga Yogyakarta*, ed. by Muhammad Damami (Yogyakarta: Pusat Penelitian IAIN Sunan Kalijaga, 2000), pp. 217–71

Daneshgar, Majid, 'The Study of Qur'ān Interpretation in the Malay-Indonesian World: A Select Bibliography', in *The Qur'ān in Malay-Indonesian World: Context and Interpretation*, ed. by Majid Daneshgar, Peter G. Riddell, and Andrew Rippin (London, New York: Routledge, 2016), pp. 7–21

Daneshgar, Majid, Peter G. Riddell, and Andrew Rippin, eds., *The Qur'ān in Malay-Indonesian World: Context and Interpretation* (London, New York: Routledge, 2016)

Darmaputera, Eka, 'Pancasila and The Search for Identity and Modernity in Indonesian Society: A Cultural and Ethical Analysis' (unpublished doctoral dissertation, Boston Collegee, 1982)

Departemen Agama Republik Indonesia, *Al-Quräan dan Terdjemahnja*, 3 vols (Jakarta: Jamunu', 1965), I

—, *Al-Quräan dan Terdjemahnja*, 3 vols (Jakarta: Jamunu', 1967), II

—, *Al-Qur'an dan Terjemahannya* (Jakarta: Lajnah Pentashihan Mushaf Al-Qur'an, 2019)

al-Dhahabī, Muḥammad Ḥusain, *al-Tafsīr wa al-mufassirūn*, 3 vols (Cairo: Maktaba Wahba, 2004), I

Dhofier, Zamakhsyari, 'The Pesantren Tradition: A Study of the Role of the Kyai in the Maintenance of the Traditional Ideology of Islam in Java' (unpublished doctoral dissertation, The Australian National University, 1980)

Djidin, M., and Sahiron Syamsuddin, 'Indonesian Interpretation of the Qur'an on Khilāfah: The Case of Quraish Shihab and Yudian Wahyudi on Qur'an, 2: 30–38', *Al-Jami'ah: Journal of Islamic Studies*, 57.1 (2019), 143–66, https://doi.org/10.14421/ajis.2019.571.143-166

Drakeley, Steven, 'Indonesia's Muslim Organisations and the Overthrow of Sukarno', *Studia Islamika*, 21.2 (2014), 197–232, https://doi.org/10.15408/sdi.v21i2.1039

Dumairieh, Naser, *Intellectual Life in the Ḥijāz before Wahhabism: Ibrāhīm al-Kūrānī's (d. 1101/1690) Theology of Sufism*, Islamicate Intellectual History: Studies and Text in the Late Medieval and Early Modern Periods, 9 (Leiden - Boston: Brill, 2022)

Dzuhayatin, Siti Ruhaini, 'Gender and Pluralism in Indonesia', in *The Politics of Multiculturalism: Pluralism and Citizenship in Malaysia, Singapore, and Indonesia*, ed. by Robert W. Hefner (Honolulu: University of Hawaii Press, 2001), http://www.redi-bw.de/db/ebsco.php/search.ebscohost.com/login.aspx%3fdirect%3dtrue%26db%3dnlebk%26AN%3d104410%26site%3dehost-live

—, 'Pergulatan Pemikiran Feminis dalam Wacana Islam di Indonesia', in *Rekonstruksi Metodologis Wacana Kesetaraan Gender dalam Islam*, PSW IAIN Sunan Kalijaga Yogyakarta (Yogyakarta: Pustaka Pelajar, 2002), pp. 3–26

Dzuhayatin, Siti Ruhaini, Budhy Munawar-Rachman, Nasaruddin Umar, Zaitunah Subhan, Hamim Ilyas, and H. Akh Minhaji, *Rekonstruksi Metodologis Wacana Kesetaraan Gender dalam Islam*, PSW IAIN Sunan Kalijaga Yogyakarta (Yogyakarta: Pustaka Pelajar, 2002)

Effendy, Bakhtiar, *Islam dan Negara: Transformasi Gagasan dan Praktik Politik Islam di Indonesia*, trans. by Ihsan Ali-Fauzi and Rudy Harisyah Alam, Digital (Democracy Project, 2011)

Faizin, Hamam, 'Colored-Text Qur'anic Mushaf in Modern Indonesia' (Jakarta, 2017)

—, *Sejarah Penerjemahan Al-Quran di Indonesia* (Ciputat: Gaung Persada, 2022)

Fealy, Greg, *Ijtihad Politik Ulama: Sejarah NU 1952–1967*, trans. by Farid Wajdi and Mulni Adelina Bachtar (Yogyakarta: LKiS, 2011)

Federspiel, Howard M., *Indonesian Muslim Intellectuals of the 20th Century*, Southeast Asia Background Series, no. 8 (Singapore: Institute of Southeast Asian Studies, 2006)

Federspiel, Howard. M., *Popular Indonesian Literature of the Qur'an*, 72nd edn (Ithaca, New York: Cornell Modern Indonesia Project, 1994)

Feener, R. Michael, 'Indonesian Movements for the Creation of a "National Madhhab"', *Islamic Law & Society*, 9.1 (2002), 83–115

—, 'Notes Towards the History of Qur'anic Exegesis in Southeast Asia', *Studia Islamika*, 5.3 (1998), https://doi.org/10.15408/sdi.v5i3.739

—, 'Southeast Asian Qurʾānic Literature', ed. by Jane Dammen McAuliffe, *Encyclopaedia of the Qurʾān* (Leiden; Boston; Köln: Brill, 2006), 98–101, http://referenceworks.brillonline.com/entries/encyclopaedia-of-the-quran/southeast-asian-quranic-literature-EQCOM_00190

Feillard, Andrée, 'Traditionalist Islam and the State Indonesia: The Road to Legitimacy and Renewal', in *Islam in an Era of Nation-States: Politics and Religious Renewal in Muslim Southeast Asia*, ed. by Robert W. Hefner and Patricia Horvatich (Honolulu: University of Hawaii Press, 1997), pp. 129–55, http://web.a.ebscohost.com/ehost/ebookviewer/ebook/bmxlYmtfXzM5MDEyX19BTg2?sid=e44de59c-0406-45a5-b9af-50ca961dd135@sdc-v-sessmgr03&vid=0&format=EB&rid=1

Fogg, Kevin W., 'The Fate of Muslim Nationalism in Independent Indonesia' (unpublished doctoral dissertation, Yale University, 2012)

—, 'The Standardisation of the Indonesian Language and Its Consequence for Islamic Communities', *Journal of Southeast Asian Studies*, 46.1 (2015), 86–110, https://doi.org/doi:10.1017/S0022463414000629

Gallop, Annabel Teh, Wan Ali Wan Mamat, Ali Akbar, Vladimir Braginsky, Ampuan Hj Brahim bin A.H. Tengah, Ian Caldwell, and others, 'A Jawi Sourcebook for the Study of Malay Palaeography and Orthograpy', *Indonesia and the Malay World*, 43.125 (2015), 13–171, https://doi.org/10.1080/13639811.2015.1008253

Gilliot, Claude, 'Exegesis of the Qur'ān: Classical and Medieval', ed. by Jane Dammen McAuliffe, *Encyclopaedia of the Qur'ān* (Leiden; Boston; Köln: Brill, 2002), 99–124

Gunawan, Fahmi, 'The Effect of Translation Technique to Its Quality at The Holy Book of Indonesian Moslem Society', *Lisan: Jurnal Bahasa dan Linguistik*, 8.2 (2019), 101–09, https://doi.org/10.33506/jbl.v8i2.377

Gusmian, Islah, 'Bahasa dan Aksara dalam Penulisan Tafsir Al-Qur'an di Indonesia Era Awal Abad 20 M', *Mutawatir*, 5.2 (2015), 223–47

—, *Khazanah Tafsir Indonesia: dari Hermeneutika hingga Ideologi* (Yogyakarta: LKiS, 2013)

—, *Tafsir Al-Qur'an dan Kekuasaan di Indonesia: Peneguhan, Kontestasi, dan Pertarungan Wacana* (Yogyakarta: Yayasan Salwa Indonesia, 2019)

Haleem, M. A. S. Abdel, *The Qur'an* (Oxford: Oxford University Press, 2004)

Hamayotsu, Kikue, 'The Limits of Civil Society in Democratic Indonesia: Media Freedom and Religious Intolerance.', *Journal of Contemporary Asia*, 43.4 (2013), 658–77

Hamka, *Urat Tunggang Pantjasila* (Jakarta: Pustaka Keluarga, 1951)

Hanafi, Muchlis Muhammad, 'Problematika Terjemahan Al-Qur'an Studi Pada Beberapa Penerbitan Al-Qur'an dan Kasus Kontemporer', *SUHUF Jurnal Pengkajian Al-Qur'an dan Budaya*, 4.2 (2011), 169–95, https://doi.org/10.22548/shf.v4i2.53

Hasan, Noorhaidi, 'Religious Diversity and Blasphemy Law: Understanding Growing Religious Conflict and Intolerance in Post-Suharto Indonesia', *Al-Jāmi'ah: Journal of Islamic Studies*, 55.1 (2017), 105–26, https://doi.org/10.14421/ajis.2017.551.105-126

Hasyim, Syafiq, 'Fatwa Aliran Sesat dan Politik Hukum Majelis Ulama Indonesia (MUI)', *Al-Ahkam*, 25.2 (2015), 241–66, https://doi.org/10.21580/ahkam.2015.25.2.810

—, 'The Council of Indonesian Ulama (Majelis Ulama Indonesia, MUI) and Religious Freedom', in *Les Notes de l'Irasec n'12 - Irasec's Discussion Papers #12* (Bangkok: IRASEC, 2011)

Hefner, Robert W., 'Indonesia in the Global Scheme of Islamic Things: Sustaining the Virtuous Circle of Education, Associations and Democracy', in *Islam in Indonesia: Contrasting Images and Interpretations*, ed. by Jajat Burhanudin and Kees van Dijk, ICAS Publication Series (Amsterdam: Amsterdam University Press, 2013), XVI, 49–62

Hermawan, Bayu, 'Netizen Dihebohkan dengan "Berubahnya" Tafsir Al Maidah Ayat 51', *Republika Online*, 22 October 2016, section Nasional, http://www.republika.co.id/berita/nasional/umum/16/10/22/offxlk354-netizen-dihebohkan-dengan-berubahnya-tafsir-al-maidah-ayat-51

Hosen, Nadirsyah, 'Behind the Scenes: Fatwas of Majelis Ulama Indonesia (1975–1998)', *Journal of Islamic Studies*, 15.2 (2004), 147–79

—, 'Meluruskan Sejumlah Tafsir Surat Al-Maidah 51', *NU Online Suara Nahdlatul Ulama*, 2016, http://www.nu.or.id/post/read/71937/meluruskan-sejumlah-tafsir-surat-al-maidah-51

—, 'Race and Religion in the 2012 Jakarta Gubernatorial Election: The Case of Jokowi Ahok', in *Religion, Law and Intolerance in Indonesia*, ed. by T. Lindsey and H. Pausacker, Routledge Law in Asia (London, New York: Taylor & Francis, 2016), pp. 180–94

—, 'Tafsir Awliya': Bagaimana Kita Harus Bersikap?', *Mengkaji ISLAM Kontekstual Bersama Gus Nadir*, 2017, http://linkis.com/nadirhosen.net/multi/oHlq2

Humas Dewan Da'wah Islamiyah Indonesia, 'Menista Islam Ahok Menghitung Hari', *Dewan Da'wah News*, October 2016

al-Husain, Bariq, 'The Translation of Mutashaabih, Ambiguous, and Muḥkam Quranic Verses: A Contrastive Study' (unpublished doctoral dissertation, Western Sydney University, 2018)

Ibn Fāris, Abū Ḥasan Aḥmad, *Muᶜjam Maqāyis al-luga*, ed. by ᶜAbd al-Salām Muhammad Hārun, 6 vols (Beirut: Dār al-Fikr, 1979), VI

Ibn Kathīr, ᶜImād al-Dīn Abū al-Fidāᵓ Ismāᶜīl, *al-Tafsīr al-qurᵓān al-ᶜaẓīm*, 15 vols (Giza: Muᵓassasa Qurṭuba, 2000), iv

—, *al-Tafsīr al-qurᵓān al-ᶜaẓīm*, 15 vols (Giza: Muᵓassasa Qurṭuba, 2000), I, III, V, VI

Ichwan, Moch. Nur, 'Differing Responses to an Ahmadi Translation and Exegesis: "The Holy Qur'ân" in Egypt and Indonesia', *Archipel*, 2001, 143–61, https://doi.org/10.3406/arch.2001.3668

—, 'MUI, Gerakan Islamis, dan Umat Mengambang', *Jurnal Maarif*, Setelah 'Bela Islam': Gerakan Sosial Islam, Demokratisasi, dan Keadilan Sosial, 11.2 (2016), 87–104

—, 'Negara, Kitab Suci dan Politik: Terjemahan Resmi Al-Qur'an di Indonesia', in *Sadur Sejarah Terjemahan di Indonesia dan Malaysia*, ed. by Henri Chambert-Loir (Jakarta: Kepustakaan Populer Gramedia, 2009), pp. 417–33

—, 'Official Reform of Islam: State Islam and the Ministry of Religious Affairs in Contemporary Indonesia, 1966–2004' (unpublished doctoral dissertation, Tilburg University, 2006), https://pure.uvt.nl/portal/en/publications/official-reform-of-islam(f07a60f1-bf55-4979-8ea1-bab6e45a42ac).html

—, 'The End of Jawi Islamic Scholarship? Kitab Jawi, Qur'anic Exegesis, and Politics in Indonesia', in *Rainbows of Malay Literature and Beyond: Festschrift in Honour of Professor Md. Salleh Yaapar* (Pulau Pinang: Penerbit Universiti Sains Malaysia, 2011), pp. 82–101

—, 'The Making of a Pancasila State: Political Debates on Secularism, Islam and the State in Indonesia', in *SOIAS Research Paper Series*, 6 (Japan: Institute of Asian Cultures, 2012)

—, 'Towards a Puritanical Moderate Islam: The Majelis Ulama Indonesia and the Politics of Religious Orthodoxy', in *Contemporary Development in Indonesian Islam: Explaining the 'Conservative Turn'*, ed. by Martin van Bruinessen (Singapore: ISEAS Publishing, 2013), pp. 60–104

Ikhwan, Munirul, 'Challenging the State: Exegetical Translation in Opposition to the Official Religious Discourse of the Indonesian State', *Journal of Qur'anic Studies*, 17.3 (2015), 157–121, https://doi.org/10.3366/jqs.2015.0214

Ilyas, Yunahar, *Feminisme dalam Kajian Tafsir Al-Qur'an Klasik dan Kontemporer* (Yogyakarta: Pustaka Pelajar, 1997)

Ismail, Faisal, 'Islam, Politics, and Ideology in Indonesia: A Study of The Process of Muslim Acceptance of the Pancasila' (unpublished doctoral dissertation, McGill University, 1995)

Jainuri, Achmad, 'The Formation of the Muḥammadīyah's Ideology, 1912–1942' (unpublished doctoral dissertation, McGill University, 1997)

'"Jiplak-Menjiplak" Tafsir Qur'an', *Majalah Tempo*, 12 January 1974, p. 49

Johns, Anthony H., 'Quranic Exegesis in the Malay World: In Search of a Profile', in *Approaches to the History of the Interpretation of the Qur'ān*, ed. by Andrew Rippin (Oxford: Clarendon Press, 1988), pp. 257–87

—, 'Qur'ān Exegesis in the Malay-Indonesian World: An Introductory Survey', in *Approaches to The Qur'an in Contemporary Indonesia.*, ed. by Abdullah Saeed (Oxford: Oxford University Press, 2005), pp. 17–41

Kasiri, Julizar, Siti Nurbaiti, and Wahyu Muryadi, '"Penjahat Besar" atau Pembesar yang Jahat', *Majalah Tempo*, 25 April 1992, pp. 77–78

Keane, Webb, 'Divine Text, National Language, and Their Publics: Arguing an Indonesian Qur'an', *Comparative Studies in Society and History*, 60.4 (2018), 758–85, https://doi.org/10.1017/S0010417518000282

'Kemenag akan Luncurkan Alquran Terjemahan 3 Bahasa Daerah', *Republika Online*, 2018, https://republika.co.id/share/pjk6tr384

Kersten, Carool, *A History of Islam in Indonesia: Unity in Diversity*, The New Edinburgh Islamic Surveys (Edinburgh: Edinburgh University Press, 2017)

—, *Islam in Indonesia: The Contest for Society, Ideas and Values* (London: C. Hurst & Co., 2015)

Khoiron, 'Penjelasan tentang Dugaan Kesalahan Terjemah Al Quran Kementrian Agama', *Kementrian Agama Republik Indonesia*, 2017, https://kemenag.go.id/berita/read/504945/penjelasan-tentang-dugaan-kesalahan-terjemah-al-quran-kementerian-agama

—, 'Soal Terjemahan Awliyā sebagai "Teman Setia", Ini Penjelasan Kemenag', *Kementrian Agama Republik Indonesia*, 2016, https://kemenag.go.id/berita/read/417806/soal-terjemahan-awliy---sebagai----teman-setia-----ini-penjelasan-kemenag

Kidway, Abdur Raheem, 'Muhammad Marmaduke Pickthall's English Translation of the Quran (1930): An Assessment', in *Marmaduke Pickthall: Islam and the Modern World*, ed. by Geoffrey P. Nash (Leiden; Boston: Brill, 2017), pp. 231–48

Kridalaksana, Harimurti, 'Spelling Reform 1972: A Stage in the Process of Standardisation of Bahasa Indonesia', in *Papers from the Conference on the Standardisation of Asian Languages, Manila, Philiphines. Pacific Linguistic*, ed. by AQ Perez, AO Santiago, and Nguyen Dang Liem, C, 47 (Canberra: Australian National University, 1974), pp. 305–17, http://sealang.net/archives/pl/pdf/PL-C47.305.pdf

Laffan, Michael Francis, *Islamic Nationhood and Colonial Indonesia: The Umma Below the Winds* (London, New York: RoutledgeCurzon, 2003)

—, *The Makings of Indonesian Islam: Orientalism and the Narration of a Sufi Past* (Princeton: Princeton University Press, 2011)

Lajnah Pentashihan Mushaf Al-Qur'an, 'Panduan Kajian Revisi Al-Qur'an dan Terjemahnya Kementrian Agama Tahun 2016'

—, 'Sejarah - Lajnah Pentashihan Mushaf Al-Qur'an', *Lajnah Pentashihan Mushaf Al-Qur'an Badan Litbang dan Diklat Kementerian Agama Republik Indonesia*, https://lajnah.kemenag.go.id/profil/sejarah

—, *Tafsir Ringkas Al-Qur'an al-Karim*, 2 vols (Jakarta: Lajnah Pentashihan Mushaf Al-Qur'an, 2015), I

Lawrence, Bruce B., *The Koran in English: A Biography*, Lives of Great Religious Books (Princeton and Oxford: Princeton University Press, 2017)

Lay, Cornelis, 'Pancasila, Soekarno, dan Orde Baru', *Prisma*, 2013, 43–61

Leeuwen, Lizzy van, 'Onderzoek De Zaak-Buni Yani "Hij Ging Met Niemand Om"', *De Groene Amsterdammer*, 2017, https://www.groene.nl/artikel/hij-ging-met-niemand-om

'Lema "Pembesar"—Tesaurus Tematis Bahasa Indonesia', http://tesaurus.kemdikbud.go.id/tematis/lema/pembesar

Liddle, R. William, 'The Islamic Turn in Indonesia: A Political Explanation', *The Journal of Asian Studies*, 55.3 (1996), 613–34, https://doi.org/10.2307/2646448

Lubis, Isma'il, *Falsifikasi Terjemahan Al-Qur'an Departemen Agama Edisi 1990* (Yogyakarta: Tiara Wacana, 2001)

Lukens-Bull, Ronald A., *Islamic Higher Education in Indonesia: Continuity and Conflict* (New York: Palgrave Macmillan, 2013)

Lukman, Fadhli, 'Epistemologi Intuitif dalam Resepsi Estetis H.B. Jassin terhadap Al-Qur'an', *Journal of Qur'an and Hadith Studies*, 4.1 (2015), 37–55, https://doi.org/10.15408/quhas.v4i1.2282

—, 'Studi Kritis atas Teori Tarjamah Al-Qur'an dalam 'Ulūm al-Qur'ān', *Al-A'raf: Jurnal Pemikiran Islam dan Filsafat*, 13.2 (2016), 167–90

—, 'Telaah Historiografi Tafsir Indonesia: Analisis Makna Konseptual Terminologi Tafsir Nusantara', *SUHUF Jurnal Pengkajian Al-Qur'an dan Budaya*, 14.1 (2021)

Machasin, 'Prof. Mr. R.H.A Soenarjo', in *Lima Tokoh IAIN Sunan Kalijaga Yogyakarta*, ed. by Muhammad Damami (Yogyakarta: Pusat Penelitian IAIN Sunan Kalijaga, 2000), pp. 71–102

Madjid, Nurcholish, *Islam: Doktrin dan Peradaban* (Jakarta: Paramadina, 1992)

al-Maḥallī, Jalāl-u-dīn Muḥammad ibn Aḥmad ibn Muḥammad, and Jalāl-u-dīn ᶜAbd-l-raḥmān ibn Abī Bakr al-Ṣuyūṭī, *Tafsīr al-Imāmayn al-jalīlayn* (Dār Ibn Kathīr)

Majid, M. Dien, *Berhaji di Masa Kolonial* (Jakarta: CV. Sejahtera, 2008)

Majma' al-Lugha al-'Arabiya, *Mu'jam al-Waṣīṭ*, 4th edn (Cairo: Maktaba al-Syurūq al-Duwaliya, 2004)

Mandhūr, Ibn, 'Waliya', *Lisān al-'arab* (Cairo: Dār al-Ma'ārif, 1981), pp. 4920–26

Mansyur, Moh., 'Studi Kritis terhadap Al-Qur'an dan Terjemahnya Departemen Agama Republik Indonesia' (unpublished doctoral dissertation, IAIN Syarif Hidayatullah, 1998)

al-Marāghī, Aḥmad Muṣṭafā, *Tafsīr al-Marāghī*, 30 vols (Cairo: Muṣṭafā al-Bāb al-Ḥalab wa Awlāduh, 1946), V

Marcoes-Natsir, Lies M, and Johan Hendrik Meuleman, eds., *Wanita Islam Indonesia dalam Kajian Tekstual dan Kontekstual: Kumpulan Makalah Seminar*, INIS, 1 (Jakarta: INIS, 1993)

Matanggui, Junaiyah H., *Bahasa Indonesia Serba Sekilas* (Jakarta: Indra Press, 1984)

McRae, Dave, 'Talking Indonesia: Ahok, Race, Religion, and Democracy', Talking Indonesia, http://indonesiaatmelbourne.unimelb.edu.au/talking-indonesia-ahok-race-religion-and-democracy/

Media, Kompas Cyber, 'Kementerian Agama Resmi Luncurkan Aplikasi Al Quran Digital Pertama', *KOMPAS.com*, 2016, https://nasional.kompas.com/read/2016/08/30/22125031/kementerian.agama.resmi.luncurkan.aplikasi.al.quran.digital.pertama

'Menag Luncurkan Alquran Terjemah Tiga Bahasa Daerah', *Republika Online*, 2017, https://republika.co.id/share/p18slr335

Menchik, Jeremy, '"Do Not Take Unbelievers as Your Leaders" The Politics of Translation in Indonesia', *Mizan*, 2016, http://www.mizanproject.org/do-not-take-unbelievers-as-your-leaders/

—, *Islam and Democracy in Indonesia: Tolerance without Liberalism* (Cambridge: Cambridge University Press, 2016)

—, 'Productive Intolerance Godly Nationalism in Indonesia', *Comparative Studies in Society and History*, 56.3 (2014), 591–621, https://doi.org/httpdx.doi.org10.1017S0010417514000267

Mohammad, Herry, 'Alih Bahasa Mengungkap Makna', *Majalah Gatra*, 8 September 2010, pp. 78–79

Mohammad, Herry, Ade Faisal Alami, and Arif Koes Hernawan, 'Mundur Bukan karena Uzur', *Majalah Gatra*, 11 July 2012, pp. 90–91

M.P.R.S dan Departemen Penerangan, *Ringkasan Ketetapan Madjelis Permusjawaratan Rakjat Sementara—Republik Indonesia* (Jakarta: M.P.R.S dan Departemen Penerangan, 1961)

M.P.R.S, and Departemen Penerangan, *Ringkasan Ketetapan Madjelis Permusjawaratan Rakjat Sementara-Republik Indonesia No. I dan II/MPRS/1960* (M.P.R.S dan Departemen Penerangan, 1961)

Mubarok, Husni, 'Babak Baru Ketegangan Islam dan Kristen di Indonesia (Book Review)', *Studia Islamika*, 21.3 (2014), 579–601

Muhajir, Ahmad, 'Fahira Idris Benarkan Ada Perubahan Terjemah Al-Qur'an', *Gontornews*, 2016, http://gontornews.com/2016/10/24/fahira-idris-benarkan-ada-perubahan-terjemah-al-quran/

Mui, Editor, 'Pendapat dan Sikap Keagamaan MUI terkait Pernyataan Basuki Tjahaja Purnama', *Majelis Ulama Indonesia*, 2017, http://mui.or.id/id/berita/pendapat-dan-sikap-keagamaan-mui-terkait-pernyataan-basuki-tjahaja-purnama/

Mukti, Hafizd, 'FPI: Pemeriksaan Terbuka, Langkah Jowoki Lindungi Ahok', *CNN Indonesia*, 5 October 2016, https://cnnindonesia.com/nasional/20161105213504-12-170576/fpi-pemeriksaan-terbuka-langkah-jokowi-lindungi-ahok/

Munawar-Rachman, Budhy, 'Penafsiran Islam Liberal atas Isu-Isu Gender dan Feminisme', in *Rekonstruksi Metodologis Wacana Kesetaraan Gender dalam Islam*, PSW IAIN Sunan Kalijaga Yogyakarta (Yogyakarta: Pustaka Pelajar, 2002), pp. 27–84

Munjid, Ahmad, 'Building A Shared Home: Investigating The Intellectual Legacy of The Key Thinkers of Inter-Religious Dialogue in Indonesia' (unpublished doctoral dissertation, The Temple University Graduate Board, 2014)

Murad, Jama'in Abdul, *Tafsīr Juzʾ ʿAmmā Bahasa Melayu* (Patani - Thailand: Maṭbaʿa ibn Halabī)

Murtadha, 'Penjelasan kenapa "Awliya" Pernah Diterjemahkan "Pemimpin" di Masa ORBA by @Nadir_Monash', *Chirpstory*, 2016, https://chirpstory.com/li/333681

Mustaqim, Abdul, 'The Epistemology of Javanese Qurʾanic Exegesis: A Study of Ṣāliḥ Darat's Fayḍ al-Raḥmān', *Al-Jāmi'ah: Journal of Islamic Studies*, 55.2 (2017), 357–90, https://doi.org/10.14421/ajis.2017.552.357-390

Naim, Mochtar, 'The Nahdlatul-Ulama Party (1952–1955): An Inquiry into the Origin of Its Electoral Success' (unpublished Thesis, McGill University, 1960)

Noer, Deliar, 'The Rise and Development of the Modernist Muslim Movement in Indonesia During the Dutch Colonial Period (1900–1942)' (unpublished doctoral dissertation, Cornell University, 1963)

Notosoetardjo, Achmad, *Amnesti Abolisi Ditinjau dari Adjaran Nabi Muhammad S.A.W.* (Jakarta: Jajasan Pemuda, 1961)

—, *Bung Karno Mencari dan Menemukan Tuhan* (Jakarta: Jajasan Pemuda, 1963)

—, *Kata-Kata Penumpas Menentang Imperialisme Kolonialisme jang Selalu Dipakai Bung Karno* (Jakarta: Lembaga Penggali dan Penghimpun Sedjarah Revolusi - Endang - Pemuda, 1963)

—, *Menggali Api Revolusi dari 11 Amanat Bung Karno* (Jakarta: Lembaga Penggali dan Penghimpun Sedjarah Revolusi - Endang - Pemuda, 1962)

—, *Peranan Agama Islam dalam Revolusi Indonesia* (Jakarta: Lembaga Penggali dan Penghimpun Sedjarah Revolusi - Endang - Pemuda, 1963)

Nurdin, Nasrullah, 'Terorisme dan Teks Keagamaan: Studi Komparatif atas Terjemah Al-Qur'an Kemenag RI dan Terjemah Tafsiriyah MMI' (unpublished master's thesis, Universitas Islam Negeri Syarif Hidayatullah, 2016)

Nurmila, Nina, *Women, Islam and Everyday Life: Renegotiating Polygamy in Indonesia*, Women in Asia (New York: Routledge, 2009)

Nurtawab, Ervan, 'Jalalayn Pedagogical Practice: Styles of Qur'an and Tafsir Learning in Contemporary Indonesia' (unpublished doctoral dissertation, Monash University, 2018)

—, 'Qur'anic Translation in Malay, Javanese, and Sundanese: A Commentary or Substitution', in *The Qurʾān in Malay-Indonesian World: Context and Interpretation*, ed. by Majid Daneshgar, Peter G. Riddell, and Andrew Rippin (London, New York: Routledge, 2016), pp. 39–57

—, 'Tafsīr al-Jalālayn at the Crossroads: Interpreting the Qur'ān in Modern Indonesia', *Australian Journal of Islamic Studies*, 6.4 (2021), 4–24, https://doi.org/10.55831/ajis.v6i4.429

Pink, Johanna, 'Classical Qur'anic Hermeneutics', in *The Oxford Handbook of Qur'anic Studies*, ed. by Mustafa Shah and M. A. S. Abdel Haleem (Oxford: Oxford University Press, 2020), pp. 818–31

—, 'Form Follows Function: Notes on the Arrangement of Texts in Printed Qur'an Translations', *Journal of Qur'anic Studies*, 19.1 (2017), 143–54, https://doi.org/10.3366/jqs.2017.0274

—, '"Literal Meaning" or "Correct ʿaqīda"? The Reflection of Theological Controversy in Indonesian Qur'an Translations', *Journal of Qur'anic Studies*, 17.3 (2015), 100–20

—, *Muslim Qur'ānic Interpretation Today: Media, Genealogies, and Interpretive Communities*, Themes in Qur'ānic Studies (Sheffield: Equinox, 2019)

—, 'The Fig, the Olive, and the Cycles of Prophethood: Q 95:1–3 and the Image of History in Early 20th-Century Qura'nic Exegesis', in *Islamic Studies Today: Essays in Honor of Andrew Rippin*, ed. by Majid Daneshgar and Walid A. Saleh (Leiden; Boston: Brill), pp. 317–38

—, 'The "Kyai's" Voice and the Arabic Qur'an; Translation, Orality, and Print in Modern Java', *Wacana*, 21.3 (2020), 329–59, https://doi.org/10.17510/wacana.v21i3.948

—, 'Tradition and Ideology in Contemporary Sunnite Qur'ānic Exegesis: Qur'ānic Commentaries from the Arab World, Turkey, and Indonesia and Their Interpretation of Q 5:51', *Die Welt Des Islams*, 50 (2010), 3–59, https://doi.org/10.1163/157006010X489801

—, 'Tradition, Authority and Innovation in Contemporary Sunnī Tafsīr: Towards a Typology of Qur'an Commentaries from the Arab World, Indonesia and Turkey', *Journal of Qur'anic Studies*, 12.1/2 (2010), 56–82

—, 'Translation', in *The Routledge Companion to the Qur'ān*, ed. by Daniel A Madigan and Maria Dakake (London: Routledge, 2021), pp. 364–76

'PTIQ Jakarta Gagas Tafsir Kebangsaan – INSTITUT PTIQ JAKARTA', 2018, https://ptiq.ac.id/2018/03/05/ptiq-jakarta-gagas-tafsir-kebangsaan/

Purnama, Basuki Tjahaja, *Merubah Indonesia: The History of Basuki Tjahaja Purnama* (Jakarta: Center for Democracy and Transparency, 2008)

'Putusan Nomor 1537/Pid.B/2016/PN.Jkt Utr. Tahun 2017 Ir. BASUKI TJAHAJA PURNAMA Alias AHOK' (Jakarta: Direktori Putusan Mahkamah Agung Republik Indonesia, 2017), https://putusan.mahkamahagung.go.id/putusan/e8b1049e890f1bf53511d70ffa120602

Rahman, Yusuf, 'The Controversy Around H.B. Jassin: A Study of His Al-Quranu'l-Karim Bacaan Mulia and Al-Qur'an al-Karim Berwajah Puisi', in *Approaches to the Qur'an in Contemporary Indonesia*, ed. by Abdullah Saeed (Oxford: Oxford University Press, 2005), pp. 85–105

Rais, Amin, 'Amien Rais: Bung Jokowi, Selesaikan Skandal Ahok', *Republika Online*, 29 October 2016, section Khazanah, http://www.republika.co.id/berita/dunia-islam/islam-nusantara/16/10/28/ofqben385-amien-rais-bung-jokowi-selesaikan-skandal-ahok

Rasmussen, Anne K., *Women, the Recited Qur'an, and Islamic Music in Indonesia* (Berkeley: University of California Press, 2010)

al-Rāzī, Fakhr al-Dīn, *Mafātīḥ al-ghayb*, 32 vols (Beirut: Dār al-Fikr, 1981), X

—, *Mafātīḥ al-ghayb*, 32 vols (Beirut: Dār al-Fikr, 1981), XXIX

—, *Mafātīḥ al-ghayb*, 32 vols (Beirut: Dār al-Fikr, 1981), IX

—, *Mafātīḥ al-ghayb*, 32 vols (Beirut: Dār al-Fikr, 1981), XII

—, *Mafātīḥ al-ghayb*, 32 vols (Beirut: Dār al-Fikr, 1981), XIII

Ricci, Ronit, 'Reading between the Lines: A World of Interlinear Translation', *Journal of World Literature*, 1.1 (2016), 68–80, https://doi.org/10.1163/24056480-00101008

Ricklefs, M. C., *A History of Modern Indonesia* (New York: Palgrave Macmillan, 2008)

Riḍā, Rashīd, *Tafsīr al-Manār*, 11 vols (Cairo: Dār al-Manār, 1947), IV

Riddell, Peter G., 'Classical Tafsīr in the Malay World: Emerging Trends in Seventeenth-Century Malay Exegetical Writing', in *The Qurʾān in Malay-Indonesian World: Context and Interpretation*, ed. by Majid Daneshgar, Andrew Rippin, and Peter G. Riddell (London, New York: Routledge, 2016)

—, *Malay Court Religion, Culture and Language: Interpreting the Qur'ān in 17th Century Aceh*, Texts and Studies on the Qur'ān, 12 (Leiden; Boston: Brill, 2017)

—, 'Menerjemahkan Al-Qur'an Ke dalam Bahasa-bahasa di Indonesia', in *Sadur Sejarah Terjemahan di Indonesia dan Malaysia*, ed. by Henri Chambert-Loir (Jakarta: Kepustakaan Populer Gramedia, 2009), pp. 397–416

—, 'Translating the Qurʾān into Indonesian Languages', *Al-Bayān – Journal of Qurʾān and Ḥadīth Studies*, 12.1 (2014), 1–27, https://doi.org/10.1163/22321969-12340001

Rohmana, Jajang A, 'Negosiasi, Ideologi, dan Batas Kesarjanaan: Pengalaman Penerjemah dalam Proyek Terjemahan Al-Qur'an Bahasa Sunda', *SUHUF Jurnal Pengkajian Al-Qur'an dan Budaya*, 12.1 (2019), 21–55, https://doi.org/10.22548/shf.v12i1.407

Rohmana, Jajang A., and Muhamad Zuldin, 'Negara Kitab Suci: Pewacanaan Al-Qur'an di Jawa Barat', *KALAM*, 12.1 (2018), 127–58, https://doi.org/10.24042/klm.v12i1.1945

Ropi, Ismatu, *Religion and Regulation in Indonesia* (Singapore: Springer Singapore, 2017), https://doi.org/10.1007/978-981-10-2827-4

Royal Aal al-Bayt Institute for Islamic Thought, 'Tafsīr al-Jāmiᶜ li aḥkām al-qurʾān / al-Qurṭubī (d. 671 AH) Sūrat al-Anᶜām 123', *Altafsir.Com*, https://www.altafsir.com/Tafasir.asp?tMadhNo=0&tTafsirNo=5&tSoraNo=6&tAyahNo=123&tDisplay=yes&UserProfile=0&LanguageId=1

—, 'Tafsīr al-Jāmiᶜ li aḥkām al-qurʾān / al-Qurṭubī (d. 671 AH) Sūrat al-Nisāʾ 85', *Altafsir.Com*, https://www.altafsir.com/Tafasir.asp?tMadhNo=0&tTafsirNo=5&tSoraNo=4&tAyahNo=83&tDisplay=yes&UserProfile=0&LanguageId=1

—, 'Tafsīr al-Muntakhab fī tafsīr al-qurʾān al-karīm / Lajna al-qurʾān wa al-sunna Sūrat al-Māʾida 48', *Altafsir.Com*, https://www.altafsir.com/Tafasir.asp?tMadhNo=9&tTafsirNo=65&tSoraNo=5&tAyahNo=48&tDisplay=yes&UserProfile=0&LanguageId=1

—, 'Tafsīr al-Muntakhab fī tafsīr al-qur'ān al-karīm / Lajna al-qur'ān wa al-sunna Sūrat al-Nisā' 83', *Altafsir.Com,* https://www.altafsir.com/Tafasir.asp?tMadhNo=9&tTafsirNo=65&tSoraNo=4&tAyahNo=83&tDisplay=yes&UserProfile=0&LanguageId=1

—, 'Tafsīr Anwār al-tanzīl wa asrār al-ta'wīl / al-Bayḍāwī (d. 685 AH) Sūrat al-Anᶜām 123', *Altafsir.Com,* https://www.altafsir.com/Tafasir.asp?tMadhNo=0&tTafsirNo=6&tSoraNo=6&tAyahNo=123&tDisplay=yes&UserProfile=0&LanguageId=1

—, 'Tafsīr Maḥāsin al-ta'wīl / Muḥammad Jamāl al-Dīn al-Qāsimī (d. 1332 AH) sūrat al-Mā'ida 51', *Altafsir.Com,* https://www.altafsir.com/Tafasir.asp?tMadhNo=0&tTafsirNo=102&tSoraNo=5&tAyahNo=51&tDisplay=yes&UserProfile=0&LanguageId=1

—, 'Tafsīr Maᶜālim al-tanzīl / al-Baghawī (d. 516 AH) Sūrat al-Anisā' 85', *Altafsir.Com,* https://www.altafsir.com/Tafasir.asp?tMadhNo=0&tTafsirNo=13&tSoraNo=4&tAyahNo=83&tDisplay=yes&UserProfile=0&LanguageId=1

—, 'Tafsīr Maᶜālim al-tanzīl / al-Baghawī (d. 516 AH) Sūrat al-Anᶜām 123', *Altafsir.Com,* https://www.altafsir.com/Tafasir.asp?tMadhNo=0&tTafsirNo=13&tSoraNo=6&tAyahNo=123&tDisplay=yes&UserProfile=0&LanguageId=1

S, Sadhewo, and Hartoyo W.H., 'Quran yang Terpelihara', *Majalah Tempo,* 25 April 1992, p. 77

Saeed, Abdullah, 'Towards Religious Tolerance Through Reform in Islamic Education: The Case of The State Institute of Islamic Studies of Indonesia', *Indonesia and the Malay World,* 27.79 (1999), 177–91

Saenong, Faried F., 'Nahdlatul Ulama (NU): A Grassroots Movements Advocating Moderate Islam', in *Handbook of Islamic Sects and Movements,* ed. by Muhammad Afzal Upal and Carole M. Cusack, Brill Handbook on Contemporary Religion, 21 (Leiden - Boston: Brill, 2021), pp. 129–50

Sahal, Akhmad, 'Haramkah Pemimpin Non Muslim?', *Majalah Tempo,* 16 August 2012

—, 'Haramkah Pemimpin Non Muslim?', *Koran Tempo,* 25 April 2016

Sahal, Akhmad, and Munawir Aziz, eds., *Islam Nusantra: Dari Ushul Fiqh Hingga Paham Kebangsaan* (Bandung: Mizan, 2015)

Saidurrahman, and Azhari Akmal Tarigan, *Rekonstruksi Peradaban Islam Perspektif Prof. K.H. Yudian Wahyudi, Ph.D.* (Jakarta: Prenadamedia Grup, 2019)

Saleh, Walid A., 'Preliminary Remarks on the Historiography of Tafsir in Arabic: A History of the Book Approach', *Journal of Qur'anic Studies,* 12 (2010), 6–40, https://doi.org/10.3366/E146535911000094X

—, *The Formation of The Classical Tafsīr Tradition: The Qur'ān Commentary of al-Thaᶜlabī (d. 427/1035)* (Leiden; Boston: Brill, 2004)

—, 'The Qur'an Commentary of al-Bayḍāwī: A History of Anwār al-tanzīl', *Journal of Qur'anic Studies*, 23.1 (2021), 71–102, https://doi.org/10.3366/jqs.2021.0451

Salim, Agus, *Ketuhanan Yang Maha Esa* (Jakarta: Bulan Bintang, 1977)

Sardar, Ziauddin, *Reading the Qur'an: The Contemporary Relevance of the Sacred Text of Islam* (Oxford: Oxford University Press, 2011)

Shiddiqi, Nourouzzaman, 'Prof. Dr. Tengku Muhammad Hasbi Ash-Shiddieqy', in *Lima Tokoh IAIN Sunan Kalijaga Yogyakarta*, ed. by Muhammad Damami (Yogyakarta: Pusat Penelitian IAIN Sunan Kalijaga, 2000), pp. 149–214

Shihab, M. Quraish, 'Konsep Wanita Menurut Quran, Hadis, dan Sumber-Sumber Ajaran Islam', in *Wanita Islam Indonesia dalam Kajian Tekstual dan Kontekstual: Kumpulan Makalah Seminar*, ed. by Lies M Marcoes-Natsir and Johan Hendrik Meuleman, INIS, 1 (Jakarta: INIS, 1993), pp. 3–18

Shohib, H. Muhammad, 'Implementasi Pemahaman Memelihara Al-Qur'an di Indonesia: Studi tentang Upaya Pemerintah Republik Indonesia dalam Memelihara Al-Qur'an Melalui Kegiatan Lajnah Pentashih Mushaf Al-Qur'an' (unpublished Thesis, Perguruan Tinggi Ilmu Al-Qur'an, 2003)

Shohib, H. Muhammad, and Zaenal Arifin Madzkur, eds., *Sejarah Penulisan Mushaf Al-Qur'an Standar Indonesia* (Jakarta: Lajnah Pentashihan Mushaf Al-Qur'an, 2013)

Sila, M. Adlin, 'Kerukunan Umat Beragama di Indonesia: Mengelola Keragaman dari Dalam', in *Kebebasan, Toleransi, dan Terorisme: Riset dan Kebijakan Agama di Indonesia*, ed. by Ihsan Ali-Fauzi, Zainal Abidin Bagir, and Irsyad Rafsadi (Jakarta: PUSAD Paramadina, 2017), pp. 117–58

al-Sinkīlī, ᶜAbd al-Raᶜūf ibn ᶜAlī al-Fanṣūrī, *Tarjumān al-mustafīd* (Singapore: Sulaymān Marᶜī, 1951)

Siroj, Said Agil, 'Mendahulukan Cinta Tanah Air', in *Nasionalisme dan Islam Nusantara*, ed. by Abdullah Ubaid and Bakir (Jakarta: Kompas, 2015)

Small, Keith E., *Qur'āns Books of Divine Encounter* (Oxford: Bodleian Library, 2015)

Sneddon, James, *The Indonesian Language: Its History and Role in Modern Society* (Sydney: UNSW Press, 2003)

Soekarno, 'Alqurän Membentuk Manusia Baru' (Djawatan Penerangan Agama Departemen Agama, 1961)

—, 'Inilah Kehidupan Islam di Indonesia: Tidak akan Terdjadi Demikian Dinegara-negara Lain' (Departemen Agama R.I, 1965)

—, *Kalau akan Mentjari Tuhan Batjalah Al-Qur'an* (Jakarta: Departemen Agama R.I, 1963)

Sokah, Umar Asasuddin, 'Prof. Dr. H. Mukhtar Yahya', in *Lima Tokoh IAIN Sunan Kalijaga Yogyakarta*, ed. by Muhammad Damami (Yogyakarta: Pusat Penelitian IAIN Sunan Kalijaga, 1998), pp. 107–46

Steenbrink, Karel A., *Kaum Kolonial Belanda dan Islam di Indonesia (1596–1942)*, trans. by Suryan A. Jamrah (Yogyakarta: Gading Publishing, 2017)

Steinhauer, Hein, 'The Indonesian Language Situation and Linguistics; Prospects and Possibilities', *Bijdragen Tot de Taal-, Land- En Volkenkunde / Journal of the Humanities and Social Sciences of Southeast Asia*, 150.4 (1994), 755–84, https://doi.org/10.1163/22134379-90003070

Subhan, Zaitunah, *Tafsir Kebencian: Studi Bias Gender dalam Tafsir Qur'an* (Yogyakarta: LKiS, 1999)

Sudjana, Eggi, 'Perbaikan Permohonan Perkara Nomor: 58/PUU-XV/2017', 15 September 2017

Sulaiman, Setyadi, *Sang Begawan Bahasa Arab: Potret Perjalanan Prof. Dr. Bustami Abdul Gani* (Ciputat: Adabia Press, 2013)

Supriadi, Akhmad, Moch. Nur Ichwan, and Syihabuddin Qalyubi, 'Menuju Kesetaraan Ontologis dan Eskatologis?: Problematika Gender dalam Perubahan Terjemahan Ayat-ayat Penciptaan Perempuan dan Pasangan Surgawi dalam Al-Qur'an dan Terjemahnya', *SUHUF Jurnal Pengkajian Al-Qur'an dan Budaya*, 12.1 (2019), 1–20, https://doi.org/10.22548/shf.v12i1.395

Syatri, Jonni, Ali Akbar, Abdul Hakim, Zarkasi, Mustopa, Ahmad Jaeni, and others, 'Sikap dan Pandangan Masyarakat terhadap Terjemahan Al-Qur'an Kementerian Agama', *SUHUF Jurnal Pengkajian Al-Qur'an dan Budaya*, 10.2 (2017), 227–62

Syihab, Al-Habib Muhammad Rizieq Bin Husein, 'Pengaruh Pancasila terhadap Penerapan Syariah Islam di Indonesia' (unpublished doctoral dissertation, Universiti Malaya, 2012)

al-Ṭabarī, Abū Jaʿfar Muḥammad ibn Jarīr, *Jāmiʿ al-bayān ʿan taʾwīlī āyi al-qurʾān*, ed. by ʿAbullāh ibn ʿAbd al Muḥsin al-Turkī, 24 vols (Cairo: Dār Hijr, 2001), VI

—, *Jāmiʿ al-bayān ʿan taʾwīlī āyi al-qurʾān*, ed. by ʿAbullāh ibn ʿAbd al-Muḥsin al-Turkī, 24 vols (Cairo: Dār Hijr, 2001), VIII

—, *Jāmiʿ al-bayān ʿan taʾwīlī āyi al-qurʾān*, ed. by ʿAbullāh ibn ʿAbd al-Muḥsin al-Turkī, 24 vols (Cairo: Dār Hijr, 2001), IX

—, *Jāmiʿ al-bayān ʿan taʾwīlī āyi al-qurʾān*, ed. by ʿAbullāh ibn ʿAbd al-Muḥsin al-Turkī, 24 vols (Cairo: Dār Hijr, 2001), VII

'[Tafsir Al Misbah] Surah Al Maidah Ayat 051–054 Part 02', *Youtube,* https://www.youtube.com/watch?v=QT23mUC8Aes

Tafsīr al-Muyassar (Medina: Mujammaᶜ al-Malik Fahd li Ṭibāᶜāt al-Muṣḥaf al-Sharīf, 2008)

Tagliacozzo, Eric, *The Longest Journey: Southeast Asian and the Pilgrimage to Mecca* (Oxford: Oxford University Press, 2013)

Tardi, 'Koherensi Terjemahan Al-Qur'an: Analisis Struktural Terjemahan al-Qur'an Depag Edisi Tahun 2002' (unpublished master's thesis, Universitas Islam Negeri Syarif Hidayatullah, 2008)

Thalib, Muhammad, *Koreksi Tarjamah Harfiyah Al-Qur'an Kemenag RI: Tinjauan Aqidah, Syariah, Mu'amalah, Iqtishadiyah* (Yogyakarta: Ma'had An-Nabawy, 2011)

—, 'Tarjamah Harfiyah Mengundang Masalah', *Majalah Gatra*, 29 September 2010, p. 36

—, *Tarjamah Tafsiriyah: Memahami Makna Al-Qur'an Lebih Mudah, Cepat dan Tepat* (Yogyakarta: Ma'had An-Nabawy, 2011)

Thalib, Muhammad, Abu Muhammad Jibril Abdurrahman, Irfan S Awwas, and M. Shabbarin Syakur, *Panduan Daurah Syar'iyyah untuk Penegakan Syari'at Islam* (Yogyakarta: Markas Majelis Mujahidin Pusat, 2010)

Tim Pengembang Pedoman Bahasa Indonesia, *Pedoman Umum Ejaan Bahasa Indonesia* (Jakarta: Badan Pengembang dan Pembinaan Bahasa Kementerian Pendidikan dan Kebudayaan, 2016)

Tim Penyusun Kamus Pusat Bahasa, 'Lindung', *Kamus Bahasa Indonesia* (Jakarta: Pusat Bahasa, 2008), p. 864

—, 'Pembesar', *Kamus Bahasa Indonesia* (Jakarta: Pusat Bahasa, 2008), p. 189

Ubaid, Abdullah, and Bakir, eds., *Nasionalisme dan Islam Nusantara* (Jakarta: Kompas, 2015)

Umar, Nasaruddin, *Argumen Kesetaraan Gender Perspektif Al-Qur'ān* (Jakarta: Paramadina, 1999)

—, 'Kajian Kritis terhadap Ayat-ayat Gender (Pendekatan Hermeneutik)', in *Rekonstruksi Metodologis Wacana Kesetaraan Gender dalam Islam*, PSW IAIN Sunan Kalijaga Yogyakarta (Yogyakarta: Pustaka Pelajar, 2002), pp. 107–49

—, *Ketika Fikih Membela Perempuan* (Jakarta: Gramedia, 2014)

—, 'Metode Penelitian Berperspektif Gender tentang Literatur Islam', in *Rekonstruksi Metodologis Wacana Kesetaraan Gender dalam Islam*, PSW IAIN Sunan Kalijaga Yogyakarta (Yogyakarta: Pustaka Pelajar, 2002), pp. 85–106

'Website Alquran Kementerian Agama', https://quran.kemenag.go.id/index.php/about

Wild, Stefan, 'Muslim Translators and Translations of the Qur'an into English', *Journal of Qur'anic Studies*, 17.3 (2015), 158–82, https://doi.org/10.3366/jqs.2015.0215

Wilson, M. Brett, *Translating the Qur'an in an Age of Nationalism: Print Culture and Modern Islam in Turkey* (London: Oxford University Press, 2014)

—, 'Translations of the Qur'an: Islamicate Languages', in *The Oxford Handbook of Qur'anic Studies*, ed. by Mustafa Shah and M. A. S. Abdel Haleem (Oxford: Oxford University Press, 2020), pp. 552–64

Wirayudha, Randy, 'FOKUS: Keteguhan Ribuan Santri Ciamis Long March 300 Km Ke Jakarta', *Okezone News*, 29 November 2016, section National, https://news.okezone.com/read/2016/11/29/337/1554370/fokus-keteguhan-ribuan-santri-ciamis-long-march-300-km-ke-jakarta

Yahya, Mohamad, 'Analisis Genetik-Objektif atas Al-Qur'an Karim: Tarjamah Tafsiriyyah Karya Muhammad Thalib' (unpublished master's thesis, State Islamic University Sunan Kalijaga, 2012)

Yakubovych, Mykhaylo, 'Qur'an Translations into Central Asian Languages: Exegetical Standards and Translation Processes', *Journal of Qur'anic Studies*, 21.1 (2022), 89–115, https://doi.org/10.3366/jqs.2022.0491

Ya'qub, Ali Mustafa, *Makan Tak Pernah Kenyang* (Jakarta: Pustaka Firdaus, 2012)

Yunus, Mahmud, *Kamus Arab-Indonesia* (Jakarta: Hidakarya Agung, 1989)

Yusuf, Choirul Fuad, 'Pengantar Kepala Puslitbang Lektur dan Khazanah Keagamaan Badan Litbang dan Diklat Kementerian Agama', in *Al-Qur'an dan Terjemahnya Bahasa Minang* (Jakarta: Puslitbang Lektur dan Khazanah Keagamaan, 2015), pp. vii–viii

Zadeh, Travis, *The Vernacular Qur'an: Translation and the Rise of Persian Exegesis* (New York: Oxford University Press, 2012)

al-Zamakhsharī, Ibn ᶜUmar, *al-Kashshāf ᶜan ḥaqāʾiq ghawāmiḍ al-tanzīl wa ᶜuyūn al-aqāwīl fī wujūh al-taʾwīl*, 6 vols (Riyad: Maktaba al-'Abīkān, 1998), II

Zaman, Muhammad Qasim, 'Ahl al-ḥall wa-l-ᶜaqd', ed. by Kate Fleet, Gudrun Krämer, Denis Matringe, John Nawas, and Everett Rowson, *Encyclopaedia of Islam* (Koninklijke Brill NV), https://doi.org/10.1163/1573-3912_ei3_COM_0027

Zulkarnain, Iskandar, *Gerakan Ahmadiyah di Indonesia* (Yogyakarta: LKiS, 2005)

Zulkifli, *The Struggle of The Shiᶜis in Indonesia*, Islam in Southeast Asia Series (Canberra: ANU E Press, 2013)

Index

ᶜAbduh, Muhammad 43–44, 46
ABI, Aksi Bela Islam xix, 237, 269–270, 279, 299–300
ᶜadl 203, 208, 224
ahl al-sunna wa al-jamāᶜa 27, 48
Ahmadiyya xix, 22, 25, 27–28, 35, 42–43, 52–58, 66, 74, 87, 125, 146, 179
Ahmad, Mirza Bashir-ud-din Mahmud 57, 66–67, 144
Ahok 244, 269–288, 290–297, 300, 302. *See also* Purnama, Basuki Tjahaja
al-Afghānī, Jamāl al-Dīn 43
Ali, Abdullah Yusuf 77, 173
Ali, Abdul Mukti 51, 70, 118
Ali, Muhammad 56, 61, 71, 179
al-Māʾida 51 239, 274, 277–280, 283
Al-Muslimun (periodical) 240, 243, 245–246
Al-Qur'an dan Maknanya 80, 178, 182
Al-Qur'an dan Tafsirnya 12, 71, 95, 100–101, 170, 195, 254–255, 258
Al-Qur'an palsu 294, 298
ambiguity 125, 196, 225, 238, 242, 252, 261
Amin, K.H. Ma'ruf 51, 79, 282, 288
anthropomorphic 153, 167
Anwār al-tanzīl 33–34, 179, 261
Api Islam xix, 1, 109–110, 113–116, 138
asas tunggal 41, 118
aṣḥab al-jāwiyīn 28, 31
Ash-Shiddieqy, Hasbi 34, 70, 128, 151–152, 178, 180, 183–184
Ashᶜarī, Abū al-Ḥasan 43
Ashᶜarī 27, 43, 46, 185, 239
Ashᶜarite 184
ᶜAsqalānī, Ibn Ḥajar 31
authority 5–6, 12–13, 24, 42, 46, 55, 74–77, 79, 82, 84–85, 102, 104, 126, 132, 136, 141, 143–144, 154–156, 161, 168, 181, 185, 221, 227, 233–234, 237, 244–246, 250, 254–255, 257, 259, 262, 264, 267, 283, 299, 301–304, 306–308
awliyāʾ 5–6, 10, 100, 215, 227, 238–253, 261–262, 268, 270, 272, 285–293, 296, 298, 300, 302
Awwas, Irfan S. 126–127

Baghdad 34
Baghdādī, Junayd 43
bahriyya 88–89
Bantānī, Muḥammad Nawāwī 32, 34, 180, 182
Baswedan, Anies Rasyid 91, 271
Battuta, Ibn 28
Bayḍāwī 33–34, 179, 182–185, 251, 260–261
Biblical translation 17
Bidāyat al-mujtahid 35
bidᶜa 46, 48
Bintang Hindia 134
blasphemy 35–36, 231, 244, 269–270, 275–280, 282, 285–286, 288, 290–296, 299, 301–302
Bombay 88–89
BPUPKI xix, 37
brackets 19, 97, 128, 211, 222. *See also* parenthesis
Bugis 85–86, 135
Bulūgh al-marām 32

Cairo 29, 43, 184–185
caliphate 42, 228, 234–237
Carakan 86

Christians 5–6, 39, 48, 53, 78, 96, 216, 218–221, 238–242, 245, 247–250, 269–272, 274, 276, 280, 284, 287, 290–291, 301
churafat 46
classical commentaries 18–19, 152, 196, 244
collective work 12, 127, 148, 186
  collective *ijtihād* 151–152. *See also* *ijtihād*
colonialism 36, 39–40, 45, 48, 52–53, 56, 60, 86, 90, 104, 107, 133, 136, 248–251, 253, 273
  colonization 104, 132, 134, 248–249
  post-colonial 11, 36, 86, 136, 139
  pre-colonial 36
communism 41, 51, 107, 117, 120
  communists 41, 51, 106–108, 117, 132, 245, 275
conservatism 35, 53–54, 123, 269

Darul Islam 41, 106, 123–124
Darussalam 64
DDI xix, 44
democracy 38, 41–42, 115, 122–124, 129, 216, 245, 247, 287, 303
  demokrasi terpimpin 106
  Guided Democracy 50, 64, 106–107, 109–111, 115, 232, 304
desukarnoization 117, 119–120, 232
Dhahabī, Husein 145, 157, 181
Dokuritsu Junbi Chōsakai. *See* BPUPKI
Durrat al-nāṣiḥīn 32
Dutch. *See* Netherlands (Dutch)

editors 184
  editorial 65, 76, 79, 82, 138, 149–150, 222
Egypt 3, 26, 29, 43, 55, 57–58, 88, 179, 184–185, 245
Ejaan Pembaruan 90
Ejaan yang Disempurnakan (EYD) 91–92, 102
elections 10–11, 24, 49–50, 105, 206, 216–217, 237, 241, 244–245, 247, 269–277, 284–285, 291–293, 301, 308
  gubernatorial elections 10, 24, 237, 244, 247, 269–271, 275, 285, 301, 308
encyclopaedic commentary 18–19, 21, 152
equivalence 8, 21–22, 139, 157, 164, 168, 172, 213, 215, 231, 238, 280, 304
esa 10, 24, 37, 39, 227–234, 237–238, 268, 307
Eve (Hawa) 190–197, 284

Falimbānī, ʿAbd al-Ṣamad 31
Fansuri, Hamzah 59, 232
Fatḥ al-muʿīn 32
Fatḥ al-qarīb 32
Fatḥ al-wahhāb 32
fatwa 35, 53–54, 126, 151, 280
Fiqh al-sunna 35
footnotes 19, 81, 85, 95, 97, 128, 143, 146–147, 153, 156, 164, 178, 192, 195–197, 202, 204–205, 208, 221, 237, 252, 256, 261, 265
foreignization 158, 169, 172
forewords 8, 10, 65, 72–74, 98, 103–104, 113, 115–117, 119–121, 126, 130, 137–138, 140–141, 232–233, 268, 305–306, 308
FPI (Front Pembela Islam) xix, 131, 238, 272, 279–282, 286, 300
freedom 26, 37, 41, 48, 122–123, 151, 205, 209, 231, 235, 245, 307
  freedom of expression 205, 209, 235
  freedom of faith 26
  freedom of speech 41

Gatra 125–129
gender 15–16, 188–190, 196, 201, 206–207, 212, 214–216, 225
genealogy 18–19, 22, 31, 107, 170, 304
genre 18–21, 59–60, 62, 98–99, 143–144, 153–154, 168–169, 186, 309
Ghani, Bustami Abdul 70
Ghāya wa al-taqrīb 32
Ghazālī, Abū Ḥāmid 43, 251
  Ghazalian 27
glosses 78, 96, 98–100, 102, 147, 172, 202, 237, 264

Godly nation 26
Godly nationalism 26, 42, 304
government 1, 3, 7–8, 10–11, 15–16, 23, 26–27, 35, 40–42, 45, 47–50, 52–55, 63–64, 72–73, 86, 88, 94, 102–105, 111–112, 117–119, 121, 123–124, 126, 133, 135–136, 139–141, 148, 169, 201, 216, 223, 227–228, 231–234, 247, 250, 253, 257–258, 262, 267–268, 273–274, 276–277, 281, 294, 296–300, 303–308
gubernatorial elections. *See* elections: gubernatorial elections
Guru Ordonnantie 48
Gus Dur. *See* Wahid, Abdurrahman

ḥajj 29–30, 36, 42, 44, 95, 187
Hamidy, Zainuddin 61, 180, 183–184, 233
Hamka 34, 111–112, 180, 184, 233–234, 244, 249, 286, 288
Hanafi, Muchlis M. xii–xiii, 61, 68, 75, 82–83, 127–129, 139, 154, 158, 185, 189, 221, 252, 298–299
hard copy 119
Hassan, Ahmad 34, 61, 98, 128, 136, 180, 232, 244, 246, 249
Hatta, Mohammad 39
Hawa. *See* Eve (Hawa)
heresy 28, 35, 42, 46, 53
hermeneutics 2–3, 9, 18, 21–24, 46, 77, 143, 147–148, 154, 156, 164–165, 170, 175, 181, 184–186, 189–190, 220, 238, 244, 253, 270, 273, 299–302, 306, 308–309
Hijāz 47
Hilali, Muhammad Taqiuddin 77
Holy Qur'an, The xx, 13, 56–57, 61–63, 66–67, 71, 120, 125, 179, 243
Hs., Fakhruddin 61, 180, 183–184, 233
HTI (Hizbut Tahrir Indonesia) xix, 227, 234–238, 281, 299

IAIN xix, 7, 69–71, 84, 118, 144, 188–189, 206–207, 214–215, 329
identity politics 10, 269
ideology 6, 10, 23–24, 41, 51, 60, 103–105, 107–108, 110–111, 113, 115–119, 121, 127, 137–138, 141, 185–186, 201, 227–228, 231–233, 237–239, 245, 247, 253, 257, 261, 267–268, 299, 302–307
Idris, Fahira 296–298, 300
ijtihād 44, 46, 151–152. *See also* collective work: collective *ijtihād*
Ilyas, Yunahar 193, 224–225, 282–283, 289
Imam Mohammad ibn Saud Islamic University 76
India 26, 29, 43, 52, 88
indoctrination 41
Indonesian (language). *See* language: Indonesian language
industry 12, 64, 75–76, 88–89, 102, 149, 155, 178, 297, 305
inimitability 2, 17, 57, 145, 157, 282, 309
institutionalization 22, 32, 188, 222–223, 263, 308
intelligentsia 44, 53, 56
interlinear translation 31, 60, 96, 98–100, 168, 171–173
interreligious harmony 221, 223, 227, 247–248
interreligious relationships 3
interreligious tensions 223
Introduction to the Study of the Holy Qur'an, The 57, 66–67
(in)visibility. *See* visibility
Iran 27, 29, 35
Irshād al-Islāmiyya 64
Islam xii, xix–xx, 1–2, 6, 8, 11, 13, 16, 22–23, 25–32, 34–54, 56, 66, 70, 77, 105–110, 112–118, 121, 123–124, 129–133, 135–136, 138, 141–142, 144, 151–152, 155–156, 158, 166, 168, 171, 188–189, 193–194, 199, 203–208, 210, 214–216, 220–225, 228–229, 234–238, 240, 245, 249, 258, 261, 263, 269, 272–273, 275, 279–281, 286–287, 291, 323
Islamic discourse 7, 15, 26, 129, 187, 303–304. *See also* standard Islamic discourse
Islamic thought 10, 35, 187, 209, 307
Islamic higher education 23, 69–70, 112, 151, 154, 187–188, 224, 306

Islamic University of Medina 76
Islamism 11, 26, 41, 44–47, 53, 117–118, 123–124, 132, 234, 238, 245, 281, 294, 302, 306
Islamization 22, 25, 27–29, 36, 42, 238
Islam Nusantara 129–133, 141
Istiqlal Mosque 76, 112, 255
Itḥāf al-dhākī 31
Iᶜānat al-ṭālibīn 32

Jahja, Muchtar 70
JAI (Jemaat Ahmadiyah Indonesia) xix, 53, 110
Jakarta Charter. *See* Piagam Djakarta (Jakarta Charter)
Jalālayn. *See Tafsīr al-Jalālayn*
Jami'ah al-Islamiyah al-Hukumiyah 70
Jāmiᶜ al-bayān 145, 181, 198, 239, 254, 262
Jamᶜiyya Iḥyāᵓ al-Turāth al-Islāmī 64
Japan 36, 40, 48–49, 104, 135
Javanese 17, 33, 36, 56, 59–60, 84, 110, 131–132, 134–135, 168, 172, 183
Jawi 28, 43, 60, 86, 135–136, 249
Jews 5–6, 78, 96, 125, 218–221, 238–242, 270, 272, 274, 280, 290–291
Jokowi. *See* Widodo, Joko (Jokowi)
Jong Indonesie 134
Jong Islamieten Bond 54
Jong Java 134

Kahf (manuscript) 34, 59, 182–183, 232
Kathīr, Ibn 145, 159–160, 183–185, 190, 197, 199, 203, 210, 212, 219–220, 239–240, 254, 260, 262–263
kaum muda 44
kaum tua 44
Kementerian Urusan Islam Khusus 40
Ketuhanan Yang Maha Esa 37, 39, 228–229, 231–234
Khan, Muhammad Muhsin 77
Khāzin 34, 182
KHI xx, 189, 205, 224
King Fahd Complex for the Printing of the Holy Qur'an 13, 61, 64, 68–69, 74–79, 81–82, 89, 97–98, 126, 149, 153, 166, 219–221, 304–307
kitab kuning 43, 55
Kitab Logat Melajoe 90
Komite Hijaz. *See* Hijāz
Kūrānī, Ibrāhīm 29, 31, 34

language 1–2, 4–5, 14, 23, 60–61, 76, 81, 84, 86, 90, 133–135, 138–139, 172–173, 176, 219, 285, 288, 306, 309. *See also* Javanese; *See also* Madurese (language); *See also* Persian (language); *See also* Sundanese (language); *See also* Malay (language)
  Indonesian language 23, 60–61, 76, 78, 85, 90, 111, 128, 133–135, 137–138, 142, 149, 152, 157, 162–164, 169, 173, 196, 201, 212, 305
  national language 13, 23, 63, 111, 133–135, 139, 181
  regional languages 23, 60, 63, 69, 83–86, 101, 130, 133, 135, 139–142, 180, 305–306
layout 9, 23, 62, 96–100, 102, 171, 305
leadership 3, 5–6, 10–11, 24, 49, 51, 56, 65, 76, 79, 81, 103, 105, 108, 110, 112, 121–122, 124, 129, 131, 137, 141, 188, 209–216, 235, 237, 240–241, 243–246, 250–253, 257, 259–261, 268, 272, 274–275, 280–281, 285–292, 300–301, 306
literacy 139
  illiteracy 137, 139
literary culture 21, 135
literature 5–6, 14, 18, 25, 28, 32, 34, 60, 67, 87–88, 120, 133, 138, 158, 170, 176–177, 179, 184, 250, 309
lithographic text 88
Lontara 86
LPMQ xii, xx, 12, 61–65, 68, 74–76, 80–85, 89, 92, 100, 102, 127–129, 149, 152–155, 185, 189, 219, 221, 298
LPPKSA xx, 62–63, 69–70, 120

madhhab 27, 30–32, 35, 43, 151–152, 224
Madjdy, Busjairi 70
Madjid, Nurcholish 138, 222–223, 225
madrasa 18–19, 21, 29, 33, 35, 50, 55
Madurese (language) 33

maghḍūb 78, 219–220
Maksum, K.H. Ali 70–71
Malay-Indonesian states 27–31, 33, 36, 59–60, 91, 131, 171, 182–183, 238
Malay (language) 33–34, 56–57, 59–60, 90, 111, 133–134, 136, 139, 229–230, 250
Manār 44, 55, 61, 191, 194, 203
Maqassarī, Yūsuf 31, 36
Maraḥ labīd 34, 180, 183. *See also Tafsīr al-Munīr li maʿālim al-tanzīl*
marriage 5, 24, 48, 188–189, 197–199, 202–207, 224–225, 245, 307
Marriage Law 189, 204–205, 224, 307
Masyumi xx, 41, 44, 49–51, 105–106, 108, 111, 117–118, 123, 136–137, 233
Māturīdī, Abū Manṣūr 43
mawḍūʿī 207. *See also* themes: thematic
Mecca 29–30, 32, 36, 43, 47, 64, 75, 109
Medina 34, 43, 64, 74, 76, 89–90, 109, 160, 166, 220
Melindo 91
MIAI xx, 48
Middle East 28, 30–31, 36, 123, 182–183
Minangkabawī, Aḥmad Khaṭīb 32
Ministry of Religious Affairs (MORA) xii, 10–15, 23–24, 26–27, 36–37, 39–40, 42, 49–51, 53, 62–64, 67–70, 75–77, 80, 83–86, 89, 94–95, 97–98, 100–101, 107, 109, 111, 118, 120, 122–125, 127, 129, 132, 140–141, 148–149, 151, 154–155, 170, 188–189, 221, 223–226, 229, 231, 240, 248, 252, 255, 258, 291, 296–300, 303–305, 307–308
Mirʾat al-ṭullāb 32
MMI (Majelis Mujahidin Indonesia) xx, 13, 124, 126–127, 129, 141, 298–299, 306
mobile 100–102, 296
modern 2, 4, 13, 17, 33–34, 52, 55, 57, 87, 96, 98, 113, 133, 137, 142–145, 158, 168, 170, 172, 176, 181, 184–186, 197, 199, 216, 219, 229, 248–249, 263, 274, 306
  modernism 116
  modernists 25, 35, 44–51, 54–55, 58, 106, 116, 118, 146, 197, 225–226, 245
  modernization 13, 52, 55, 182, 249, 307
monogamy 199, 203–205
monovalence 19, 21, 293
MPRS xx, 69, 103, 111–112, 116–117, 121, 137, 308
MS Or.li.6.45 59
MTQ (*Musabaqah Tilawatil Qur'an*) 121
Muchtar, Kamal 70, 255
Muhammadiyah 22, 26–27, 35, 41, 44–52, 54, 64, 68, 77, 82, 113, 124, 151–152, 154, 180, 241, 282
MUI xix–xx, 27, 35–36, 53–54, 76, 82–83, 124, 151–152, 241, 255, 262, 280–282, 292, 294–296, 298–299, 302
  GNPF MUI xix, 280–282, 292, 296–297, 299
Musaddad, K.H. Anwar xiii, 70
mushaf xvii, 12, 61–62, 75, 80, 85, 88–90, 98–101, 295, 297, 299, 305
  Mushaf Standar Indonesia 12, 89
mysticism 27, 43

nafs wāḥida 190–196
Nahdlatul Ulama (NU) xx, 22, 26–27, 35, 41, 43–46, 48–51, 68, 70–71, 77, 79, 82, 105–106, 110–111, 122, 124, 129–132, 151, 245, 275, 282, 284, 286, 288–289
Nahdlatul Wathan 44
Nahra, Mustafa 294–298
Nasakom 51, 107, 109–111, 115, 117, 141, 306
nationalism 26, 37, 38, 42, 51, 107, 108, 111, 132, 133, 134, 138, 231, 245, 304. *See also* Godly nation: Godly nationalism
  nationalist 37–39, 41, 134, 138, 245
Netherlands (Dutch) 36, 39–40, 45, 48, 53–57, 59–60, 71, 90, 104–108, 132–136, 179, 229, 248–249
Netherlands Indies Parliament 40
New Order 13–14, 16, 25, 41, 47, 51, 53, 63, 65, 72, 104, 110, 116–123, 132, 141, 201, 209, 216, 227–228, 247–248, 250, 257–258, 268, 304

Noor, Masuddin 71

official Qur'an translation xvii, 4, 6–16, 19–25, 57–58, 61–69, 71–82, 84–90, 92–95, 97–104, 110–113, 115–117, 119–121, 125–133, 137–138, 140–152, 154–158, 160, 164–171, 173–176, 178–189, 191, 195–197, 199, 201–205, 208–212, 214–217, 219, 221–228, 230–233, 236–238, 241, 244, 247–255, 257–258, 261–262, 265–268, 270–272, 292–294, 297–309
  officiality 7–8, 15, 271, 294, 301–302
  official reform 187, 197, 209, 224
Old Order 13–14, 65, 72, 104, 119–120, 248, 250
Omar, Toha Jahja 70
online 23, 30, 54, 62, 83, 100–102, 286, 297, 299
Ophuijsen, Ch. A. Van 90–92
Ottoman Empire 29–30, 43

Pancasila xix, 23–24, 26, 36–41, 106–107, 117–119, 121–122, 124–125, 129, 132, 228–229, 231–236, 238
  BP7 xix, 122
  BPIP xix, 236
paraphrasing 96, 168
paratext 10, 23, 62, 67, 103–104, 116, 133, 140, 186
parenthesis 78, 146, 156, 161, 163–164, 174, 192, 197, 201, 213–214, 220, 237, 265–266. *See also* brackets
Parmusi xx, 47
pedagogy 17, 31, 33, 57, 100, 135, 171–172
Pegon 23, 60, 86, 135
Pelita 67, 121, 254–255, 258
Pendapat dan Sikap Keagamaan 280–281
penguasa 10, 237, 259, 288
Persian (language) 17, 31, 52, 168
Persis (Persatuan Islam) xx, 44, 54, 82, 151, 180, 240, 245
Perti xx, 44
pesantren 23, 32, 35, 47, 50, 60, 64, 82–83, 98, 151–152, 171, 181–182
Piagam Djakarta (Jakarta Charter) 38–40, 105, 109, 118, 123, 232, 235
pilgrims 13, 29, 64, 75–76, 132, 218
Pink, Johanna xi, 2, 4, 9, 12, 15, 17, 20, 52, 54–55, 78, 96, 156, 168, 172, 181, 183, 238, 244, 248–249
plagiarism 66–67
pluralism 24, 126, 188, 217, 222–223, 225
policy 3, 10, 37, 42, 48, 50–51, 82, 86, 92, 102–103, 112, 118–119, 121–122, 133, 142, 204, 248, 287, 303–304, 308–309
politics 4, 7, 10, 14–16, 22, 47–50, 70, 87, 108, 110, 132, 136, 248, 261, 267, 269, 286
  political agenda 8, 141
  politicization 8, 16, 24, 42, 121, 228, 241, 245, 257, 262, 267–269, 284, 286, 292, 301–302, 308
  politics of translation 7
polygamy 3, 24, 48, 188, 197–199, 202–210, 224–225, 262
polyvalence 18, 152, 238
power 5–6, 10, 23–24, 26–27, 40–42, 46–47, 49–51, 60, 68, 72, 79, 104–105, 108, 116–117, 140, 216, 228, 245–246, 248, 254, 259, 262, 265–266, 300, 304
private publishers 64–65, 76, 80, 97–99, 146
PUEBI xx, 91–92
Purnama, Basuki Tjahaja 244, 269, 273–274, 280, 301. *See also* Ahok
Puslitbang LKKMO 63, 84–86

QT (*Al-Qur'an dan Terjemahnya*). *See* official Qur'an translation

Rais, Amien 281, 286
Rānirī, Nūr al-Dīn 59
rasm imlāʾī 88
rasm uthmānī 88
Rāzī, Fakhr al-Dīn 34, 152, 165–166, 183–185, 190, 193, 239, 259–261, 263, 267
reception 6, 8–10, 12, 24, 83, 143, 185, 254, 294, 300
reforms 10, 24, 26, 44–45, 69, 90–91, 107, 151–152, 187–189, 197, 209,

224–225, 229. *See also* official Qur'an translation: official reform
educational reforms 187–189
Reformasi 35, 122–123, 139, 231, 235–236, 238, 241, 269
Reformation 11, 13–14, 65, 104, 139
reformists 44, 52, 58, 125, 136, 138, 185, 225
religious reforms 10, 45
replication 17
revision 9, 13, 23, 39, 61–62, 65–68, 74–78, 80–83, 87, 125, 128, 138, 144, 149–150, 152–153, 166, 176, 178, 204–205, 216–217, 248, 255–258, 262, 293, 297, 305
ad hoc revision 65, 68, 78, 256
ribāṭ 29
Riḍā, Rashīd 44, 46, 55, 184, 191, 194–195, 197–199, 207, 210
Riyāḍ al-ṣāliḥīn 32
Roman script 85, 138
rujūᶜ ilā al-Qurʾān wa al-sunna 43, 46

Sābiq, Sayyid 35
Saifuddin, Lukman Hakim 298
Saleh, Walid 18–19, 33–34, 152, 179, 183–185, 220, 288
Samudra Pasai 28
Sani, Asrul 71
SARA 155, 274
Sarekat Islam xx, 46, 48, 50, 52, 107
Saudi Arabia 3, 13, 68–69, 74–79, 82, 89, 101–103, 126, 145, 148–149, 155, 157, 161, 165–167, 177, 191–192, 195, 200, 203, 208, 211, 218–223, 242–243, 265, 272, 292–293, 296–297, 300, 304–305, 307
scripts 23, 60, 85–90, 95, 102, 133, 135–138, 146, 249, 277. *See also Carakan*; *See also Lontara*; *See also* Roman script
secularism 26, 37–39, 105, 108, 118, 125, 231, 288
Shāfiᶜī 27–28, 30–32, 34, 43
Shibghatullāh 30–31
Shihab, Quraish xii, 34, 80, 82–83, 158, 178–182, 194, 197, 214–217, 236, 244, 287
Shinnawī, Aḥmad 30–31
Shīᶜism 25, 27, 29, 35, 42, 125
Shīᶜī 25, 28, 179
Shūmubu 40
Singkīlī, ᶜAbd al-Raʾūf 31–32, 34, 36, 182, 232
sīra 87, 176–177
sīra nabawiyya 87, 176
Siswopranoto, S. 71
SKB (1987) 94–95
Soedewo 56–57, 71, 144, 178–179
Soenarjo, R.H.A. 67, 69, 71, 120, 128, 144, 148, 156–157, 178
Soewandi 90–93, 102
Southeast Asia 14, 27–31, 33–34, 36, 39, 43, 54, 86, 88, 120, 131, 135, 139, 183, 224, 249–250, 317
spelling xvii, xx, 8–9, 23, 62, 87, 90–94, 102, 160–161, 305
standard Islamic discourse 7, 15, 26, 129, 187, 303–304. *See also* Islam: Islamic discourse
standardization 12, 15, 80, 85–86, 89–90, 100–101, 303
standardized *mushaf*. *See mushaf*: Mushaf Standar Indonesia
states 1, 3–15, 22–27, 29–30, 35–42, 49–51, 69–70, 72, 74, 76, 79, 84–87, 90, 94, 101–115, 117–118, 121–124, 127, 129–130, 132–135, 137–138, 140–142, 153–156, 173–174, 176, 185, 187–189, 204–205, 208–209, 221, 223–225, 227–229, 231–236, 238, 240, 245–246, 249, 257, 261–262, 267–268, 271–272, 283, 288, 290–292, 294, 299–309
Islamic states 6, 36, 41, 85, 106, 123–124, 234
nation-states 3–4, 11, 123, 235
Subhan, Zaitunah 194–195, 224–225
substitution 17–18, 128, 157, 169, 213, 261, 299
Sufism 29, 44

Suharto 11, 23, 35, 41, 51, 53, 72–73, 91, 103–104, 116–124, 130, 132, 139, 141, 205, 227, 229, 232, 247–248, 304, 306
Sukarno 1, 4, 11, 23, 38, 40–41, 50–51, 55–56, 65, 69, 72–73, 94, 103–104, 106–117, 119–122, 125, 134, 137–138, 141, 232, 240, 248, 262, 288, 304, 306. *See also* desukarnoization
Sukarnoputri, Megawati 216, 270
Sullam al-tawfīq 32
Sumatrāʾī, Shams al-Dīn 59
Sundanese (language) 33, 56, 60, 85, 135, 229
Sunnī 2, 12, 22, 24–25, 27, 31, 34–35, 42–43, 53, 55, 79, 155–156, 178–179, 181–186, 223, 225, 262, 303–304, 307–308
  Sunnism 16, 22, 25, 27–28, 30–32, 34, 43, 303–304
surau 32, 60, 182
Syarfuan, Junanda P. xii, 80–82
Syihab, Muhammad Rizieq 131, 234–235, 281–283, 286, 291

Ṭabarī 145, 181, 185, 197–198, 239, 253–254, 260, 262–264
tabular layout 96–97, 102
tachayyul 46
tafsīr 2–3, 5–8, 10, 12, 18–24, 32–34, 59–60, 65, 70, 80, 85, 87, 100, 131, 141, 143–145, 149, 151–154, 159, 162, 164, 166–171, 174, 179, 181–186, 188, 191, 201, 206–208, 219–221, 231, 237–239, 243–244, 250–251, 253, 257–258, 261–262, 264–268, 287, 289–290, 304, 307–309
  as genealogical tradition 18
  institutional *tafsīr* 2–3, 12
  tafsīr tradition 8, 10, 18–24, 33, 80, 141, 143, 145, 152, 154, 162, 167, 169–170, 181–182, 185–186, 219–221, 231, 237–238, 244, 250–251, 253, 258, 261–262, 264–267, 287, 304, 307–309
  visiblity of. *See* visibility: of *tafsīr*
Tafsīr al-Jalālayn 32–33, 182
Tafsīr al-Kabīr 34, 183
Tafsīr al-Munīr li maʿālim al-tanzīl 34, 180, 183
taḥlīlī 206–209
tajwīd 12, 100–101
TAP MPRS 69
taqlīd 44, 46
ṭarīqa 44
tarjama ḥarfiyya 17, 126, 128
tarjama tafsīriyya 17
Tarjumān al-mustafīd xii, 33–34, 59–60, 182–183, 232, 250–251
taṣawwuf 32, 43
taṣḥīḥ 62, 129
Taymiyya, Ibn 46, 177, 185
Tempo 66
Thaib, Gazali 71
Thalib, Muhammad 7, 124–130, 141, 233, 299–300
Thawalib 44
themes 95, 144–146, 188, 217, 267
  thematic 12, 145, 178, 207, 266–267
Tim Sembilan 38
Tjokroaminoto, H.O.S. 55–57, 61
tradition 6, 8, 10–11, 18–24, 28, 30–33, 35, 43–44, 55, 57, 60, 80, 86–87, 98, 100, 103, 114–115, 137, 141, 143–145, 152, 154, 160, 162, 167–171, 173, 181–182, 185–186, 188, 193, 195, 197, 210, 219–221, 231–232, 237–238, 244, 248, 250–251, 253, 258, 261–262, 264–267, 287, 289, 303–304, 307–309
  traditionalism 25, 44–45, 47–51, 55, 106, 116, 136–138, 185
translation theories 17, 158, 169, 309
transliteration xvii, 9, 23, 62, 85, 90, 92–95, 97, 102, 146, 166–167, 265–266, 305
typesetting 8, 95, 98, 305

UIN xi–xii, xx, 84, 188, 236
ulama xvii, 20, 24, 42–44, 47–49, 57, 62, 70–71, 83, 85, 102, 108, 112, 115, 128, 141, 149, 152, 154–156, 185–186, 208, 224, 250, 262–264, 279–280, 283, 298, 303–304, 306–308
ʿulūm al-Qurʾān 87–88, 158, 176–177, 184

Umar, Nasaruddin 193–194, 196, 206–207, 215, 224–225
University of Ummu al-Qurā 76
untranslatability 57, 157

visibility
  of *tafsīr* 22, 309
  of translators 18, 22, 168, 307, 309

Wadud, Amina 208
Wahhabism 46, 79
Wahhāb, Muḥammad ibn ᶜAbd 43
Wahid, Abdurrahman 50, 79, 122, 216, 275
Wahyudi, Yudian 236–237
Western education 45, 55
Widodo, Joko (Jokowi) 51, 65, 122, 129–130, 132, 141, 240–241, 244, 250–251, 269, 272, 275, 281, 296
women 24, 99–100, 188–190, 192, 196–202, 204–206, 208–216, 225, 305
words, choice of 7–8, 13, 264

Yamin, Mohammad 38
Yamunu' 63, 68
Yani, Buni 277–279, 283
Yayasan Iman Jama' Jakarta 80
Youth Pledge 111, 134, 138
YPPA xx, 63, 120
Yunus, Mahmud 57–58, 61, 98, 146, 180, 232–233, 244, 246, 249

Zarkashī 145
zawiya 33
Zubair, K.H. Maimun 71
Zuhri, Saifuddin 72–73, 109–110, 119
Zulkarnain, Tengku 295–298

About the Team

Alessandra Tosi was the managing editor for this book.

Helen Blatherwick edited the manuscript. Melissa Purkiss proof-read, typeset and indexed the work.

Anna Gatti designed the cover. The cover was produced in InDesign using the Fontin font.

Luca Baffa produced the paperback and hardback editions. The text font is Tex Gyre Pagella; the heading font is Californian FB. Luca produced the EPUB, AZW3, PDF, HTML, and XML editions — the conversion is performed with open source software such as pandoc (https://pandoc.org/) created by John MacFarlane and other tools freely available on our GitHub page (https://github.com/OpenBookPublishers).

The Global Qur'an

ISSN Print: 2753-8036 • ISSN Digital: 2753-8044

The Global Qur'an is a new book series that looks at Muslim engagement with the Qur'an in a global perspective. We publish studies that focus on the translation and interpretation of the Qur'an or on the social, cultural, pedagogical, aesthetic, and devotional place of the Qur'an in Muslim societies worldwide. We particularly encourage comparative studies, investigations of transregional dynamics, and interactions between local and global contexts. Contributions from scholars outside Western Europe and North America are especially welcome.

Editorial Board

Call for proposals

Scholars interested in publishing work in this series and submitting their monographs and/or edited collections should contact the General Editor, Johanna Pink (johanna.pink@orient.uni-freiburg.de). If you wish to submit a contribution, please read and download the submission guidelines.

OpenBook Publishers

www.ingramcontent.com/pod-product-compliance
Lightning Source LLC
Chambersburg PA
CBHW040745020526
44114CB00049B/2927
* 9 7 8 1 8 0 0 6 4 3 9 8 7 *